"The world of coaching is privileged to have this gift of a book now. *The Digital and AI Coaches' Handbook* is a must-have for any coach, leader of human development or practitioner who wants to stay abreast of fast-paced changes in this and related spaces."

Dr Dumi Magadlela, *ICF Global Chair*

"What an amazing array of relevant topics for Digital and AI coaches, provided by a broad range of subject experts!"

Stephen Murphy, *EMCC Global VP Thought Leadership & Development*

"*The Digital and AI Coaches' Handbook* brings together the leading experts from across the field to provide a comprehensive, informative text – a must buy for those in the future of coaching."

Dr Natalie Lancer, *Chair of the British Psychological Society's Division of Coaching Psychology*

"This book will have an immense impact helping create knowledge, understanding, and the development of digital and AI within the coaching sector. It will help the reader stay abreast with the revolution impacting our sector."

Mohau Mphomela, *President, COMENSA*

"Grounded in research, this book defines exactly what digital coaching is, what it isn't, but most importantly, it provides the science and theoretical knowledge behind how and when to use these tools for maximum effect. The ever-growing use of technologies is changing by the second, which means continual evolution of the way we work to match the pace of change. This book supports that approach, and it is why *The Digital and AI Coaches' Handbook* is on my recommended list of books to read in 2024!"

Catherine Pearson, *PCC Executive Coach, Executive Director, Leadership and Executive Coaching, Global Investment Bank*

The Digital and AI Coaches' Handbook

This comprehensive practitioner guide supports coaches in developing their understanding of digital technologies and how to work in ever-changing digital environments, and shows coaches how to craft their own practices to take advantage of working online.

The practice of coaching is undergoing significant change, with technology widely embedded and used in professional coaching services today. Coaching practitioners worldwide are adapting to digital environments, and a host of new technological tools have come into play, from the developments in virtual reality to AI-informed coaching, and from coaching bots to workplace apps. Edited by Jonathan Passmore, Sandra J. Diller, Sam Isaacson, and Maximilian Brantl, this third book in the acclaimed *Coaches' Handbook Series* brings together internationally respected coaching experts and practitioners to share the most up-to-date know-how. The book takes you through key technical developments, the critical factors in making digital coaching successful, and how to build a coaching business using these technologies. The book also considers the impacts on the wider industry and concludes with a number of case studies of global coaching organisations and their experiences of using digital techniques, including CoachHub and EZRA.

Aimed at coach practitioners, their supervisors, trainers, and student coaches on accreditation programmes or undertaking training for a certificate in coaching, this book showcases best practice, new ideas, and the science behind the digital revolution within coaching practice and the coaching industry.

Jonathan Passmore is an international respected chartered psychologist, researcher, and writer in the field of coaching. He has published widely over the past two decades including 40 books and over 250 scientific articles and book chapters.

Sandra J. Diller is Assistant Professor for Organizational Psychology at the University of Seeburg, a Coach and Trainer at the LMU Center for Leadership and People Management, and a Research Affiliate at the Institute of Coaching, Harvard Medical School.

Sam Isaacson is an independent coach and consultant co-founder of AIcoach.chat and founder of the Coachtech Collective, a global community of coaches grappling with the cutting edge of technology. He writes widely around the intersection of coaching with technology.

Maximilian Brantl is a seasoned consultant focused on strategy advisory of Fortune Global 500 companies on management and supervisory board level, and is a certified coach, currently writing his dissertation in the field of digital coaching. He specialised in orchestrating holistic organisational and cultural transformations as well as strategic reinvents. He also designs and executes leadership assessments and development journeys for C-suite executives.

The Coaches' Handbook Series

Series Editor: Jonathan Passmore

This series provides an accessible and comprehensive set of handbooks for all who are new to coaching and those who want to enhance their coaching skills. Edited by a global authority on executive coaching, Jonathan Passmore, it includes books and chapters from leading coach practitioners from across the world.

The Coaches' Handbook
The Complete Practitioner Guide for Professional Coaches
Edited By Jonathan Passmore

The Ethical Coaches' Handbook
A Guide to Developing Ethical Maturity in Practice
Edited By Wendy-Ann Smith, Jonathan Passmore, Eve Turner, Yi-Ling Lai, David Clutterbuck

The Digital and AI Coaches' Handbook
The Complete Guide to the Use of Online, AI, and Technology in Coaching
Edited by Jonathan Passmore, Sandra J. Diller, Sam Isaacson, and Maximilian Brantl

For more information about this series, please visit: www.routledge.com/The-Coaches-Handbook-Series/book-series/Coaches

The Digital and AI Coaches' Handbook

The Complete Guide to the Use of Online, AI, and Technology in Coaching

Edited by Jonathan Passmore, Sandra J. Diller, Sam Isaacson, and Maximilian Brantl

Routledge
Taylor & Francis Group

LONDON AND NEW YORK

Designed cover image: Getty Images / Vitalii Gulenok

First published 2024
by Routledge
4 Park Square, Milton Park, Abingdon, Oxon OX14 4RN

and by Routledge
605 Third Avenue, New York, NY 10158

Routledge is an imprint of the Taylor & Francis Group, an informa business

© 2024 selection and editorial matter, Jonathan Passmore, Sandra J. Diller,
Sam Isaacson, and Maximilian Brantl; individual chapters, the contributors

British Library Cataloguing-in-Publication Data
A catalogue record for this book is available from the British Library

ISBN: 978-1-032-43190-1 (hbk)
ISBN: 978-1-032-46904-1 (pbk)
ISBN: 978-1-003-38374-1 (ebk)

DOI: 10.4324/9781003383741

Typeset in Sabon
by Newgen Publishing UK

Contents

Editors

Jonathan Passmore is Professor of Coaching and Behavioural Change at Henley Business School, UK and Senior Vice President EZRA, LHH. He is a chartered psychologist, holds five degrees, is an EMCC Master Coach, ICF PCC, and holds qualifications in coaching supervision and team, board, and systemic coaching. He has published widely with over 250 scientific papers and book chapters, and 40 books on coaching, leadership, mindfulness, and I/O psychology included *The Coaches' Handbook*, *The Ethical Coaches' Handbook*, *The Health & Wellbeing Coaches' Handbook*, *Becoming a Coach: The Essential ICF Guide*, and three volumes in the *Coaching Tools* series. He is a member of the coaching Global Gurus list and Marshall Goldsmith's Coaching Thinkers 50.

Sandra J. Diller is Professor for Organisational Psychology at the Seeburg Castle University and an Institute of Coaching Research Affiliate, Harvard Medical School. Sandra is a certified coach, trainer, and mentor and has worked in coaching since 2011. Her several publications (papers, books, coaching tools) focus on coaching and coaching interventions from a psychological perspective, and ethics in organisations and leadership as an essential component for excellence.

Sam Isaacson is an enthusiastic Coachtech thought leader, as well as being an active coach and coach supervisor. He writes a popular LinkedIn newsletter and has written two books on the topic. He is the founder of the Coachtech Collective, a global community of coaches grappling with technology, and works closely with the big coaching professional bodies on the development of thinking around technology and ethics. He is also Chair of the Coaching Professional apprenticeship, the biggest coaching qualification in England. With a background in professional services and a disruptive coaching technology startup, he now supports organisations across the planet in maturing coaching ecosystems and enhancing coaching using technology.

Maximilian Brantl is a seasoned consultant focused on strategy advisory of Fortune Global 500 companies on management and supervisory board level and certified coach, who is writing his dissertation in the field of digital coaching. He specialised in orchestrating holistic organisational and cultural transformations as well as strategic reinvents. Furthermore, he designs and executes leadership assessments and development journeys for C-suite executives.

Contributors

Michael Beale works with clients as a Marshall Goldsmith stakeholder coach and Richard Bandler, NLP trainer and coach trainer. He also works with The Henley Business School to help coaches start and market their coaching practices.

Clare Beckett-McInroy is an award-winning coach specialising in systemic executive and team coaching as well as supervision. She is an ICF & EMCC Master Coach, agile coach, accredited supervisor, and researcher.

Brajesh Bajpai has 25+ years of professional experience across three industries, 14 cities on three continents. He has been coaching for over 15 years and has an ongoing research interest in 'Coaching in the Digital Age'.

Carol Braddick has over 20 years of successful coaching partnerships with global leaders. She supports coaches and organisational buyers of coaching on their learning curve about technology for coaching.

Stephen Brown is a professional coach, consultant, and creative. He is also a coach educator and accredited with the EMCC at Senior Practitioner level.

David Clutterbuck is Co-dean of the Global Team Coaching Institute, Co-founder of the EMCC and author or co-author of 70 books.

Joel DiGirolamo is Vice President of Research and Data Science for the International Coaching Federation (ICF). He is the author of two books and several research papers and book chapters and is an Associate Editor for *Consulting Psychology Journal*.

Nancy Doyle is Occupational and Coaching Psychologist, Visiting Professor at Birkbeck, University of London, Founder of Genius Within and Neurodivergent thinker.

Tünde Erdös holds a PhD in Business and Organisation Management, an Ashridge MSc in Executive Coaching, an Ashridge PgD in Coaching and Organisational Supervision. She is an ICF MCC and an EMCC Senior Practitioner as well as the recipient of the ICF Coaching Impact Award 2023. Tünde has published in high-ranking scientific papers and authored three books, specialising on presence and complexity in organisations.

Rosie Evans-Krimme is a coach and behavioural scientist, specialised in digital coaching. She has spoken at global conferences and leads the Innovation Lab at CoachHub,

Alexandra J.S. Fouracres runs her own coaching and mentoring practice in addition to working as a cybersecurity consultant and academic and is the author of *Cybersecurity for Coaches and Therapists*.

Dr. Alina Gales works as diversity manager at the Technical University of Munich is a speaker on the intersections of diversity, discrimination, and digitalization. In her research, she focuses on the mutual influence of technology, society, and gender.

Harald Geißler is a Professor of vocational and corporate education and training at Helmut Schmidt University in Hamburg. He has published extensively in the field of coaching, mostly in German, including a chapter in the *International Handbook of Evidenced based Coaching* on E-Coaching.

Eva Gengler is a researcher at the Friedrich-Alexander-Universität Erlangen-Nürnberg with focus on AI, power, and feminism as well as an entrepreneur, speaker, board member, and voice for feminist AI.

Nick Goldberg is Co-founder and CEO of EZRA Coaching and was previously CEO UKI for LHH. He has a background in business psychology and leadership.

Dr. Ilse Hagerer is a researcher at the Technical University of Munich (TUM), Germany. Her research focuses on higher education organisation, diversity, management, and digitalisation.

Rachel Hawley is Leadership Associate at the NHS Leadership Academy and co-author of *Values and Ethics in Coaching*.

Alex Haitoglou's mission is to improve human connection by expanding coaching and improving communication skills, using AI to help us get better.

Priya Hunt is an executive coach, PhD researcher in Henley Business School and published author with 30 years of experience as a senior corporate leader in the airline, telecommunications, utilities, and healthcare industries.

Ioanna Iordanou is Reader in Human Resource Management (Coaching and Mentoring) at Oxford Brookes Business School, and co-author of *Values and Ethics in Coaching* and *The Practitioner's Handbook of Team Coaching*.

Simone Kauffeld holds the chair for Industrial/Organisational and Social Psychology at TU Braunschweig and is the author of multiple books and papers on coaching.

Pam Krulitz is Founder and CEO of Optify. She is an ICF accredited coach and served on the faculty of Georgetown Leadership Coaching program.

Amit Kumar is the Founder and CEO of uExcelerate, and a UC Berkeley and XIMB alumnus with 15+ years of experience in human resources.

Michelle Lucas is Accredited Master Executive Coach and Accredited Master Coach Supervisor based in Weymouth, Dorset and author of *Creating the reflective habit*, published by Routledge.

Olivier Malafronte cofounded PocketConfidant AI in 2016, one of the first AI Coach app, and Rypple.ai in 2024. Certified coach, academic researcher and entrepreneur with an interest in human development and disruptive technologies, Olivier is also an active member in the ICF Global AI Coaching Standards Working Group.

Auriel Majumdar is a creative coach, supervisor, and educator. An EMCC Accredited Master Practitioner, she specialises in leadership and team development in the arts sector.

Lori Mazan is Co-founder, President, and Chief Coaching Officer at Sounding Board, the most adaptive solution for leadership development on the market. She is the author of *Leadership Revolution: The Future of Developing Dynamic Leaders*.

Natalie M. Michalik is an occupational and organisational psychologist and behavioural psychotherapist. Her research interests focus on the opportunities and consequences of the digitalisation of coaching.

JD Meier is an Agile leader, author, coach, entrepreneur, futurist, innovator, productivity specialist, project leader, and strategist. He was the head coach for Satya Nadella's innovation team at Microsoft.

Matti Niebelschütz is Serial Entrepreneur and Founder of the global digital coaching platform CoachHub, funded with over $330M in venture capital.

Yannis Niebelschütz has worked for LinkedIn as well as starting multiple business with his brother Matti before founding CoachHub.

Harry Novic is Founder of Rocky.ai and a pioneer in AI coaching and personal development platforms.

Alex Pascal is an I/O Psychologist and Founder of Coaching.com.

Naeema Pasha is a Visiting Fellow at Henley Business School and is an independent consultant, researcher, and advisor on AI and DEI.

Jack Prevezer is the COO and Co-Founder at EZRA, part of the Adecco Group. He has a background in consulting and new ventures.

Stefanie Rödel is Professor of Coaching & Supervision at IU International University and head of the Human Resources Department. She is a leadership coach and author of several books and articles.

Rebecca Rutschmann is a Coaching AI entrepreneur and the Founder and CPO of evoach AI coaching companions. She is also EMCC VP Accreditation Germany and an EMCC Global approved Assessor.

Sam Samarasinghe is Founder of Delenta.com, an experienced global tech entrepreneur, with an MBA from the Australian IOB, and experience of working in four continents.

Carsten C. Schermuly is Professor of Business Psychology at SRH University of Applied Sciences Berlin. His main research focuses on new ways of working from a psychological perspective and the effectiveness of coaching processes.

Hannes Schilling is a doctoral student of Industrial/Organizational and Social Psychology at TU Braunschweig.

Benita Stafford-Smith is Managing Consultant for an Oman HR Consultancy, Takatuf. She holds an International Coaching Federation, Master Certified Coaching credential.

Andrew Strange is Chairman, Non Exec, Tech Entrepreneur, Investor, Innovator – throughout the last two decades of developing digital innovation agencies Andrew has been building and supporting solutions in 3D content in collaborative immersive environments.

Christine Tao is a Co-founder and CEO, Sounding Board, Inc, Previous SVP Sales at Tapjoy, a high growth startup and past Googler, Christine brings her years of revenue growth experience and her belief in the impact of coaching to Sounding Board.

Tammy Tawadros is a coach, supervisor, OD practitioner, and work psychologist. She is a member of adjunct faculty at Ashridge and at the Blavatnik School of Government at Oxford University.

Nicky Terblanche is Senior Lecturer Associate Professor and AI researcher at Stellenbosch Business School. He has published more than 30 academic papers and is the creator of coachvici.com.

Eve Turner is a global master accredited coach and supervisor, co-author or co-editor of 4 books including The Ethical Coaches' Handbook, writing extensively on ethics, contracting, systemic working, and societal challenges, and has co-founded 2 free, global communities, the GSN and the CCA.

Woody Woodward is an executive coach, organisational psychologist, speaker, and programme director for the coaching programme at New York University.

Introduction
Coaching in the digital era

*Jonathan Passmore, Sandra J. Diller, Sam Isaacson, and
Maximilian Brantl*

Introduction

Embedding and using technology in professional coaching services has become common-place across the entire planet. This trend is nurtured by the paradigm and mindset shift that was accelerated by the COVID-19 pandemic starting in the spring of 2020, which has forced practitioners worldwide to adapt to digital environments (Passmore et al., 2023, 2024). While the integration of technology has already become part of coaches' day-to-day business, the pace of technological innovations sets an ongoing need for scientific understanding. Thus, the present chapter intends to lay the foundation for a deeper understanding of digital coaching and its future evolution.

To develop a better understanding of the drivers and roadblocks of digital coaching, we will first go back in history and outline the emergence of digital coaching. As a second step, we will shed light on the benefits, particularities, and challenges of digital coaching today. Third, we outline a picture of future capabilities of coaches for digital coaching. Finally, we will discuss the major trends shaping the coaching industry to remain ahead of the wave of transformation.

Coaching in transformation and as a key enabler of change

Coaching, having its roots in different movements and traditions (e.g., sports coaching, Griffiths, 1926; debating, Trueblood, 1911; workplace coaching; Gordy, 1937), was broadly established in the 1980s, becoming a central tool for personal development in the business context (Hudson, 1999; Kampa-Kokesch & Anderson, 2001). Coaching has gained increasing popularity during the past decades (ICF, 2016, 2020, 2022) as a methodology that focuses on providing tailor-made support, fostering the client's self-reflection, self-awareness, and self-change in order to attain self-valued goals (Diller et al., 2021; Greif & Rauen, 2022).

Yet, the coaching industry is entering a phase of rapid transformation due to digitalisation and the integration of technology into the coaching service (Passmore et al., 2023). This change started with the use of telephone coaching in 1990s (e.g. Dutton, 1997; Berry, 2005) and continued with the use of other digital technologies in the 2010s (Sherpa Executive Coaching Survey, 2012, 2020). Particularly since the COVID pandemic, the use of digital technologies in coaching has risen (Diller & Passmore, under

DOI: 10.4324/9781003383741-1

review; ICF, 2023) and new emerging technologies like artificial intelligence (AI) provide completely new potential applications (Grassmann & Schermuly, 2021; Passmore & Tee, 2023).

This digitalisation of coaching has been driven by economic considerations and a change in client needs. Digital coaching has several advantages in terms of easily accessible and on-demand support with reduced travel and costs that potentially enhance inclusivity for people who cannot travel or do not have coaching available in their geographical location (Diller & Passmore, under review). However, digital coaching may also have potential risks, as coaching is an unregulated profession which can lead to an uncontrollable competitive landscape (Fietze, 2016). Secondly, coaches fear that digital coaching negatively impacts the coach–client relationship (Heller et al., 2018), which is considered a crucial success factor for coaching outcomes (e.g., de Haan et al., 2016; Mannhardt & de Haan, 2022). However, research has shown that using digital media in coaching does not appear to adversely affect the coach–client relationship (e.g., Berry et al., 2011; Ghods, 2009; Passarelli et al., 2020, 2022). Moreover, the perceived *quality of communication* was positively correlated with the perceived *quality of the relationship* and the perceived *trustworthiness of the coach* (Passarelli et al., 2020, 2022). In other words, the coach's behaviour was more important than the coaching setting or tools used. Yet, before the COVID pandemic, most coaches preferred in-person coaching (Middendorf, 2016). This has changed rapidly due to the pandemic: During the pandemic, "98,3% of coaches had used online coaching during the 2019–21 period" (Passmore, 2021). Furthermore, even after the pandemic, in 2021, as restrictions were lifted, more than 80% of the coaches expected to continue using digital coaching as their post-pandemic modus operandi. Thus, the coaching landscape shifted sustainably towards online services: in the period between 2019 and 2021, more than 70% of the coaches used either online tools, telephone coaching, or emails as their primary way to provide their coaching services (Figure 0.1, Passmore, 2021). Since then, digital coaching services such as BetterUp, CoachHub, and EZRA have seen significant growth in clients, and have been able to secure millions of venture capital, investing in the belief of continued market growth (Handelsblatt, 2021, 2022). Figure 0.1 provides an overview of the different modalities and how this position is changing with technology playing an increasing role in coaching delivery.

There is not one approach to digital coaching. To understand the impact of technology on coaching, a nuanced perspective needs to be taken, considering the purpose, extent of use, and particularities of a specific technology. First, the purpose or role of technology for coaching needs to be clarified, e.g., are digital tools only used to enable communication between the coach and coachee, or are they used as problem-solving tools (cf. Geißler, 2022; Geißler & Rödel, 2023). In general, there are three roles that technologies can have in coaching sessions: (1) They can be used to enable the coach–client dialogue (e.g., video-conference coaching in times of social distancing), (2) to support specific interventions or methods (e.g., recording of a presentation of the client, shadowing), or (3) to replace the physical coach by a machine-human interaction partly or entirely (e.g., self-coaching apps, AI-based coaching formats). In addition, technology can streamline administrative processes (e.g., scheduling, documentation, accounting, etc.), facilitate the coach's self-reflection process, and help coaches to attract new clients (e.g., by leveraging digital marketing). Second, the extent of technology use (e.g., whether technology

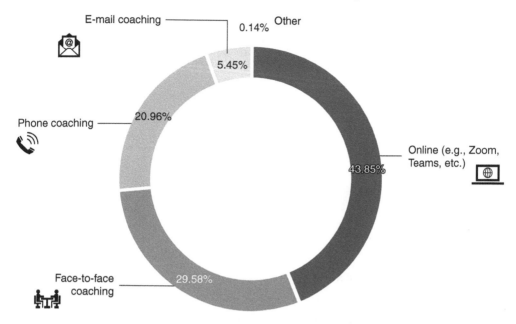

Coaching modalities 2019–21: A sustainable shift towards digital coaching

Figure 0.1 The coaching landscape is sustainably shifting towards digital coaching.

is only used for specific exercises or to facilitate the entire coaching process) and its methodological implementation into the coaching process must be considered. The involvement level of technology in a coaching process is inherently defined by its role. Still, the involvement level can vary according to the preferences of the coach and coachee (e.g., video conferences could be the only way a coach and coachee interact, be a fallback solution, or be integrated into a blended coaching approach). Finally, the specific technologies or media (e.g., text-based, audio, audio-visual, and interactive) that are used have different implications for the coaching process and the coach–client interaction (e.g., in telephone coaching, visual cues are not available). Therefore, the type of medium defines the communication type (e.g., asynchronous vs. synchronous) and the variety of available sense data (cues: hear, see, taste, smell, and feel). In Figure 0.2 we illustrate some of the ways technology can be used in coaching, from enabling conversations to replacing the human coach.

To successfully deliver the benefits and opportunities of technology for coaching, the coach needs to be clear about the role of technology, how to embed it in the coaching process, and understand the particularities and limits of the specific technology used.

Benefits, opportunities, particularities, and challenges of digital coaching

Digital coaching, in general, provides practical benefits and opportunities that go beyond the economic advantages of cost and time saving and therefore create new opportunities

Technology in coaching can be used differently

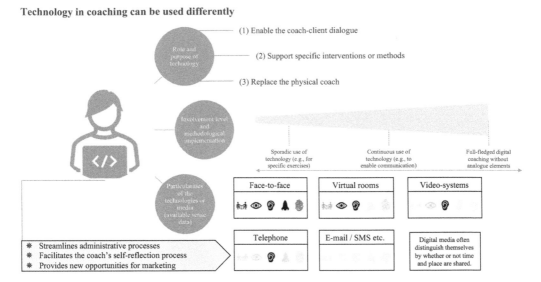

Figure 0.2 Three key elements define how technology is used in coaching.

for coaches and clients but also new challenges. Some of the upsides of digital coaching refer equally to the coach and coachee, whereas others are specific to one or the other party. For example, the global accessibility of coaching allows clients in Asia to identify the best coach for their problem regardless of the coach's location. In contrast, coaches, on the other hand, can expand their potential client base irrespective of the location. In the following section we will review some of the benefits which digital coaching can deliver, alongside aspects of the relationship which coaches need to manage.

Cost and time savings: The use of technology, e.g., video conferences, enables coaching without a physical presence. Therefore, coaches and clients can save travel time and expenses, reducing the overall time and costs associated with coaching. Moreover, based on the reduced costs, organisations can provide coaching services to a larger number of employees with lower overall cost. Finally, digital coaching is also associated with reducing administrative and inefficient activities (Kinnunen & Georgescu, 2020).

Flexibility and accessibility: In accordance with location-independent coaching, using technology facilitates scheduling appointments as digital coaching increases the flexibility of integrating coaching into packed meeting schedules by reducing time barriers and allowing short-notice scheduling. Furthermore, coaching can be executed despite different time zones and long distances, enabling an optimal coach–client-fit (e.g., McLaughlin, 2013; Deniers, 2019; Berninger-Schäfer, 2018; Ribbers & Waringa, 2015): Clients are able to select the coach based on the coach's educational background, professional expertise, and approach, regardless of their geographical location. Moreover, it enables building long-term client relationships even when clients need to travel or move abroad, e.g., for short time business meetings or relocation. Finally, location-independent coaching enables coaches to increase their scope as they do not need to limit their services based on geographical proximity.

Frequency: Based on the increased flexibility and accessibility, digital coaching can be executed on a frequency aligned with the coachee's preferences as on-demand coaching becomes feasible, and it takes fewer coordination efforts to reschedule cancelled coaching sessions. Furthermore, digital tools and platforms provide the opportunity to apply asynchronous communication (e.g., based on emails, SMS, writing online journals) between the coaching sessions, allowing a continuous interaction between coach and client.

Practice transfer support: Based on the opportunity to maintain a continuous dialogue, digital coaching provides new opportunities to support clients in transferring insights from coaching to the 'real world'. For example, coaches can remind clients of their action items and empower them before a critical situation takes place (e.g., an annual performance review meeting).

Structure: Technologies provide new opportunities to structure the coaching process by integrating workflows or allowing the coach to review past notes, relevant models, or other scientific frameworks in a digital library accessible in a more convenient manner.

Digital documentation: Finally, integrating digital forms for the initial interview with clients, self-surveys (e.g., with an automated evaluation), or digital journals reduce the time coaches need to invest in the documentation. Also, digital scheduling tools (e.g., Doodle) or digital assistants reduce the administrative efforts of coaches.

Sustainability: In almost all cases, using technology reduces the negative impact on the planet. As organisations increasingly recognise their responsibility to care for the natural world, technology offers an opportunity to achieve this goal.

Furthermore, digital coaching provides opportunities that need to be understood in more detail as they can also be considered as tradeoffs (e.g., a stronger feeling of anonymity may lead to more openness by the client) or are based on the maturity of the technology in the coaching process (e.g., using VR or AR to simulate specific situations).

Anonymity, disinhibition, and increased safety: Especially text-based coaching but also video-conference coaching and self-coaching apps increase the feeling of anonymity of the client and increase the psychological safety of the client. For example, even in video-conference coaching, the client can turn off the camera while performing a specific self-reflection task. Furthermore, the client can choose an environment that makes them feel safe and confident. Some research proposes that a feeling of anonymity and increased safety nurtures disinhibition (Suler, 2004) and therefore leads to more openness during the coaching. Nevertheless, this phenomenon needs to be understood more in detail as the bond between coach and coachee is success-critical for the coaching outcome, and the concept of anonymity at least can be understood as a hurdle to strengthening personal bonds.

Creativity and innovation: The broad range of digital creative tools enables coaches to engage in more innovative coaching practices with their coachees (e.g., digital picture cards, AI-generated artwork, and multi-sensory experiences, Isaacson, 2022; see also Schwartzman & Boswell, 2020).

Finally, based on the particularities of specific technologies, new challenges arise depending on the role, level of integration, and type of technology used, having direct implications on ethics and professional standards of digital coaching.

Technical excellence: During the coaching, the coach takes the role of a process expert or 'process consultant' (Schein, 1999). Therefore, clients expect a frictionless and seamless integrated self-evaluation journey. If either a technological problem arises (e.g., a broken internet connection, frequent crashes of software) or the coach lacks the experience in using specific tools (e.g., the explanation of how to move in a VR is not clear enough or the coach cannot answer specific questions on the tools), the coaching process can be slowed down, or the trust in the coach can be impacted.

Increased impact and opportunities by new tools: Furthermore, digital coaching provides new opportunities to enable interventions as technology can be easily embedded into existing methods (e.g., recording the presentation of the client to support the analyses of how they are perceived during a presentation or speech) and provides new opportunities (e.g., confronting clients with challenging situations by VR; this, for example, is already being integrated into exposure therapy for anxiety disorders, Powers & Emmelkamp, 2008).

Lack of physical presence: "Presence is the quality of a therapist connecting with his/her patient" (Rogers, 1979, 1980) and, therefore, by many practicians (e.g., Iliffe-Wood, 2014; Du Toit, 2014; Silsbee, 2008) and professional coaching associations (cf. ICF, e.g., Bhattacharya, 2018) considered an essential element in coaching. Digital coaching, based on the applied media, provides other forms of presence, e.g., telepresence. Telepresence can be described as "A set of technologies that allows a person to feel as if he/she was present, to give the appearance of being present, or to have an effect at a place other than the true location of that person' (Collins et al., 2020). Nevertheless, the opportunity of creating a feeling to have an impact in remote coaching settings depends on the media used and the coach.

Reduction of cues: One of the central challenges in digital coaching consists of the fact that, based on the chosen type of media, only a reduced variety of sense data is available. Whereas coaches efficiently synthesise the fact-based information and all the information of their five senses (sight, smell, hearing, taste, and touch) during in-person face-to-face coaching, text-based coaching, for example, provides no additional information. Therefore, coaches need to develop strategies and techniques to compensate for the lack of additional information. Berry et al. (2011), for example, recommended that the absence of visual cues in telephone-based coaching can be compensated by a more robust working alliance.

Data security and confidentiality: As in a coaching process, sensitive and personal-related information is exchanged, confidentiality has always been a prerequisite for coaching services. Given the required transfer of information in communications technologies, coaches need to be aware that they cannot guarantee that client information will be kept safe while using technology, as they face new risks in the form of cyber-crimes. The risk of cyber-crimes can be mitigated, but not eliminated. Therefore, coaches must assess the data security of their digital tools and implement specific measures to partially mitigate risks through strong information security controls and compliance with data privacy legislation (e.g., General Data Protection Regulation, GDPR).

Over-reliance on technology: As technology encroaches deeper into the territory of coaching conversations, historically held exclusively by the coach, the nature of the coaching relationship becomes more influenced from an ontological design perspective by the technology than by the coach. Holding closely to coaching ethics while feeling a need to adapt to a digital tool will introduce new challenges.

Ethical challenges: Finally, new ethical challenges arise with digital coaching, and coaches need to develop a clear concept of how to address them. For example, the always accessibility of a coach by SMS-based communication can, in extreme situations, lead to similar challenges psychotherapists are facing: Do I need to reply to an urgent text message from my client who seems to be at the edge of an existential crisis at 1 am on a Friday? Furthermore, coaching clients at home via video conferences also provides a new dimension of insights into the clients' private life that may be worrisome: How do you deal with a picture of multiple empty wine bottles in the background or signs of domestic violence happening in the background? With the expansion of conversational AI technology, new ethical challenges will be experienced such as the tools that gave tips on drug misuse to children.

Taking the opportunities and challenges into consideration, it is evident that coaches need to develop new skills and adopt a lifelong-learning mindset to integrate state-of-the-art technology into their coaching service portfolio, leveraging the benefits of digital coaching.

Needed skills and mindset in a new era

Defining the future skills and mindset that are needed in coaching is quite difficult. As Michael Cavanagh (ICF, 2022) pointed out, there is no jointly acknowledged and scientifically based interaction framework of coaching capabilities:

> I wasn't able to find a single experimental randomised controlled study of coaching competencies. What I did find was a whole bunch of different frameworks and all different sorts of qualitative studies, but really what they are is mostly at the level of collated opinion. You get a whole bunch of experts together, and you say, well, what are the competencies, and then that becomes a competency framework.

Even though an encompassing evolution path cannot be described as there is no joint basis, and the further evolution of new technologies may add further skills and new challenges, it is needed to prepare for the future in several ways.

Most essential to thrive in the future is the development of a new mindset regarding coaching, in the sense that coaches need to internalise that it will be success-critical for the future to continuously explore the opportunities and limits of new technology in order to select and integrate technology seamlessly at the right time. Thus, the future coach needs to develop a new self-concept that goes beyond the role of a 'process consultant' (Schein, 1999), but they need to understand themselves as an advanced user of the technology, tools, and media used during the coaching process. This implies not only that they master the technologies used but are capable of explaining and enabling their clients to use them. As an indispensable prerequisite, coaches need to develop a positive attitude towards the use of technology in coaching: Developing the needed skills and gathering experience in using media can positively affect our perception of the media's richness (e.g., D'Urso & Rains, 2008; Timmermann & Madhavapeddi, 2007) and our attitude towards it. Therefore, continuous exploration of new technologies and their application will lay the foundation for thriving as a digital coach.

Furthermore, coaches need to mature in their ability to develop and test hypotheses based on the cues and sense data available to them, for example, by becoming more sensitive to language in writing when communicating predominantly through text messaging. In digital environments that lack visual cues, there may be other information available that can support the coach in decoding the needs and motives of a client. In addition to this, coaches need to become more agile and flexible as they need to be capable of adapting their coaching style not only in light of their client but also in light of the (digital) coaching setting and the technologies used. Based on the available cues and sense data defined by the technologies used, the coach needs to use different strategies to develop a strong and fruitful relationship with the client, establish and show empathy, guide the process, and enable problem-solving. This also means that coaches need to extend their toolbox beyond solely mastering the use of technologies.

Finally, communication in different forms (e.g., facilitating the client's thinking by asking the right questions, Clutterbuck, 2020; showing empathy by active listening, Diller et al., 2021; Will et al., 2016; remaining silent to provide the needed room for ideas to evolve) will remain the central tools for coaches even in digital coaching. Considering that communication has different levels (e.g., Watzlawick et al., 1967; Schulz von Thun, 2009) and that especially emotions are most powerfully conveyed non-verbally (Roter & Hall, 2006), coaches should compensate for non-verbal communication cues in settings that lack visual and paralingual sense data through the development of more lively, visual, and descriptive language. Furthermore, coaches need to be aware that the development of language is impacted by the evolution of technology and new forms of non-verbal communication are being established, for example, by the application of emojis (Gee & Hayes, 2011), the use of capital letters, or exclamation marks (Harris & Paradice, 2007; Riordan & Kreuz, 2010), and the implementation of avatars. Therefore, coaches need to be able to decode these new forms of non-verbal communication contextually. Nevertheless, the meaning and application of these new forms of non-verbal communication are not universal. For example, the application of emojis is related to the cultural context (Park et al., 2014). Thus, coaches need not only to learn to understand the new forms of non-verbal communication that are evolving but also to develop an awareness of the cultural and individual application of these expressions.

Whereas the basics for digital coaching, like developing a more pictorial and vivid language or mastering specific technologies, can be successfully acquired by training, the development of the needed capabilities (e.g., having the right strategies for different digital coaching settings and tools to establish a fruitful coach–client relationship) and mindset (e.g., perceiving technologies as opportunities for coaches and clients) needs a more deliberate self-reflection process. Therefore, supervision as a tool to support the own self-reflection process will become even more important for coaches in the future.

Future trends in coaching

The coaching industry is at the dawn of a radical and continuous transformation that will sustainably shape and refine fundamental core beliefs, competencies, and ways of working for coaches. Even though the transformation pace will vary between geographic locations and specific client segments, there are three trends that will define the future of coaching:

(1) Digitalisation and democratisation of the majority of coaching services.
(2) Refinement of the definition of coaching and differentiation from other interventions such as counselling and training.
(3) Scientific-based updates of competency models for coaches and related training programmes.
(4) Organisational people agendas including mental wellbeing, inclusion strategies, leadership approaches based on shared responsibility, and the transformation of knowledge work will remain as 'hot topics'.

(1) Digitalisation and democratisation of the majority of coaching services

The digital evolution of coaching will continue at a rapid pace (Passmore, 2021), and the coaching industry, in general, will enter the fourth stage of its development: production (see Figure 0.1; Passmore & Evans-Krimme, 2021). Integrating emerging technologies will create new opportunities and challenges for coaches. For example, the challenges that are associated with a lack of physical presence can be offset as VR and AR evolve. Moreover, these technologies already facilitate a new form of telepresence and client's self-reflection by changing the perspective (Woods, 2018) through 'teleportation' or allowing the client to experience critical situations through simulation. As these technologies mature and become part of our everyday life, creating a 'real world' experience, they will sustainably

The evolution of coaching

Figure 0.3 The coaching industry's evolution is now entering stage 4, 'productisation'.
Source: Passmore & Evans-Krimme (2021).

shape future coaching methods. Furthermore, with the growing demand for coaching services reaching across all grades within organisations, coaching will continue on its journey of being 'democratised'. This results in consolidation and standardisation for a large majority of coaching services by a few online large-scale platforms (e.g., BetterUp, CoachHub, EZRA), enabling "low-cost and on-demand access to coaching services informed by science, in multiple languages" (Passmore & Evans-Krimme, 2021, p. 5). As conversational AI technology continues to improve, this is likely to further impact the industry.

(2) Scientifically based update of the competency model for coaches and training

Today, there is only limited insight into what behaviour of the coach leads to successful coaching outcomes, even though many researchers claimed that this is needed (e.g., de Haan et al., 2016; Jones, Woods, & Guillaume, 2016). In order to build a scientifically based competency model for coaching, it is necessary to understand the impact of the coach's behaviour on the known success factors and derive the needed skillset. This call for action becomes even more important as only 50% of competencies identified in surveys or Delphi techniques in management and leadership literature can be proven to have a relevant impact in follow-up research (Boyatzis, 1982). Moreover, 25% of the identified competencies seem irrelevant, and another 25% seem counterproductive to performance (Boyatzis, 1982; Spencer & Spencer, 1993). Thus, to enable coaching to develop into a mature profession based on scientific evidence, it is necessary to link the identified success factors in coaching to concrete behaviours of the coach and then develop a comprehensive competency model synthesising the insights. This becomes even more relevant as different (digital) coaching settings will need different strategies and competencies (e.g., Berninger-Schäfer, 2020; Geißler, 2020; Friesenhahn & Taylor, 2019) and therefore, coaches need to alternate their behaviour in different contexts successfully.

In terms of research, this means also a more structured approach is needed, including randomised control trials and longitudinal studies, specifically exploring coaching competencies as well as the components of generally accepted success factors, like the coach–client relationship, trust, and empathy. These studies need to consider especially the interaction, mediation, and moderation of success factors and the particularities of the differences in digital coaching settings to provide structured guidance for coaches on how to thrive in a digital environment. Moreover, organisations long for transparency and objective, measurable outcomes of coaching success. To meet these needs, coaching research needs to focus more deliberately on objective, measurable coaching outcomes for both coachees and sponsors. Finally, even though developing an integrated model of coaching competencies is indispensable, there will be no 'one size fits all' solution. Coaches need to continuously develop their competencies in light of the accelerated evolution of technology.

(3) Organisational people agendas including mental wellbeing, inclusion strategies, leadership approaches based on shared responsibility and the transformation of knowledge work will remain the 'hot topics'

Events of the recent past, like the COVID-19 pandemic, global inflation, and the war in Ukraine, have shown the possibility of repeated large-scale disruptive events in the future (e.g., Irving, 2021). Therefore, the perceived level of uncertainty has increased significantly, and people need to learn how to deal with this. This development is fostered by the transformation of knowledge work in light of the integration of new technologies, redefining the division of labour and required capabilities and skills. Thus, one central topic for coaches in the future will be enabling people to successfully thrive in a rapidly changing world by acquiring the capabilities needed for a fast-track adaption as well as learning how to successfully cope with stress induced by multiple sources (e.g., Passmore, 2021).

Furthermore, the awareness of mental health issues has risen, leading to intensive research and development of applications focused on health behaviour change (Brinkman, 2016). Taking into consideration that work-life balance plays an important role in mental health, e.g., people who perceive a good balance between their work life and private life report better physical and mental health (Brough et al., 2014; Haar et al., 2012; Lunau et al., 2014), especially enabling a good work-life balance will remain one of the central themes of coaching in the future (e.g., Passmore, 2021).

Organisations' increasing acceptance of the role the workplace – physical, virtual, and/or hybrid – in employees' lived experience has impacted on expected coaching topics and outcomes. As the continual development of new technology leads to greater reliance on those skills that technology cannot replace yet, coaching will need to keep on adapting.

The present book

The present book is divided into seven parts. Each section sheds light on a specific aspect of coaching in a digital environment and combines state-of-the-art research with insights from seasoned practitioners.

The first part outlines what digital coaching is in general, how it is defined in contrast to face-to-face coaching, and how the emerging practice of digital coaching is embedded in the overall transformation of the world. In particular, light will be shed on how the world of working will change and what skills are needed in the future to thrive as a coach, and how the demands of clients will change. Furthermore, it will explore how digital technologies can enable coaches to gain new clients in a more competitive world and provide world-class services, unleashing the full potential of digital coaching.

In the second part, a deep dive into the different technologies that can be used in digital coaching will be provided, exploring established technologies like video-conference coaching and developing a clearer picture of the future potential of new technologies. In addition the opportunities, and limitations of artificial intelligence and virtual reality will also be discussed. Furthermore, the use of technologies for nurturing creativity and fostering self-reflection will be outlined.

In the third part, coaches will be provided with clear guidance on how to thrive in developing their digital coaching practice and align with data-security standards. We will also discuss how success factors of coaching are affected by a digital environment and how coaches can nurture them. In particular, light will be shed on how to develop trust, show empathy, and nurture a fruitful relationship in a digital environment. Moreover, new challenges that arise with digital coaching are discussed and how ethics can be managed online.

The fourth part will explicitly discuss how digital coaching can foster inclusion and diversity while considering the new challenges that emerge with the use of artificial intelligence. Thus, coaches will be provided with clear guidance on how technology can be used to include marginalised groups and what pitfalls need to be avoided. Thus, this section will illuminate one of the most important social factors of our time.

The fifth part will provide the big picture of digital coaching and outline the evolution of the coaching industry over the next years. The most important trends and the changing competitive landscape will be discussed as well as the disruptive potential of artificial intelligence for a new era of coaching.

The sixth part will provide tangible case studies of how to apply digital coaching in traditional one-to-one settings and show how coaching can enable teams in a digital workplace. Furthermore, best practices in terms of providing and participating in digital supervision will be discussed.

The final section of the book will provide first-hand perspectives from entrepreneurs and leaders in the digital and AI coaching sector. These mini chapters provide a unique insight into the minds of those leading the digital coaching revolution.

We hope, this book will enable coaches to better understand and adapt to a new era of digital coaching, helping them to develop the skills needed to thrive in the future of the new coaching industry.

References

Alaoui, O., & Passmore, J. (2022). Is it time to embrace the technology of transformation of coaching? *Coaching Perspectives, (33)*, 8–11.

APA. (2023). Different approaches to psychotherapy. Psychologists generally draw on one or more theories of psychotherapy. Retrieved on 20th March 2023 from www.apa.org/topics/psychother apy/approaches

Atad, O. I., & Grant, A. M. (2021). How does coach training change coaches-in-training? Differential effects for novices. Experienced 'skilled helpers'. *Coaching: An International Journal of Theory, Research, and Practice, 14*(1), 3–19. https://doi.org/10.1080/17521882.2019.1707246

Berninger-Schäfer, E. (Ed.). (2018). *Online-Coaching.* Wiesbaden: Springer.

Berninger-Schäfer, E. (2020). *Online-coaching.* Fakten & Mythen. Coaching-Magazin Online.

Berry, M. R. (2005). *A comparison of face-to-face and distance coaching practices: The role of the working alliance in problem resolution.* Unpublished doctoral dissertation, Georgia State University, Atlanta, Georgia.

Berry, R. M, Ashby, J. S., Gnilka, P. B., & Matheny, K. B. (2011). A comparison of face-to-face and distance coaching practices: Coaches' perception of the role of the working alliance in problem resolution. *Consulting Psychology Journal: Practice and Research, 63*, 243–253.

Bhattacharya, S. (2018). The gift of coaching presence. International Coaching Federation. Retrieved on 20th March 2023 from https://coachingfederation.org/blog/gift-coaching-presence

Boyatzis, R. E. (1982). *The competent manager: A model for effective performance.* John Wiley & Sons.

Boyatzis, R. E., Hullinger, A., Ehasz, S. F., Harvey, J., Tassarotti, S., Gallotti, A., & Penafort, F. (2022). The grand challenge for research on the future of coaching. *Journal of Applied Behavioral Science, 58*(2), 202–222. https://doi.org/10.1177/00218863221079937

Brinkman, W.-P. (2016). Virtual health agents for behavior change: Research perspectives and directions. In *Proceedings of the Workshop on Graphical and Robotic Embodied Agents for*

Therapeutic Systems (GREATS16) Held During the International Conference on Intelligent Virtual Agents (IVA16) (pp. 1–17). http://ii. tudelft.nl/willem-paul/. Online at www.macs.hw.ac. uk/$ruth/ greats16-programme

Brough, P., Timms, C., O'Driscoll, M. P., Kalliath, T., Siu, O.-L., Sit, C., & Lo, D. (2014). Work–life balance: A longitudinal evaluation of a new measure across Australia and New Zealand workers. *International Journal of Human Resource Management, 25*(19), 2724–2744. https://doi.org/10.1080/09585192.2014.899262

Clutterbuck, D. (1998). *Learning alliances: Tapping into talent.* London: Institute of Personnel & Development.

Clutterbuck, D. (2020). Questions in coaching. In J. Passmore (Ed.), *The coaches handbook. The complete practitioner guide for professional coaches.* Oxon: Routledge.

Collins, J. W. et al. (2020). Utilising an accelerated Delphi process to develop guidance and protocols for telepresence applications in remote robotic surgery training. *European Urology Open Science, 22,* 23–33. https://doi.org/10.1016/j.euros.2020.09.005

de Haan, E., Grant, A., Burger, Y., & Eriksson, P.-O. (2016). A large-scale study of executive coaching outcome: The relative contributions of working relationship, personality match, and self-efficacy. *Consulting Psychology Journal: Practice and Research, 68,* 189–207.

Deniers, C. (2019). Experiences of receiving career coaching via Skype: An interpretative phenomenological analysis. *International Journal of Evidence Based Coaching and Mentoring, 17,* 72–81. doi:10.24384/r4j8-hm94

Deutschland Funk. (2020). Folgen der Coronakrise. Was in unserer Gesellschaft wirklich systemrelevant ist. Retrieved on 15th March 2022 from www.deutschlandfunk.de/folgen-der-coronakrise-was-in-unserer-gesellschaft-wirklich-100.html

Deutscher Verband für Coaching und Training e.V. (2016). E-Learning – Angebot folgt wachsender Nachfrage. Abgerufen am 12.08.2019: www.dvct.de/aktuelles/dvct-pressemitteilungen/artikel/e-learning-angebot-folgt-wachsender-nachfrage

Diller, S. J. (2024). Ethics in digital and AI coaching. *Human Resource Development International,* in advance of print. https://doi.org/10.1080/13678868.2024.2315928

Diller, S. J., Muehlberger, C., Braumandl, I., & Jonas, E. (2021). Supporting students with coaching or training depending on their basic psychological needs. *International Journal of Mentoring and Coaching in Education, 10*(1), 84–100. https://doi.org/10.1108/IJMCE-08-2020-0050

Diller, S. J., Mühlberger, C., Löhlau, N., & Jonas, E. (2021). How to show empathy as a coach: The effects of coaches' imagine-self versus imagine-other empathy on the client's self-change and coaching outcome. *Current Psychology, 42,* 11917–11935. https://doi.org/10.1007/s12144-021-02430-y

Diller, S. J., & Passmore, J. (2023). Defining digital coaching: A qualitative inductive approach. *Frontiers in Psychology, Section Organizational Psychology, Special Issue: Advancing Coaching Scholarship, 14.* https://doi.org/10.3389/fpsyg.2023.1148243

D'Urso, S. C., & Rains, S. A. (2008). Examining the scope of channel expansion: A test of channel expansion theory with new and traditional communication media. *Management Communication Quarterly, 21*(4), 486–507.

Du Toit, A. (2014). *Making sense of coaching.* Los Angeles, CA: Sage.

Dutton, Gail. (Feb. 1997). Executive coaches call the plays. *Management Review, 86*(2), 39+. *Gale Academic OneFile,* link.gale.com/apps/doc/A19109940/AONE?u=anon~748ce089&sid=googleScholar&xid=06768dfa.

Ebermann, D. (2017). Coaching im Digitalen Wandel. Teil 1: Wie verändern sich Branche und Markt? *Coaching Magazin, 10*(1), 9–11.

Fietze, B. (2016). Coaching in der reflexiven Moderne. In R. Wegener, S. Deplazes, M. Hasenbein, H. Künzli, A. Ryter, & B. Uebelhart (Eds.), *Coaching als individuelle Antwort auf gesellschaftliche Entwicklungen* (S. 36–44). Wiesbaden: Springer.

Friesenhahn, J., & Taylor, M. (2019). Chancen und Grenzen von Online-Coaching. *Coaching-Magazin, 12*(3), S. 50–54. Retrieved on 1st January 2023 from www.coaching-magazin.de/wisse nschaft/chancen-und-grenzen-von-online-coaching

Gee, J. P., & Hayes, E. (2011). *Language and learning in the digital age.* Routledge. https://doi.org/ 10.4324/9780203830918

Geißler, H. (2020). Digitalisierung von Coaching und Coaching-Ausbildungen. *Coaching-Magazin Online.* Retrieved on 1st January 2023 from www.coaching-magazin.de/beruf-coach/digitalisier ung-von-coaching-und-coaching-ausbildungen

Geißler, H. (2022). E-coaching: An overview. In S. Greif, H. Möller, W. Scholl, J. Passmore & F. Müller (Eds.), *International handbook of evidence-based coaching* (pp. 269–280). Cham: Springer Nature Switzerland.

Geißler, H., & Rödel, S. (2023). *Praxishandbuch professionelles Online-Coaching.* Weinheim, Basel: Beltz.

Ghods, N. (2009). *Distance coaching: The relationship between the coach-client relationship, client satisfaction and coaching outcomes.* Unpublished doctoral dissertation, Alliant International University, San Diego, CA.

Gordy, C. (1937). Everyone gets a share of the profits. *Factory Management and Maintenance, 95,* 82–83.

Grant, A. (2011). Developing an agenda for teaching coaching psychology. *International Coaching Psychology Review, 6*(1), 84–99.

Grant, A. M. (2003). The impact of life coaching on goal attainment, metacognition and mental health. *Social Behavior and Personality, 31*(3), 253–264.

Grant, A. M. (2012). Making positive change: A randomized study comparing solution-focused vs. problem-focused coaching questions. *Journal of Systemic Therapies, 31*(2), 21–35. https://doi. org/10.1521/jsyt.2012.31.2.21

Grant, A. M., & Cavanagh, M. J. (2004). Toward a profession of coaching: Sixty-five years of progress and challenges for the future. *International Journal of Evidence Based Coaching and Mentoring, 2*(1), 1–16.

Graßmann, C., & Schermuly, C. C. (2021). Coaching with artificial intelligence: Concepts and capabilities. *Human Resource Development Review, 20*(1), 106–126. https://doi.org/10.1177/ 1534484320982891

Green, S., & Palmer, S. (2019). Positive psychology coaching. In S. Green & S. Palmer (Eds.), *Positive psychology coaching in practice* (pp. 1–20). Routledge.

Greif, S., & Rauen, C. (2022). Self-reflection in coaching. In S. Greif, H. Möller, W. Scholl, J. Passmore & F. Müller (Eds.), *International handbook of evidence-based coaching.* Cham: Springer. https:// doi.org/10.1007/978-3-030-81938-5_69

Greif, S., Möller, H., Passmore, J., & Müller, F. (Eds.). (2022). *International handbook of evidence-based coaching.* Cham: Springer. https://doi.org/10.1007/978-3-03081938-5_14

Griffiths, C. R. (1926). *Psychology of coaching: A study of coaching methods from the point of view of psychology.* New York: Charles Scribner's and Sons.

Haar, J. M., Roche, M., & Taylor, D. (2012). Work–family conflict and turnover intentions of indigenous employees: The importance of the whanau/family for Maori. *International Journal of Human Resource Management, 23*(12), 2546–2560.

Handelsblatt. (2021). US-Start-UP; BetterUp sammelt weitere 300 Millionen Dollar ein und greift deutsche Coaching Plattformen an. Retrieved on 5th May 2022 from www.handelsblatt.com/ unternehmen/dienstleister/us-start-up-betterup-sammelt-weitere-300-millionen-dollar-ein-und-greift-deutsche-coaching-plattformen-an/27690138.html

Handelsblatt. (2022). Coaching für jeden Mitarbeiter: Coachhub will zum globalen Marktführer warden Über die digitale Plattform können Firmen ihren Mitarbeitern persönliche Beratung bieten. Investoren setzen darauf, dass der Trend weiter an Fahrt gewinnt. Retrieved on 30th July

2023 from www.handelsblatt.com/technik/it-internet/start-up-check-coaching-fuer-jeden-mita
rbeiter-coachhub-will-zum-globalen-marktfuehrer-werden/28878342.html

Harris, R., & Paradice, D. (2007). An investigation of the computer-mediated communication of emotions. *Journal of Applied Sciences Research, 3*, 2081–2090.

Heller, J., Triebel, C., Hauser, B., & Koch, A. (2018). *Digitale Medien im Coaching*. Berlin, Heidelberg: Springer.

Hudson, F. (1999). *The handbook of coaching*. San Francisco, CA: Jossey-Bass.

ICF. (2016). Global coaching study executive summary. Retrieved on 28 February 2023 from https://coachfederation.org/app/uploads/2017/12/2016ICFGlobalCoachingStudy_Executive Summary-2.pdf

ICF. (2020). Global coaching study – executive summary. Retrieved on 21st December 2022 from https://coachingfederation.org/app/uploads/2020/09/FINAL_ICF_GCS2020_ExecutiveSumm ary.pdf

ICF. (2022). Updated competency models improve coaching's effectiveness. Retrieved on 20th February 2023 from https://thoughtleadership.org/research-needs-on-coaching-competencies/

ICF. (2023). *ICF Global Coaching Study 2023 Final Report*. https://coachingfederation.org/

Iliffe-Wood, M. (2014). *Coaching presence: Building consciousness and awareness in coaching interventions*. London: Kogan Page Publishers.

Irving, J. (2021). How have workplace coaches experienced coaching during the Covid-19 pandemic? *International Journal of Evidence Based Coaching & Mentoring, 15*.

Isaacson, S. (2021). *How to thrive as a coach in a digital world*. Maidenhead: Open University Press-McGraw-Hill.

Isaacson, S. (2022). *Superhuman coaching*. London: Hanwell Publishing.

Jones, R. J., Woods, S. A., & Guillaume, Y. R. (2016). The effectiveness of workplace coaching: A meta-analysis of learning and performance outcomes from coaching. *Journal of Occupational and Organizational Psychology, 89*(2), 249–277.

Kampa-Kokesch, S., & Anderson, M. (2001). Executive coaching: A comprehensive review of the literature. *Consulting Psychology Journal: Practice and Research, 53*, 205–228.

Kinnunen, J., & Georgescu, I. (2020). Disruptive pandemic as a driver towards digital coaching in OECD countries. *RevistaRomaneasca Pentru Educatie Multidimensionala, 12*(2Sup1), 55–61. https://doi.org/10.18662/rrem/12.2Sup1/289

Korthagen, F. A., Hoekstra, A., & Meijer, P. C. (2013). Promoting presence in professional practice: A core reflection approach. *Perspectives on theory U: Insights from the field* (pp. 77–96). DOI: 10.4018/978-1-4666-4793-0.ch006

Lunau, T., Bambra, C., Eikemo, T. A., van der Wel, K. A., & Dragano, N. (2014). A balancing act? Work–life balance, health and well-being in European welfare states. *European Journal of Public Health, 24*(3), 422–427. https://doi.org/10.1093/eurpub/cku010

Mannhardt, S. M., & de Haan, E. (2022). The coaching relationship. In S. Greif, H. Möller, & W. Scholl (Eds.) *International handbook of evidenced based coaching*. Cham: Springer.

McLaughlin, M. (2013). Less is more: The executive coach's experience of working on the telephone. *International Journal of Evidence Based Coaching and Mentoring, 7*, 1–13.

Michalik, N. M., & Schermuly, C. C. (2022). Is technostress stressing coaches out? The relevance of technostress to coaches' emotional exhaustion and coaches' perception of coaching success. *Coaching: An International Journal of Theory, Research and Practice, 16*(2), 155-172. https://doi.org/10.1080/17521882.2022.2128386

Middendorf, J. (2016). 14. Coaching-Umfrage Deutschland 2015/2016. Retrieved on 25th April 2020 from https://coachingumfrage.files.wordpress.com/2017/04/ergeb-coaching-umfrage-2015.pdf

Mühlberger, M. D., & Traut-Mattausch, E. (2015). Leading to effectiveness: Comparing dyadic coaching and group coaching. *The Journal of Applied Behavioral Science, 51*(2), 198–230. https://doi.org/10.1177/0021886315574331

Neck, C. P., & Houghton, J. D. (2017). Two decades of self-leadership theory and research: Past developments, present trends, and future possibilities. *Journal of Vocational Behavior, 100*, 88–97.

OECD. (2004). *Lifelong learning*. Policy Brief February 2004. Paris: OECD.

Park, J., Baek, Y. M., & Cha, M. (2014). Cross-cultural comparison of nonverbal cues in emoticons on twitter: Evidence from big data analysis. *Journal of Communication, 64*, 333–354. https://doi.org/10.1111/jcom.12086

Passarelli, A., Trinh, M. P., Van Oosten, E. B., & Varley, M. (2020). Can you hear me now? The influence of perceived media richness on executive coaching relationships. *Academy of Management Proceedings, 2020*(1), 13211.

Passarelli, A. M., Trinh, M. P., van Oosten, E. B., & Varley, A. (2022). Communication quality and relational self-expansion: The path to leadership coaching effectiveness. *Human Resource Management*. Advance online publication.

Passmore, J. (2021). *Global Coach Survey 2021– Passmore*. Retrieved on 30th December 2022 from www.researchgate.net/profile/Jonathan-Passmore/publication/355491476_Global_Coach_Survey_2021_Passmore/links/617593c0a767a03c14a90752/Global-Coach-Survey-2021-Passmore.pdf

Passmore, J., & Evans-Krimme, R. (2021). The future of coaching: A conceptual framework for the coaching sector from personal craft to scientific process and the implications for practice and research. *Frontiers in Psychology, 12*, 1–8. https://doi.org/10.3389/fpsyg.2021.715228

Passmore, J., & Fillery-Travis, A. (2011). A critical review of executive coaching research: A decade of progress and what's to come. *Coaching: An International Journal of Theory, Research and Practice, 4*(2), 70–88. https://doi.org/10.1080/17521882.2011.596484

Passmore, J., Saraeva, A., Money, K., & Diller, S. J. (2024). *Trends in Digital and AI Coaching: Executive Report*. Henley-on-Thames: Henley Business School and EMCC International. Retrieved on March 24, 2024 from https://www.jonathanpassmore.com/technical-reports/future-trends-in-digital-ai-coaching-executive-report

Passmore, J., & Lai, Y.-L. (2019). Coaching psychology: Exploring definitions and research contribution to practice? *International Coaching Psychology Review, 14*(2), 69–83. ISSN 1750-2764

Passmore, J., Liu, Q., Tee, D., & Tewald, S. (2023). The impact of COVID-19 on coaching practice: Results from a global coach survey. *Coaching: An International Journal of Theory, Research and Practice, 16*(2), 173–189. https://doi.org/10.1080/17521882.2022.2161923

Passmore, J., & Tee, D. (2023). Can chatbots like GPT-4 replace human coaches: Issues and dilemmas for the coaching profession, coaching clients and for organisations. *The Coaching Psychologist, 19*(1), 47–54. https://doi.org/10.53841/bpstcp.2023.19.1.47

Powers, M. B., & Emmelkamp P. M. (2008). Virtual reality exposure therapy for anxiety disorders: A meta-analysis. *Journal of Anxiety Disorders, 22*(3), 561–569.

Rauen, Christopher. (2017). Wie die Industrie 4.0 Coaching und Weiterbildung verändern wird. *RAUEN Coaching-Newsletter, 17*(4), S. 1–4.

Ribbers, A., & Waringa, A. (2015). *E-Coaching: Theory and practice for a new online approach to coaching*. London: Routledge.

Riordan, M. A., & Kreuz, R. J. (2010). Emotion encoding and interpretation in computer-mediated communication: Reasons for use. *Computers in Human Behavior, 26*(6), 1667–1673. https://doi.org/10.1016/j.chb.2010.06.015

Rogers, C. R. (1979). The foundations of the person-centered approach. *Education, 100*, 96–107.

Rogers, C. R. (1980). *A way of being*. Boston, MA: Houghton Mifflin.

Roter, D. L., & Hall, J. A. (2006). *Doctors talking with patients/patients talking with doctors. Improving communication in medical visits*. Westport: Praeger.

Schein, E. (Ed.). (1999). *Process consultation revisited: Building the helping relationship*. Reading, MA: Addison-Wesley Publishing Inc.

Schulz von Thun, F. (2009). Miteinander Reden 1: Stöörungen und Klärungen. *Allgemeine Psychologie der Kommunikation*. 16. Auflage. Hamburg: rororo.

Schwartzman, C. M., & Boswell, J. F. (2020). A narrative review of alliance formation and outcome in text-based telepsychotherapy. *Practice Innovations, 5*(2), 128–142. https://doi.org/10.1037/pri0000120

Sherman, S., & Freas, A. (2004). The wild west of executive coaching. *Harvard Business Review, 82*(11), 82–93.

Sherpa Executive Coaching Survey. (2012). Seventh annual report. Retrieved on 20th March 2020 from https://libraryofprofessionalcoaching.com/wp-app/wp-content/uploads/2012/01/Coaching-Survey-2012-Executive.pdf

Sherpa Executive Coaching Survey. (2020). Fifteenth annual report. Retrieved on 5th July 2021 from www.beachtig.com/dl/a6474fcf26b396d472885d637ac793ef/2020_Executive_Coaching_Survey_EXECUTIVE_SUMMARY_FINAL.pdf

Silsbee, D. (2008). *Presence-based coaching: Cultivating self-generative leaders through mind, body & heart.* San Francisco, CA: Jossey-Bass Inc.

Sonesh, S. C., Coultas, C. W., Lacerenza, C. N., Marlow, S. L., Benishek, L. E., & Salas, E. (2015). The power of coaching: A meta analytic investigation. *Coaching: An International Journal of Theory, Research and Practice, 8*(2), 73–95. https://doi.org/10.1080/17521882.2015.1071418

Spencer, L. M., & Spencer, S. M. (1993). *Competence at work: Models for superior performance.* Hoboken: John Wiley & Sons.

Stanton, M. V., Maher, E. J., & Salmon, J. (2018). Effectiveness of online weight loss coaching versus in-person counseling in a commercial weight loss program: A randomized trial. *International Journal of E-Learning & Distance Education, 32*(1), 1–16.

Suler, J. (2004). The online disinhibition effect. *CyberPsychology & Behavior, 7*(3), 321–326. https://doi.org/10.1089/1094931041291295

Thakkar, J., Kurup, R., Laba, T. L., Santo, K., Thiagalingam, A., Rodgers, A., & Woodward, M. (2016). Mobile telephone text messaging for medication adherence in chronic disease: A meta-analysis. *Journal of Medical Internet Research, 18*(11), e330.

Timmermann, S. E., & Madhavapeddi, S. N. (2007). Perceptions of organizational media richness: Channel expansion effects for electronic and traditional media across richness dimensions. *IEEE Transactions on Professional Communication, 51*(1), 18–32.

Toffler, A. (1970). *Future shock.* New York: Random House, Inc.

Trueblood, T. C. (1911). Coaching a debating team. *Public Speaking Review, 1,* 84–85.

Watzlawick, P., et al. (1967). Some tentative axioms of communication. In P. Watzlawick et al. (Eds.), *Pragmatics of human communication: A study of interactional patterns, pathologies, and paradoxes* (p. 282). New York: W. W. Norton & Co. https://pdfs.semanticscholar.org/e998/92445f8215bdaad067f2ba85aa9bb3ec35fe.pdf

Will, T., Gessnitzer, S., & Kauffeld, S. (2016). You think you are an empathic coach? Maybe you should think again. The difference between perceptions of empathy vs. empathic behaviour after a person-centred coaching training. *Coaching: An International Journal of Theory, Research and Practice, 9*(1), 53–68.

Woods, N. (2018). *Coaching and the use of technology.* Research paper, Sydney Business School, University of Wollongong, Australia.

Part I

Coaching practice

Chapter 1

Defining digital and AI coaching

Jonathan Passmore and Sandra J. Diller

Introduction

The term 'digital coaching' is widely used, but has been applied to multiple different formats of coaching. Further, other terms, including 'online coaching', virtual coaching, 'technology coaching', and 'remote coaching' have all been used over the past decade, sometimes to mean the same things or sometimes something similar but different. The same is true for the term 'AI coaching': with the term used for technology being used to support the coaching process, such as matching or learning nudges, as well as coachbots. In this chapter we aim to explore the variety of terms and provide clear definitions which can act as the basis for future research and writing in this area of theory and practice.

We start by exploring the key aspects of digital and artificial intelligence (AI), review the wide range of terms, and offer explicit definitions for each mode of coaching delivery, including face-to-face, digital coaching, and AI coaching. We argue that in many of these modes, research is needed to explore the efficacy and to examine when one mode may be preferable to another, hypothesising that some modes may be better suited to certain types of individuals and specific types of presenting issues.

The development of technology in coaching

Coaching has emerged over the past two decades as a popular topic and effective human resource development intervention. The 2020–21 global pandemic raised questions over the potential future of coaching, as a face-to-face personalised development intervention. While digital tools had been used to deliver coaching in the early decades of the century (Charbonneau, 2002), using tools such as Skype, which gained prominence for digital business communication in 2008 (Cowling, 2016), the widespread adoption of digital technologies remained comparatively slow until 2020, with most coaches continuing to work face-to-face (König et al., 2017; Passmore et al., 2021). The arrival of Covid-19 in early 2020, however, witnessed coaching switch to online delivery together with many workplace practices (ICF 2021; Passmore, 2021). This pivot in the mode of coaching delivery has generated new interest in the implications for coaching practice and the coaching industry (Passmore & Evans-Krimme, 2021).

However, digital coaching has so far not been the subject of in-depth review or discussion within the literature. Digital coaching remains a loosely defined term. There remains confusion about the term itself (digital coaching) and multiple other terms which have been used in the literature. In most cases the terms are vaguely defined. They include

DOI: 10.4324/9781003383741-3

'e-coaching' (Ribbers & Waringa, 2015), 'virtual coaching' (Rock et al., 2011), 'distance coaching' (Berry, 2005; Berry et al., 2011), 'online coaching' (Fielden & Hunt, 2011), or 'remote coaching' (Crawford et al., 2021). The lack of clarity echoes the debate in coaching in the early 1990s, prior to the emergence of professional bodies when there was a lack of a consensus definition for 'coaching'. While a broad consensus has emerged about the term 'coaching' (Passmore & Lai, 2019), a consensus has yet to emerge around the use of the term 'digital coaching', a perspective noted by other writers: "As the discourse on e-coaching is recent, there is an apparent lack of consensus around its meaning" (p. 166; Geissler et al., 2014). As this practice grows in scale, resolving this ambiguity is important.

Not only is there a variety in the discussion of which term is used for digital coaching but also a lack of clarity about the boundary: When should the intervention be called 'digital training' or 'digital mentoring', and when 'digital coaching'? Is the only difference between coaching and digital coaching that digital coaching takes place via a digital communication platform, or could digital coaching also include conversations involving a coachbot (a non-human coach)? This lack of a shared definition of digital coaching not only complicates theory development but also empirical exploration:

> Without an agreed upon explicit definition which outlines underlying assumptions and boundaries of the concept, it is challenging, if not impossible, for the literature to develop further. Clear conceptualization is required to ensure that attention can be turned to the development and subsequent testing of a theory [...]. Such a conceptualization is also essential for enabling organisations to understand what exactly they are purchasing and why
>
> (p. 62; Jones et al., 2019)

This chapter seeks to resolve these questions and provide a shared understanding of terminology from which practice and research can build.

Definitions

Defining coaching

It may be helpful to spend a short while reviewing what we mean by coaching. As we mentioned there is a broad consensus which has emerged as to what constitutes coaching. However, in reality different definitions are still widely quoted. The most popular is John Whitmore's practice definition: "Coaching is unlocking a person's potential to maximise their own performance. It is helping them to learn rather than teaching them" (p. 8; Whitmore, 2002). In his deeper reflection on coaching Whitmore went on to suggest that fundamentally coaching was about enhancing personal responsibility and deepening self-awareness.

A second popular definition, widely used, is from a professional body, the International Coaching Federation (ICF): Coaching involves "partnering with clients in a thought-provoking and creative process that inspires them to maximise their personal and professional potential. The process of coaching often unlocks previously untapped sources of imagination, productivity and leadership" (ICF, 2021).

A final and more academic definition has been offered by Passmore & Tee (2023), building on Passmore and Fillery-Travis' academic definition (2011). Passmore and Tee sought to address the challenge posed by Bachkirova and Kauffman (2009) of universality and unique: How can a definition both apply to the multiple applications of coaching, and also clearly delineate coaching from other similar development interventions such as mentoring, training, and group facilitation.

They proposed the following formal definition Coaching is "a voluntary intervention involving a series of future-focused, structured, purposeful conversations characterised by open questions, listening, summaries, reflections and affirmations intended to facilitate the client in generating and acting upon strategies which result in developing greater self awareness, enhancing personal responsibility and achieving meaningful progress towards a desired change" (Passmore & Tee, 2023).

These definitions however do not cast coaching as a process in stone. Instead we might argue that a lively and continuous debate about the nature of coaching reflects the dynamic and lively nature of a profession which is creative, curious, and continuing to develop.

The digital coaching debate

Given these definitions, coaching has differentiated itself from other formats like training or consulting as an intervention to empower clients to attain their self-determined goals through a conversation process employing open questions or active listening, which as a by-product also enhances self-awareness and personal responsibility of the participant (Diller et al., 2020; Grant et al., 2010; Greif et al., 2018; Passmore & Fillery-Travis, 2011). Thus, coaching is individualised support, similar to counselling/psychotherapy in its use of questions, but differs in that counselling/psychotherapy is focused on clients whose needs may be defined through a formal diagnosis, and with a focus towards healing and stabilising a client. In contrast, coaching is about empowering a healthy and stable client towards planning and achieving future desires (Crowe, 2017; Passmore & Lai, 2019). Prior to the emergence of technology-enabled conversations, synchronicity was not considered a factor, as coaching has taken place mostly face-to-face (König et al., 2017).

Digital coaching has become a term used to include the same coach–client relationship – but the term has been used for both *synchronous* media (e.g., audio, video, and text-based live chats) and *asynchronous* media (e.g., instant text messaging). Further, the intervention could be exclusively conversation or could include digital coaching tools (e.g., whiteboards, VR). Besides this problem, the term digital coaching has been applied variously to include coachbot conversations, where the human client engages with an interaction partner (e.g., Allemand & Flückiger, 2022; Allemand et al., 2020; Nahum-Shani et al., 2018; Kettunen et al., 2022; Schueller et al., 2013; Stieger et al., 2021; Treblanche et al, 2022). As Graßmann and Schermuly (2021) noted: "every aspect of learning or any other feature of intelligence can in principle be so precisely described that a machine can be made to simulate it" (p. 12; McCarthy et al., 2006). Thus, AI could "learn based on a large data set of coaching processes to get more efficient in helping clients to achieve their goals, such as by the best selection of tools and exercises or questions to ask" (p. 109; Graßmann & Schermuly, 2021). In sum, no clear data-driven definition and differentiation of digital coaching exist. Based on this confusing and jumbled collection of terms, we sort to explore and categorise this growing diversity of applications and terminologies.

As a starter for this book we thought it thus may be helpful to offer some definitions of the various terms used in this book. We have provided a summary of key definitions in Table 1.1.

Table 1.1 Digitally-enabled coaching terminology

Term	Definition
Online coaching / virtual coaching / e-coaching	These terms have been used to apply to different forms of coaching that are delivered through digital communications, combining audio and visual channels. They have largely been replaced by the term 'digital coaching'.
Telephone coaching	This is coaching using an audio channel only. Once popular in the US where distances are large, but now almost completely replaced by online communications.
Digital coaching	A synchronous, personal conversation using DT-enabled audio and video channels of communication between a human coach and a human client to empower the client in their self-development (Diller & Passmore, 2023).
Coaching platform	A provider of software that enables audio and visual communications, usually combined with other tools to facilitate record keeping, diary management, and learning.
AI coachbot	A computer-generated response, which either follows a predetermined script or LLM from which the software selects a response.
AI coaching	The process of delivering a synchronous or or asynchronous coaching using a computer as the coach instead of a human coach.
VR (virtual reality)	VR is the term used for computer-generated 3D environments which are presented using head-worn computer devices that occlude the physical world, enabling the user to explore and interact with the content. True VR is created using two different content streams, one presented to each eye, thus creating depth of perception so that the user has a sense of being immersed in the digital experience. VR content can be 3D generated or filmic, interactive or passive, and can be a personal experience or shared by many users connecting to the same digital environment across a network.

The emergence of digital learning environments

Given the rapid emergence of global digital coaching providers, such as BetterUp, CoachHub, or EZRA, as well as the widespread use of digital coaching, coaching science needs to catch up. Billions of dollars have already been invested in these new businesses by venture capitalists, and the period 2024–30 is likely to see one or more of these companies come to the market as IPOs with a multi-billion valuation (Bersin, 2022). Without clear evidence of efficacy, long-term investors may be more cautious about an investment than their high-risk venture capital investors. With a clear definition and categorisation, we hope this chapter will both set the scene for this book and also provide a first step in building both theory and research in this new field by distinguishing between different digitally-enabled interventions and creating a shared language for researchers, practitioners, and investors.

Coaching, however, is not unique but is part of a wider trend across multiple fields, where digital technologies are impacting on delivery, from entertainment to learning and development.

Prior to the 2020 Covid pandemic, over 60% of learning was technology-based, though most times classroom training was still included in this blended form; this changed massively after Covid-19 to half of the offers being completely virtual learning environments (Sugrue & Rivera, 2005; The Ken Blanchard Companies, 2020). The advantage of technology is its ability to enable just-in-time and on-demand learning, development, and support (Sugrue & Rivera, 2005; Sullivan, 2005) as well as to interact with others around the world (Taylor et al., 2008). Furthermore, artificial intelligence as virtual interaction partners can reduce impression management and fear of negative evaluation in users (Gratch, 2014). Accordingly, digital learning environments have been widely adopted by organisations as they are perceived as being low in cost but still high in impact (Bierema & Hill, 2005; Ensher et al., 2003; Stone, 2004; Tahmincioglu, 2004).

Possible advantages of coaching using digital technologies

The rapid growth in digital coaching is part of a shift to just-in-time learning and performance support with the wider application of digital technologies to the learning and development industry (Brandenburg & Ellinger, 2003; Hernez-Broome et al., 2007; Kim et al., 2005). Likewise, coaching, delivered through digital technologies has increased as these technologies have become more widespread and reliable while alternatives have become less attractive or are not available, particularly during the Covid-19 pandemic (ICF, 2021; Passmore, 2021). Digital technologies have provided "a variety of means for synchronous and asynchronous communication [which can] alter the timing, scheduling, and formality of the coaching process" (p. 7; Frazee, 2008). We use the term coaching with digital technologies to include digital coaching but also a wide range of other digitally-enabled coaching formats from coachbots to phone coaching and email coaching. Coaching with digital technologies can enable new opportunities for individual support and behaviour change, as it can be independent of space and potentially independently of time (Allemand & Flückiger, 2022; Allemand et al., 2020; Nahum-Shani et al., 2018; Kettunen et al., 2022; Schueller et al., 2013). Even more so, digital technologies can help reduce time and travel expenses of attending a coaching session, as well as help people who would not be able to travel (e.g., disabilities, or reduced travel options) (e.g., long distance) (Amichai-Hamburger et al., 2014). Consequently, coaching with digital technologies can broaden access to coaching, offering consistency, scalability, and cost-effective coaching solutions (Barbian, 2002; Charbonneau, 2002): At an average cost of around $300 plus per hour in 2023 [for face-to-face coaching], not all organisations can afford to have everybody in their company coached. These costs are inflated by the addition of travel time, which can easily double the total time of the coach invested in each session. In contrast, digital coaching allows organisations to increase the number of people coached, by making the most efficient use of the coaches' time. It's bringing together the technologies and delivery in a cost-effective way. Similarly, coaching using digital technologies does not only increase the options for clients but can also increase the coach pool, providing great diversity and choice to clients (Hamilton & Scandura, 2003; Sparrow, 2006). In other words, coaching delivered through digital technologies creates what we call the '*Polly Pocket* Coach': A coach, human or otherwise, accessible via a digital device, in your pocket, whenever they are needed. To sum up, digitalisation offers benefits for both cost-conscious enterprise organisations and individuals living in rural or remote areas. Thus, practitioners believe that digital-enabled coaching is very effective and has vast potential (Frazee, 2008).

In addition, digital technologies support more flexible and open communication due to options for when, how (often), and between whom communication takes place (Hamilton & Scandura, 2003; Stone, 2004; Wainfan & Davis, 2004). Digital technologies also have the potential of monitoring behaviors, thoughts, or feelings from the frequency of use, to the length of the conversation, and also the potential to record the communication for more in-depth analysis, from examining voice tone for emotion to verbal content (Allemand et al., 2022; Harari et al., 2020; Marsch et al., 2014; Trull & Ebner-Priemer, 2014; Tausczik & Pennebaker, 2010). This online material of recorded interactions can further be used as a resource or future reference (Rossett & Marino, 2005). Moreover, not only the client's progress but also the process can be monitored, such as via digital recording of sessions for coach supervision, shared, and accessed via the cloud (Amichai-Hamburger et al., 2014). Such recordings can also be used for AI learning, to enhance and develop coachbots. For some users, digital environments are perceived as safer and more secure spaces than face-to-face environments (Amichai-Hamburger & Hayat, 2013; Hamburger & Ben-Artzi, 2000). This 'safe space' can further help test out situations or scenarios via virtual reality before applying in a real world situation (e.g., virtual reality therapy; Miyahira et al., 2012). For instance, an avatar can even help the user to feel stronger when the avatar is displayed as a strong person (proteus effect; Yee & Bailenson, 2007). This can also foster opportunities to explore different roles and identities, such as other genders or cultures (Slater et al., 2010) as well as virtual embodiment, when individuals are seeking to explore body image topics (Hänsell et al., 2011; Normand et al., 2011; Riva, 2011). In sum, digital technologies could offer enhanced possibilities in the coming decade, as digital technologies such as VR (virtual reality), AR (augmented reality), and MR (mixed reality) emerge.

Disadvantages of coaching using digital technologies

However, there is also criticism of digital interventions. For instance, 'digital therapy' has been criticised, as the technologies not only leads to differences in space and time but can also reduce the visibility of non-verbal cues, potentially impacting the development of trust and adversely impacting the working alliance. The effects of such changes could be a reduction in intimacy, openness, client commitment, and goal attainment (Amichai-Hamburger et al., 2014; Lester, 2006; Scharff, 2013; Wells et al., 2007; Wenger, 1998). Coaches, therefore, fear that communication barriers may hinder coaching success in digital settings (Hebert & Vorauer, 2003). For example, coaches have noted the challenges in phone coaching, that active listening can become difficult, as pauses can be interpreted in several ways when body language is absent from the communication. Others have highlighted that some clients find it difficult to express their issues as well over the phone in comparison to face-to-face (Frazee, 2008). Others, also from 2008 research, highlighted a preference for a face-to-face coaching session to start building the trust and ownership (Frazee, 2008).

Further criticism includes issues of confidentiality, privacy, ethics, and legal concerns (Ragusea & VandeCreek, 2003). These issues are closely related to the topic of disruptions not only in the room but also via the digital tool, such as via delays in video or voice, technical faults with the software or connection, failures in power supply, incoming email notifications, or automated software updates (Amichai-Hamburger et al., 2014).

There is also some evidence of what has become labelled 'Zoom fatigue'. This phenomenon describes the increased occurrence of emotional and physical exhaustion from participating in long or multiple video calls. The suggested explanation for this phenomenon is that the user has to constantly look at the screen in order to appear present. However in face-to-face conversation looking away is a natural part of the conversation and provides both an opportunity for the vision to move from short to medium and long distance and for a rest from the intensity of engagement (Shockley et al., 2021). The phenomenon has been increasingly studied in the context of work, with a focus on businesses (e.g., Shockley et al., 2021). 'Zoom fatigue' is likely to also affect digital coaching, as both the client and the coach have to be highly attentive. A qualitative study by Feijt et al. (2020) showed that mental health practitioners found digital sessions with their clients were more tiring than face-to-face sessions. Furthermore, it is more difficult to create interpersonal proximity and a connection with the client, as a part of non-verbal communication, emotions, facial expressions, and gestures are reduced, in part due to a reduced vision of the whole person and an over concentration on the face (Feijt et al., 2020; Kellner et al., 2020). In sum, the digital coaching experience may see reduced communication, and a subsequent negative impact on the working alliance.

However, we note that much of the writing and discussion of the potential of digital coaching occurred before 2020. The impact of the 2020–22 global lockdowns has changed attitudes, competency, and engagement with digital tools, as employees initially were forced, and more lately have chosen to, switch from the office to home-digital working. Covid-19 led to a step change in users' perceptions of what can be achieved online (Passmore, 2021; Passmore et al., 2023).

Digital coaching effectiveness

For these reasons, research and discussion on the effectiveness of digital technology-enabled coaching compared to face-to-face coaching is essential and is a key driver for this textbook. However as we have noted this term includes a wide range of different methods. To date only a few studies have taken place involving digital technologies, most of these are relatively old, and employed phone coaching.

In one example, a small sample study offered both telephone and face-to-face coaching compared to a control group without coaching. It showed that participants who received coaching reported higher goal clarification and goal attainment (Hernez-Broome, 2002). Similarly, a telephone coaching programme led to a good coach–client relationship and coaching satisfaction (Ghods, 2009). As these studies have their limitations in terms of missing a face-to-face coaching group as a comparison, the specificity of coaching offer, or a small sample size, it is difficult to interpret these first findings. In 2011, Berry et al. compared telephone coaching with face-to-face coaching. The study showed there was no difference between the two with regard to the establishment of a working alliance. In reviewing parallel disciplines such as telemedicine and counselling research, the evidence suggests that aspects such as the working alliance are unaffected as a result of the switch to phone-based interventions (Cook & Doyle, 2002; Day & Schneider, 2002; Sucala et al., 2012).

Besides telephone coaching, online coaching via text messages has been investigated. For example, Poepsel (2011) translated a tested format of face-to-face coaching based on Green et al. (2006) into a digital setting and compared it to a control group. The digital setting included a professional coach that exclusively communicated online with the clients over a website with discussion forums, supporting content (e.g., exercise instructions), and chat options with not only the coach but also other clients. The researcher found positive effects on goal-striving, subjective well-being, and hope from the intervention compared to the control group. Such text-based interventions seem to be particularly valuable after training to secure further self-development (Wang, 2000). In addition, recent research found that a completely app-based approach with artificial intelligence or a computer as the interaction partner showed positive outcomes like short-term personality change and an increase in self-control (e.g., Allemand & Flückiger, 2022; Allemand et al., 2020; Nahum-Shani et al., 2018; Kettunen et al., 2022; Schueller et al., 2013; Stieger et al., 2021).

The development of app-based coachbots, like Ovida, using AI to improve and enhance human coaching conversations, has witnessed new streams of research. AI coaching is likely to be a major feature of writing and research during the 2020s as organisations seek to leverage the potential it offers to further reduce cost and enhance accessibility of coaching.

Conclusion

In this chapter we have briefly explored the topic of digital coaching, offering some insights into its development, advantages, and disadvantages of its use and definitions of the key terms. However we acknowledge that different authors continue to use different terms, and this is likely to happen as the technology continues to evolve and the application of coaching extends into new and different arenas.

References

Allemand, M., & Flückiger, C. (2022). Personality change through digital-coaching interventions. *Current Directions in Psychological Science, 31*(1), 41–48. https://doi.org/10.1177/0963721421 1067782

Allemand, M., Keller, L., Gmür, B., Gehriger, V., Oberholzer, T., & Stieger, M. (2020). MindHike, a digital coaching application to promote self-control: Rationale, content, and study protocol. *Frontiers in Psychiatry, 11*, Article 575101. https://doi.org/10.3389/fpsyt.2020.575101

Amichai-Hamburger, Y., & Hayat, Z. (2013). *Internet and personality. The social net: Understanding our online behavior.* Oxford: Oxford University Press.

Amichai-Hamburger, Y., Klomek, A. B., Friedman, D., Zuckerman, O., & Shani-Sherman, T. (2014). The future of online therapy. *Computers in Human Behaviour, 41*, 288–294. https://doi.org/10.1016/j.chb.2014.09.016

Bachkirova, T., & Kauffman, C. (2009). The blind men and the elephant: Using criteria of universality and uniqueness in evaluating our attempts to define coaching [Editorial]. *Coaching: An International Journal of Theory, Research and Practice, 2*(2), 95–105, https://doi.org/10.1080/17521880903102381

Barbian, J. (2002). Screenplay. *Online Learning Magazine, 6*(5), 12–16.

Berry, R. M. (2005). *A comparison of face-to-face and distance coaching practices: The role of the working alliance in problem resolution.* (Publication No. 3221700) [Doctoral dissertation, Georgia State University]. ProQuest Dissertations & Theses Global.

Berry, R. M., Ashby, J. S., Gnilka, P. B., & Matheny, K. B. (2011). A comparison of face-to-face and distance coaching practices: Coaches' perceptions of the role of the working alliance in problem resolution. *Consulting Psychology Journal: Practice and Research, 63*(4), 243–253. https://doi.org/10.1037/a0026735

Bersin (2022, January 26). *Online coaching is so hot it's now disrupting leadership development.* JOSH BERSIN Insights on Corporate Talent, Learning, and HR Technology. Retrieved January 9, 2023, from https://joshbersin.com/2022/01/online-coaching-is-so-hot-its-now-disrupting-lea dership-development/

Bierema, L. L., & Hill, J. R. (2005). Virtual mentoring and HRD. *Advances in Developing Human Resources, 7*(4), 556–568. https://doi.org/10.1177/1523422305279688

Brandenburg, D. C., & Ellinger, A. D. (2003). The future: Just-in-time learning expectations and potential implications for human resource development. *Advances in Developing Human Resources, 5*(3), 308–320. https://doi.org/10.1177/1523422303254629

Charbonneau, M. A. (2002). *Media selection in executive coaching: A qualitative study.* (Publication No. 3077435) [Doctoral dissertation, Alliant International University]. ProQuest Dissertations & Theses Global.

Cook, J. E., & Doyle, C. (2002). Working alliance in online therapy as compared to face-to-face therapy: Preliminary results. *CyberPsychology & Behavior, 5*(2), 95–105. http://dx.doi.org/10.1089/109493102753770480

Cowling, J. (2016, February 9). *A brief history of Skype –The peer-to-peer messaging service.* Retrieved January 9, 2023, from https://content.dsp.co.uk/history-of-skype

Crawford, A., Varghese, C., Hsu, H.-Y., Zucker, T., Landry, S., Assel, M., Monsegue-Bailey, P., & Bhavsar, V. (2021). A comparative analysis of instructional coaching approaches: Face-to-face versus remote coaching in preschool classrooms. *Journal of Educational Psychology, 113*(8), 1609–1627. https://doi.org/10.1037/edu0000691

Crowe, T. (2017). Coaching and psychotherapy. In T. Bachkirova, G. Spence, & D. Drake (Eds.), *The Sage handbook of coaching* (pp. 85–101). Sage.

Day, S. X., & Schneider, P. L. (2002). Psychotherapy using distance technology: A comparison of face-to-face, video, and audio treatment. *Journal of Counseling Psychology, 49*(4), 499–503. https://doi.org/10.1037/0022-0167.49.4.499

Diller, S. J., Muehlberger, C., Braumandl, I., & Jonas, E. (2020). Supporting students with coaching or training depending on their basic psychological needs. *International Journal of Mentoring and Coaching in Education, 10*(1), 84–100. https://doi.org/10.1108/IJMCE-08-2020-0050

Diller, S. J., & Passmore, J. (2023). Defining digital coaching: A qualitative inductive approach. *Frontiers in Psychology, 14*, 1148243. https://doi.org/10.3389/fpsyg.2023.1148243

Ensher, E. A., Heun, C., & Blanchard, A. (2003). Online mentoring and computer-mediated communication: New directions in research. *Journal of Vocational Behavior, 63*(2), 264–288. https://doi.org/10.1016/S0001-8791(03)00044-7

Feijt, M., De Kort, Y., Bongers, I., Bierbooms, J., Westerink, J., & IJsselsteijn, W. (2020). Mental health care goes online: Practitioners' experiences of providing mental health care during the COVID-19 pandemic. *Cyberpsychology, Behavior, and Social Networking, 23*(12), 860–864. https://doi.org/10.1089/cyber.2020.0370

Fielden, S. L., & Hunt, C. M. (2011). Online coaching: An alternative source of social support for female entrepreneurs during venture creation. *International Small Business Journal, 29*(4), 345–359. https://doi.org/10.1177/0266242610369881

Frazee, R. V. (2008). *E-coaching in organizations: A study of features, practices, and determinants of use* (Publication No. 3314978) [Doctoral dissertation, San Diego State University and University of San Diego]. ProQuest Dissertations & Theses Global.

Geissler, H., Hasenbein, M., Kanatouri, S., & Wegener, R. (2014). E-coaching: Conceptual and empirical findings of a virtual coaching programme. *International Journal of Evidence-Based Coaching and Mentoring, 12*(2), 165–187.

Ghods, N. (2009). *Distance coaching: The relationship between the coach-client relationship, client satisfaction, and coaching outcomes.* [Unpublished doctoral dissertation]. San Diego University.

Graßmann, C., & Schermuly, C. C. (2021). Coaching with artificial intelligence: Concepts and capabilities. *Human Resource Development Review, 20*(1), 106–126. https://doi.org/10.1177/1534484320982891

Grant, A. M., Passmore, J., Cavanagh, M. J., & Parker, H. (2010). The state of play in coaching. *International Review of Industrial & Organizational Psychology, 25,* 125–168.

Gratch, J. (2014). Virtual humans for interpersonal processes and skills training. *AI Matters, 1*(2), 24–25.

Green, L. S., Oades, L. G., & Grant, A. M. (2006). Cognitive-behavioral, solution-focused life coaching: Enhancing goal striving, well-being, and hope. *Journal of Positive Psychology, 1*(3), 142–149. https://doi.org/10.1080/17439760600619849

Greif, S., Möller, H., & Scholl, W. (2018). Coachingdefinitionen und-konzepte [Coaching definitions and concepts]. In Greif, S., Möller, H., & Scholl, W. (Eds.), *Handbuch Schlüsselkonzepte im Coaching* [*Handbook key concepts in coaching*] (pp. 1–9). Cham, Switzerland: Springer. https://doi.org/10.1007/978-3-662-49483-7_7

Hamburger, Y. A., & Ben-Artzi, E. (2000). The relationship between extraversion and neuroticism and the different uses of the Internet. *Computers in Human Behavior, 16*(4), 441–449. https://doi.org/10.1016/S0747-5632(00)00017-0

Hamilton, B. A., & Scandura, T. A. (2003). E-Mentoring: Implications for organizational learning and development in a wired world. *Organizational Dynamics, 31*(4), 388–402. https://doi.org/10.1016/S0090-2616(02)00128-6

Hänsell, A., Lenggenhager, B., von Känel, R., Curatolo, M., & Blanke, O. (2011). Seeing and identifying with a virtual body decreases pain perception. *European Journal of Pain, 15*(8), 874–879. https://doi.org/10.1016/j.ejpain.2011.03.013

Harari, G. M., Vaid, S. S., Müller, S. R., Stachl, C., Marrero, Z., Schoedel, R., Bühner, M., & Gosling, S. D. (2020). Personality sensing for theory development and assessment in the digital age. *European Journal of Personality, 34*(5), 649–669. https://doi.org/10.1002/per.2273

Hebert, B. G., & Vorauer, J. D. (2003). Seeing through the screen: Is evaluative feedback communicated more effectively in face-to-face or computer-mediated exchanges? *Computers in Human Behavior, 19*(1), 25–38. https://doi.org/10.1016/S0747-5632(02)00031-6

Hernez-Broome, G. (2002). *In it for the long haul: Coaching is key to continued development.* Greensboro: Center for Creative Leadership.

Hernez-Broome, G., Boyce, L. A., & Whyman, W. (2007, April 27). *Critical issues of coaching with technology.* In E-coaching: Supporting leadership coaching with technology [conference presentation]. *22nd Annual conference of the Society for Industrial and Organizational Psychology,* New York, NY.

ICF (International Coaching Federation). (2021). *Covid-19 and the coaching industry.* Retrieved Dec 17, 2022, from https://coachingfederation.org/app/uploads/2020/09/FINAL_ICF_GCS2 020_COVIDSt udy.pdf

Jones, R. J., Napiersky, U., & Lyubovnikova, J. (2019). Conceptualizing the distinctiveness of team coaching. *Journal of Managerial Psychology, 34*(2), 62–78. https://doi.org/10.1108/JMP-07-2018-0326

Kellner, T., Albrecht, T., & Löffl, J. (2020). *Wie arbeitest du heute? Veränderungen von Arbeits- und Organisationtionsstrukturen durch die Einführung von Home-Office in Zeiten der Covid-19*

Pandemie [How do you work today? Changes in work and organizational structures through the introduction of home office in times of the Covid-19 pandemic]. Technische Hochschule Ostwestfalen-Lippe University of Applied Sciences and Arts Institut für Wissenschaftsdialog [Ostwestfalen-Lippe University of Applied Sciences and Arts Institute for Science Dialogue]. https://doi.org/10.13140/RG.2.2.24636.05767

The Ken Blanchard Companies. (2020). *2021 Trends: Learning and development in a COVID world.* https://resources.kenbl anchard.com/research-insights/2021-trends-report

Kettunen, E., Kari, T., & Frank, L. (2022). Digital coaching motivating young elderly people towards physical activity. *Sustainability, 14*(13), Article 7718. https://doi.org/10.3390/su1 4137718

Kim, K. J., Bonk, C. J., & Zeng, T. (2005). Surveying the future of workplace e-learning: The rise of blending, interactivity, and authentic learning. *eLearn, 2005*(6), 2.

König, V., Schiemann, S., Brockmeier, S., & Lindschau, J. (2017). *eCoaching.* XING Coaching Kompendium.

Lester, D. (2006). E-therapy: Caveats from experiences with telephone therapy. *Psychological Reports, 99*(3), 894–896. https://doi.org/10.1089/109493101753235142

Marsch, L., Lord, S., & Dallery, J. (2014). *Behavioral healthcare and technology: Using science-based innovations to transform practice.* Oxford: Oxford University Press. https://doi.org/10.1093/med/9780199314027.001.0001

McCarthy, J., Minsky, M. L., Rochester, N., & Shannon, C. E. (2006). A proposal for the Dartmouth summer research project on artificial intelligence, August 31, 1955. *AI Magazine, 27*(4), 12. https://doi.org/10.1609/aimag.v27i4.1904

Miyahira, S. D., Folen, R. A., Hoffman, H. G., Garcia-Palacios, A., Spira, J. L., & Kawasaki, M. (2012). The effectiveness of VR exposure therapy for PTSD in returning warfighters. *Studies in Health Technology and Informatics, 181,* 128–132.

Nahum-Shani, I., Smith, S. N., Spring, B. J., Collins, L. M., Witkiewitz, K., Tewari, A., & Murphy, S. A. (2018). Just-in-time adaptive interventions (JITAIs) in mobile health: Key components and design principles for ongoing health behavior support. *Annals of Behavioral Medicine, 52*(6), 446–462. https://doi.org/10.1007/s12160-016-9830-8

Normand, J. M., Giannopoulos, E., Spanlang, B., & Slater, M. (2011). Multisensory stimulation can induce an illusion of larger belly size in immersive virtual reality. *PloS One, 6*(1), Article e16128. https://doi.org/10.1371/journal.pone.0016128

Passmore, J. (2021). *Future trends in coaching: Executive report 2021.* Henley-on-Thames: Henley Business School and EMCC International. https://assets.henley.ac.uk/v3/fileUploads/Future-Tre nds-in-Coaching.pdf

Passmore, J., & Evans-Krimme, R. (2021). The future of coaching: A conceptual framework for the coaching sector from personal craft to scientific process and the implications for practice and research. *Frontiers in Psychology, 12,* Article 715228. https://doi.org/10.3389/fpsyg.2021.715228

Passmore, J., & Fillery-Travis, A. (2011). A critical review of executive coaching research: A decade of progress and what's to come. *Coaching: An International Journal of Theory, Practice & Research, 4*(2), 70–88. https://doi.org/10.1080/17521882.2011.596484

Passmore, J., & Lai, Y. (2019). Coaching psychology: Exploring definitions and contribution to coaching research and practice? *International Coaching Psychology Review, 14*(2), 69–83. https://doi.org/10.1002/9781119656913.ch1

Passmore, J., Liu, Q., Tee, D., & Tewald, S. (2023). The impact of Covid-19 on coaching practice: Results from a global coach survey. *Coaching: An International Journal of Theory, Practice and Research, 16*(2), 173–189. https://doi.org/10.1080/17521882.2022.2161923

Passmore, J., Liu, Q., & Tewald, S. (2021). Future trends in coaching: Results from a global coaching survey 2021. *The Coaching Psychologist, 17*(2), 40–51.

Passmore, J., & Tee, D. (2023). Can chatbots like GPT-4 replace human coaches: Issues and dilemmas for the coaching profession, coaching clients and for organisations. *The Coaching Psychologist, 19*(1), 47–54. doi:10.53841/ bpstcp.2023.19.1.47

Poepsel, M. (2011). *The impact of an online evidence-based coaching program on goal striving, subjective well-being, and level of hope.* (Publication No. 3456769) [Doctoral dissertation, Capella University]. ProQuest Dissertations & Theses Global.

Ragusea, A. S., & VandeCreek, L. (2003). Suggestions for the ethical practice of online psychotherapy. *Psychotherapy: Theory, Research, Practice, Training, 40*(1–2), 94–102. https://doi.org/ 10.1037/0033-3204.40.1-2.9

Ribbers, A., & Waringa, A. (2015). *E-coaching: Theory and practice for a new online approach to coaching.* Abingdon: Routledge.

Riva, G. (2011). The key to unlocking the virtual body: Virtual reality in the treatment of obesity and eating disorders. *Journal of Diabetes Science and Technology, 5*(2), 283–292. https://doi. org/10.1177/193229681100500213

Rock, M. L., Zigmond, N. P., Gregg, M., & Gable, R. A. (2011). The power of virtual coaching. *Educational Leadership, 69*(2), 42–48.

Rossett, A., & Marino, G. (2005). If coaching is good, then e-coaching is. *T AND D, 59*(11), 46–49.

Scharff, J. S. (2013). Technology-assisted psychoanalysis. *Journal of the American Psychoanalytic Association, 61*(3), 491–510. https://doi.org/10.1177/00030651134854

Schueller, S. M., Muñoz, R. F., & Mohr, D. C. (2013). Realizing the potential of behavioral intervention technologies. *Current Directions in Psychological Science, 22*(6), 478–483. https://doi. org/10.1177/0963721413495872

Shockley, K. M., Gabriel, A. S., Robertson, D., Rosen, C. C., Chawla, N., Ganster, M. L., & Ezerins, M. E. (2021). The fatiguing effects of camera use in virtual meetings: A within-person field experiment. *Journal of Applied Psychology, 106*(8), 1137–1155. https://doi.org/10.1037/ apl0000948

Slater, M., Spanlang, B., Sanchez-Vives, M. V., & Blanke, O. (2010). First person experience of body transfer in virtual reality. *PloS One, 5*(5), Article e10564. https://doi.org/10.1371/journal. pone.0010564

Sparrow, S. (2006). Stuck in the middle with E. *Training & Coaching Today, 22.* Retrieved on 6 March 2024 from www.personneltoday.com/hr/stuck-in-the-middle-with-e/. The article was published on 14 June 2006.

Stieger, M., Flückiger, C., Rüegger, D., Kowatsch, T., Roberts, B. W., & Allemand, M. (2021). Changing personality traits with the help of a digital personality change intervention. *Proceedings of the National Academy of Sciences, 118*(8), Article e2017548118. https://doi.org/10.1073/ pnas.2017548118

Stone, F. M. (2004). *The mentoring advantage: Creating the next generation of leaders.* London: Kaplan Business.

Sucala, M., Schnur, J. B., Constantino, M. J., Miller, S. J., Brackman, E. H., & Montgomery, G. H. (2012). The therapeutic relationship in e-therapy for mental health: A systematic review. *Journal of Medical Internet Research, 14*(4), Article e2084. https://doi.org/10.2196/jmir.2084

Sugrue, B., & Rivera, R. J. (2005). *State of the industry report.* Retrieved December 10, 2007, from http://hdl.voced.edu.au/10707/142249

Sullivan, J. (2005). *World-class talent development: How learning organizations align talent development with organizational objectives.* Retrieved December 12, 2022, from https://de.scribd. com/document/6824655/wpaper-TalentDev

Tahmincioglu, E. (2004). Looking for a mentor? Technology can help make the right match. *Workforce Management, 83*(13), 63–65.

Tausczik, Y. R., & Pennebaker, J. W. (2010). The psychological meaning of words. LIWC and computerized text analysis methods. *Journal of Language and Social Psychology, 29*(1), 24–54. https://doi.org/10.1177/0261927X09351676

Taylor, T. K., Webster-Stratton, C., Feil, E. G., Broadbent, B., Widdop, C. S., & Severson, H. H. (2008). Computer-based intervention with coaching: An example using the Incredible Years program. *Cognitive Behaviour Therapy, 37*(4), 233–246. https://doi.org/10.1080/1650607080 2364511

Terblanche, N., Molyn, J., de Haan, E., & Nilsson, V. O. (2022). Comparing artificial intelligence and human coaching goal attainment efficacy. *PloS One, 17*(6), Article e0270255. https://doi.org/10.1371/journal.pone.0270255

Trull, T. J., & Ebner-Priemer, U. (2014). The role of ambulatory assessment in psychological science. *Current Directions in Psychological Science, 23*(6), 466–470. https://doi.org/10.1177/0963721414550706

Wainfan, L., & Davis, P. K. (2004). *Challenges in virtual collaboration: Videoconferencing, audio-conferencing, and computer-mediated communications.* Santa Monica, CA: Rand Corporation.

Wang, L. (2000). *The relationship between distance coaching and transfer of training.* [Unpublished doctoral dissertation]. University of Illinois at Urbana-Champaign.

Wells, M., Mitchell, K. J., Finkelhor, D., & Becker-Blease, K. A. (2007). Online mental health treatment: Concerns and considerations. *CyberPsychology & Behavior, 10*(3), 453–459. https://doi.org/10.1089/cpb.2006.9933

Wenger, E. (1998). Communities of practice: Learning as a social system. *Systems Thinker, 9*(5), 2–3.

Whitmore, J. (2002). *Coaching for performance*: London: Nicholas Brealey.

Yee, N., & Bailenson, J. (2007). The Proteus effect: The effect of transformed self- representation on behavior. *Human Communication Research, 33*(3), 271–290. https://doi.org/10.1111/j.1468-2958.2007.00299.x

Chapter 2

The future of work is the future for coaches

Carsten Schermuly, Max Brantl, and Sandra J. Diller

Introduction

Today's working environment is transforming at an unprecedented pace and is characterised by several significant transformations. Digitalisation, globalisation, demographic change, and knowledge explosion reshape the ways of working in organisations. This pace and strength of transformation lead to a so-called VUCA (volatility, uncertainty, complexity, and ambiguity) world (Millar et al., 2018). In line with the organisational transformation, new ways of working are emerging, and the demands on the workforce are evolving. Thus, excellent soft skills, the mastery of abstract skills, and the ability to apply these skills in different and digital contexts will be critical for success. Thus, employees need to develop so-called 21st-century skills (van Laar et al., 2020) to thrive. This chapter outlines how the four megatrends will transform the world of work, how organisations will need to adapt and evolve to maintain their competitiveness, and what specific skills employees and coaches will need to develop to thrive in tomorrow's working world.

Working in the new normal

Today's working world is characterised by four megatrends that redefine the guardrails of economic success and collaboration and, therefore, create an imperative for organisational and personal evolution:

1. *Digitisation*: Since computers were invented in the 1980s, "information and communication technologies have spread to practically all workplaces and also to virtually every aspect of non-work lives" (Korunka & Kubicek, 2017, p. 1). Mobile devices and cloud computing further allow people to work outside their offices and alter traditional communication habits. Thus, coaches and clients can connect digitally on virtual platforms. In addition, big data enables extensive analyses, while social media creates new avenues to initiate contact and cultivate relationships between clients, customers, and service providers (e.g., coaches). Furthermore, artificial intelligence (AI) has made rapid progress in different professions in the last years (Stone et al., 2016) and conversational AI coachbots are already used (e.g., AIMY; CoachHub, 2024coaching platform CoachHub).

2. *Globalisation*: The buzzword globalisation (Wilpert, 2009) defines the closer integration and connection of countries and their people (Stiglitz, 2002). This closer connection has fostered global competition, changed the worldwide division of labour,

DOI: 10.4324/9781003383741-4

and lead to intercultural teams (Korunka & Kubicek, 2017; Zink, 2011). The high intercultural diversity challenges not only the employees' intercultural skills but also their cultural identity (Schermuly, 2021; Wilpert, 2009). These challenges produce new coaching demands, such as a new level of intercultural communication and collaboration skills across time and place (van Laar et al., 2020). In contrast to the globalisation trend, there is also a trend of glocalisation: Global trade is reduced in some industries and political deglobalisation is taking place, driven by geopolitical tensions (Blatter, 2013). Thus, in some areas, production and supply chains become more regional again and critical elements are relocated domestically (e.g., production of vaccines or chips). Thus, there is a multipolar world order of both globalisation and glocalisation (O'Sullivan, 2019).

3. *Demographic change:* A demographic change was produced due to a longer life span and decreasing birth rates, especially in economically well-developed countries (Fraccaroli & Deller, 2015). The longer life span lead to a highly age-diverse workforce: "For the first time in history, most organisations have four distinct generations with an age range spanning more than 60 years working together" (Calk & Patrick, 2017, p. 131). The decreasing birth rates uncover an even bigger challenge for the future of work: The baby-boomer generation will retire soon, resulting in severe specialist shortage in many countries (Dychtwald, Erickson, & Morison, 2006). Thus, skilled workers become scarce and younger generations are unable to fill the gaps in the high-producing labour market as it is structured now. Furthermore, the present social pension system faces significant challenges due to the aging population (Alessie et al., 2013). Thus, age-related poverty can become a pressing concern in many societies worldwide. While the risks of the aging population are well-known, little has been done towards gender equality in order to widen the talent pool and reduce the risks of age-related poverty (Chen et al., 2021; Veremchuk, 2020). Furthermore, immigration as a solution (Serrano et al., 2011) has led to resistance (Houte et al., 2021).

4. *Knowledge explosion*: Last but not least, the world is experiencing a significant expansion of knowledge. For example, science results are growing exponentially (Tabah, 1999; Bornmann & Mutz, 2015) due to more international competition and collaboration (Zang, Powell, & Baker, 2015). This knowledge growth leads to higher complexity and shorter product cycles. Dynamic markets speed up changes and make high organisational flexibility necessary (Zink, 2011). The knowledge growth and the need for more agile ways of working result in high work intensity and flexibility (Zink, 2011), which might also lead to new challenges and topics for workplace coaching. Furthermore, more and more jobs are dominated by intellectual instead of physical work demands (Wilpert, 2009). These knowledge workers need to invest in further education, specialisation, and cooperation to master their jobs (Schermuly, 2019). Furthermore, an additional dynamic emerged with generative artificial intelligence, such as ChatGPT, that can be implemented in apps, software, and other products (Hughes, 2023) and accelerates knowledge production even further.

All four megatrends accelerate the transformation speed across industries and force organisations and individuals to adapt to a new, ever-changing working world. As a result, the market for coaches supporting change and transformation will grow at an unprecedented pace and the needs and topics in workplace coaching will change sustainably (see

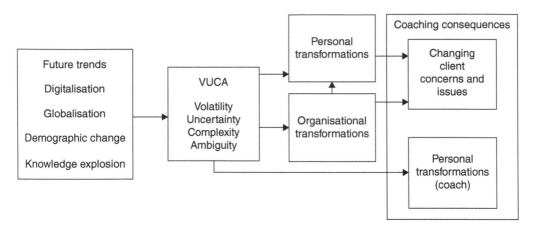

Figure 2.1 Model for the future of coaching.

Figure 2.1). The situation resulting from the simultaneous actions of various megatrends is often summarised with the acronym VUCA.

The acronym VUCA consists of the following components (Millar et al., 2018):

V = volatility
U = uncertainty
C = complexity
A = ambiguity

Volatility refers to a dynamic and unstable character (Ratter & Treiling, 2008). The actual state, the target state, and possible solutions change without intervention (Schermuly, 2021). *Uncertainty* arises from too little knowledge or from too much knowledge, which can no longer be overviewed and can no longer be mastered. The consequence is the same: Uncertainty triggers fear (Schermuly, 2021). *Complexity* means that a system consists of many hardly manageable elements that have additional complicated relationships with each other (Schermuly, 2021). A complex system thus has a complicated constitution. Everything seems to be connected to everything else; the rules of how the system functions with its elements and relationships are unknown (Ratter & Treiling, 2008). "Ambiguity characterizes situations where there is doubt about the nature of cause-and-effect relationship" (Ratter & Treiling, 2008, p. 316). This makes it extremely difficult to find a proper intervention to change the situation. From a psychological perspective, ambiguity means that situations can be interpreted in different ways. There is no clarity; thus, different interpretations and subjective truths arise from different perspectives for the same situation. The ambiguity in the VUCA world stresses people with a low tolerance for ambiguity (Schermuly, 2021).

Embracing change to thrive in the VUCA world

When organisations are confronted with a dynamic and complex external world, they often mirror this world intra-organisationally (Schermuly, 2021). Technology, in particular, is considered as one of the key drivers of this transformation. On the one hand, technological innovation results in the creation of new jobs, such as product innovation, for example, and allows employees to concentrate on more intricate and abstract tasks. Also, digital tools, for instance, make it easier and quicker to visualise complex financial data in various ways, enabling managers to focus on important discussions related to the 'so-what' and 'root cause' and decision-making. On the other hand, technology also subsidises jobs by automating traditional and more simple tasks, e.g., by increasing process efficiency (Dosi & Mohnen, 2018). At the same time, many organisations work with organisational systems like steep hierarchies that date back to the 19th century. In steep hierarchies, knowledge is exchanged more slowly between departments because communication and cooperation take place more vertically than horizontally. Upper management levels thus become a bottleneck, limiting the speed of cooperation and communication. Hierarchical systems can thus lead to poorer performance (Berdahl & Anderson, 2005) as well as more conflicts. These conflicts arise mainly because not all employees agree with their rank in the hierarchy (Anderson, Ames, & Gosling, 2008).

To tackle these challenges and shortcomings of steep hierarchies, new ways of working are applied in many organisations. In Germany, every year, the New Work Barometer is conducted. In this survey, more than 500 companies provide information about their understanding of new work and what practices they use in this area (Schermuly & Meifert, 2022). Figure 2.2 gives an overview of which practices have been applied by organisations in the years 2020–22. The results show a decline in new work practices during the extreme phases of the pandemic. Only mobile working benefited clearly in 2021. It seems that companies experienced difficulties in implementing new work practices such as agile project work or new leadership styles while the workforce worked so many days from home. In 2022, however, the practices were increasingly used again. This includes measures such as work time autonomy, mobile technologies, agile project work (e.g., Scrum), self-organisation, open error culture, agile leadership, open office concepts, flattening of hierarchies, self-determined learning, digital leadership, or Kanban (see Figure 2.2).

Skills needed for the VUCA world

These future trends and the VUCA world are changing jobs and their requirements. It is not new that professions evolve and, therefore, workforce requirements change. For instance, Wegman et al. (2016) conducted a cross-temporal meta-analysis concerning the job characteristic model (Hackman & Oldham, 1975). They analysed the changes in autonomy, task identity, task significance, skill variety, and feedback from the job since 1975 and found that especially autonomy and skill variety increased in the last 40 years (Wegman et al., 2016). New competencies are needed to cope with the challenges of the VUCA world, the changing job demands, and the new ways of working. Which skills are needed?

Having in mind that the transformation pace in organisations is accelerating, it is reasonable that soft skills (i.e., in particular, the skills that are needed to apply hard skills in a working context; Windels et al., 2013) become essential (Trudeau-Poskas, 2020). Since the beginning of the 21st century, it has been widely acknowledged among management boards that a growth mindset, as defined by Carol Dweck (2006), is a crucial factor for employees to thrive in the VUCA world. To provide a more comprehensive understanding of the specific skills required in today's and tomorrow's working world, various frameworks have been developed. In a systematic literature review, van Laar et al. (2017)

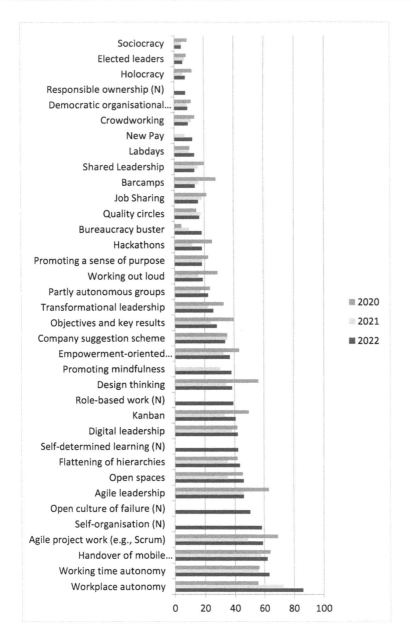

Figure 2.2 Organisational practices and their change between 2020 and 2022.

Source: Schermuly & Meifert (2022).

analysed these frameworks and identified seven core skills with digital components that are essential for employees in the 21st century. These skills include technical, information, communication, collaboration, creativity, critical thinking, and problem solving. These skills are considered to be universal to a certain extent, making them applicable not only across industries and functions but also in analogue and digital working environments (van Laar et al., 2020).

Technical skills: Technical skills refer to the ability to successfully understand and use technical devices or applications (e.g., Ng, 2012; van Deursen et al., 2016). While even in the analogue working world, basic technical skills, like turning on an electronic device or answering emails, are required across all industries, mastering new software, systems, and applications becomes significantly more important in a digital working world. Utilising technologies for successful communication via basic messaging (e.g., email) or video-conferencing tools (e.g., Microsoft Teams, Zoom) builds, for example, the foundation of collaboration in the digital world. In addition, editing platforms (e.g., Google Drive) and the ability to technically share information across company boundaries can significantly improve the quality of digital collaboration. In light of the advancing digitalisation that goes beyond the mere transformation of analogue tasks into a digital environment by, for example, enabling communication between digital devices via IoT, employees need to keep up with technical skills and languages to succeed in tomorrow's working world (Lemke, 2002).

Information skills: But as Peter Drucker said, "executives have become computer-literate … but not many executives are information literate" (Drucker, 2005, Section 1), or in other words, technical skills are not enough to thrive in a VUCA world. The call for information literacy is not new; for example, the National Forum on Information Literacy was formed in 1989 in the United States of America. And although Peter Drucker referred explicitly to executives, finding, extracting, and organising information is of utmost importance for all knowledge workers and coaches for different reasons (e.g., to educate themselves on the latest scientific insights in coaching, to identify the best ways to deliver services in a digital world, etc.). While there are many different terms for describing the information skill (cf., information competence, Mossberger et al., 2003; information literacy, Bawden, 2001), they all refer to the ability to recognise when information is needed, where it is located, and how to evaluate and utilise it (cf., Correia & Teixeira, 2003). This skill becomes even more relevant in a fast-changing and interconnected world when events on the other side of the world (e.g., the COVID-19 outbreak) can have significant and long-lasting impacts on the business (e.g., lockdowns, supply chain). Furthermore, the advent of the internet, the rise of social media, and AI (e.g., ChatGPT) have significantly changed the way information is produced, searched, structured, and evaluated. On one hand, the amount of available information on the internet has reached unprecedented levels as the total amount of data created, captured, copied, and consumed globally summed up to a total of 64.2 zettabytes (one zettabyte is equal to a trillion gigabytes) in 2020 (Statista, 2022). On the other hand, the rise of social media and just-in-time news has blurred the lines between producers and consumers of information (Jenkins, 2006; Park, 2013), paving the way for fake news. Thus, today, information and knowledge are available from various sources, and different people, who have diverse intentions and skills, publish them (Starkey, 2011). Therefore, it is crucial for individuals to have the ability to search, organise, structure (Catts & Lau, 2008), and filter information effectively (Dede, 2010).

Critical thinking skills: Furthermore, future knowledge workers need to look beyond the information itself and assess the quality of the information based on the source and learn to 'read between the lines' to unveil disinformation and fake news. A central prerequisite of these abilities is to judge unbiasedly or, in other words, to draw conclusions independently of one's prior beliefs and opinions (e.g., Baron, 2008; Sternberg, 1997). Therefore, it is necessary that people develop an awareness of the aspects that unconsciously drive their thinking and judgement and develop strategies on how to minimise these biases. Thus, the combination of identifying the information needed from a business perspective and extracting the right pieces of information based on critical thinking will be essential in the new normal.

Communication skills: As the success of organisations no longer depends only on tangible assets (e.g., land, capital), knowledge has become the primary production factor (Beijerse, 1999) and the key strategic resource of an organisation (Grant, 1996); it is reasonable that communication as the central way to share knowledge (van den Hooff & de Ridder, 2004) is one of the critical skills of the 21st century. Thus, it is no surprise that communication skills have become a priority in the hiring process (National Association of Colleges and Employers, 2016). In general, communication skills can be divided into written and oral communication skills. In terms of written communication skills, especially the right use of grammar plays an important role, as grammatical mistakes have a negative impact on the writer's credibility (Beason, 2001). Furthermore, other product-specific elements like persuasiveness and the design of documents (Jones, 2011), as well as the skills to produce a specific written outcome, e.g., reports, proposals, memos, etc. (Wardrope, 2002), have been identified as important aspects. In contrast, oral communication focuses on both product-oriented elements (e.g., presenting effectively; Reinsch & Gardner, 2014) and behaviour-oriented skills (e.g., listening, asking questions, discussing, etc.; Keyton et al., 2013). Moreover, communication is not only an essential part of knowledge management (van den Hooff & de Ridder, 2004) but critical for the day-to-day business as it impacts any interaction, from informal coffee chats over meetings to presentations – in an analogue and digital environment. As the variety of formats that can be used for communication internally and externally has increased rapidly, ranging from traditional in-person meetings over Yammer posts on the intranet to podcasts, videos, and live Q&A sessions using video-conference tools, it is important that employees understand and are capable of communicating effectively using different media (Lewin & McNicol, 2015; Wang et al., 2012). Finally, people need to be able to adapt their communication in light of the audience (Ananiadou & Claro, 2009) and their relationship with the audience.

Collaboration skills: Moreover, fostered by a new philosophy regarding remote work, the need for cross-organisational collaboration, and the emergence of the gig economy (Petriglieri, Ashford, & Wrzesniewski, 2019), the workforce of tomorrow needs to be capable of sharing information, developing relationships, and interacting with others regardless of their geographical location and time zone (Yu et al., 2010). In other words, the skill to collaborate globally is and will remain of utmost importance (cf., Singh-Gupta & Troutt-Ervin, 1996) as a single employee cannot possess all knowledge and skills to solve complex problems in today's working world (Wang, 2010). Collaboration itself can be either seen as a method to acquire knowledge or solve a problem or as a process in the sense of a domain-general skill (Kuhn, 2015). In the context of the future skills of employees, collaboration will be considered as a domain-general skill. Collaboration itself is characterised by three central elements: (1) two or more people work interdependently,

(2) all engage in a genuine task with a joint goal, and (3) they pool their knowledge, skills, and efforts (Child & Shaw, 2019; Lai, 2011). Although there is no joint definition of collaboration (Dillenbourg, 1999; Lai, 2011), four aspects of the collaboration skill are consistently considered relevant across different sources (Evans, 2020):

(1) The ability to plan activities that are focused on achieving a jointly agreed goal, define clear roles and responsibilities among team members, and facilitate group decisions by solving conflicts.
(2) The ability to constructively respond to other opinions, using perspective taking and seeking honesty to understand others, and to engage all members of the group in subject-relevant discussions.
(3) The ability to take responsibility for joint outcomes, actively engage in the joint endeavour, and contribute to the success by sharing ideas and providing resources.
(4) The ability to adjust processes and methods – individually and on group-level – based on a reflection of the effectiveness and efficiency of the collaboration and to initiate an open dialogue with the other team members on this topic.

While technology can be seen as an enabler of global collaboration, as, for example, tools like Microsoft 365 and Google Docs allow people to work on documents regardless of time and place simultaneously, it is also transforming the nature of teamwork fundamentally (Fan & Yen, 2004). Thus, the skill to understand, structure, and manage collaboration globally in analogue and digital environments – in the sense that it is more than the technical know-how of using these tools – becomes even more relevant (Bălău & Utz, 2017).

Creativity skills: The ability to transform knowledge is a critical skill in collaboration and is often associated with creativity as a central element (Kaufman, 2013). Creativity refers to the "novel combination of old ideas" (Boden, 1996, p. 75) as well as to a "process of 'making up' something new and valuable by transforming what is into something better" (Young, 1985, p. 77). Thus, creativity is seen as a prerequisite or pre-outcome for innovation (Patrício et al., 2018) and correlates with entrepreneurship positively (Durnali, Orakci, & Khalili, 2023). Therefore, creativity is perceived as a central lever for long-term organisational success (DiLiello & Houghton, 2008) as it fosters organisational performance, product quality, and innovation power (Anderson et al., 2014; Liu et al., 2016). This becomes even more relevant when companies face existential threats: Businesses across all industries need to scrutinise their business model, value creation, and supply chain in light of the green transition and the evolving multipolar world order. On an individual level, creativity is perceived as a fluid state of mind most affected by intrinsic motivation that can be strengthened by habits and specific thinking patterns (Claxton et al., 2006). These include, for example, the curiosity to solve complex problems, an open-minded but systemic approach to tackle challenges (e.g., scientific experimenting), the ability to concentrate intensively and effortlessly (cf. flow concept; Csikszentmihalyi, 1990) as well as a certain degree of resilience against failure and setbacks. Furthermore, creativity is often connected with the capability of thinking critically (Lai, 2011), and with problem-solving (Mayer & Wittrock, 2006).

Problem-solving skills: Based on existential crises we need to face, such as health issues and pandemics, political conflicts and wars, as well as global warming and resulting nature threats, we need to deal with more and more challenging problems (Autor et al., 2003). Thus, we need specific knowledge and skills to deal effectively with them (Funke et al., 2018). This specific knowledge and skills are what is conceptualised as problem-solving. Therefore, it goes beyond a specific knowledge domain and describes the ability to develop a holistic view and apply a solution-oriented approach to challenges. This entails defining actions, identifying possible gaps, and gathering the information needed (Rausch & Wuttke, 2016). Hereby, it is essential to develop a skill for problem identification in order to not only find a solution but also find a solution for the exact problem. To thrive in problem-solving, it is necessary that people can transfer their knowledge and skills in a way that is applicable to an unfamiliar situation (Barak, 2018).

In summary, these seven domain-general skills are needed for thriving in both analogue and digital environments and are critical for individual – and in the end, organisational – success in a VUCA world. Thus, coaches need to (1) develop scientifically based approaches to empower their clients' personal growth along these seven skills and (2) reflect themselves on their own skill set.

Implications

Coaches are affected by these future trends and the VUCA world in two ways. The first way (see Figure 2.1) is the direct influence of these future trends: Coaches do not work shielded from future trends but are directly affected by them in their jobs. The coaching job is exposed to the same transformational challenges as those of other knowledge workers (Schermuly et al., 2022).

For example, in Germany, digital coaching increased from 8% in 2020 to 45% in 2022 (Rauen et al., 2022). In addition, AI is already used on coaching platforms, such as CoachHub, EZRA, and Betterup. In addition, for coaches more and more knowledge is available. For instance, several meta-analyses have been published on coaching effectiveness in the past years (e.g., de Haan & Nilsson; 2023, Graßmann et al., 2020; Theeboom et al., 2013; Jones et al., 2015). Thus, future coaches need to provide services using new technology and stay up to date with scientific insights and deal with shifts in their clients' needs and environments, communicate their services across different platforms, and engage in fruitful and collaborative working alliances without meeting their clients in person. Furthermore, coaches are affected by the demographic change, as both young and baby boomer generations work in the field and need to work together in order to exchange their knowledge.

In addition, coaches are affected indirectly by these trends via their clients (see Figure 2.1). "When the world becomes complex and uncertain, more people might seek help and need coaching" (English et al., 2019). In the future, coaches might therefore have more clients seeking help to cope with transformations in the business world. "New topics might emerge, and perhaps, new client types might begin coaching" (Schermuly et al., 2022, p. 246). When, for example, organisations flatten their hierarchies or introduce agile project management, the leadership roles change dramatically, and coaches should have the expertise and knowledge to support these. Future leaders also need to lead more virtually compared to the past and this means adapting communication, leadership mechanisms, and attitudes towards leadership, which leads to new coaching concerns. New coaching topics for managers could also result from diversity issues that are produced by demographic change and globalisation. Managers are confronted with younger generations and with team members, which have their origins in different cultures. Moreover, people will seek more support in developing the seven skills of the 21st century to thrive as job roles will continue to evolve. Thus, coaches need to reflect now on the question of which of the seven future skills are most important to their clients and develop scientifically based approaches to nurture them. In summary, coaches will be challenged in two ways in the future: They have to cope with new coaching concerns and foster new client competencies, and, at the same time, coaches themselves have to keep pace with the changes in the working world.

Reflective questions

1. How will the coaching industry adapt in light of the megatrends that shape our future?
2. What are the skills that I need to foster in order to thrive in a VUCA world?
3. How can coaching effectively nurture the necessary future skill set?

Conclusion

In navigating the future of work, coaches are tasked with confronting the VUCA world themselves while also empowering their clients and aiding companies in maintaining competitiveness amidst technological advancements. To achieve this, coaches must adopt innovative approaches to assist both organisations and individuals in transforming their work methodologies, fostering 21st-century skill sets within a digital landscape. Particularly, emphasis must be placed on enhancing abstract skills like communication, creativity, and problem-solving. As these skills necessitate not only formal education but also introspection and self-awareness, coaching emerges as a pivotal tool for their cultivation. Consequently, coaching is poised to remain indispensable for personal development within organizations, demanding coaches to gain a profound understanding of the nuances and evolving demands of the VUCA environment.

References

Alessie, R., Angelini, V., & Santen, P. (2013). Pension wealth and household savings in Europe: Evidence from sharelife. *European Economic Review, 63*, 308–328. https://doi.org/10.1016/j.euroecorev.2013.04.009

Ananiadou, K., & Claro, M. (2009). *21st century skills and competences for new millennium learners in OECD countries* (OECD Education Working Papers No. 41). Paris, France: OECD Publishing. https://doi.org/10.1787/218525261154

Anderson, C., Ames, D. R., & Gosling, S. D. (2008). Punishing hubris: The perils of overestimating one's status in a group. *Personality and Social Psychology Bulletin, 34*(1), 90–101. https://doi.org/10.1177/0146167207307489

Anderson, N., Potočnik, K., & Zhou, J. (2014). Innovation and creativity in organizations. *Journal of Management, 40*, 1297–1333. https://doi.org/10.1177/0149206314527128

Autor, D. H., Levy F., & Murnane R. J. (2003). The skill content of recent technological change: An empirical exploration. *Quarterly Journal of Economics, 118*(4), 1279–1333. https://doi.org/10.1162/003355303322552801

Bălău, N., & Utz, S. (2017). Information sharing as strategic behaviour: The role of information display, social motivation and time pressure. *Behaviour & Information Technology, 36*(6), 589–605. https://doi.org/10.1080/0144929X.2016.1267263

Barak, M. (2018). Are digital natives open to change? Examining flexible thinking and resistance to change. *Computers & Education, 121*, 115–123. https://doi.org/10.1016/j.compedu.2018.01.016

Baron, J. (2008). *Thinking and deciding* (4th ed.). New York: Cambridge University Press.

Bawden, D. (2001). Information and digital literacies; a review of concepts. *Journal of Documentation, 47*, 218–259.

Beason, L. (2001). Ethos and error: How business people react to errors. *College Composition and Communication, 53*, 33–64.

Beijerse, R. (1999). Questions in knowledge management: Defining and conceptualizing a phenomenon. *Journal of Knowledge Management, 3*(2), 94–110.

Berdahl, J. L., & Anderson, C. (2005). Men, women, and leadership centralization in groups over time. *Group Dynamics: Theory, Research, and Practice, 9*(1), 45–57. https://doi.org/10.1037/1089-2699.9.1.45

Blatter, J. (2013). Glocalization | Understanding global & local markets. *Encyclopedia Britannica.* www.britannica.com/money/topic/glocalization

Boden, M. A. (1996). What is creativity? In M. A. Boden (Ed.), *Dimensions of creativity* (pp. 75–118). Cambridge, MA: MIT Press.

Bornmann, L., & Mutz, R. (2015). Growth rates of modern science: A bibliometric analysis based on the number of publications and cited references. *Journal of the Association for Information Science and Technology, 66*(11), 2215–2222. https://doi.org/10.1002/asi.23329

Calk, R., & Patrick, A. (2017). Millennials through the looking glass: Workplace motivating factors. *Journal of Business Inquiry, 16*(2), 131–139. http://161.28.100.113/index.php/jbi/article/view/81

Catts, R., & Lau, J. (2008). *Towards information literacy indicators: Conceptual framework paper.* Paris, France: UNESCO.

Chen, M., Fu, Y., & Chang, Q. (2021). Life satisfaction among older adults in urban china: does gender interact with pensions, social support and self-care ability?. *Ageing and Society, 42*(9), 2026–2045. https://doi.org/10.1017/s0144686x20001877

Child, S. F. J., & Shaw, S. (2018). Towards an operational framework for establishing and assessing collaborative interactions. *Research Papers in Education, 34*(3), 276–297. https://doi.org/10.1080/02671522.2018.1424928

Claxton, G., Edwards, L., & Scale-Constantinou, V. (2006). Cultivating creative mentalities: A framework for education. *Thinking Skills and Creativity, 1*(1), 57–61.

Correia, R. A. M., & Teixeira, J. C. (2003). Information literacy: An integrated concept for a safer Internet. *Online Information Review, 27*, 311–320.

Csikszentmihalyi, M. (1990). *Flow.* New York: Harper & Row.

Dede C. (2010). Comparing frameworks for 21st century skills. In J. Bellanca & R. Brandt (Eds.), *21st century skills* (pp. 51–76). Bloomington, IN: Solution Tree Press.

de Haan, E., & Nilsson, V. (2023). What can we know about the effectiveness of coaching? A meta-analysis based only on randomized controlled trials. *Academy of Management Learning and Education.* https://doi.org/10.5465/amle.2022.0107

DiLiello, T. C., & Houghton, J. D. (2008). Creative potential and practiced creativity: Identifying untapped creativity in organizations. *Creativity and Innovation Management, 17*(1), 37–46. https://doi.org/10.1111/j.1467-8691.2007.00464.x

Dillenbourg, P. (1999). What do you mean by "collaborative learning?" In P. Dillenbourg (Ed.), *Collaborative learning: Cognitive and computational approaches* (pp. 1–19). Oxford, UK: Elsevier.

Dosi, G., & Mohnen, P. (2018). Innovation and employment: An introduction. *Industrial and Corporate Change, 28*(1), 45–49. https://doi.org/10.1093/icc/dty064

Drucker, P. (2005). Be data literate – Know what to know. *The Wall Street Journal.* www.wsj.com/articles/SB113208395700897890 (Original work published 1992).

Durnali, M., Orakci, Ş., & Khalili, T. (2023). Fostering creative thinking skills to burst the effect of emotional intelligence on entrepreneurial skills. *Thinking Skills and Creativity, 47,* 101200. https://doi.org/https://doi.org/10.1016/j.tsc.2022.101200

Dweck, C. S. (2006). Mindset: The new psychology of success. *Choice Reviews Online, 44*(04), 44–2397. https://doi.org/10.5860/choice.44-2397

Dychtwald, K., Erickson, T. J., & Morison, R. (2006). *Workforce crisis: How to beat the coming shortage of skills and talent.* https://ci.nii.ac.jp/ncid/BA7700712X

English, S., Sabatine, J. M. & Brownell, P. (2019). *Professional coaching: Principles and practice.* New York: Springer Publishing Company pages (pp. 293–303).

Evans, C. M. (2020). *Measuring student success skills: A review of the literature on collaboration.* Dover, NH: National Center for the Improvement of Educational Assessment.

Fan, X., & Yen, J. (2004). Modeling and simulating human teamwork behaviors using intelligent agents. *Physics of Life Reviews, 1*(3), 173–201.

Fraccaroli, F., & Deller, J. (2015). Work, aging, and retirement in Europe: Introduction to the special issue. *Work, Aging and Retirement, 1*(3), 237–242. https://doi.org/10.1093/workar/wav017

Funke, J., Fischer, A., & Holt, D. V. (2018). Competencies for complexity: Problem solving in the twenty-first century. In Care, E., Griffin, P., Wilson, M. (Eds.), *Assessment and teaching of 21st century skills. Educational assessment in an information age* (S. 41–53). Cham: Springer International Publishing. https://doi.org/10.1007/978-3-319-65368-6_3

Graßmann, C., Schölmerich, F., & Schermuly, C. C. (2019). The relationship between working alliance and client outcomes in coaching: A meta-analysis. *Human Relations, 73*(1), 35–58. https://doi.org/10.1177/0018726718819725

Grant, R. M. (1996). Toward a knowledge-based view of the firm. *Strategic Management Journal, 17,* 109–122.

Guilford, J. P. (1967). *The nature of human intelligence.* New York: McGraw-Hill.

Hackman, J. R., & Oldham, G. R. (1975). Development of the job diagnostic survey. *Journal of Applied Psychology, 60,* 159–170.

Houte, M., Leerkes, A., Slipper, A., & Breuls, L. (2021). Globalised citizenship and the perceived legitimacy of immigration control: narratives and acts of resistance in immigration detention. *Migration Studies, 9*(3), 1269–1291. https://doi.org/10.1093/migration/mnaa034

Hughes, A. (2023). ChatGPT: Everything you need to know about OpenAI's GPT-4 tool. BBC Sciencefocus. Retrieved October 8, 2023, from www.sciencefocus.com/future-technology/gpt-3/

Jenkins, H. (2006). *Convergence culture: Where old and new media collide.* New York: New York University Press.

Jones, C. (2011). Written and computer-mediated accounting communication skills. *Business and Professional Communication Quarterly, 74*(3), 247–271. https://doi.org/10.1177/1080569911413808

Jones, R. J., Woods, S. A. & Guillaume, Y. R. F. (2015). The effectiveness of workplace coaching: A meta-analysis of learning and performance outcomes from coaching. *Journal of Occupational and Organisational Psychology, 89,* 249–277. https://doi.org/10.1111/joop.12119

Kaufman, K. J. (2013). 21 ways to 21st century skills: Why students need them and ideas for practicalimplementation. *Kappa Delta Pi Record, 49*(2), 78–83. https://doi.org/10.1080/00228958.2013.786594

Keyton, J., Caputo, J. M., Ford, E. A., Fu, R., Leibowitz, S. A., Liu, T., . . . Wu, C. (2013). Investigating verbal workplace communication behaviors. *International Journal of Business Communication, 50,* 152–169. https://doi.org/10.1177/0021943612474990

Korunka, C., & Kubicek, B. (2017). Job demands in a changing world of work. In C. Korunka & B. Kubicek (Eds.), *Job demands in a changing world of work* (pp. 1–5). Springer International Publishing/Springer Nature. https://doi.org/10.1007/978-3-319-54678-0_1

Kuhn, D. (2015). Thinking together and alone. *Educational Researcher, 44*(1), 46–53.

Lai, E. (2011). *Collaboration: A literature review.* Princeton, NJ: Pearson.

Lemke, C. (2002). *enGauge 21st century skills: Digital literacies for a digital age.* Naperville, IL: North Central Regional Educational Laboratory (NCREL).

Lewin, C., & McNicol, S. (2015). The impact and potential of iTEC: Evidence from large-scale validation in school classrooms. In F. Van Assche, L. Anido, D. Griffiths, C. Lewin, & S. McNicol (Eds.), *Re-engineering the uptake of ICT in schools: The iTEC project* (pp. 163–186). Amsterdam: Springer Verlag.

Liu, D., Jiang, K., Shalley, C. E., Keem, S., & Zhou, J. (2016). Motivational mechanisms of employee creativity: A meta-analytic examination and theoretical extension of the creativity literature. *Organizational Behavior and Human Decision Processes, 137,* 236–263. https://doi.org/10.1016/j.obhdp.2016.08.001

Mayer, R., & Wittrock, M. (2006). Problem-solving transfer. In D. Berliner & R. Calfee (Eds.), *Handbook of educational psychology* (pp. 47–62). Mahwah, NJ: Erlbaum.

Millar, C. C. J. M., Groth, O., & Mahon, J. F. (2018). Management innovation in a VUCA world: Challenges and recommendations. *California Management Review, 61*(1), 5–14.

Mossberger, K., Tolbert, C. J., & Stansbury, M. (2003). *Virtual inequality: Beyond the digital divide.* Washington, DC: Georgetown University Press.

National Association of Colleges and Employers. (2016). *Job outlook 2017.* Retrieved from NACE website: www.naceweb.org/store/2017/job-outlook-2017/

Ng, W. (2012). Can we teach digital natives digital literacy? *Computers & Education, 59*(3), 1065–1078. https://doi.org/10.1016/j.compedu.2012.04.01

O'Sullivan, M. (2019). *The levelling: What's next after globalization.* Hachette UK.

Park, Y. J. (2013). Digital literacy and privacy behavior online. *Communication Research, 40,* 215–236.

Patrício, L., Gustafsson, A., & Fisk, R. (2018). Upframing service design and innovation for research impact. *Journal of Service Research, 21*(1), 3–16.

Petriglieri, G., Ashford, S. J., & Wrzesniewski, A. (2019). Agony and ecstasy in the Gig economy: Cultivating holding environments for precarious and personalized work identities. *Administrative Science Quarterly, 64*(1), 124–170. https://doi.org/10.1177/0001839218759646

Ratter, B., & Treiling, T. (2008). Komplexität – oder was bedeuten die Pfeile zwischen den Kästchen? In: Heike Egner, Beate Ratter und Richard Dikau (Hg.), *Umwelt als System – System als Umwelt? Systemtheorien auf dem Prüfstand* (S. 23–38). München: Oekom.

Rauen, C. et al. (2022). RAUEN Coaching-Marktanalyse 2022. Version as of 31st of May 2022. Available at www.rauen.de/cma/

Rausch, A., & Wuttke, E. (2016). Development of a multi-faceted model of domain-specific problem-solving competence and its acceptance by different stakeholders in the business domain. *Unterrichtswissenschaft, 44*(2), 164–189.

Reinsch, N. L., Jr., & Gardner, J. A. (2014). Do communication abilities affect promotion decisions? Some data from the C-Suite. *Journal of Business and Technical Communication, 28,* 31–57. https://doi.org/10.1177/1050651913502357

Schermuly, C. C. (2019). New Work und Coaching – psychologisches Empowerment als Chance für Coaches. *Organisationsberat Superv Coach, 26,* 173–192. https://doi.org/10.1007/s11613-019-00599-7

Schermuly, C. C. (2021). *New Work – Gute Arbeit gestalten.* https://doi.org/10.34157/9783648150030

Schermuly, C. C., & Meifert, M. (2022). Auf dem Wg ins postagile Zeitalter. *Personalmagazin, 9*(22), 24–30.

Serrano, F., Eguía, B., & Ferreiro, J. (2011). Public pensions' sustainability and population ageing: Is immigration the solution?. *International Labour Review, 150*(1–2), 63–79. https://doi.org/10.1111/j.1564-913x.2011.00105.x

Singh-Gupta, V., & Troutt-Ervin, E. (1996). Preparing learners for teamwork through collaborative writing and peer-review techniques. *Teaching English in the Two Year College, 23,* 127–136.

Starkey L. (2011). Evaluating learning in the 21st century: A digital age learning matrix. *Technology, Pedagogy and Education, 20*(1), 19–39. https://doi.org/10.1080/1475939X.2011.554021

Statista. (2022). *Total data volume worldwide 2010–2025.* Statista. www.statista.com/statistics/871513/worldwide-data-created/

Sternberg, R. J. (1997). *Successful intelligence.* New York: Plume.

Stiglitz, J. E. (2002, September 1). *Integration of unemployment insurance with retirement insurance.* https://papers.ssrn.com/sol3/papers.cfm?abstract_id=330338

Stone, P., Brooks, R., Brynjolfsson, E., Calo, R., Etzioni, O., Hager, G., Hirschberg, J., Kalyanakrishnan, S., Kamar, E., Kraus, S., Leyton-Brown, K., Parkes, D., Press, W., Saxenian, A., Shah, J., Tambe, M., & Teller, A. (2016). *"Artificial Intelligence and Life in 2030."* One Hundred Year Study on Artificial Intelligence: Report of the 2015–2016 Study Panel, Stanford University, Stanford, CA, September 2016. Doc: http://ai100.stanford.edu/2016-report. Accessed: September 6, 2022.

Tabah, A. N. (1999). Literature dynamics: Studies on growth, diffusion, and epidemics. *Annual Review of Information Science and Technology, 34,* 249–286. https://eric.ed.gov/?id=EJ635524

Theeboom, T., Beersma, B., & Van Vianen, A. (2013). Does coaching work? A meta-analysis on the effects of coaching on individual level outcomes in an organizational context. *Journal of Positive Psychology, 9*(1), 1–18. https://doi.org/10.1080/17439760.2013.837499

Treffinger, D. J., Young, G. C., Selby, E. C., & Shepardson, C. (2002). Assessing creativity: A guide for educators. Guide prepared for the National Research Center on the Gifted and Talented. Available online at: https://files.eric.ed.gov/fulltext/ED505548.pdf

Trudeau-Poskas, D. (2020). *Soft skills are 2020's hard skills.* Forbes. www.forbes.com/sites/forbescoachescouncil/2020/01/29/soft-skills-are-2020s-hard-skills-heres-how-to-master-them/?sh=2eee34dd70f2

van den Hooff, B. & de Ridder, J. A. (2004). Knowledge sharing in context: The influence of organizational commitment, communication climate and CMC use on knowledge sharing. *Journal of Knowledge Management, 8*(6), 117–130.

van Deursen, A. J. A. M., Helsper, E. J., & Eynon, R. (2016). Development and validation of the Internet Skills Scale (ISS). *Information Communication & Society, 19*(6), 804–823. https://doi.org/10.1080/1369118X.2015.1078834.

van Laar E., Van Deursen, A. J. A. M., Van Dijk, J. A. G. M., & De Haan, J. (2017). The relation between 21st-century skills and digital skills: A systematic literature review. *Computers in Human Behavior, 72,* 577–588. https://doi.org/10.1016/j.chb.2017.03.010

van Laar, E., Van Deursen, A. J. A. M., Van Dijk, J. A. G. M., & De Haan, J. (2020). Determinants of 21st-century skills and 21st-century digital skills for workers: A systematic literature review. *Sage Open, 10*(1), 1–14. https://doi.org/10.1177/2158244019900176

Veremchuk, A. (2020). Gender gap in pension income: cross-country analysis and role of gender attitudes. *SSRN Electronic Journal.* https://doi.org/10.2139/ssrn.3662968

Wang, Q. (2010). Using online shared workspaces to support group collaborative learning. *Computers & Education, 55*(3), 1270–1276. https://doi.org/10.1016/j.compedu.2010.05.023

Wang, Q., Fink, E. L., & Cai, D. A. (2012). The effect of conflict goals on avoidance strategies: What does not communicating communicate? *Human Communication Research, 38*(2), 222–252. https://doi.org/10.1111/j.1468-2958.2011.01421.x

Wardrope, W. J. (2002). Department chairs' perceptions of the importance of business communication skills. *Business Communication Quarterly, 65*(4), 60–72. https://doi.org/10.1177/1080569 90206500406

Wegman, L. A., Hoffman, B. J., Carter, N. T., Twenge, J. M., & Guenole, N. (2018). Placing job characteristics in context: Cross-temporal meta-analysis of changes in job characteristics since 1975. *Journal of Management, 44*(1), 352–386. https://doi.org/10.1177/0149206316654545

Wilpert, B. (2009). Impact of globalization on human work. *Safety Science, 47*(6), 727–732. https://doi.org/10.1016/j.ssci.2008.01.014

Windels, K., Mallia, K., & Broyles, S. (2013). Soft skills: The difference between leading and leaving the advertising industry? *Journal of Advertising Education, 17*(2), 17–27. https://doi.org/10.1177/109804821301700204

Young, J. G. (1985). What is creativity? *Journal of Creative Behavior, 19*(2), 77–87.

Yu, A. Y., Tian, S. W., Vogel, D. R., & Kwok, R. C. (2010). Can learning be virtually boosted? An investigation of online social networking impacts. *Computers & education, 55*(4), 1494–1503. https://doi.org/10.1016/j.compedu.2010.06.015

Zhang, L., Powell, J. J. W., & D. P. Baker. (2015). Exponential growth and the Shifting Global Center of Gravity of Science Production, 1900–2011. *Change: The Magazine of Higher Learning, 47*(4), 46–49. https://doi.org/10.1080/00091383.2015.1053777

Zink, E. (2011) *Flexible science: An anthropology of scientists, society and nature in Vietnam.* Uppsala: Uppsala University.

Chapter 3

Keeping up-to-date with technology change

Priya Hunt

Introduction

There are various definitions of digital coaching prevalent among coaches. It's been described simply as "coaching assisted by digital media" (Kanatouri, 2020, p.10). Some coaches see it as covering every synchronous technology (audio or video) that enables the coach and client to communicate. But it can also cover other aspects, such as using artificial intelligence (AI) to coach or the use of asynchronous technologies that enable further communication between the coach and client. This chapter uses the definition by Diller & Passmore (2023, p.05) to describe it as "a synchronous, personal conversation using Digital-Technology-enabled audio and/or video channels of communication between a human coach and a human coachee to empower the coachee in their self-development". It also covers the use of asynchronous digital technologies as supporting material and uses the term 'Coachtech' as coined by Isaacson (2022, p.180) to refer to any technology used, in its broadest sense, by a coach for coaching purposes.

The chapter explores how coaches can navigate the digital landscape without compromising their values and essence as a coach. This digital world is acknowledged as rapidly changing (Braddick, 2021) with the influx of technologies that are constantly evolving. The presented applications thereby focus on individual coaches and the steps they can take to stay well-informed in this dynamic digital environment.

Growth in technology

There has been a significant proliferation of technology in coaching, making it more accessible, flexible, and cost-effective while also potentially increasing the coach's capacity, capability, and competence (Otte et al., 2014; Kanatouri, 2020; Isaacson, 2022). This has been strengthened by the move to more flexible working patterns and the greater embracing of technology precipitated by the Covid pandemic. McKinsey's study shows that 25% of workers in advanced economies and 10% in emerging economies could work from home three to five days a week (Lund et al., 2021) and this trend is corroborated in terms of preference, ease, and productivity by many others (Barrero et al., 2021; Felstead & Reuschke, 2020; Forbes, 2020). This type of work needs virtual collaboration using technology and individuals have started expecting this flexibility in all fields, including coaching, illustrated by the significant increases in coaches using audio-video platforms (International Coaching Federation, 2021: Passmore, 2021).

DOI: 10.4324/9781003383741-5

However, many coaches still approach technology with a healthy dose of scepticism, feeling it can undermine spontaneity, creativity, and trust (Otte et al., 2014). There are accepted disadvantages such as loss of non-verbal cues, disruptions, and additional requirements of the coach (Diller & Passmore, 2023). Given that technology is here to stay and constantly changing, coaches need to adapt to it in an agile fashion and understand how human relationships change in the digital world, much like any other industry (Bellis et al., 2022). Acknowledging that every individual's needs and approach will differ, this chapter provides a framework rather than a recipe. It is suggested that coaches tailor this to suit their personal needs, preferences, and the coaching situation.

The framework includes four areas to explore how coaches can stay agile and invest in their continuous professional development in this digital world while also staying true to their coaching ethos (Figure 3.1):

(a) Attitude and approach to technology
(b) Using different information channels to learn
(c) Practice and preparation
(d) Holding tools lightly

Figure 3.1 Framework for keeping abreast of technology in coaching.

Attitude and approach towards technology

Resistance to change is a normal human phenomenon based on four reasons why people resist change: fear of the unknown, lack of trust, fear of failure, and lack of control (Kotter & Schlesinger, 1979). Technology change is seen as complex and multi-faceted and requires a nuanced understanding of societal impacts (Kraus et al., 2021). Therefore, attitude to this change is arguably the most important and the first element to consider.

A global coach survey on the impact of COVID-19 illustrates that those least able to transition to an online environment during the pandemic reported a greater detrimental impact (Passmore et al., 2023). Many will be aware of Dweck's mindset theory (1999), where she illustrates how people function better or worse, based on their attitudes and approaches.

People with a growth mindset are more likely to be open and flexible to learning, whereas those having a fixed mindset (i.e., 'I am not good with technology, I am too old to learn this, I will never understand it' etc.) can be self-defeating. Interestingly, this is also valid for consumer behaviour, where people with a growth mindset are more likely to adopt products aligned with their goals to learn and grow (Murphy & Dweck, 2016). There is evidence that there is no significant relationship between positive attitudes and gender or age (Otte et al., 2014), but it is true that usage builds proficiency (making the section on practice even more important to those who are not naturally drawn to technology). In the domain of digital coaching, coaches approach technology with a dual perspective: as learners and as consumers. Consequently, it is essential for coaches to evaluate where they are on the spectrum of fixed and growth mindsets and explore methods to transition towards the latter. Encouragingly, ample evidence, as exemplified by Dweck's research (1999), indicates that such a shift is attainable once individuals become aware of their existing mindset.

The Coachtech attitudes matrix (Isaacson, 2022) can be employed as a suitable tool for the evaluation of technology attitudes due to its user-friendly nature and comprehensibility. This matrix examines the coach's affinity for technology (*y*-axis) and overlays it with their proficiency (*x*-axis) within the context of their coaching practice.

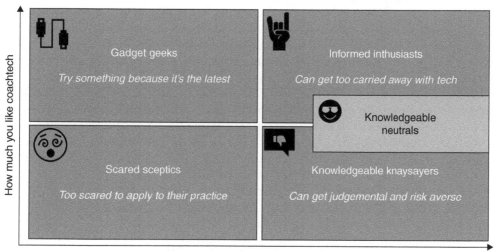

Figure 3.2 Coachtech attitudes matrix.
Source: Adapted from Isaacson (2022).

Starting from the bottom left of Figure 3.2, the 'Scared Sceptics' (low on both liking and understanding technology) can be intimidated by technology and tend to avoid it where possible. If the coach is here, it is worth channelling their inner Dweck to see if they can move towards a growth mindset – they may not be able to understand this technology *yet* – but there is plenty of help available and research that shows that human brains are malleable enough to learn more (Schulz & Hausmann, 2017). Two ways to do this would be the following:

1. Accept imperfections as uniqueness and set goals towards intentional learning. Irrespective of how much one learns, focusing on the process of learning in manageable chunks can help people stay in the growth mindset (Dweck, 1999).

2. Lines (2021, p. 380) comments on how "coaches exist in service of their clients" and reminding themselves that coaching clients are seeking the flexibility offered by digital coaching in the hybrid world is a good way for coaches to make this mindset shift. Digital technology also enables coaching to become more inclusive and accessible to people who need it, which makes it another very good reason to embrace it (Kanatouri, 2020).

The top left box in Figure 3.2 is also a version of a fixed mindset where the coach loves technology but knows little about it and can be enamoured by the latest shiny toy. If the coach is a 'Gadget Geek', it is not a bad thing as they have a passion for technology, and they could channel this passion for learning more about it. In this space, supervision, with peers or with a supervisor, can help. Reflecting on whether the coaching sessions move the client's thinking forward, tools and techniques are used only when needed, and the coach considers the client's preferences and needs, is a good way to temper the love for technology from overtaking the coach's way of being. Another good mechanism would be to learn more about the use of technology by being part of a coach community that regularly shares best practice.

The top right space of 'Informed Inthusiasts' are people who love technology but also are very well-informed about it. Such people would make an excellent buddy or mentor for those in the less knowledgeable sections. Coaches in this quadrant are advised to observe themselves to check if they have the tendency to use fancier tools, e.g., one only needs a hammer to hit a nail on the head, not a Swiss army knife. Using supervision to reflect on this and taking a humanistic, person-centred approach will enable the coach to keep themselves focused. Coaches could also become aligned with a professional coaching body (e.g., International Coaching Federation or European Mentoring & Coaching Council) and use this as an opportunity to participate or even initiate a special interest group on digital coaching. For coaches who are seeking 'Informed Inthusiasts' to network with, it is worth exploring the platforms provided by digital coaching firms that normally hire experts in this space. These firms also provide resources (blogs, whitepapers, webinars) that can offer coaches this informed perspective.

The 'Knowledgeable Knaysayers' (bottom right box) are also very aware of technology but understand it so well that they may dwell more on the security issues and flaws of the various systems. While it is sensible to be aware of the risks of Coachtech, it is important to maintain a balanced outlook, as being overly focused on the negatives will have a direct impact on the mindset and the ability to stay creative. Using a mix of reflection, supervision, and a growth mindset could help here. It is also worth evaluating whether the coach is falling into thinking traps (Beck, 1967) and focusing only on the negatives. These coaches can keep themselves balanced by getting into the habit of logically and explicitly identifying the positives alongside the negatives each time.

Maintaining Isaacson's phonetic play on the English language, a new category called 'kNowledgeable Neutrals' has been created, which is the space we recommend coaches occupy. This is a space where coaches are knowledgeable but neutral to technology so that they can hold tools lightly and stay unattached. While this sounds simple, it can be uncomfortable to move out from one attitudinal position to another. Given that growth and learning lie outside the comfort zone (Senninger, 2000), it is recommended that coaches learn to sit with this discomfort as they adapt to the optimal spot in the Coachtech attitudes matrix in order to increase their knowledge and self-efficacy. This increase in self-efficacy can also foster a positive attitude (Otte et al., 2014), becoming a virtuous cycle. The next section focuses on various information channels that coaches can reach out to improve their knowledge and understanding of these tools.

Information channels for keeping up-to-date

Keeping abreast of the latest advancements in the field is not only an ethical obligation but also crucial for delivering optimal services to clients. This aspect holds particular significance in disciplines characterised by interpretive subject matter, such as nursing, medicine, coaching, counselling, and teaching (Moon, 2013). Failing to stay updated can result in a loss of enthusiasm, complacency, or disinterest (Mann & Webb, 2022).

In today's information-driven world, the challenge lies not in accessing information but rather in discerning its credibility and relevance to our objectives. This process closely mirrors the evaluation of accreditation and training undertaken by coaches. Employing a structured approach to assess the source's reliability before incorporating the information becomes essential to uphold credibility and trust, thereby aligning with ethical coaching standards. Mandalios (2013) proposes the RADAR structure as a practical mnemonic to evaluate web sources:

- Relevance
- Authority
- Date
- Appearance
- Reason

This mnemonic serves as a convenient tool to validate online sources and align the acquired information with one's specific requirements. The internet is widely recognised as a valuable learning resource, with research indicating its popularity among coaches and their clients (Koh et al., 2018). The advancements in online search engines have made it effortless to find precise information promptly and then sift through the results to identify credible and pertinent sources. Social media platforms further facilitate the process by providing comments and endorsements from various individuals, including fellow coaches, thereby instilling confidence in the content being reviewed. However, discerning whose opinions to trust remains a challenge.

The advent of artificial intelligence has led to the proliferation of specialised research platforms capable of delivering query results along with source papers and an assessment of their trustworthiness. Additionally, platforms like YouTube host expert users who create concise and accessible videos utilising Coachtech, available free of charge. Numerous podcasts, webinars, and online training courses are readily accessible, although exploring these resources can be time-consuming and frustrating for those lacking a specific passion for technology. Capitalising on our expertise as coaches to pose insightful questions, one can leverage advanced technologies like ChatGPT as an initial reference point to explore available technologies and generate ideas for further research. However, it is vital to evaluate the answers provided by intelligent search engines like ChatGPT before accepting them (Box 3.1, myth 3).

A more viable alternative presents itself in the form of establishing or engaging in a learning community. Learning communities are characterised as "a heterogeneous collective endeavour aimed at fostering and perpetuating a system of knowledge creation" (Senge & Scharmer, 2006, p. 197). Various avenues exist to either join or initiate a community. Professional coaching associations offer membership forums and special interest groups where individuals can actively participate. Additionally, maintaining informal connections with fellow colleagues from the same coaching course or certification programme serves as a valuable means of reconnecting with like-minded individuals sharing similar interests.

In the realm of digital coaching, certain authors have ventured into establishing paid-for communities, which can be discovered on business-oriented social media platforms like LinkedIn. Research indicates that innovative learning methods and the existence of a robust and diverse membership can contribute to the growth and advancement of such communities (Lepistö & Hytti, 2021). Moreover, these communities can offer varied perspectives, thereby enhancing the reflective process. Engaging in a coach community can provide ways to discover new tools and techniques utilised by fellow professionals. While it is prudent for the community's focus to encompass all aspects of coaching, it is crucial to ensure that digital and Coachtech-related discussions receive adequate attention. Within these sessions, individuals representing different positions on the Coachtech attitudes matrix (Figure 3.1) can be found, making it advantageous to establish partnerships or request presentations from 'Informed Inthusiasts' who possess a profound passion for technology. The beauty of such sessions lies in the ability of participants across various quadrants to offer a balanced perspective, tempering enthusiasm with practical considerations.

Practice and preparation

It makes sense for coaches to aim for the saying practice makes proficient rather than practice makes perfect, as perfectionism can be maladaptive to successful learning (Osenk et al., 2020). Perfection is a moot point and if coaches are tempted to go in that direction, it is worth evaluating if they need to adjust any behaviour or thinking to temper their passion for technology. Reminding themselves that they are here in the service of the client in the first place rather than in the service of their mastery over technology may be a useful method.

If there's an argument on why practice is even needed, there is the evidence mentioned earlier about how technology self-efficacy and a systematic approach to it can encourage a positive attitude and, therefore, a growth mindset (Otte et al., 2014). Regular practice of the technology outside the coaching environment enables a coach to bring Coachtech into a coaching process with minimal effort and disruption. This may involve some level of training, but the bulk will be practical, i.e., how to integrate technology in your coaching sessions rather than focusing on using it.

How much practice is good practice? In the context of digital coaching, the determination of an appropriate amount of practice is a challenging task, as it varies depending on factors such as the coach's existing technical competency, coaching skills, and the specific technology they aim to practise. When self-assessing one's skills on a scale of 0 to 10, with 10 representing an extremely competent level and 0 representing the opposite, it is recommended to engage in practice until the competency level increases by 2–3 points or reaching a reasonable level of competence. Striving for perfection with a rating of 9 or 10 may not be necessary and could be driven by an excessive pursuit of flawlessness.

To enhance competency, individuals can leverage freely available online resources provided by technology enthusiasts or the technology providers themselves. Additionally, digital coaching firms may offer training opportunities to associate coaches, although these programs typically align with the firm's specific processes and platforms.

Several training firms provide online coach training and digital coaching certifications. However, it should be noted that these entities are not affiliated with professional coaching bodies. Professional coaching bodies, such as the International Coaching Federation, European Mentoring and Coaching Council and Association for Coaching, offer valuable resources in the form of articles, blogs, and webinars related to various aspects of digital coaching. It is important to recognise that the field of digital coaching is constantly evolving, and new developments are expected to emerge.

From a practical standpoint, it is crucial for coaches to possess a reasonable level of proficiency with technology during coaching sessions. To facilitate this, it is recommended to test the technology in a secure and controlled environment. One effective approach is to utilise a coaching circle, wherein coaches engage in peer-coaching sessions and have the opportunity to test new tools, provided there is prior agreement among participants. However, if one is not involved in such a setup or is unable to join one, the only alternative is to introduce the tool during a regular coaching session, preferably on a pro-bono basis, with the client's explicit permission and subsequent feedback.

Engaging in self-reflection after employing a new tool in a coaching session is beneficial in uncovering additional insights regarding its application. Utilisation of coaching circles is more acceptable than conducting experiments with paying clients, even if the clients are agreeable to it. Research has demonstrated the effectiveness of peer coaching in various interpretive professions, such as education and nursing, and it stands to reason that similar benefits can be derived within the coaching field as well (Bai et al., 2019; Shelton et al., 2021; Waldrop & Derouin, 2019).

For individuals who are not fond of technology, engaging in practice can often become an arduous task, leading them to seek alternative distractions as a means of avoidance. Drawing inspiration from the Japanese concept of Kaizen, which has become synonymous with continuous improvement across various industries and businesses (Imai, 1986), one can embrace the notion of everyday improvement. The core principle of Kaizen entails making small daily changes to foster habit formation and enhance proficiency. By applying a similar approach, dedicating just 15 minutes each day to delve into the realm of Coachtech is more likely to yield favourable outcomes compared to sporadic, lengthy sessions. This approach is particularly advantageous for individuals who lack an inherent enthusiasm for technology. Research suggests that short, focused bursts of learning may prove more effective than prolonged study sessions (Rohrer & Pashler, 2010). Moreover, recognising and aligning one's learning habits with one's circadian rhythm can significantly enhance overall effectiveness (Pink, 2019; Schwartz et al., 2011).

In cases where individuals struggle with commitment, the importance of seeking support resources cannot be overstated. As previously discussed, the establishment of learning communities is invaluable. Finding a like-minded buddy who possesses a genuine passion for technology and is willing to dedicate time to mutual growth (potentially in exchange for a coaching session) serves as a productive approach to enhancing and practising skills. Paradoxically, coaches often overlook the fact that coaching itself serves as a valuable means of augmenting self-efficacy (Jones & Andrews, 2022). Collaborating with another coach to foster self-efficacy in Coachtech can yield remarkable outcomes, as research indicates that partnering with peers can be an effective strategy for technology learning, particularly when combined with other approaches (Carvalho & Santos, 2020; Kaluyu & Ndiku, 2020).

In addition to consistent practice, adequate preparation before coaching sessions is essential. This entails logistical planning and consideration of potential tools to be utilised during the session. This does not necessarily mean to predetermine the tools to be employed, as coaching is a collaborative process that is co-created with the client, based on the discussion at hand. However, it is advisable to have a selection of simple resources readily available, such as blank templates for useful matrices. If conducting a face-to-face session, one may choose to carry relevant materials that could potentially be utilised. Coachtech can be an integral part of this toolkit, and it is beneficial to contemplate how and when it could be employed if the opportunity arises. For example, downloading templates on an iPad makes it convenient to physically review them in face-to-face sessions. If conducting sessions via videoconferencing, it is advisable to consider downloading associated apps that enhance the interactive whiteboarding experience in advance.

A valuable tip to bear in mind is that many technology tools operate on a subscription model, often offering a free version as well. Engaging with the free version and gaining clarity on which specific technologies to commit to is a prudent and cost-effective approach. While the allure of multiple subscriptions may be tempting, with each individual subscription being a relatively small expense, it is important to consider the cumulative cost. As a coach-entrepreneur, it is crucial to evaluate the return on investment, and therefore, adopting a 'try-before-you-buy' mindset becomes a sensible strategy. Additionally, maintaining a list of all technology investments allows for periodic evaluation, enabling the discontinuation of subscriptions that are under-utilised. This cautious approach serves as a warning to those prone to being enticed by the latest gadgets or being overly enthusiastic about staying informed, as they may be more inclined to invest in software or hardware with higher specifications. It is important to note that this decision may not be relevant for individuals operating within a larger coaching ecosystem where the technology is predetermined and provided.

Holding tools lightly

Having a variety of tools in their repertoire allows coaches to be more adaptable and responsive to their clients' needs, preferences, and requirements in real-time. Coaches understand that the success of a coaching partnership relies significantly on the client relationship, with theory and technique contributing to only approximately 15% of the overall impact (McKenna & Davis, 2009). Hence, it is crucial to develop the ability to effortlessly use technology, allowing coaches to maintain their focus and attention on what truly matters – the client.

Finding a balance between the challenges posed by technology and one's skills is essential to achieve a state of Flow – an effortless state of focus and absorption (Csikszentmihalyi, 1990). Flow necessitates clear goals, unwavering concentration, and immediate feedback, qualities that coaches strive for in every session. Why is Flow relevant? Research has linked this state to both well being and performance. In a decade-long study involving over 5000 executives, McKinsey identified that Flow enhances productivity by up to 500% (Cranston & Keller, 2013). While coaching may not solely aim to improve productivity, the state of effortless absorption associated with Flow creates an environment where coaches can be fully present and engaged with their clients during coaching sessions.

Thus, being knowledgeable about Coachtech and continuously improving skills through practice are vital to effectively move the clients' thinking forward using these tools. However, it is equally important to maintain a balanced perspective and avoid becoming overly attached to the tools themselves. Leach and Passmore (2021, p. 125) caution that tools can sometimes become a hindrance or a 'distinct disadvantage', obstructing the client–coach relationship and detracting from serving the client's needs. This brings us back to the significance of practice and preparation. Coaches must invest sufficient effort to ensure that their attention remains focused on the client, rather than being consumed by the application of tools or techniques. The 'five top tips' for using tools and techniques in coaching, as developed by Leach and Passmore (2021, p. 130), adapted to digital coaching, may help. In this, a new tip has been added, emphasising the need for coaches to regularly self-evaluate their attitude and approach towards technology to ensure its alignment with serving the client effectively.

Making ethical considerations while maintaining a balanced approach to digital coaching tools involves contemplating data security and protection. Coaches must actively educate themselves about data security, including compliance with policies and regulations such as the General Data Protection Regulation (GDPR). Passmore and Sinclair (2020) highlight that coaches may adopt different approaches to note taking and reflection, which become more complex when utilising digital media. Therefore, it is recommended that coaches dedicate time to developing an approach that aligns with national and international guidelines on data protection and disposal.

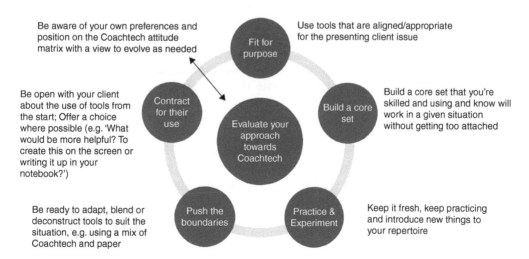

Figure 3.3 Top tips for using tools/techniques.

Source: Adapted from Leach & Passmore (2021, p. 130).

Several factors require consideration, including the following:

- *Security for oneself and the client*: Implementing measures such as virus protection and firewalls to ensure the confidentiality and integrity of information. Investing in robust security measures is crucial in the digital landscape.
- *Back-up and access*: Determining secure storage options to prevent data loss due to hardware failure. Coaches need to audit the various applications they use, considering where co-created whiteboards and PowerPoint templates are stored and who has access to the data.
- *Approach to data storage and deletion*: Coaches should consider whether they retain any data or transfer it to the client, ensuring its deletion from their own devices. Communicating this approach and contracting with clients can provide reassurance that their data remains confidential. Co-created tools can be designed in a way that limits understanding to the coaching pair or is password-protected, serving as an additional safeguard. When deleting data, coaches should verify that clients have received and saved the necessary files to prevent accidental loss.

For those who may struggle with or hold reservations about technology, it becomes essential, from an ethical standpoint, to confront these challenges to best serve clients. Prioritising personal mindset transformation through coaching support becomes paramount before tackling other aspects of staying abreast of technology (see Figure 3.1).

Key implications

In a rapidly evolving digital landscape, the process of learning Coachtech can appear overwhelming, particularly for individuals who did not grow up using technology. On the other hand, those who are fascinated by technology may find themselves more captivated by its allure than fully present in the moment, requiring a significant shift in mindset. Coaches understand that human beings possess the capacity to adapt and transform beyond their perceived limitations. Therefore, it is only fitting for coaches to apply this transformative process to themselves.

By approaching this transformation systematically and utilising the framework presented in this chapter, individuals can alleviate the anxiety associated with new technology while gaining a deeper awareness of their own attitudes toward it. Tackling one section at a time and dedicating a small portion of daily time to the learning process are effective strategies to avoid being overwhelmed.

Van Nieuwerburgh (2017) provides a concise depiction of the three key elements of effective coaching. He contends that while skills and processes can be taught, the coach's way of being represents the most critical aspect. Acquiring knowledge about technology becomes essential for coaches to enhance their skills and adapt their coaching processes to align with the demands of the digital world. However, it is important to strike a balance and not allow technology to overshadow the fundamental coaching approach. Maintaining a conscious and self-aware stance is crucial for continually evolving and maximising coaching effectiveness.

Engaging in reflective practice is one method of cultivating self-awareness, a practice that skilled coaches already embrace. Jones (2021) distinguishes between rumination, which focuses on negative aspects, threats, and losses, and reflection, which involves challenging self-limiting beliefs and cultivating awareness of latent strengths. When exploring personal attitudes towards Coachtech, it is valuable to assess whether rumination or genuine reflection predominates, with the aim of fostering the latter. Utilising coaching tools such as force-field analysis and the GROW model to evaluate facilitators and barriers to becoming more knowledgeable about digital technology can provide valuable support and resources.

Feedback from clients, including their experiences with tools and their perception of progress in their thinking, along with the coach's reflection on digital coaching sessions during supervision, can offer additional perspectives. Recording coaching sessions that employ technology (with appropriate permission) and subsequently observing and rating one's presence throughout the session, as well as cues on the client's level of thinking and progress, can serve as a useful resource for identifying areas that require attention. By recognising moments of diminished presence or inadequate listening, coaches can determine whether further skill development in using tools and techniques, as well as additional practice, is necessary. If a sense of nonchalance towards the technology or a failure to keep pace with the client's progress is observed, it may be imperative to prioritise the evolution of one's attitude and approach, either by holding tools more lightly or adopting a growth mindset.

Coaches already possess many of the skills and processes required to coach themselves toward greater proficiency with technology, while ensuring that it remains a tool wielded lightly and in service of the client. Box 3.1 provides an illustration of some common myths and evidence to assist in this endeavour. This is not an exhaustive list but provides a snapshot and indication of how the digital coaching space can be peppered with misconceptions and reiterates the need to use data and research to validate popular stories.

Reflective questions

As coaches embark on their digital coaching journey, it can be beneficial to reflect on the following three questions that facilitate staying up-to-date with technological advancements:

1. Does my attitude toward technology contribute to my client's progress in their thinking?
2. Am I striking a balance in the use of technology, ensuring that my client is not disadvantaged by either its absence or overuse in coaching sessions?
3. How should Coachtech be incorporated into my continuous professional development?

Conclusion

The adoption of digital coaching provides numerous notable advantages, encompassing enhanced accessibility, structured guidance, innovative approaches, and flexible convenience (Kanatouri, 2020). In the contemporary context, technology has become an indispensable component of coaching, as clients anticipate its seamless integration within their coaching experiences. Nonetheless, it is imperative to recognise that Coachtech is

---

Box 3.1   Myth-busting digital coaching

Myth 1: Digital coaching is worse (or superior) – False

Digital coaching is as effective as traditional coaching as indicated by studies on behavioural change (Gershkowitz et al., 2020), self-efficacy (Kettunen et al., 2019), and clinical outcomes (Rasulnia et al., 2017). Tests against face-to-face coaching have shown similar outcomes (Rethorn, 2021) and offering digital tools to complement telephone coaching shows an increase in satisfaction with coaching (Muuraiskangas et al., 2020). It's important to note that the effectiveness will depend on the context as found in a study in shadow education (Meço, 2023) and while it is a viable alternative, it needs to be considered against the context and the needs of the client.

Myth 2: Digital coaching needs significant financial investment – False

Studies suggest that Coachtech does not require significant financial investment by the coach (Bachmann & Fietze, 2018; Heller & Koch, 2018). As mentioned throughout the chapter, there are many free resources available on the internet and most paid-for resources offer a free trial which is recommended prior to committing. It is also possible to take subscriptions for a period of time and stopping this subscription if the technology is not working for you. If the coach is tempted to always invest in the latest applications, it is worth reviewing the intention behind this – is it their attitude or a real need for the tool that is driving this approach?

Myth 3: Information sources that are easily accessible are unreliable – Partially True

The internet is a vast source of information – but the context, validity, and the relevance of the information needs to be checked before use. Studies indicate that even artificial intelligence apps (e.g., ChatGPT) can provide correct and partially correct answers only in 44% of the cases and correct and partially correct explanations in 57% of cases (Jalil et al., 2023). While technology will continue to evolve and become better, it is clear that there is a need to undertake an evaluation before using data. If the internet can be used to sift through a large quantity and filter to the ones that need further investigation, it can be used as a relatively reliable source for searching for preliminary information.

---

merely a tool in the coaching repertoire and should not be regarded with fear or excessive attachment. By fostering a mindful and adaptable mindset toward technology, actively seeking valuable resources, refining skills through deliberate practice, and maintaining a balanced approach, coaches can harness its potential as a potent asset. Embracing digital technology in this manner empowers coaches to elevate their coaching presence and propel clients' transformative thinking with heightened effectiveness.

References

Bachmann, T., & Fietze, B. (2018). The digitization of coaching – Thoughts from the perspective of participant observation. *Superv Coach, 25*, 281–292. https://doi.org/10.1007/s11613-018-0561-5.

Bai, B., Song, H., & Zhang, Q. (2019). Catering for teachers' individual teaching differences in China: Ihe case of forming reciprocal coaching circles supported by university-based teacher educators. *Journal of Education for Teaching, 45*(2), 214–218.

Barrero, J. M., Bloom, N., & Davis, S. (2021). *Why working from home will stick.* NBER Working paper. Retrieved from: www.nber.org/papers/w28731.pdf.

Beck, A. T. (1967). *Depression: Causes and treatment.* Philadelphia, PA: University of Pennsylvania Press.

Bellis, P., Trabucchi, D., Buganza, T., & Verganti, R. (2022). How do human relationships change in the digital environment after COVID-19 pandemic? The road towards agility. *European Journal of Innovation Management, 25*(6), 821–849.

Braddick, C. (2021). Emerging conversations about technology and coaching. In Watts, M. & Florance, I. (Eds.), *Emerging conversations in coaching and coaching psychology*, pp. 125–140. Abingdon: Routledge.

Carvalho, A. R., & Santos, C. (2020). The impact of a digitally enhanced peer-learning program on peer teacher students' academic performance: A study developed under Educational Design Research. *2020 15th Iberian Conference on Information Systems and Technologies* (CISTI) (pp. 24–27). Seville, Spain. https://doi.org/10.23919/CISTI49556.2020.9141111

Cranston, S., & Keller, S. (2013). Increasing the meaning quotient of work. *McKinsey Quarterly, 1*, 48–59.

Csikszentmihalyi, M. (1990). *Flow: The psychology of optimal experience.* New York: Harper & Row.

Diller, S., & Passmore, J. (2023). Defining digital coaching: A qualitative inductive approach. *Frontiers in Psychology, 14*, 1148243. doi:10.3389/fpsyg.2023.1148243.

Dweck, C. S. (1999). *Self-theories: Their role in motivation, personality and development.* Philadelphia, PA: Taylor & Francis/Psychology Press.

Felstead, A., & Reuschke, D. (2020). Homeworking in the UK: Before and during the 2020 lockdown. *WISERD Report*, Cardiff: Wales Institute of Social and Economic Research.

Forbes. (2020). *Working from home; It's now a thing.* Retrieved from: www.forbes.com/sites/enriquedans/2020/06/06/working-from-home-its-now-athing/?sh=3da4ac045d54 [Accessed: 01 Nov 2022].

Gershkowitz, B. D., Hillert, C. J., & Crotty, B. H. (2020). Digital coaching strategies to facilitate behavioural change in type 2 diabetes: A systematic review. *Journal of Clinical Endocrinology & Metabolism, 106*(4), 1513–1520. https://doi.org/10.1210/clinem/dgaa850

Heller, J., & Koch, A. (2018). Digitization in coaching. In: Heller, J., Triebel, C., Hauser, B., & Koch, A. (Eds.), *Digitale Medien im Coaching.* Springer, Berlin, Heidelberg. https://doi.org/10.1007/978-3-662-54269-9_1

Imai, M. (1986). *Kaizen* (Vol. 201). New York: Random House Business Division.

International Coaching Federation. (2021). *Covid 19 and the coaching industry.* Retrieved from: COVID-19 and the Coaching Industry – International Coaching Federation [Accessed: 01 Nov 2022].

Isaacson, S. (2022). *Superhuman Coaching: Ten technologies that expand coaching beyond what's humanly possible.* London, UK: Hanwell.

Jalil, S., Rafi, S., LaToza, T. D., Morgan, K., & Lam, W. (2023). ChatGPT and software testing education: Promises & perils. Paper presented at *2023 IEEE International Conference on Software Testing, Verification and Validation Workshops (ICSTW).* https://doi.org/10.48550/arXiv.2302.03287

Jones, R. J. (2021). *Coaching with research in mind.* Abingdon: Routledge.

Jones, R. J., & Andrews, H. (2022). *Can one-to-one coaching improve selection success and who benefits most? The role of candidate generalised self-efficacy.* Unpublished manuscript. Henley Business School, University of Reading. Corresponding author: r.j.jones@henley.ac.uk.

Jung, C. G. (1928). Analytical psychology and education. In H. G. Baynes & F. C. Baynes (Eds.), *Contributions to Analytical Psychology* (pp. 313–382). London: Trench Trubner.

Kaluyu, V., & Ndiku, J.M. (2020). Pedagogy and information technology integration as strategies for improving academic performance in STEM subjects: A critical literature review. *International Knowledge Sharing Platform, 11*(21). https://doi.org/10.7176/JEP/11-21-21

Kanatouri, S. (2020). *The digital coach.* Abingdon: Routledge.

Kettunen, E., Kari, T., Makkonen, M., Critchley, W., & Sell, A. (Eds.). (2019). *Humanizing technology for a sustainable society: Proceedings of the 32nd Bled eConference, Bled, Slovenia, 16–19 June 2019.* Bled: University of Maribor.

Koh, K. T., Lee, T. P., & Lim, S. H. (2018). The Internet as a source of learning for youth soccer coaches. *International Journal of Sports Science & Coaching, 13*(2), 278–289.

Kotter, J. P., & Schlesinger, L. A. (1979). Choosing strategies for change. *Harvard Business Review*, March–April, 106–114. Harvard Business School Publishing Corporation. Available at: https://projects.iq.harvard.edu/files/sdpfellowship/files/day3_2_choosing_strategies_for_change.pdf [Accessed: 24 June 2023].

Kraus, S., Jones, P., Kailer, N., Weinmann, A., Chaparro-Banegas, N., & Roig-Tierno, N. (2021). Digital transformation: An overview of the current state of the art of research. *Sage Open, 11*(3), 21582440211047576.

Leach, S., & Passmore, J. (2021). Tools and techniques in Coaching. In: Passmore, J. (Ed.), *The coaches' handbook*. Abingdon: Routledge.

Lepistö, T., & Hytti, U. (2021). Developing an executive learning community: Focus on collective creation. *Academy of Management Learning & Education, 20*(4), 514–538.

Lines, S. (2021). Supervision in coaching. In: Passmore, J. (Ed.), *The coaches' handbook: The complete practitioner guide for professional coaches*. Abingdon, Oxon: Routledge. Retrieved from: https://search.ebscohost.com/login.aspx?direct=true&db=nlebk&AN=2574240&site=ehost-live [Accessed: 8 April 2023].

Lund, S., Madgavkar, A., Manyika, J., Smit, S., Ellingrud, K., Meaney, M., & Robinson, O. (2021). *The future of work after COVID-19.* McKinsey Global Institute. Retrieved from: www.mckinsey.com/featured-insights/future-of-work/the-future-of-work-after-covid-19 [Accessed: 12 Aug 2022].

Mandalios, J. (2013). RADAR: An approach for helping students evaluate Internet sources. *Journal of Information Science, 39*(4), 470–478.

Mann, S., & Webb, K. (2022). Continuing professional development: Key themes in supporting the development of professional practice. In: Schwab, G., Oesterle, M., & Whelan, A. (Eds.), *Promoting professionalism, innovation and transnational collaboration: A new approach to foreign language teacher education* (pp. 15–44). Research-publishing.net. Retrieved from: https://doi.org/10.14705/rpnet.2022.57.1382 [Accessed: 09 April 2023].

McKenna, D. D., & Davis, S. L. (2009). Hidden in plain sight: The active ingredients of executive coaching. *Industrial and Organizational Psychology, 2*(3), 244–260.

Meço, G. (2023). Comparison of digital coaching centers and face-to-face coaching centers in the context of shadow education institutions: Student and teacher perceptions and academic achievements of students. *Preprints* 2023, 2023051231. https://doi.org/10.20944/preprints202305.1231.v1

Moon, J. A. (2013). *Reflection in learning and professional development: Theory and practice.* Abingdon: Routledge.

Murphy, M. C., & Dweck, C. S. (2016). Mindsets shape consumer behavior. *Journal of Consumer Psychology, 26*(1), 127–136. www.jstor.org/stable/26618124

Muuraiskangas, S.T., Honka, A. M., Junno, U. M., Nieminen, H., & Kaartinen, J. (2020). A technology-assisted telephone intervention for work-related stress management: Pilot randomized controlled trial. *Journal of Medical Internet Research, 24*(7), e26569. https://doi.org/10.2196/26569

Osenk, I., Williamson, P., & Wade, T. D. (2020). Does perfectionism or pursuit of excellence contribute to successful learning? A meta-analytic review. *Psychological Assessment, 32*(10), 972–983. https://doi.org/10.1037/pas0000942

Otte, S., Bangerter, A., Britsch, M., & Wüthrich, U. (2014). Attitudes of coaches towards the use of computer-based technology in coaching. *Consulting Psychology Journal: Practice and Research, 66*(1), 38.

Passmore, J. (2021). *Future trends in coaching: Executive report 2021.* Henley-on-Thames: Henley Business School.

Passmore, J., Liu, Q., Tee, D., & Tewald, S. (2023). The impact of Covid-19 on coaching practice: Results from a global coach survey. *Coaching: An International Journal of Theory, Research and Practice, 16*(2), 173–189. https://doi.org/10.1080/17521882.2022.2161923

Passmore, J., & Sinclair, T. (2020). *Becoming a coach.* Cham: Springer International Publishing.

Pink, D. H. (2019). *When: The scientific secrets of perfect timing.* New York: Penguin Random House.

Rasulnia, M., Burton, W. S., Ginter, R. P., Wang, T. Y., Pleasants, R. A., Green, C. L., & Lugogo, N. (2017). Assessing the impact of a remote digital coaching engagement program on patient-reported outcomes in asthma. *Journal of Asthma, 55*(7), 795–800. https://doi.org/10.1080/02770903.2017.1362430

Rethorn, Z. D. (2021). Telehealth and wellness coaching: Mirage or mainstay? *Developmental Medicine & Child Neurology, 63*(6), 631.

Rohrer, D., & Pashler, H. (2010). Recent research on human learning challenges conventional instruction strategies. *Educational Researcher, 39*(5), 406–412. https://doi.org/10.3102/0013189X10374770.

Schulz, J. B., & Hausmann, L. (2017). The malleable brain: Plasticity of neural circuits and behaviour. *Journal of Neurochemistry, 142*(6), 788–789.

Schwartz, T., Gomes, J., & McCarthy, C. (2011). *Be excellent at anything: The four keys to transforming the way we work and live.* London: Simon & Schuster.

Senge, P. M., & Scharmer, C. O. (2006). Community action research: Learning as a community of practitioners, consultants and researchers. In: Reason, P., & Bradbury, H. (Eds.), *Handbook of action research* (pp. 195–207). Thousand Oaks, CA: Sage.

Senninger, T. (2000). The learning zone model. ThemPra Social Pedagogy. Retrieved from: The Learning Zone Model – ThemPra Social Pedagogy [Accessed: 18 Nov 2022].

Shelton, D. S., Delgado, M. M., Greenway, E. V., Hobson, E. A., Lackey, A. C., Medina-García, A., Reinke, B. A., Trillo, P. A., Wells, C. P., & Horner-Devine, M. C. (2021). Expanding the landscape of opportunity: Professional societies support early-career researchers through community programming and peer coaching. *Journal of Comparative Psychology, 135*(4), 439.

Van Nieuwerburgh, C. (2017). *An introduction to coaching skills – A practical guide* (2nd ed.). London: Sage.

Waldrop, J., & Derouin, A. (2019). The coaching experience of advanced practice nurses in a national leadership program. *Journal of Continuing Education in Nursing, 50*(4), 170–175.

Chapter 4

Marketing a digital coaching business

Michael Beale and JD Meier

Introduction

Marketing has always been a critical challenge for coaches, and the same is true for anyone coaching in the digital sphere. This challenge will grow as the cost of entry for a coach remains low while technology significantly extends their reach. Weiss and Larter (2022, p 7) describe marketing as the "creation of need into which you can position your product and service as the best alternative". This chapter considers the key elements of marketing digital coaching business, addressing the above. We start with the critical elements of brand, niche, proposition, business model, content, and marketing plan questions, which can be used to help develop a marketing plan. These elements are needed by all coaches, both digital and traditional. Developing a marketing plan is an iterative process. An effective start to this process is to articulate an approach to all the highlighted areas. We then consider the various technologies, including websites, content platforms, and tools that can be used. We consider the significant impact AI will have on marketing coaching services. The chapter ends with an exploration of the mindset and actions that are essential for success in the coaching market. This includes setting the scene for testimonials, referrals, and case studies at the beginning of the programme and asking for them at the end.

The fundamentals of a marketing strategy

Brand

A coach's brand is their online personality, described by Weiss and Larter as "What people say about you when you're not there" (Weiss & Larter, 2022, p 9). For Godin (2018), branding is shorthand for customers' expectations: What promise they think they're making and is made up of all of a coach's touch points with clients and potential clients.

In determining their brand, coaches can reflect on the following questions: *What does the coach want to be famous for? What are their three top values? What's a sticky tagline that people will remember them by?*

Niche

Before developing a coaching proposition, it is wise for a coach to consider whether they want to work in a particular niche. Marketing to an established niche or a sub-niche

DOI: 10.4324/9781003383741-6

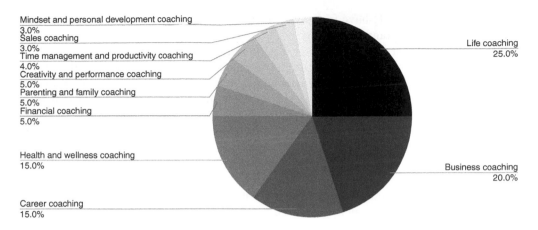

Mindset and personal development coaching
3.0%
Sales coaching
3.0%
Time management and productivity coaching
4.0%
Creativity and performance coaching
5.0%
Parenting and family coaching
5.0%
Financial coaching
5.0%

Health and wellness coaching
15.0%

Career coaching
15.0%

Life coaching
25.0%

Business coaching
20.0%

Figure 4.1 Estimated breakdown of coaching niches by demand (2023).

is more manageable. Ideally, a coach wants to be a brand leader in their sub-niche. Estimating the exact market share for each coaching niche is challenging due to the nature of the industry, which is fragmented and constantly evolving. It is possible, however, to provide a rough approximation of the market share based on the popularity and demand for each niche (see Figure 4.1).

Proposition

Who are a coach's ideal clients? What are their personas? What are their pain and pleasure points? Does the coach know their typical journey towards what they want and what they're buying now? What is the potential value that a coach offers? How will a coach reach them and get feedback so they can improve their proposition and get case studies and referrals? What's their business model? How will they name their offer?

When developing their proposition, a coach should consider each of these in detail.

A helpful starting point for a coach to identify their ideal clients is to clarify their niche, what their clients do, their seniority, their access to funds to pay for their services, and whether they have the qualities needed to get real value from what they're offering. If the coach pays to reach out to their clients, it is wise to always start with their smallest viable market and build on that.

Two ways of expressing value are the following:

1. The cost clients will incur if they don't address the implication of their pain points, plus the additional value they receive during the programme, less the total cost of any programme.
2. The benefit of any innovation achieved from the programme, plus an estimate of potential future value that the innovation will enable, less the total cost of any programme.

Rosso and McGraw (2021) have found an effective way of coaching clients to think of and communicate pain points: FUDWACA.

FUDWACA stands for frustrated, upset, disappointed, worried, angry, concerned, and anxious. List out what your clients might be frustrated with. Then repeat with the other words mentioned above; however, only use the most relevant with your clients. To amplify the pain further, you may ask your clients what the implications and cost of not addressing these implications over time will be.

There are four basic ways of attracting clients. Despite what people may say, we've found they all work for the right practitioner in the right market. It is unusual for anyone to master all four, so it is important that a coach starts with the one that works for them.

Hunting is traditional selling, directly reaching out to potential clients. Basic knowledge of sales skills is helpful for all approaches.

Attracting is at the core of social media and web marketing. Produce text, images, video, and audio that engages ideal clients, so they approach the coach first when looking for services.

Nurturing – focus on adding value to a small, select number of influencers, resulting in case studies and testimonials. These can be a significant way of bringing in new business.

Paying includes a commission on leads and sales, outsourcing sales and marketing activity, and advertising such as LinkedIn and Google ads.

It is important that a coach should only outsource when they know enough about the subject to manage and monitor their service provider(s) correctly. On top of this, it's helpful to know the revenue a typical client will bring to the coach (client lifetime value) so that they can work out an estimated ROI from all marketing activity.

Business model

What is the coach's business model? Will the numbers work?

We have summarised the models that are most likely to get traction as digital continues to grow in Table 4.1.

Content

Quality content is the cornerstone of marketing digital coaching business; when a coach produces web and social media marketing content, they must focus on several key aspects to engage their audience and effectively promote their services.

First of all, content must *attract*. A coach may choose to produce visually appealing content through images and cross-promote on multiple platforms: Utilise various social media platforms, blogs, and email marketing to reach a wider audience and maximise their online presence. Tailor their content to each platform's requirements and audience preferences.

Regardless of their approach, all content the coach produces must come from a foundation of understanding their potential clients' demographics, needs, and preferences. This will help coaches create content that resonates with them and effectively addresses

Table 4.1 Business models for coaching in 2030

1:1 coaching via Zoom, etc.	*Dominate a niche market.*
Online courses and workshops	As more people become comfortable with online learning and remote work, there will be a growing demand for self-paced online courses and workshops. Coaches can leverage technology to create and deliver high-quality, engaging content on various topics related to their coaching expertise.
Group coaching and virtual masterminds	Group coaching and virtual masterminds offer a more affordable and accessible option for clients who cannot invest in 1:1 coaching. These models also foster peer support and networking, which can be particularly valuable in a digital world.
Membership programmes	Subscription-based membership programmes can offer clients ongoing support, resources, and community engagement at an affordable price. Coaches can benefit from a more stable and predictable income source while building a loyal client base.
Hybrid coaching models	Combining various coaching formats (e.g., 1:1, group, online courses) can cater to client needs and preferences, making coaching services more accessible and appealing. Hybrid models can help coaches diversify their income streams and reach a wider audience.
Corporate coaching and well being programmes	As organisations become more aware of the importance of mental health, well being, and effective leadership, there may be a growing demand for corporate coaching services. Coaches can offer tailored programmes to organisations, targeting various levels of management, teams, or specific workplace challenges.
Niche coaching specialisations	As the coaching market becomes more saturated, coaches specialising in specific niches or industries will stand out and attract clients seeking expert guidance. Examples include health and wellness coaching, career transition coaching, or coaching for entrepreneurs in specific industries.

their concerns. Additionally, it is crucial that all content contains a call to action (CTA) – what exactly does the coach hope for their audience to *do*?

On a more strategic time frame, a long-term goal should be for the coach to establish a clear brand identity across all their online platforms. This includes their logo, colour schemes, fonts, and messaging. This helps build trust and credibility among their audience. The coach can help cultivate this image and community spirit by offering practical tips, insights, and advice their audience can apply to their lives. By sharing valuable content, they will establish themselves as an expert in their field and build trust with potential clients. Engagement is key, and a savvy coach will encourage interaction through comments, questions, and direct messages. Providing the coach is authentic and relatable, and they respond promptly to comments and messages, a sense of community will be cultivated, and the coach will have demonstrated their commitment to their clients.

Finally, a coach must know the metrics governing their online success. They must optimise for search engines (SEO) by using relevant keywords and their content to rank higher on search engine results pages (SERPs). This will help increase visibility and drive organic traffic to their website. They must regularly monitor and analyse their content's performance with online tools, fine-tune their content strategy, and improve their overall marketing efforts. They must create a content calendar: Plan and schedule their content in advance to ensure consistency in posting and maintain an organised workflow.

By focusing on these essentials, coaches can create compelling content that attracts and retains clients while boosting their online presence.

Marketing plan questions

Building a marketing plan is a useful first step to building a wider successful business. Creating a comprehensive marketing plan for a coaching business involves addressing a range of key questions that cover various aspects of marketing and business growth. By considering the following questions in Box 4.1, coaches can develop a plan that effectively attracts and retains clients, supports their business's long-term success, and helps coaches stay ahead of the competition:

Online marketing platforms

When considering platforms, coaches should evaluate their target audience, marketing goals, and available resources to determine which platforms align best with their needs. They might optimise their efforts by considering the following strategies:

Multiple platforms will reach a broader audience, diversify content formats, and increase the chances of engaging with potential clients. For example, in 2024 LinkedIn is ideal for connecting with fellow professionals, YouTube for video content, and Instagram for visual storytelling. But keep up-to-date as new technologies emerge and new trends offer the opportunity for different forms of engagement.

A coach can increase reach and engagement by posting across different platforms. A blog post can become a LinkedIn article, then create a video based on the article for YouTube and share snippets or images on Instagram. This helps to maintain a consistent brand identity which in turn attracts and helps to retain clients. Once this community has grown, authentic engagement helps build trust and credibility.

While such human qualities are important to foster, it is equally important to watch the numbers. By regularly tracking and analysing performance metrics, a coach is able to identify which platforms and content types are most effective in reaching and engaging the target audience. These insights can help to refine marketing strategies and optimise future efforts. Furthermore, it is important to keep abreast of platform updates, algorithm changes, and emerging trends to adapt marketing strategies accordingly and maintain a competitive edge.

By thoughtfully selecting platforms and employing tailored strategies, coaches can maximise their marketing efforts and successfully attract and engage their target audience. Remember that each platform serves a unique purpose, and it's crucial to understand how to use them best to achieve their marketing objectives.

Box 4.1   Key questions in marketing a coaching service

- *Target audience:* Who are my ideal clients? What are their demographics, interests, and pain points?
- *Unique selling proposition (USP):* What sets me apart from other coaches? What unique skills, experience, or approach do I bring to the table?
- *Marketing objectives:* What are my short-term and long-term goals for my coaching business? What is my brand? How many clients do I want to acquire, and how will I measure success?
- *Marketing channels:* Which marketing channels (e.g., social media, email, website, public speaking) will be most effective for reaching my target audience and achieving my objectives?
- *Content strategy:* What type of content will I create to showcase my expertise and attract clients? How frequently will I create and distribute content?
- *Partnerships and networking:* How can I collaborate with other coaches, organisations, or influencers to reach a wider audience and strengthen my brand?
- *Client referrals, testimonials, and success stories:* How can I leverage the success of my current clients to demonstrate the value of my coaching services?
- *Pricing strategy:* What pricing structure will I use for my coaching services? How do my prices compare to my competitors?
- *Promotion strategy:* How will I promote my coaching services to attract new clients? Will I offer any incentives, discounts, or referral programmes?
- *Monitoring and evaluation:* How will I track the success of my marketing efforts? Which key performance indicators (KPIs) will I use to measure progress, and how will I adjust my strategy based on the results?
- *Budget:* What resources will I allocate to marketing efforts? How will I prioritise spending across different marketing channels and initiatives?
- *Timeline:* What is the timeline for implementing my marketing plan? When will I review and revise the plan based on performance?
- *Social media strategy:* Which social media platforms will I focus on to engage with my target audience? What type of content will I share, and how often will I post?
- *SEO and website optimisation:* How will I optimise my website to rank higher in search engine results? What keywords will I target, and how will I create valuable content that appeals to both search engines and users?
- *Email marketing:* How will I use email marketing to nurture relationships with potential and existing clients? What types of email campaigns will I create, and how will I segment my mailing list?
- *Event marketing:* Will I host or participate in events (e.g., workshops, webinars, conferences) to increase brand visibility and attract new clients? How will I promote these events and measure their success?
- *Public relations:* How will I leverage media coverage, guest appearances, and other PR opportunities to enhance my brand's credibility and reach a wider audience?

- *Analytics and data:* What tools will I use to gather data on my marketing efforts and client interactions? How will I use this information to make data-driven decisions and refine my marketing strategy?
- *Crisis management:* How will I handle potential challenges or negative situations that could impact my coaching business? What is my plan for addressing client dissatisfaction, public criticism, or other unforeseen issues?
- *Continuing education and professional development:* How will I stay informed about industry trends, new coaching techniques, and marketing strategies? What resources will I use to improve my skills continually?

YouTube

YouTube enables a coach to create engaging content to showcase their expertise. As a Google-owned platform, YouTube videos can rank highly in search results. Due to its monetisation options, coaches may earn revenue through ads, sponsored content, and memberships.

However, there are many disadvantages to using YouTube that have to be acknowledged. Firstly, creating high-quality videos requires time, effort, and resources. Producing compelling videos consistently is a unique skill set that only some possess. Beyond this, YouTube's algorithm can make it difficult to reach an audience consistently and with many content creators on the platform, a coach must compete for attention.

Due to these limitations, it may be best for a coach to create educational videos, vlogs, interviews, and tutorials to attract clients and establish authority within their niche.

It is recommended that coaches create a dedicated YouTube channel for their coaching business with a clear and engaging banner, profile picture, and channel description. Ensure a coach's branding is consistent across all their online platforms to maintain a strong brand identity.

Coaches should aim to create valuable and engaging videos to show their coaching expertise. Topics include tips, tricks, how-to guides, client success stories, and live Q&A sessions. They should ensure their videos have good production quality, with clear audio and visuals.

To increase visibility, it is best practice to optimise video titles, descriptions, and tags with relevant keywords for their coaching niche. This will help their videos rank higher in search results. Additionally, create thumbnails for their videos that are visually appealing and convey the main idea.

Facebook

With billions of active users, Facebook offers an extensive reach. What's more is that Facebook allows for targeted advertising, which precisely targets your ideal audience before offering robust analytics to help a coach understand their audience.

However, it should be acknowledged that organic reach on Facebook has declined over time, making it harder to engage users without paid promotions. This, along with the high levels of competition, means that coaches and businesses compete for attention, making it difficult to stand out.

The best practice for a coach is to create a Facebook business page dedicated to their coaching services, complete with a high-quality profile picture, cover photo, and a compelling 'About' section. They would be wise to ensure their branding is consistent across all their online platforms and provide easy-to-find contact information for potential clients.

From here, a coach may choose to post a mix of informative and engaging content that showcases their expertise and offers value to their target audience. This can include articles, tips, motivational quotes, images, videos, and live streams. Facebook allows for such posts to be scheduled and automated, which should help the coach maintain a consistent posting schedule – however, the challenge is to vary the content to engage an audience.

Of course, much like YouTube, the goal of Facebook is often to foster a sort of community. This is best done by responding promptly to comments, messages, and questions to show commitment to the audience. Much like YouTube, engagement is an important success metric and can be boosted by encouraging followers to share their thoughts and experiences. A coach may consider hosting Q&A sessions, polls, or live streams to interact with your audience in real-time.

A final strength of the platform is found in Facebook Insights. This tool will help the coach to understand which types of content resonate with their audience and allow them to optimise their marketing strategy accordingly. This data can be used to make informed decisions about content, engagement strategies, and ad targeting.

LinkedIn

Whereas Facebook caters to a general audience, LinkedIn is a professional networking platform where business people can connect with potential clients and industry leaders. This means that the overall tone is more formal, and a different tone and approach should be taken as opposed to those taken with YouTube and Facebook.

The advantage of these differences is that LinkedIn's professional user base is an ideal platform for targeting executives and businesses. It provides networking opportunities and lets the coach connect with potential clients and industry leaders. It also allows coaches to use LinkedIn Learning to create and sell courses to showcase their expertise.

However, the disadvantages of using LinkedIn include its limited organic reach, which might mean that the coach needs to invest in sponsored content to increase their visibility. As a result, compared to other platforms, LinkedIn's content may need to be more engaging, specifically to professionally minded people. It should also be remembered that because many coaches and consultants use LinkedIn, it may be challenging for any individual coach to stand out.

The fundamental strategy for success on LinkedIn is to share articles, insights, and industry news to engage your audience and create a professional image. With this as the goal, it is crucial that coaches ensure that their LinkedIn profile is complete, up-to-date, and professional. It is best practice to use a high-quality profile picture, write a compelling headline, and craft a summary showcasing their coaching expertise while including relevant keywords to make it easier for potential clients to find them.

Beyond this, the coach should aim to position themselves as an authority in their field by regularly sharing high-quality, relevant content. This can include articles, blog posts, infographics, or videos. They should focus on topics that resonate with their target audience and demonstrate their expertise while providing practical tips and advice.

A common mistake is to post content without actively participating in conversations on LinkedIn. Engaging with connections and joining relevant groups to build relationships is important. A coach can establish their knowledge and personality by commenting on other people's posts, asking questions, and providing thoughtful insights.

This presence can be significantly bolstered by asking satisfied clients to write a LinkedIn recommendation. This adds credibility to a coach's profile and helps demonstrate the value and impact of their coaching services. These testimonials are shown on the coach's profile and should be considered a part of their content strategy.

Finally, to significantly improve their LinkedIn activity, coaches may choose to use LinkedIn Sales Navigator with Dux-Soup (www.dux-soup.com). Dux-Soup lets LinkedIn users automate their critical connection and lead generation activity.

How can AI help coaches market their services?

The most potent use of AI (artificial intelligence) is in content generation and research. In particular, resources such as openai.com and bard.google.com can offer several benefits to coaches looking to market their services more effectively. AI-powered tools and technologies can streamline marketing processes, optimise content, and engage a target audience.

Chief among the tasks AI can help with is content generation. However, caution is needed as the content produced by such tools is not always accurate, so it's important to verify and double check claims, as the person publishing or sharing the information is responsible, not the AI tool for the accuracy of statements made in any published content (Passmore & Tee, 2023).

AI-powered tools such as natural language generation (NLG) can be used to create blog posts, social media updates, and email marketing campaigns. AI can also recommend relevant articles, videos, and other resources to enhance the learning experience and foster personal growth. These save time and effort while maintaining a consistent brand voice.

AI-driven social media management tools are already being used to help schedule posts, analyse performance, and optimise content for each platform. You can focus on other aspects of your business and maintain a consistent online presence. Much in the same way, AI promises to improve SEO optimisation: AI can analyse search engine algorithms, user behaviour, and competition to suggest improvements in website content, structure, and keyword targeting. Optimising your online presence can increase visibility and attract more potential clients.

Finally, AI can help a coach with A/B testing: AI-driven tools can automate the process of testing various elements of a marketing campaign, such as headlines, images, and call-to-action buttons. This can improve the effectiveness of your marketing efforts and generate better results.

In summary, AI can help you enhance your effectiveness and efficiency by offering personalised coaching experiences, data-driven insights, and automation of various coaching tasks. By leveraging AI-powered tools and technologies, you can optimise your time, resources, and client outcomes, ultimately leading to a more successful coaching practice.

Mindset and actions

What is it that a coach does daily or weekly that will help market their coaching services? Godin emphasises the importance of taking daily actions whether we feel like it or not (Godin, 2020, p 18). "Your work is too important to be left to how you feel today. On the other hand, by committing to an action, we can change how we feel. If we act as though we trust the process and do the work, then the feeling will follow. Waiting for a feeling is a luxury we don't have."

Coaches should proactively and consistently market their services to attract new clients and maintain a solid online presence. In Box 4.2 we have set out some thoughts on daily and weekly activities.

By consistently executing these activities, a coach can effectively market their services, grow their client base, and establish themself as an authority.

Box 4.2   Daily & weekly marketing activities

1. Develop valuable content such as blog posts, articles, videos, podcasts, or social media posts showcasing your expertise, insights, and tips for your coaching niche.
2. Post regularly on your chosen social media platforms. Share your content, engage with your audience, respond to comments, and participate in relevant online communities or groups.
3. Send weekly or bi-weekly newsletters to your subscribers, sharing updates, valuable content, and promotional offers.
4. Networking: Attend industry events, conferences, or workshops, and engage in online networking platforms to connect with potential clients, partners, and other professionals in your field.
5. Expand your reach and credibility by partnering with other coaches, influencers, or industry experts to create guest posts, webinars, or joint ventures.
6. Encourage satisfied clients to leave positive reviews or testimonials. Regularly check online reviews and testimonials and address any negative feedback professionally.
7. Ensure your website is up-to-date, user-friendly, and optimised for search engines.
8. Use analytics tools to monitor the performance of your marketing efforts. Assess what's working and make necessary adjustments to your strategy.
9. Allocate enough time to explore and test new and updated platforms and tools.
10. Invest in learning and professional development to stay current in your field and enhance your coaching skills.
11. Set weekly marketing goals: Break down your marketing objectives into smaller, achievable tasks and goals. This helps maintain focus and ensures consistent marketing efforts.
12. Remember to ask for testimonials, case studies, referrals, and feedforward at the end of the assignment for your most successful clients. Setting a pre-frame for these at the beginning of the coaching engagement may be useful.

Mindset

Mindset refers to the collection of beliefs, attitudes, and thought patterns that shape how an individual perceives and reacts to situations. It influences motivation, behaviour, and overall success in various aspects of life, including professional endeavours.

Meier (2010) believes that mindset is a personal decision. We decide to learn and grow, or we can decide to pull up the drawbridge and to ignore the learning that comes from rejections, feedback, and challenges: As he notes: "You'll decide if no problem is personal, pervasive or permanent. Life's not static; neither are your results" (Meier, 2010, p 233).

A positive mindset for a coach in marketing their business during changing times is likely to include the following characteristics:

Adaptability. Market conditions, consumer preferences, and industry trends can shift rapidly during changing times. Embrace change and be open to adjusting their marketing strategies, messaging, or target audience as needed. This flexibility will allow a coach to navigate fluctuations in the market better and maintain relevance. Adaptability is essential for a coach marketing their business to stay relevant and effectively reach their target audience. This might involve modifying the message, exploring new marketing channels, or targeting different audience segments. Adaptable coaches are also more likely to experiment with new marketing tactics and embrace emerging technologies.

Resilience is the ability to face challenges and setbacks with determination, positivity, and the mental strength to bounce back. For coaches marketing their business during changing times, resilience is crucial for focusing on the goals and persevering through obstacles. A coach can develop resilience by maintaining a solutions-oriented mindset and focusing on what a coach can control. This involves reframing challenges as opportunities for learning and growth rather than dwelling on setbacks. Additionally, seek support from their professional network, mentors, or peers, as these connections can provide valuable insights, encouragement, and advice to help a coach.

A good approach to developing resilience in relation to apparent failure is expressed by Fenton & Waltz (2011, p 27): "I realised that failure was the halfway mark on the road to success, not a destination to be avoided but a stepping stone to get what I really wanted."

What leads to resilience? These factors are identified in Thomson and Khan (Thomson & Khan, 2008) Social support and connectedness, a sense of control, predictability, positive expectancy, meaning, purpose and spirituality, and dissipation.

Continuous learning involves staying committed to expanding one's knowledge, skills, and expertise. As the business landscape evolves, a coach must stay updated with the latest marketing trends, best practices, and emerging technologies. Investing in their professional development ensures that their marketing efforts remain practical and relevant in a constantly changing environment. This might involve participating in webinars, attending industry conferences, taking online courses, or reading marketing blogs and publications.

Growth mindset can support an individual's abilities and skills to develop and improve over time. Coaches with a growth mindset view challenges as opportunities for learning and growth rather than insurmountable obstacles. In the marketing context during changing times, adopting a growth mindset encourages embracing feedback, learning from successes and failures, and consistently improving their marketing strategy. By focusing on progress and development, a coach is more likely to stay motivated and committed to their marketing goals, even in the face of adversity.

A *growth mindset*, according to author and researcher Carol Dweck (Dweck, 2017, p 7), is "The position of stretching yourself and sticking to it, even (or especially) when it's not going well, is the hallmark of a growth mindset."

Take the initiative and consistently execute the plan. Regularly assessing marketing activities, adjusting the approach when needed, and looking for new opportunities to reach the target audience will all contribute to success.

Partnering with other coaches, industry professionals, or marketing experts to share resources and ideas and expand their reach. Collaboration can help a coach adapt to changing times more effectively.

Focus on providing value and addressing their concerns to build trust and loyalty, while keeping client's needs and preferences at the forefront.

Monitoring the impact of marketing efforts through reviewing data. Leverage insights to make informed decisions and optimise their marketing strategies.

Self-care: Prioritise well being and maintain a healthy work–life balance.

Marketing checklist

Meier (2010) brings these elements together in a marketing checklist (see Box 4.3), which can be a useful resource for coaches as they plan their approach to building and developing their business in a digital age.

Box 4.3   Meier's marketing checklist

1. What will be your digital coaching persona? What do you want to be famous for? What are your top three values that you want your brand to be about? What's a simple and sticky tagline where people will remember you?
2. What is your ideal client/customer persona/avatar? Who do you want to attract? What are their pains? What solutions are they paying for? This is the key to your offers. Will you play in the Red Ocean or the Blue Ocean? (Contested space or brand out into uncontested space.)
3. What is the journey of your ideal client? Break the path down from point A to point B for your client's perfect journey for the outcome they want to achieve. Then identify pain points and opportunities along the way. I find using simple journeys, as in 'Day in the Life' and 'Transformational Journeys', helpful.
4. What is your business model? And do the numbers work? Will you do 1:1, group coaching, online courses, affiliates, and membership sites? Tony Robbins did a lot of affiliates and partnerships early on in his coaching career.
5. Know your channels. Some channels like Medium and YouTube are more 'evergreen.' Others are 'chattier' or 'throw-away.'

---

6. Know your tools. Learn and play and experiment with tools to boost your productivity, help you make data-driven decisions, and gain interesting insights into the behaviour and intent of your target audience.
7. Optimize around your strengths: audio, video, and writing. Understand your target audiences.
8. Empathy. Without empathy, you won't connect in meaningful ways.
9. Passion. If you aren't passionate about it, you won't sustain it.
10. Name your offers in a way that your clients will recommend to others. You want the names of offers to stick in their mind and be something that sounds like a 'Must Have' versus a 'Nice to Have.'

Reflective questions

1. What is their brand, and what is their proposition?
2. What platforms and tools is the coach going to focus on?
3. What mindset will the coach develop, and what are the critical daily or weekly actions the coach will take to market their coaching practice?

Conclusion

Many opportunities exist for coaches to embrace digital coaching; two that work well for coaches are niche 1:1 business coaching worldwide and developing a worldwide niche membership community. However, there are many more. Before a coach starts marketing, they should consider their approach to these key marketing pillars. Their ideal clients, brand, proposition, business model, and content, and how they will address them. Then, they should choose which platforms and tools they will use to support their marketing. Finally, what mindset does the coach need to push through when the going gets tough and ensure they take consistent action daily and weekly? It is worth remembering to ask for testimonials, case studies, and feedforward from their most successful clients at the end of the assignment. When a coach focuses on these areas, a coach will be significantly more effective and efficient, making the process of delivering their services more enjoyable to themselves and their clients.

References

Dweck, C. S. (2017). *Mindset – Updated edition: Changing the way you think to fulfil their potential*. London: Robinson.
Fenton, R., & Waltz, A. (2011). *Go for no: Yes is the destination, no is how to get there*. London: Embassy Books.
Godin, S. (2018). *This is marketing: You can't be seen until you learn to see*. London: Portfolio Penguin.
Godin, S. (2020). *The practice: Shipping creative work*. London: Portfolio Penguin.
Meier, J. D. (2010). *Getting results the agile way*. Innovation Playhouse.

Passmore, J., & Tee, D. (2023). Can chatbots like GPT-4 replace human coaches: Issues and dilemmas for the coaching profession, coaching clients and for organisations. *The Coaching Psychologist, 19*(1), 47–54. Doi: 10.53841/bpstcp.2023.19.1.47

Rosso, J., & McGraw, M. (2021). *21st century prospecting: The authoritative playbook for new business development.* Sandler Training.

Thomson, G., & Khan, K. (2008). *Magic in practice: Introducing medical NLP – The art and science of language in healing and health.* London: Hammersmith Press Ltd.

Weiss, A., & Larter, L. (2022). *Masterful marketing: How to dominate their market with a value-based approach.* London: Bloomsbury Business.

Chapter 5

The impact and side effects of digital coaching

Natalie M. Michalik and Jonathan Passmore

Introduction

The 2020s saw an exposition in digital coaching as organisations pivoted from commissioning mainly face-to-face coaching delivery to commissioning providers delivering online. This delivery could be via Zoom, Google Meet, Microsoft Teams, or similar communications software tools, but digital coaching platforms, which had been emerging during the 2017–20 period, suddenly witnessed significant growth. In the period from 2019 to 2022, coaching went from 25–35% online delivery to 80–90% online delivery. In late 2022, the launch of ChatGPT triggered similar interest in the use of AI. However, while these technologies for coaching emerged there was relatively little research evaluating their efficacy.

This chapter aims to provide an overview about what we know about different forms of coaching delivery and what scientific evidence exists regarding face-to-face, digital (online) and also blended coaching formats using both face-to-face and digital coaching delivery. Furthermore, we aim to provide guidance for practitioners to choose the most suitable coaching setting for themselves and to eliminate existent concerns by providing possible solutions for certain challenges regarding online and blended coaching.

Defining digital coaching

There has been much confusion about the terminology used to describe digital coaching (Diller & Passmore, 2023). The terms online, virtual, e-coaching and others have all been used. This multiplicity of terms has contributed towards confusion. In response Diller and Passmore sought to create a single clear definition to support research in the field. They defined digital coaching as follows: digital coaching is a "synchronous, personal conversation using DT-enabled audio and video channels of communication between a human coach and a human client to empower the client in their self-development" (Diller & Passmore, 2023). A coaching using both face-to-face and digital coaching can be defined as blended coaching in accordance to Jones et al. (2016).

Growth of digital coaching

The traditional coaching has been equated with face-to-face meetings between a coach and a client (Jones et al., 2018), which has changed in recent years. During the early 2020s, there was a substantial increase in digital (online) coaching, accelerated by the

DOI: 10.4324/9781003383741-7

COVID-19 pandemic. For instance, in Germany digital coaching grew from 7.7 % in 2020 to 45% in 2022 while face-to-face coaching dropped from 76% to 44% in 2022 (Rauen et al., 2022). The change was even steeper across the globe, with 85% of coaches reporting a switch to digital by 2021 (Passmore et al., 2023). Even after the pandemic, when many companies returned to their normal business operations, digital coaching remains one of the most important forms of coaching in Germany, accounting for 38% (Rauen et al., 2023). According to Passmore et al. (2023), digital coaching is expected to remain the key mode for human coaching delivery in the future. Furthermore, according to the global coach survey, the majority of coaches and clients favour the digital coaching format (Passmore & Evans-Krimme, 2021).

Even though digital technologies are now part of our everyday lives, there are still reservations about the use of digital coaching. This leads to some practitioners questioning which mode they wish to use. This question mark has grown as the environmental impact of travel and the accessibility of coaching has become part of the debate (e.g., Alraja et al., 2022). One question for many practitioners is whether digital coaching can be an effective, cost-saving alternative to face-to-face coaching. Second, what downsides may result from either mode and how can these risks be mitigated?

What do we know about coaching format?

Generally speaking, coaching research has demonstrated that phone and digital coaching is not inferior to face-to-face coaching in terms of effectiveness (e.g., Berry et al., 2011; Jones et al., 2016; Doyle & Bradley, 2023; Michalik & Schermuly, 2023a). Distant coaching is nothing new and has been already around for more than a decade in terms of telephone coaching (Clutterbuck & Hussain, 2010). However, traditionally, coaching is most associated with face-to-face meetings (Jones et al., 2018) and the number of scientific articles investigating coaching format is limited. While the majority of studies pre-2020 make no reference to the format, these studies have generally concentrated on phone and face-to-face modes of delivery. The studies found no difference between face-to-face and other modes of delivery, such as phone coaching. In a 2011 study exploring working alliance and problem resolution, the researchers examined data from 102 coaches and found no differences between face-to-face and 'distance' (phone) coaching (Berry et al., 2011).

As we noted above, 2020 saw a pivot to digital delivery. Online meetings and the usage of digital format, such as Zoom, Google Meet, and Microsoft Teams, became the rule due to restrictions on face-to-face meetings and movements imposed by governments across the world in an attempt to contain the spread of COVID-19.

One study conducted during this period compared COVID (digital delivery) to pre-COVID-19 (face-to-face delivery) (Doyle & Bradley, 2022). The researchers compared face-to-face and digital coaching in three cohorts of adults with disabilities undergoing workplace coaching in a sample of 409 participants and found that the forced-remote coaching format did not make a significant difference to the positive impact of the coaching as perceived by the clients.

Another study by Hui et al. (2021) provides suggestions for media choice, coaching style, and coaching outcome. Based on a two-wave longitudinal field study of 114 employees, Hui et al. (2021) found specifically that face-to-face coaching facilitated the clients' creativity, while digital coaching benefits clients' adaptive performance. Furthermore, they found that digital coaching contributed to clients' emotional exhaustion more than face-to-face coaching.

In a global survey of 1266 coaches from 79 countries, the researchers found that about one-third of coaches perceived some disadvantages with digital coaching, which contributed to lower levels of enjoyment. These side effects included more effort to establish a relationship between coach and client and issues with connectivity (Passmore et al., 2023). At the same time, the study also identified benefits, which included cost savings and convenience, which depending on individual circumstances may outweigh the disadvantages (Passmore et al., 2023).

In a further study (Michalik & Schermuly, 2023a), the researchers compared face-to-face, blended, and digital coaching from coaches' and clients' perspectives directly. In two independent studies, they investigated differences in terms of perceived coaching success and side effects from both coaches' and clients' perspective and found no differences in terms of perceived coaching success between these formats (Michalik & Schermuly, 2023a). In terms of side effects, they found that side effects were slightly more prevalent in digital than face-to-face coaching from a coach's perspective. These side effects include frustrations with technology, such as connectivity, tiredness, and fatigue and also issues if clients had failed to set up sound or cameras to optimise the engagement. However, from clients' perspective the number of side effects was highest in the blended coaching format (Michalik & Schermuly, 2023a). The authors suggested that switching between coaching formats may cause more disruptions in the coaching process and therefore lead to more unwanted effects. The results provide further evidence, supporting previous findings that coaching is perceived as successful regardless of coaching format (Michalik & Schermuly, 2023a).

In sum, quantitative research has demonstrated that digital coaching is not inferior to in-person delivery of coaching in terms of effectiveness. These results are mainly in line with research on online psychotherapy, demonstrating that online psychotherapy is not inferior to face-to-face psychotherapy in terms of effectiveness (e.g., Lin et al., 2022). However, there is some qualitative research with mixed findings (e.g., Burrous, 2021) which we have not mentioned yet. For instance, Deniers (2019) examined a qualitative approach, based on interviews with 11 clients, showing that the presence of the camera had mixed effects. On the one hand, the camera enabled contact, on the other hand, it was found to influence the clients' self-image and perception of both themselves and their respective coaches.

Another qualitative study examined potential advantages and disadvantages of digital coaching. The researcher interviewed 19 coaches (Burrous, 2021). The results suggested, on the one hand, digital coaching offered advantages such as enhancing the comfort, convenience, and geographic reach. Clients were not dependent on a certain location and the reductions in travel time and costs, contributed to coaching being more affordable and thus increasing take up. On the other hand, digital coaching clients may experience technological problems and perceived limited connection between the coach and client (Burrous, 2021).

In summary, most empirical studies of various coaching formats have found evidence of effectiveness for face-to-face, blended, and digital coaching formats, each with potential side effects which the coach or client need to manage in order to optimise the value of the coaching encounter.

Exploring coaching side effects?

These negative effects, sometimes called 'side effects' in coaching, are defined as unwanted and potentially negative effects which are directly related to the coaching (Schermuly et al., 2014) and occur with a reasonable level of frequency (Schermuly & Graßmann, 2019). Generally, these unintended negative effects occur frequently across all coaching formats regardless of perceived coaching success. For instance, a client may quit their job as a result of the coaching and find they experience a reduction of income. On the one hand, the client may be happy because they like their new job better. Therefore, that consequence is something we would consider as a side effect. It is an unwanted consequence that was directly caused by the coaching. In terms of digital coaching and using new coaching formats, one might expect that new coaching formats may cause new side effects. Possible disadvantages of digital coaching have been discussed already (e.g., Passmore et al., 2023). For example digital coaching may cause new challenges due to poor sound quality, background disturbance, poor camera position, or limited screen frame (e.g., Passarelli et al., 2022; Riedl, 2022). Technology usage during coaches may also cause technology-related stress, 'technostress' (Michalik & Schermuly, 2023b) as coaches and clients seek to connect and communicate through the digital environment.

Theory helps provide some insights to explaining these side effects. Media naturalness theory (Kock, 2004) suggests the more natural a communication tool, the less communication obstacles occur. In terms of coaching format, Michalik and Schermuly (2023a) assumed that face-to-face coaching was the most natural way of communication with the least disruptions, followed by blended and digital coaching. Their results were not in line with their expectations. From the clients' point of view, clients in the blended coaching condition experienced an average of 7.16 side effects, significantly more side effects than clients both the face-to-face coaching condition ($M = 4.28$) and digital coaching condition ($M = 3.00$). Michalik and Schermuly (2023a) suggested clients who start with digital coaching may get used to or may prefer this format. Past experience of online meetings may also inform expectations and experience may mean they are effective in using the technology, making it more natural. However, changing formats and switching between the face-to-face and digital coaching format may cause disruptions and uncertainties which may explain the high number of experienced side effects in the blended coaching format (Michalik & Schermuly, 2023a).

In terms of side effects, Michalik and Schermuly (2023a) also identified new side effects, related to digital and blended coaching. First, clients may experience stress due to technology usage. Stress due to technology usage was experienced by 16% of the clients in the blended coaching group and 15% of the clients in the digital only coaching format. Second, there was a perception that digital environments impacted negatively on communications as some aspects of body language were missing, this accounted for 28% for clients in the blended coaching format and 18% in the digital coaching format (Michalik & Schermuly, 2023a). Finally, they found that clients might have problems with a face-to-face coaching format after switching from the digital coaching condition (Michalik & Schermuly, 2023a), and that clients experience more 'side effects' than coaches, which is in line with previous findings (Graßmann & Schermuly, 2016).

While these results may sound negative for users of digital coaching, it's important to recognise that these unintended negative effects appear across all coaching regardless of perceived coaching success and that these effects can in many cases be mitigated or managed by effected use of technology and advanced planning and preparation (Michalik & Schermuly, 2023a).

Implications for practice

It's fair to say that digital coaching represents an effective tool for coaching. Further, scientific research demonstrates that it is perceived as equally effective as the traditional face-to-face coaching. Given the growth of digital coaching during the early 2020s it now represents the most commonly used mode for the delivery of coaching in organisations. However, research also reveals there are a number of 'side effects' which can result and which can have a detrimental impact on the coaching process, and on outcomes, if these are not managed or mitigated. Michalik and Schermuly (2023a) detected three new side effects for the online and blended coaching setting: (i) 'stress due to technology usage'; (ii) 'difficulty to express myself in the digital settings due to a lack of body language'; and (iii) 'difficulty to engage in face-to-face coaching after switching from digital coaching', which we will explore in more detail.

Technology-induced stress

While individuals may be less fearful of using technology for organising meetings or coaching conversations, partly as a result of the pandemic and the flip to online working, there remains anxiety over the use of technology which lacks the stability, permanence, and reliability of a face-to-face connection. The level of anxiety may vary across different parts of the world, with some countries or regions experiencing more anxiety due to less reliability in power supply or connectivity. They may also relate to functionality, for example, the feeling of being constantly observed during a call or observing ourselves. The coach can take some steps to minimise their personal and their client's anxiety.

One suggestion is to first connect with their camera on, but to switch off the self-view function. This can help reduce self-evaluation during the call. Second, is the office and computer set-up ensuring the camera is properly located, the individual is lit from in front (as opposed from behind) preferable by natural light. Third, the coach should plan their physical location for the call – with a preference for a private space, with little or no likelihood of disturbance. Third, the coach should invite clients to plan in advance to ensure their sound, lighting, and location can all guarantee a secure and private call check, which is also well lit and with suitable camera and sound. Fourth, stress can be decreased by good quality connectivity. A secure, stable, and strong connection can all help reduce anxiety. Of course, like all events in life, the unexpected can occur. This may be a cancelled train on the way to a face-to-face coaching session, or a power line down as a result of a fallen tree. These events can impact both physical and online meetings, so having an alternative contact number can help further reduce the anxiety, allowing an exchange of text, WhatsApp, or similar messages to let the other party know of the problem and agree a time to reconnect.

An associated issue to stress was exhaustion. Individuals working online described feeling more tired after digital coaching. Another recent study by Michalik and Schermuly

(2023b) found that technology-related stress, 'technostress', was directly related to coaches' emotional exhaustion. In their study, they also found that techno-overload and techno-uncertainty are the most important technostress factors for coaches, which may also be relevant for clients. Techno-overload can occur when technology forces us to work faster and longer. For example, coaches may feel compelled to respond to inquiries or emails late at night or after hours. Furthermore, clients may text their coach, who may feel pressured to respond immediately to certain instant messages. Clients may also be technically overloaded if they receive work or personal messages during digital coaching sessions. Using a separate work phone and turning off notifications after hours could help mitigate the 'tech-overload' stressor. Another relevant stressor identified by Michalik and Schermuly (2023b) is 'techno-uncertainty', which arises when changes and updates of software lead to uncertainty. In response, individuals in digital coaching may find it beneficial to stick to a specific platform or software to avoid uncertainty around certain technologies. Coaches can also help coaches to avoid uncertainty by providing instructions or lessons learned from previous coaching sessions. For example, some software may be problematic for certain Internet browsers. By telling clients in advance which browser they can use for the best coaching experience, coaches can avoid creating technical uncertainty among clients.

In general, while technology use in digital coaching provides fertile ground for new technology-induced stress, by identifying these risks, coaches and clients can collaborate to minimise or mitigate the risks and optimise the benefits of the digital environment.

Missing body language cues

A second issue identified was the concern that the nature of digital calls results in fewer visual cues from body language. In most cases the set-up of the camera means the coach and client only see each other's faces, and thus movements off camera are not captured. While online communications cannot replicate face-to-face communications, by careful positioning of both the coach and client's camera and seating, both parties can see the upper half of each other's bodies, thus capturing hand movements and changes in position which can facilitate a deeper understanding of energy and emotion. Additionally, coaches with more experience of digital coaching will learn to pay more consciously attention to other cues during digital coaching, whether this is through voice tone or facial expression.

The challenges of switching face-to-face to digital coaching

The third issue identified by Michalik and Schermuly (2023a) was the challenges faced by the parties in switching between different modes of delivery. In our view this may result from the need to also change the mindset of what's possible when working online. Clients might have difficulties in adapting to a certain coaching setting and feel stressed when changing between face-to-face and digital coaching. We believe it's best for coach and client to jointly identify the mode which works for them and to then stick to the use of this mode, rather than seek to switch mode throughout the coaching relationship.

Reflective questions

1. Are some forms of media (digital, phone, face-to-face) more effective than others for different presenting problems?
2. Do different generational groups (such as Gen Z) benefit more or less from different coaching media?
3. Much of the research in coaching has used self-report from clients (client) or coach evaluation. How might the evidence change if the perspectives of line managers, peers, or stakeholders were included?

Conclusion

In this chapter we have reviewed the evidence for digital coaching compared with face-to-face and blended delivery. The evidence from a multiplicity of studies suggests that in the main the mode of delivery is broadly similar in terms of perceived outcomes. However, the evidence also suggests that different modes bring with them different consequences. As a result, coaches need to be mindful of these side effects and should seek to put in place appropriate mitigating actions to optimise the media they are using. Educating clients and reflecting together can also reduce unwanted negative consequences and improve coaching experience generally.

References

Alraja, M. N., Imran, R., Khashab, B. M., & Shah, M. (2022). Technological innovation, sustainable green practices and SMEs sustainable performance in times of crisis (COVID-19 pandemic). *Information Systems Frontiers, 24*(4), 1081–1105. https://doi.org/10.1007/s10796-022-10250-z

Berry, R. M., Ashby, J. S., Gnilka, P. B., & Matheny, K. B. (2011). A comparison of face-to-face and distance coaching practices: Coaches' perceptions of the role of the working alliance in problem resolution. *Consulting Psychology Journal: Practice and Research, 63*(4), 243–253. https://doi.org/10.1037/a0026735

Burrous, T. C. (2021). *A comparison study on e-coaching and face-to-face coaching* (Doctoral dissertation, University of Pennsylvania).

Clutterbuck, D., & Hussain, Z. (2010). *Virtual coach, virtual mentor.* Charlotte, NC: Information Age.

Deniers, C. (2019). Experiences of receiving career coaching via Skype: An interpretative phenomenological analysis. *International Journal of Evidence Based Coaching and Mentoring, 17*(1), 72–81. https://doi.org/10.24384/r4j8-hm94

Diller, S., & Passmore, J. (2023). Digital coaching: A qualitative inductive approach. *Frontiers in Psychology, 14*, 1148243. https://doi.org/10.3389/fpsyg.2023.1148243

Doyle, N., & Bradley, E. (2023). Disability coaching in a pandemic. *Journal of Work-Applied Management, 15*(1), 135–147. https://doi.org/10.1108/JWAM-07-2022-0042

Graßmann, C., & Schermuly, C. C. (2016). Side effects of business coaching and their predictors from the clients' perspective. *Journal of Personnel Psychology, 15*(4), 152–163. https://doi.org/10.1027/1866-5888/a000161

Hui, R. T. yin, Law, K. K., & Lau, S. C. P. (2021). Online or offline? Coaching media as mediator of the relationship between coaching style and employee work-related outcomes. *Australian Journal of Management, 46*(2), 326–345. https://doi.org/10.1177/0312896220914383

Jones, R. J., Woods, S. A., & Guillaume, Y. R. (2016). The effectiveness of workplace coaching: A meta-analysis of learning and performance outcomes from coaching. *Journal of Occupational and Organizational Psychology, 89*(2), 249–277.

Jones, R. J., Woods, S. A., & Zhou, Y. (2018). Boundary conditions of workplace coaching outcomes. *Journal of Managerial Psychology, 33*(7–8), 475–496. https://doi.org/10.1108/JMP-11-2017-0390

Kock, N. (2004). The psychobiological model: Towards a new theory of computer-mediated communication based on Darwinian evolution. *Organization Science, 15*(3), 327–348.

Lin, T., Heckman, T. G., & Anderson, T. (2022). The efficacy of synchronous teletherapy versus in-person therapy: A meta-analysis of randomized clinical trials. *Clinical Psychology: Science and Practice, 29*(2), 167–178. https://doi.org/10.1037/cps0000056

Michalik, N. M., & Schermuly, C. C. (2023a). Online, offline, or both? The importance of coaching format for side effects in business coaching. *Journal of Managerial Psychology*, Ahead of print. https://doi.org/10.1108/JMP-01-2023-0068

Michalik, N. M., & Schermuly, C. C. (2023b). Is technostress stressing coaches out? The relevance of technostress to coaches' emotional exhaustion and coaches' perception of coaching success. *Coaching: An International Journal of Theory, Research and Practice, 16*(2), 155–172.

Passarelli, A. M., Trinh, M. P., Van Oosten, E. B., & Varley, A. (2022). Communication quality and relational self-expansion: The path to leadership coaching effectiveness. *Human Resource Management, 62*(4), 661–680. https://doi.org/10.1002/hrm.22156

Passmore, J., & Evans-Krimme, R. (2021). The future of coaching: A conceptual framework for the coaching sector from personal craft to scientific process and the implications for practice and research. *Frontiers in Psychology, 12*. https://doi.org/10.3389/fpsyg.2021.715228

Passmore, J., Liu, Q., Tee, D., & Tewald, S. (2023). The impact of COVID-19 on coaching practice: Results from a global coach survey. *Coaching: An International Journal of Theory, Research and Practice, 16*(2), 173–189. https://doi.org/10.1080/17521882.2022.2161923

Rauen, C., Barczynski, D., Ebermann, D., Plath, A., & Tanzil, I. (2022). RAUEN Coaching – Marktanalyse 2022. Retrieved September 15, 2023, from www.rauen.de/cma/

Rauen, C., Barczynski, D., Ebermann, D., Plath, A., & Tanzil, I. (2023). RAUEN Coaching – Marktanalyse 2023. Retrieved September 15, 2023, from www.rauen.de/cma/

Riedl, R. (2022). On the stress potential of videoconferencing: Definition and root causes of Zoom fatigue. *Electronic Markets, 32*(1), 153–177. https://doi.org/10.1007/s12525-021-00501-3

Schermuly, C. C., & Graßmann, C. (2019). A literature review on negative effects of coaching–what we know and what we need to know. *Coaching: An International Journal of Theory, Research & Practice, 12*(1), 39–66. https://doi.org/10.1080/17521882.2018.1528621

Schermuly, C. C., Schermuly-Haupt, M. L., Schölmerich, F., & Rauterberg, H. (2014). For risks and side-effects read ... Negative effects of coaching. *Zeitschrift Fur Arbeits – Und Organisationspsychologie, 58*(1), 17–33. https://doi.org/10.1026/0932-4089/a000129

Part II

Technologies

Chapter 6

Video-mediated coaching

Tammy Tawadros

Introduction

Video-mediated coaching (VMC) offers mutual convenience for coaches and clients. It allows easy access to meet in real-time, regardless of physical location. This chapter focuses on the use of video meetings for one-to-one coaching involving a coach and client. It draws on the existing literature and research to highlight three principal areas of VMC practice, specifically preparing and contracting, establishing, and sustaining relational connection and emotional presence of the coach. In this chapter, we suggest that by systematically attending to these principal areas, coaches may be able to optimise the experience and practice of VMC. Preparing and advance contracting for VMC lay the preliminary foundations for the work. Establishing and sustaining relational connection is key to the success of coaching, regardless of modality. However, in VMC, the sense of presence and realism when interacting in the virtual video space is of primary importance. The coach may need to consider how to boost various dimensions of presence, as well as how they might mitigate some negative aspects associated with the use of video meetings. The coach's emotional presence is also crucially important. In VMC, it may be beneficial to pay special attention to enhancing deep listening, empathic responsiveness, and interpersonal attunement, with the potential impact of the limitations and distortions of video meetings in mind. In the chapter conclusion, we capture and summarise key insights and we offer a practical checklist, together with some questions for reflection.

Preparing and contracting

In this section, we define what we mean by VMC, and set out what we believe to be the baseline conditions for optimising use of the technology which enables VMC meetings. We recommend some of the ways that the coach and client need to prepare before embarking on VMC. We suggest that in the first place, it is important to consider carefully whether the medium of video is suitable for the individual needs of the client, and to establish that both parties feel comfortable to work in this way. Also, we recommend that the coach systematically prepares for using VMC in their practice, by checking the practical set-up they have in place, along with the physical and virtual setting. In addition, we propose that it is helpful for the coach to contract on issues that relate specifically to the use of video technology with their clients. Preparation and advance contracting lay the foundations for rapport and relational connection.

DOI: 10.4324/9781003383741-9

What is video mediated coaching?

Video-conferencing technology enables real-time (synchronous) face-to-face communication between two (or more) remote participants over the internet that simulates an in-person meeting. It requires a computer connection, audio, and video camera. Typically, the video meeting takes place using a software-based platform such as Zoom, Google Meet, Microsoft Teams, or via a coaching platform.

VMC is coaching that is enabled using digital technology. This means that a coach and a client can meet for sessions from different locations. It offers the possibility of connecting across geographical distance and confers many advantages including the saving of time and commuting costs. One key advantage of video over audio only, may be that some non-verbal cues are mutually visible to the parties involved, though the psychological evidence base for this has yet to emerge.

As with other digital means of communication, the rate at which we build a systematic evidence base, and a nuanced understanding about the use of video meetings, lags behind the rate of development and adoption of the video-conferencing technology. Moreover, because of the rapid changes in technology and work practices, we see video coaching becoming increasingly used, while direct research on its use is continuing to emerge. That said, our knowledge and understanding about the psychology of video mediated communication from other parallel domains such as health care and counselling is steadily evolving. In this chapter, we suggest that video is a fundamentally different context for coaching; one which gives rise to a particular set of practical, psychological, and relational conditions. The sections below will draw on available research to highlight some key considerations for coaches to take into account when using video coaching.

The decision to use video conferencing

Many coaches use video meetings to work with their clients, as a medium of choice. Much of the time, it isn't only practically expedient but also expected as the norm. By and large, coaches and clients have become habituated to using video conferencing for remote meetings, but it is important not to take it for granted that video conferencing will always be the most appropriate medium for the individuals involved.

Firstly, both coach and client need to feel comfortable meeting via video. Some may not be, for a variety of reasons. It is important for the coach to make sure that they are both comfortable and confident about the medium of video conferencing, and to ensure that their would-be clients are too, in advance of agreeing to work together. We would recommend that the coach reflect on their own level of comfort and confidence in the first place, and that they explore the same in a pre-contracting, 'chemistry', or 'intake' meeting or call with the would-be client.

Second, it is especially important to take account of practical IT issues that may affect the quality of connectivity. For example, there may be intermittent, or poor WI-FI coverage in a particular geographical location, an existing long-term problem with the means for connecting with the internet (such as faulty cabling, wiring or router), or access to reliable video-conferencing software. As a minimum requirement, both coach and client need to have reliable access to video-conferencing software and a high-speed internet connection. It is essential for the coach to ensure that this requirement is in place for both parties before considering or committing to working via video. This is because the virtual presence of both the coach and the client, and the extent to which feel like they are having a one-to-one, in-person meeting, depends on the quality of the audio and video output, and the degree the quality of the technology is able to provide a sense of real, physical interaction.

Third, there may be a range of sensory and psychological needs that may make video meetings less suitable. For example, where the individuals involved have a sensory impairment or a neurodivergence that is not amenable to adjustments, and which would impact their access or limit the quality of communication via video. Other additional factors to consider and 'test out' before embarking on the coaching work may be to do with needs arising from different personal and contextual factors. For example, it may be that the person's past experiences and their perception of, and unique associations with digital technology use, may mean that they are more or less open or well-disposed to video-based coaching. Misgivings or reservations about the efficacy of meeting online, whether on the part of the client or indeed the coach, would clearly present difficulties for starting or maintaining a coaching relationship. Another consideration may be to do with the degree of technostress that the person is experiencing. Technostress is a term which refers to the negative stress that can result from digital technology use. Where the coach or client is experiencing high levels of technostress, extreme fatigue or burnout caused by the extended use of video conferencing and other online technology use, it may be useful to explore the potential value of in-person, telephone, or 'walk and talk' coaching as alternatives to video.

Advance contracting

As well as agreeing administrative terms, goals, and approach to the coaching work, it is useful for the coach to contract with the client in advance, in other areas that relate specifically to the use of video-conferencing technology. These might include the following:

1. *Checking that the basic requirements are in place.* Ensuring that the client has the minimum requirements of reliable access to video-conferencing software and a high-speed internet connection in place, for the foreseeable duration of the coaching engagement.
2. *Contingencies.* How to handle poor quality audio or visual output, or complete loss of connection. For example, having an advance agreement to revert to using the telephone to continue a session, if connectivity or quality issues are likely to disrupt the session.
3. *Recurring connectivity and quality issues.* What to do when technical glitches such as time delay, or the distortion or temporary loss of video image or voice audio are intermittent or recurring and disrupt the coaching sessions. For example, having an advance contingency plan (as above), as well as an in-principle agreement to shift to using another medium such as the telephone or to in-person meetings.

Establishing and sustaining relationships

A strong and positive relational connection and relationship is an essential foundation for the coaching process. It positively impacts the effectiveness and outcomes for the client (see, for example, de Haan & Nilsson, 2023). In this section we consider how the coach might lay the groundwork for a strong and positive relational connection in video-mediated sessions by attending to a number of factors that relate specifically to the video meeting medium itself.

Technical quality

The technical quality of the video call is the single most important factor in determining how real and natural the experience of the meeting feels to the coach and the client. The sense of 'realness' afforded by high-quality visual and audio input, is often referred to as presence. Presence makes it more likely that the overall experience of the meeting will be more psychologically and socially satisfying, and in this way, it contributes to the ability of the coach and the client to build rapport, relational connection, and to develop a productive relationship.

Quality of the setting

The quality of the setting is also crucially important for the quality of presence during a video meeting. Although it may seem obvious, it is nevertheless important to make sure that as well as having their own camera on, the coach encourages the client to have theirs on too. Also, the coach may need to encourage and reinforce the basic expectations for an 'enabling' physical and virtual setting. This may encompass the need to minimise background noise, to ensure good lighting, keeping the camera at eye level, in addition to the need to avoid multi-tasking, distractions, and interruptions of various kinds, including those from automatic alerts and notifications.

Video presence

The literature distinguishes between two types of presence that contribute to video meetings feeling real and therefore satisfying. As with other types of video meetings, without the enlivening, animating experiences of presence, VMC meetings can feel rather cold, stilted, and alienating. Many of us may be familiar with the experience. One dimension of overall presence is telepresence, that is, having a feeling of 'being there' (Suler, 2016). Telepresence is about how real and present the individual feels in the meeting. A person can experience a low level of telepresence, wherein they may feel like a passive and uninvolved observer. When experiencing a high level of telepresence, a person might feel fully connected and immersed in the virtual video environment. The other dimension of presence is the idea of social presence. Over the years, the concept of social presence has been defined in several overlapping ways (see, for example, Short, Williams, and Christie (1976) who advanced the original theory, and subsequently developed by Gunawardena and Zittle (1997)). In the context of one-to-one video coaching, social presence may be summarised as being about how real and present the other person and this meeting feels to the participant. It is about how they perceive and experience the other person and the meeting, and how real they feel in the interaction.

Countering fatigue

Much has been written about so-called 'Zoom fatigue'. Experience and research point to this being a widespread phenomenon. It happens in part because the amount of perceptual and other information which we must take in on a video call can outstrip our brain's natural information processing capacity. In other words, keeping track, particularly of the many bits of visual data on the screen, causes cognitive and perceptual overload, which can be exhausting. As one Stanford researcher notes, before the regular use of video for meetings, the only time we might have looked so intently at another person's face would have been if we were squaring up to hit them, or moving close enough to kiss them (Leighton, 2021). Although we may be able to habituate to some degree to the cognitive and perceptual input that such proximity and constant looking at another person on screen involves, there is nevertheless a limit to the amount of information we are able to process without becoming fatigued. In addition, the cognitive and emotional effort involved in producing non-verbal cues, as well as tracking, interpreting, and responding attentively to another person, can be exhausting. Contracting in advance to schedule regular comfort and screen breaks, and ensuring that they happen during the course of a session, can help both the client and the coach to counter tiredness, as well as to maintain attention and involvement in the video session.

Countering disembodiment

Sitting or standing still, with a restricted range of movement for extended periods, can lead to a sense of detachment from one's own body and physical being. This is because limited movement and the absence of feedback from subtle physical cues in the environment may erode our awareness of our bodily position and posture – a neuro-muscular sense known as proprioception. The erosion of bodily awareness can also be compounded by the absence of accurate depth and spatial perception during video conferencing. Regardless of the quality of the video call, it relies on a two-dimensional (2D) visual representation, which inevitably offers a limited visual experience. The 2D nature of the experience, in turn, contributes to the disruption of proprioception. There is a good deal of indirect evidence from medical research and neuropsychology, to suggest that physical activity and good sensory information play a vital role in maintaining our somatic sense of self, and sense of bodily well being. Crucially, our self-awareness and self-understanding are themselves both shaped, to a large extent, by the experience of our own corporeality (see, for example, Gallagher, 2005).

Having rituals and routines that promote a sense of embodiment in the coach can enhance their sense of well being and alertness and enable them to be more attentive to the client's verbal and non-verbal cues. The coach may suggest using the same activities to the client, at the beginning of the session, or as needed during a session. These may include (but are not confined to) the following: breathing exercises that intentionally slow down and deepen breathing patterns; building physical and bodily awareness through mindful body scanning; holding a few moments of meditative silence to bring focused attention and awareness to the here and now experience of the self, and of being in coaching the session; sensory awareness building techniques that bring attention to each of the five senses in turn; and gentle stretching and movement routines. Regular movement at intervals during a session can also help counter Zoom claustrophobia, that is, feelings of being physically trapped, because of the need to stay within the camera's field of view and centred within the screen.

Mitigating the impact of mirror anxiety and hyper gaze

The phenomenon and experience of 'mirror anxiety', that is, feeling self-conscious or distressed about how we may look or appear in the video meeting, is being increasingly recognised and researched. As a result of this type of experience, the sense of trust and interpersonal connection in the coaching relationship may take longer to build. It is important for the coach to take sensitive note of the available cues and possible indicators that the client may be uncomfortable or worried about being 'on show' or 'looking OK'. It may be appropriate for the coach to gently inquire about the client's experience, and to explore their concerns, and the possible ways to resolve their anxiety. In some cases, the client's distress may warrant consideration of specialist psychological support. In others, turning off the video self-view may offer a direct and simple way to mitigate any mild distress. This can help because it immediately removes the source of mirror and presentational anxiety.

Hyper gaze is another potentially distressing phenomenon associated with video meetings, although its impact may be greater in meetings involving multiple participants. Hyper gaze refers to the experience of having another person's eyes in your field of view, and being in their direct gaze. Being stared at while speaking can engender feelings of anxiety and stress. It is much less likely to occur in an in-person, three-dimensional visual environment, for the simple reason that there is more to look at in a physical setting. Reducing the time spent in the video coaching session, taking regular screen breaks, as well as practising the habit of looking away periodically, can all help to reduce the physiological and psychological impacts of hyper gaze. It may also be helpful for coaches to schedule video coaching sessions with the potential impact of cumulative, sustained, or prolonged periods of time spent in group video meetings in mind.

Amplifying communication and expressiveness

During video meetings, we may experience feelings of passivity, akin to watching television, as well as growing physically tired. These can both erode the energy and vivacity of participants on a call. When this happens, it can be useful for the coach to be more purposeful and deliberate in the way they use non-verbal communication during VMC, as this can help to enhance social presence. Social presence, in turn, helps the client to feel more engaged and to experience the coach as more present. Being more expressive, for example, by using gestures and movements, facial expressions, eye contact, and a warm tone of voice make for more meaningful and satisfying interaction between the coach and the client. Becoming overly self-conscious or mechanistic when seeking to amplify communication and expressiveness can often lead to the coach exaggerating their actions, which may convey a note of insincerity. By contrast, the judicious use of amplification is more likely to enhance communication and reinforce the overall sense of the coach's presence. The more relaxed and the more 'embodied' awareness the coach feels, the more likely they are to move more easily and naturally, allowing for more genuine facial and other expressions that convey their interest and engagement with the client and the video meeting. Some studies of video-based therapy indicate that it may be easier to establish rapport and connection when the therapist's upper body and arms are in view, as this conveys more natural non-verbal cues and gestures.

Building co-presence and trust

Many social scientists have emphasised the cognitive 'leap of imagination' that is required for individuals to construct a sense of co-presence when they are online. Co-presence refers to the sense of being together in a physically intangible setting. (For a sociological account of co-presence, see Zhao, 2003.) That we are able to mentally 'bridge' the physical separation while being together on a video call, and to overcome the potentially dissonant experience of being in 'a room together without a room', is testament to our imaginative and social abilities as human beings. Several neuroscientific studies have highlighted our unique human capacity to imagine the visuo-spatial perspective (VPT) of another, precisely in situations where we are not in the bodily physical presence of the other person (see, for example, Hamilton et al. (2015) and Kessler et al. (2014)). This type of perspective taking is not about the inferences we make, rather, it involves a kind of mental 'simulation' that in some way represents and embodies the other. Taken together, these studies seem to suggest that all things being equal, we may be naturally well-equipped to achieve a basic sense of 'being with' another person in the video coaching setting.

With regard to establishing trust online, the views in the literature are mixed, and the evidence points to a complex set of interacting factors. Several scholars, such as Ess (2014; 2020) for example, contend that embodied co-presence is essential for establishing and sustaining relational trust. Moreover, for some clients, the online environment may well be inhibiting or limiting. There may be sensory, brain, or personality differences, or indeed past experiences that make the person more cautious or guarded. Some clients may particularly miss getting fuller sensory information and combining it to get a 'read out' of the coach and the relational 'climate' between them. Without physical presence, there are some clients who may feel at least partially disconnected from the video coaching experience, and distanced from the relationship with their coach. This may be, in part, mediated by the client's lived experience and/or their attachment style. We can infer from attachment style research (see, for example, Mikulincer & Shaver, 2007) that clients with insecure attachment styles may find that the remote video context presents additional challenges to establishing and maintaining trust with their coach. Depending on what else may be happening in the client's life and work, the sense of the coach's physical absence may prevail, and consequently impact the working alliance with the coach, and the potential for coaching to bring about the desired learning and change.

Although there is little, if any research which compares trust within in-person and VMC, many practitioners contend that the basic conditions for optimising trust in real-world coaching relationships are essentially the same. These conditions include showing genuine interest, curiosity, and concern, as well as being authentic, congruent, reliable, consistent, and respectful. Being able to be vulnerable in the presence of another is also key to building trust. Additionally, as Brown's work has shown, vulnerability can be a core condition for growth and self-exploration (Brown, 2012). It follows that the coach showing something of their own vulnerability, as well as creating a safe and supportive environment for the client to share their vulnerability, is likely to engender greater relational trust, but also promote the client's development. Intentionally sharing information about themselves, about the setting and about the coach as a person, models ordinary human vulnerability, and reinforces mutuality.

The coach's emotional presence

In this section, we will outline and explore some of the ways the coach can enhance their ability to fully engage and attune to the emotional world of the client in the video mediated context. The coach's emotional presence serves to further deepen the quality of the relationship with the client, which in turn can create greater trust and safety in the virtual space. With greater trust and safety, the client will feel more comfortable to share their aspirations, concerns, and feelings, and to co-create a productive relationship which supports the achievement of their goals. Developing and honing the skills of deep listening and empathic responsiveness in the video meeting space can enhance the emotional presence of the coach and increase the potential for a deeper and more effective coaching relationship.

Deep listening

It goes without saying that active and deep listening, as well as asking questions that demonstrate their understanding and build on what the coach has heard, convey that the coach is fully present in the virtual space. Conveying this capacity to receive, and to respond to what the client is saying, goes beyond parroting or indeed using paraphrasing or clarifying interventions alone. Rather, it requires, as a first step, that the coach is able to perceive the client clearly, unfiltered and unattenuated by audio and visual quality that is subpar. Second, it requires that the coach be able to 'read' and 'register' the emotional state of the client. As the emotional realm tends to manifest more through body posture and other non-verbal cues than it does through the words which client utters, video mediated communication is thought to be a relatively rich digital medium. Consequently, some authors (see, for example, Grondin et al. (2019)), underline the value of video because it offers richer information, additively combining voice cues such as intonation and rhythm, with visual ones. This suggests that where the quality of connection and audio-visual transmission is optimal, it may be easier for the video coach to use a combination of voice and visual cues to listen deeply, in order to recognise the emotional state of the client. The implication is that to develop the capacity for deep listening with empathy, the video coach would need to hone their ability to closely observe and track both the non-verbal visual and voice cues of the client, simultaneously, in real-time. Further, the coach would also benefit from practising making direct verbal statements that consciously and explicitly test their 'reading' of the client's emotions.

Some authors, however, underline the importance and primacy of voice as a portal into the emotional world of the client. These practitioners and researchers (see, for example, Caulet (2004; 2012), and Gilligan (2006)) emphasise that centring on voice improves the quality of deep listening. The implication here is that far from augmenting the coach's capacity to attune to the video client's emotions, the presence of visual cues detracts from deep listening and empathic attunement. They recommend practising listening attentively to the quality of the client's voice, and over time, getting to know their individual habits and patterns of speech so that they can better access and understand their internal world.

Empathic responsiveness

Empathy is a core condition for a strong and effective coaching relationship, and a predictor of positive outcomes. There is evidence from video therapy research (cited in Grondin et al., 2019) to suggest that being perceived to be empathic by clients may rest more on the non-verbal vocal utterances and non-verbal visual cues than on the precise verbal interventions that the coach makes. The literature also suggests that responding through vocal intonations and inflexions, as well as visual cues such as nods and facial expressions that are somewhat amplified, may be helpful. This further reinforces the important role that amplifying communication and expressiveness plays to create a greater sense of presence and realism in the video coaching context (see above). Another dimension of empathic responsiveness concerns the ability to accurately match the emotional state of the client, by adapting communication style. Matching requires that the coach observe the client's verbal and non-verbal communication style carefully and accurately, and then to reflect back to the client what they observe. For example, the coach might match the pace, tone, and volume of the client's speech, or they might match the client's body language, facial expressions, and eye contact. As with deep listening, the video coach can best develop their capacity for empathic responsiveness through repeated observation, practice, and experimenting, gauging the impact of their empathic responses and matching behaviours by monitoring how their clients' reactions, and adjusting what they do as necessary.

Synchrony and attunement

Several neuroscientific studies have suggested that narrative and storytelling enable our brains to 'synchronise' helping us to feel more relationally in tune. These research studies typically use brain imaging techniques to investigate the effects of sharing narratives whether through listening to stories, telling stories, or even watching a film together (see, for example, Hasson et al. (2008; 2012); Numennaa et al. (2014); and Stephens et al. (2010)). Taken together, this research demonstrates how shared narratives create a shared neural representation which causes our brain activity patterns to become synchronised. This shared experience strengthens emotional engagement, emotional resonance, and social connection.

Encouraging narrative exchange between coach and client is likely to be very helpful in creating and reinforcing the interpersonal relationship. It probably needs to go beyond small talk and chatting to break the ice. Rather, it may require a more deliberate, structured, and mutually agreed approach to facilitate a sustained exchange and/or several iterations of story exchange. For example, with the coach telling a story about themselves and encouraging the client to do the same. Another option might involve using a narrative format to describe a work scenario, to explore a real-life experience, or to take the perspective of another person.

Dealing with ruptures and micro-ruptures

Some tensions in the collaborative coaching endeavour may arise as a direct result of the medium of video itself. For example, non-verbal cues such as head orientation and direction of gaze may be more ambiguous and difficult to interpret. The video-specific phenomena, of mirror anxiety and hyper gaze; the feeling of being on show and watched in high definition and in real-time, may also lead or contribute to misunderstandings, and ruptures, which challenge the working relationship between coach and client. It is helpful for the coach to acknowledge and explore these experiences.

From time to time, technical glitches and poor transmission can affect the quality of the video image and voice audio, causing time delay, and the filtering of communication, for example. As a result, these may lead to disruptions and micro (small) ruptures in the video coaching relationship, arising from a sense of disorientation, or from misunderstanding and miscommunication. Drawing on the therapy literature points to the importance of the coach instigating communication and working with the client to repair the rupture by acknowledging the miscommunication and sharing their feelings and thoughts honestly, as well by showing understanding and compassion for the client's feelings and perspective on the micro-rupture. Having an advance contract in place with the client, about what to do in the event of a loss of technical quality and/or connection can also be immensely valuable. On a psychological level, contracting for glitches and contingencies primes the client to expect and accept that technical difficulties may happen, and provides a degree of assurance in having some pre-planned, mutually agreed, practical steps to take to improve or resume the session.

Table 6.1 Checklist

Planning ahead
1. Check the tech. Gently explore the client's efficacy and confidence about using the hardware and/or meeting software or platform.
2. Disposition. What is the client's preference? What is their past experience of video conferencing and VMC? Is the client techno stressed/or at risk of techno burnout?
3. Are there any sensory or brain differences that need to be considered?
4. Are there any likely home, life, work, or other factors that will impact the physical environment that the client will be in, and which may become a hindrance or a barrier to the coaching work?

During the work
5. Is the client experiencing video stress? Are they spending prolonged periods in video meetings? Are they feeling anxious or distressed in the moment?
6. Is the client distracted or stressed by something in their physical environment?
7. Is there any evident tension or discomfort impacting the interaction and/or the working relationship?

In case of poor connectivity or disconnection
• Have you checked systematically for possible causes?
• Have you tried resuming the meeting and been unsuccessful?
• What contingency plan or fallback do you have in place?

Reflective questions

1. What am I doing to strengthen presence and rapport in my VMC meetings?
2. How effective am I in adapting my communication style to compensate for the limitations of non-verbal cues in the virtual video space?
3. How well do I resource myself so that I am alert and emotionally present for coaching via video?

Conclusion

Video mediated meetings offer both opportunity and convenience, enabling coaches and clients to meet without needing to be physically co-located. However, it is important to make a positive decision to use video as a medium, to ensure that it suits the needs of both parties. It is also crucial that both coach and client have access to technology that can deliver a high quality of visual and audio output, thereby providing the optimal basis for the video meeting and environment. Contracting in advance for contingencies and disruption to the enabling technology is helpful. These are arguably the baseline conditions on which the ability to establish a quality relational connection is built. Relational connection, in turn, is the foundation for coaching to be more effective in meeting the outcomes that the client seeks. When deploying video coaching it is helpful for the coach to work actively to create social presence and to make interventions that counter digital disembodiment. Together, these engender a sense of vitality and lively engagement, which can help the client and indeed the coach to feel more connected in the virtual space, and contribute to a climate of psychological safety and trust in video meetings. It is important for coaches to appreciate that it may take time to establish trust and to be aware of the potential for certain phenomena such as mirror anxiety, hyper gaze, and Zoom claustrophobia to emerge in the course of video coaching. Coaches can further enhance a supportive video coaching relationship by cultivating their virtual emotional presence through boosting their skills in deep listening, the capacity for empathic responsiveness, a more deliberate use of narrative to facilitate interpersonal neural synchrony and emotional connection, and a willingness to recognise and discuss tensions and misunderstandings that may arise.

Acknowledgments

With thanks to my colleagues, clients, and my daughter Ellie, from whom I have learnt so much about working with video.

References

Brown, B. (2012). *Daring greatly: How the courage to be vulnerable transforms the way we live, love, parent and lead*. New York: Gotham Books.
Caulat, G. (2004). *Being heard but not seen*. Ashridge Masters AMOC.
Caulat, Gh. (2012). *Virtual leadership – Learning to lead differently*. London: Libri Publishing.
de Haan, E., & Nilsson, V. (2023). What can we know about the effectiveness of coaching? A meta-analysis based only on randomized controlled trials. *Academy of Management Learning & Education, 22*(4), 1–21. DOI: 10.5465/amle.2022.0107

Ess, C. (2014). Trust, social identity, and computation. In R. H. R. Harper (Ed.), *The complexity of trust, computing, and society* (pp. 199–226), Cambridge University Press.

Ess, C. M. (2020). Trust and information and communication technologies. In J. Simon (Ed.), *The Routledge handbook of trust and philosophy* (pp. 405–420), Cambridge University Press.

Gallagher, S. (2005). *How the body shapes the mind.* New York: Oxford University Press.

Gilligan, C., Spencer, R., Weinberg, K. M., & Bertsch, T. (2006). On the listening guide. A voice-centered relational method. In S. N. Hesse-Biber (Ed.), *Emergent methods in social research* (pp. 253–254), London: Sage.

Grondin, F., Lomanowska, A. M., & Jackson, P. L. (2019). Empathy in computer-mediated interactions: A conceptual framework for research and clinical practice. *Clinical Psychology: Science and Practice, 26*(4), e12298.

Gunawardena, C. N., & Zittle, F. J. (1997). Social presence as a predictor of satisfaction within a computer mediated conferencing environment. *American Journal of Distance Education, 11*(3), 8–26.

Hamilton, A. F. d. C., Kessler, K., & Creem-Regehr, S. H. (2015). Perspective taking: Building a neurocognitive framework for integrating the "social" and the "spatial". *Frontiers in Human Neuroscience, 8,* 6–9.

Hasson, U., Ghazanfar, A. A., Galantucci, B., Garrod, S., & Keysers, C. (2012). Brain-to-brain coupling: A mechanism for creating and sharing a social world. *Trends in Cognitive Sciences, 16*(2), 114–121.

Hasson, U., Landesman, O., Knappmeyer, B., Vallines, I., Rubin, N., & Heeger, D. J. (2008). Neurocinematics: The neuroscience of film. *Projections, 2*(1), 1–26.

Kessler, K., Cao, L., O'Shea, K. J., & Wang, H. (2014). A cross-culture, cross-gender comparison of perspective taking mechanisms. *Proceedings of the Royal Society of London B: Biological Sciences, 281*(1785), 20140388.

Kirton, A. (2020). Matters of trust as matters of attachment security. *International Journal of Philosophical Studies, 28*(5), 583–602. DOI: 10.1080/09672559.2020.1802971

Leighton, J. (2021). Stanford researchers identify four causes for 'Zoom fatigue' and their simple fixes. *Stanford News.* https://news.standford.edu/2021/02/23/four-causes-zoom-fatigue-solutions/ [Google Scholar].

Mikulincer, M., & Shaver, P. R. (2007). *Attachment in adulthood: Structure, dynamics, and change.* New York: Guilford Press.

Nummenmaa, A., Saarimäki, H., Glerean, E., Gotsopoulos, A., Jääskeläinen, L. P., Hari, R., & Mikko Sams, M. (2014). Emotional speech synchronizes brains across listeners and engages large-scale dynamic brain networks. *NeuroImage, 102*(2), 498–509.

Short, J., Williams, E., & Christie, B. (1976). *The social psychology of telecommunications.* London: John Wiley & Sons.

Stephens, G. J., Silbert, L. J., & Hasson, U. (2010). Speaker–listener neural coupling underlies successful communication. *Proceedings of the National Academy of Sciences, 107*(32), 14425–14430.

Suler, J. R. (2016). *Psychology of the Digital Age: Humans become electric.* Cambridge: Cambridge University Press.

Zhao, S. (2003). Toward a taxonomy of co-presence. *Presence, 12*(5), 445–455.

Chapter 7

Artificial intelligence coaching chatbots

Nicky Terblanche

Introduction

Coaching chatbots are increasingly used to scale and democratise coaching due to their cost-effectiveness and 24/7 availability. From humble beginnings as simplistic, scripted conversation agents, coaching chatbots continue to grow in sophistication and complexity, and are able to rival human coaches in certain scenarios. To successfully create and deploy a coaching chatbot it is important to understand how to design one, which factors play a role in user adoption and importantly in which use cases they are effective. There are also numerous ethical challenges that must be considered. This chapter reviews research to shed light on the intricacies of coaching chatbots.

Conceptualising AI coaching chatbots

To understand the notion of AI coaching chatbots, we need to first consider AI itself. AI is seen by some as one of the most significant developments in human history with the potential to disrupt all aspects of human life. 'Artificial intelligence' may be defined as 'the broad collection of technologies, such as computer vision, language processing, robotics, robotic process automation, and virtual agents that are able to mimic cognitive human functions' (Bughin & Hazan, 2017, p. 4). AI is also described as a computer program combined with real-life data, which can be trained to perform a task and can become smarter about its users through experience with its users. Another perspective of AI is to view it as a science dedicated to the study of systems that, from the perspective of an observer, act intelligently (Bernardini, Sônego, & Pozzebon, 2018). AI research started in the early 1950s. It is an interdisciplinary field that applies learning and perception to specific tasks including potentially coaching.

Importantly, a distinction can be made between artificial narrow intelligence (ANI), which refers to systems that can perform only a very specific task in a narrow context; artificial general intelligence (AGI), which refers to systems that are at least as intelligent as humans and can apply their learning in different contexts; and artificial super intelligence (ASI), which refers to systems that can outperform humans in most dimensions. AGI, and especially ASI, are currently still in their infancy with no clear indication of reaching maturity in the foreseeable future. ANI, however, is showing steady signs of progress with encouraging results in specific applications, such as speech recognition, self-driving cars, and large language models.

DOI: 10.4324/9781003383741-10

A 'conversational agent' or 'chatbot system' is defined as a computer program that interacts with users via natural language either through text, voice, or both (Chung & Park, 2019). Chatbots typically receive questions in natural human language, associate these questions with a knowledge base, and then offer a response. Various terms are used to describe chatbots, including conversational agents, talkbots, dialogue systems, chatterbots, machine conversation systems, and virtual agents. The origins of chatbot type systems can be traced back to the 1950s, when Alan Turing proposed a five-minute test (also known as the Imitation Game) based on a text message conversation, where a human had to predict whether the entity, they were communicating with via text was a computer program or not.

Two famous chatbots of the past are Eliza, developed in 1966, and PARRY, developed in the 1970s. Eliza imitated a Rogerian psychologist, using simple pattern matching techniques to restructure users' sentences into questions. Notwithstanding the simplistic approach, its performance was considered remarkable, partly due to people's inexperience with this type of technology. PARRY imitated a paranoid person and when its transcripts were compared to real paranoia patients, psychiatrists were able to distinguish between the two sets only 48% of the time. More recently, chatbots have found new applications in the services industry where they are used to assist with customer queries, advice, and fulfilment of orders (Araujo, 2018). Chatbots have proliferated with one estimate of more than 300,000 chatbots operational on Facebook Messenger alone (Joselow, 2023).

As a form of narrow or weak AI and so-called 'expert system', chatbots are usually designed by a set of scripted rules (retrieval-based), AI (generative-based), or a combination of both to interact with humans. Driven by algorithms of varying complexity and optionally employing AI technologies such as machine learning, deep learning, and natural language processing, generation, and understanding (NLP, NLG, NLU), chatbots respond to users by deciding on the appropriate response given a user input.

Joining the two concepts AI and coaching chatbots, 'AI coaching chatbots' can therefore be described as a computer program that simulates a human coach. In other words, it is a software system that acts as an autonomous coaching agent that could completely replace or augment human coaches, working with human clients to simulate the process of providing a coaching service (Terblanche, 2020). There could be many incarnations of such an entity ranging from an actual physical coach robot that looks like a human, to a non-embodied conversation system. For the purpose of our discussion we will limit AI coaching to its application through chatbots.

There are numerous classifications of chatbots. A distinction can be made between rule-based (retrieval) and generative chatbots. Rule-based chatbots have a mostly hard-coded decision tree that follows a specific conversation script. Generative chatbots, on the other hand, are able to create conversations in-the-moment based on user input and the history of the conversation. Chatbots can also be classified as being open or closed domain. Open domain means the chatbot can talk about anything while closed domain chatbots can talk about only very specific things like pizza orders. Finally there are short versus long conversation chatbots where the length of the conversation determines the amount of context the bot has to remember.

Until the arrival of LLMs, most chatbots for coaching were rule-based, closed domain, short conversation bots. LLMs changed all of this, most dramatically in the generative aspect of the conversation. By 'understanding' what a human has said, LLMs can generate responses relevant to the context. The use of LLMs also means that the domain of conversation is far more open than before. We will return to the discussion of LLMs in coaching chatbots later in this chapter.

How to create an AI coaching chatbot

Given the infancy of the field, there are very few guidelines available on how to create AI coaching chatbots. In an attempt to guide the design process, Terblanche (2020) created a conceptual framework for creating AI coaching chatbots. The resulting designing AI coach (DAIC) framework captures a pragmatic approach for implementing an AI coach (Terblanche, 2020). The DAIC framework suggests the use of chatbot technology with embedded 'good' human coaching attributes, behaviours, and importantly ethics. The framework consists of two facets: effective human coaching and acknowledged chatbot design principles.

To create guidelines for the first facet (effective human coaching), a literature review of what constitutes desired coaching behaviour that promotes a strong coach–client relationship and resultant coaching success revealed that a coach should exhibit the following: trust, empathy, transparency, predictability, reliability, ability, benevolence, and integrity. A coaching chatbot should therefore aim to exhibit these types of behaviours. For example, trust can be created by avoiding the 'uncanny valley' effect. This is a phenomenon whereby a robot starts looking too similar to a human and generates a sense of eeriness or revulsion. A coaching chatbot should also be transparent about the fact that it is in fact not a human and should disclose its limitations.

Furthermore, in coaching we should all strive to base our practice on evidence. One of the criticisms often levelled at coaching is that practitioners use models and frameworks that are borrowed from other professions without having been empirically verified for the coaching context (Theeboom et al., 2013). Therefore, in addition to a strong coach–client relationship, an AI coach must also be based on theoretically-sound coaching approaches. An example is one of the original coaching chatbots (Coach Vici) that was based on goal theory and used the classical GROW model. Vici has evolved significantly since its inception, but each new feature and function is still grounded in solid, proven theory.

Ethical considerations

An AI coaching chatbot should also adhere to the highest ethical standards. In coaching, ethics are crucially important given the personal and sensitive information clients share with coaches and especially because there is often a third-party involved (the organisation). In AI coaching chatbots, the ethical aspects become even more important and specifically the following aspects: (i) privacy and data protection; (ii) autonomy; (iii) liability and division of responsibilities; (iv) biases; and (v) algorithm transparency (see Passmore & Tee, 2023a,b) for a discussion of ethical challenges).

Both the need and the ability of AI coaching systems to continuously collect, monitor, store, and process information raise issues regarding privacy and data protection. Questions such as 'who owns and can access the data obtained from a coaching session?' must be made clear to users. Autonomy raises the question of how to deal with potential manipulation by an AI coaching system. Autonomous AI coaching systems may offer users suggestions for action, thereby affecting their decision-making process. Being influenced by its decision making seems to conflict with the classical understanding of self-directedness as professed in coaching.

Third, many stakeholders of various levels of diversity, specialisation, and complex interdependencies are involved in creating an AI coaching system. Therefore, the division of liabilities and responsibilities among the relevant stakeholders involved (producers, providers, consumers, and organisations) cannot be ignored. Creating responsible AI coaches also requires alertness to the possibility that some clients need to work with a different specialist and not a coach. The acceptance of AI coaching applications will be constrained if the design and use of the system adhere to a different set of ethical principles than their intended users.

Bias is another critical consideration. Machine learning typically used in AI relies on large amounts of data. Data originates from many sources and data is not necessarily neutral. Care must be taken to ensure that potential biases inherent in data are not transferred to the AI coach via the learning process, or if not avoidable, these biases must be made explicit.

AI coaching in the organisational context presents additional ethical challenges. In traditional human-to-human coaching, contracting for coaching in organisations typically involves three parties: the coach, the client, and the sponsoring organisation paying for the coaching. Although the organisation pays for the coaching, there is usually a confidential agreement between coach and client to the exclusion of the organisation. If an AI coach is used and paid for by the organisation, the ethical question about who owns the details of the conversation must be made clear. It would potentially be unethical for the organisation to have access to the AI coach–client conversation.

Adoption factors

'Build it and they will come' does not often apply to technology. Just because individuals are able to create AI coaching chatbots does not mean people will use it. It is therefore crucial that we understand what factors influence users' adoption of AI coaching chatbots.

The first quantitative study using Coach Vici investigated what factors would influence users' adoption of this type of technology (Terblanche & Kidd, 2022). Users were invited to have a conversation with Coach Vici and then complete the standardised UTAUT (technology adoption) survey that measures the role of performance, ease of use, social influence, infrastructure required, and risk on the intent of users to use Coach Vici. The results suggested the most important predictor of using Coach Vici was the performance aspect (Terblanche & Kidd, 2022). People were more inclined to use Coach Vici if they thought it was useful – more than any other aspect. This finding points to the fact that it is critical to create AI coaches that work, as obvious as it sounds. This brings us back to the DAIC framework's requirement that coaching chatbots should be created using tried and tested theoretical frameworks applicable to coaching.

The other two aspects that were rated high are infrastructure required and social influence. Infrastructure requirements refer to the devices and software people require to use an AI coach. The most obvious devices to target are smartphones given their ubiquity.

Here the choices are between deploying the coaching chatbot via a dedicated app or using existing instant messaging services such as Facebook Messenger or WhatsApp. The advantage of a dedicated app is the rich user experience that can be created. However from a development perspective, this approach requires ongoing maintenance on various operating systems and potentially high cost to initially develop. There are also studies that show most people engage with only a few apps on their phone. Deploying the chatbot via an existing messaging platform is cheaper and faster, but the usage of various messaging services differ between regions. In an initial study the researchers used Telegram, but uptake was low due to the relative obscurity of that system. A further constraint is that in some organisations social media messaging platforms are banned or highly regulated. As a result, careful consideration needs to be given to the technology platform on which the AI coaching chatbot is deployed.

The notion of social influence in the adoption of an AI coaching chatbot was an interesting result of the research. It implies that people will use a coaching chatbot if their friends and people they trust also use it. We interpret this to suggest that when deploying such technology in an organisation it is important to have early adopters, champions, and influencers to promote its usage.

In later studies a third factor emerged: the availability of the chatbot. Individual users wanted to be able to rely on the service being constantly available whenever they needed it.

In the next section we will look at efficacy evidence.

AI chatbot coaching efficacy

AI coaching chatbots have the potential to scale coaching and make it available to under-coached people at a fraction of the cost of human coaching. But does it work? And how well does it perform compared to a human coach? There are at this stage only a few efficacy studies to draw from.

A longitudinal randomised controlled trial (RCT) looked at the ability of Coach Vici (a goal attainment coaching chatbot) to improve users' goal attainment, resilience, psychological well being, and perceived stress (Terblanche et al., 2022a). In the study a group of 200 users were randomly assigned to either the chatbot group or a control group. The chatbot group used the chatbot for 10 months while the control group received only reading material on goal attainment. For both groups the participants' goal attainment, resilience, psychological well being, and perceived stress were measured. The results show that Coach Vici was not able to improve resilience, well being, or reduce stress, however it was able to help its users at double the rate of the non-users with their goal attainment (Terblanche et al., 2022a). It was not a surprise that Vici did not improve resilience, well being, and reduce stress since it was not designed to address these aspects. Vici was designed using the DAIC framework that dictates the use of proven theoretical models, in this case goal theory. The results that showed significant goal attainment improvement relative to the control group was however a surprise and is a testimony to the power of coaching chatbots if implemented following the DAIC framework. To investigate how Vici compared to human coaches a replication study was conducted using human coaches. The results showed that Coach Vici was comparable to a human coach performance in terms of helping people with goal attainment (Terblanche et al., 2022b). Even though the chatbot was not nearly as intelligent as a human coach, the fact that it implements goal theory accurately, was always available, and regularly checked-in with users can be considered as reasons for its surprising efficacy.

A different study looked at the impact an AI coach could have on the human coach–client relationship (Terblanche, van Heerden & Hunt (2024)). It found that, in general, coaches were more sceptical of using an AI coach assistant than clients. Coaches were concerned the chatbot coach would interfere with their relationship with the client. Both parties could however see the advantages such as improved goal attainment, accountability, and always available accessibility. Interestingly some clients felt more psychologically safe speaking to the chatbot than to their human coach since they felt unjudged. A different study that investigated coaching efficacy by Ellis-Brush (2021) also found that users of a psychologically-based chatbot (WYSA) felt psychologically safe using the bot and the reported improved self-resilience.

We are at the early stages of understanding how effective AI coaching chatbots are and significantly more research is needed to explore this phenomenon. To illustrate our lack of understanding and the dangers of assumptions, one study compared a voice-based coaching chatbot with a text-based bot. Both chatbots conducted a basic GROW conversation with the user (Terblanche, Wallis & Kidd, 2023). The aim was to understand what role extraversion plays in chatbot adoption. The hypothesis was that introverts would prefer the text-based chatbot, however they in fact preferred the voice-based version. This was a surprising, non-intuitive result. Perhaps the psychological safety of a chatbot allows introverts to open up and engage more freely? There are many unanswered questions in relation to this new type of coaching technology.

Benefits and pitfalls of AI coaching chatbots

Due to its scalability, AI coaching chatbots promises numerous benefits. There are however also potential dangers and pitfalls that coaches and clients must be aware of.

Benefits

The most significant benefit of this type of technology in coaching is the promise to reduce the cost of coaching and increase the availability of this service. Coaching is expensive. The average cost of a one hour organisational coaching session is in the region of $300 in the USA, UK, and Europe (Terblanche, Passmore & Myburgh, 2021). Even in less affluent regions such as Africa the average rate of executive coaching is $100 (Terblanche et al., 2020). Combined with these prohibitive costs is the lack of availability of well-trained coaches. In Africa, for example, the ICF has fewer than 2000 members. AI coaching chatbots can provide basic coaching services at a fraction of the cost and on an almost unlimited scale to people currently excluded from this valuable service.

Another obvious benefit of AI coaching chatbots is the ubiquity and 24/7 availability compared to human coaches. Users can engage with their coaching chatbot whenever they have the need. This could be very beneficial to, for example, think through a challenging problem you are facing at the moment instead of having to wait until your next human coaching session.

Human coaches also stand to benefit from coaching chatbots. Chatbots could automate aspects of human coaching that are repetitive such as doing an initial assessment of a new client, supporting the progress of a client in between human coaching sessions and continuing the support when human coaching ends. It is also plausible that people who engage with coaching for the first time via a coaching chatbot could eventually migrate to a human coach to gain a more advanced and human-centred coaching service. Therefore, instead of being concerned that AI coaching chatbots will destroy the need for human coaches and negatively impact human coach jobs, the opposite effect is just as likely an outcome.

Pitfalls

There are three main challenges in using AI coaching chatbots. First, human coaches who rely on simplistic model-based coaching approaches could be replaced by AI coaching chatbots. This is especially true when LLMs are incorporated into these chatbots. These LLM models have instant access to an amount of information that no human could ever memorise. This implies that in the moment, an LLM-based coaching chatbot could ask an impressive array of theoretically-sound, context-aware questions and not be swayed by human emotion, projection, or transference. Of course, human coaches still have the edge when it comes to 'thinking outside the box' and drawing on their own personal learning and emotional awareness. Humans also have the ability to make new connections between concepts and events that break the rules and this is where creativity and novelty arises. Human coaches therefore have to embrace their emotional and compassionate sides but also ensure they stay abreast with knowledge and theoretical understanding of their practice.

As a profession, coaching needs regulation and standards to control AI coaching chatbots. Just like the early days of coaching was described as the 'Wild West' (Sherman & Freas, 2004) we are in for a rough ride yet again as providers and professional bodies of AI coaching chatbots try to figure out how to tame this beast. This is especially true for using LLMs. While initial versions of LLMs such as ChatGPT and Bard are immensely powerful they were not created as coaching tools. It therefore takes a significant effort to prompt-engineer (instruct them to behave in a certain way) these language models to be compliant with coaching standards and ethics, as some have noted from their testing of GPT (Passmore & Tee, 2023b). I have personally spent months 'prompt engineering' ChatGPT to be a 'proper' coach and it still takes me by surprise on occasion. The coaching community needs to apply scrutiny to ensure these LLM-based coaching chatbots do not become advice-giving mentors or pseudo coaches with hidden agendas that even the creators are not aware of.

Finally there are numerous ethical challenges to overcome. I have already discussed some of these challenges under the designing of AI coaching chatbots section. We must remain vigilant about the adherence to sound coaching ethical practice.

The future of AI coaching chatbots

Before the arrival of LLMs, it would have taken a significant amount of effort to create a generative coaching chatbot. One would have to record hundreds, probably thousands of coaching conversations and use machine learning to train a model about coaching conversations. LLMs have given us a shortcut. As it is, with quite a bit of effort one can now prompt engineer ChatGPT or Bard to more or less behave like a coach.

One future use is for AI coaching chatbots to provide development tools for coaches to enhance their practice. A second is the provision of chatbots as a mass service, like a search engine providing coaching to people who don't usually have access to coaching. The instant popularity and media coverage of ChatGPT and other similar models have made chatbots more known and acceptable. This should help improve the adoption of AI coaching chatbots in general.

At the moment there are only a handful of researchers focusing on this field. There are many unknown aspects of this emerging technology and we simply cannot assume that what worked in human coaching is transferable to AI coaching.

With regards to research AI offers great potential to fast-track our understanding of human coaching using AI. It is notoriously difficult to do large-scale studies involving human coaches due to cost and confidentiality issues. Using AI coaching chatbots is a much more cost-effective and controllable way to investigate coaching. One example would be to create a number of different AI coaches (directive vs non-directive, CBT vs narrative etc.) and then test which approach works best against different presenting issues.

Reflective questions

1. How as a coach can I use AI coaching chatbots in my practice?
2. As a coaching profession, how do we regulate and ethically manage this new technology without destroying its potential?
3. As organisations how do we help democratise coaching through the application of AI coaching chatbots?

Conclusion

AI coaching chatbots are here, whether you like it or not. The advent of LLMs have given this technology a significant boost and we will soon see remarkably eloquent and efficient coaching chatbots. This technology is likely to dramatically scale and democratise coaching and bring the proven benefits of coaching to millions of people around the world who would otherwise not have access to coaching. We have to remain engaged and vigilant with this unfolding process to ensure we manage the power of this technology in an ethically sound and responsible manner.

References

Araujo, T. (2018). Living up to the chatbot hype: The influence of anthropomorphic design cues and communicative agency framing on conversational agent and company perceptions. *Computers in Human Behavior, 85*, 183–189. https://doi.org/10.1016/j.chb.2018.03.051

Bernardini, A. A., Sônego, A. A., & Pozzebon, E. (2018, October). Chatbots: An analysis of the state of art of literature. In *Anais do I workshop on advanced virtual environments and education* (pp. 1–6). SBC.

Bughin, J., Hazan, E., Ramaswamy, S., Chui, M., Allas, T., Dahlstrom, P., ... & Trench, M. (2017). *Artificial intelligence: The next digital frontier?* www.mckinsey.com/~/media/mckin sey/industries/advanced%20electronics/our%20insights/how%20artificial%20intelligence%20 can%20deliver%20real%20value%20to%20companies/mgi-artificial-intelligence-discussion-paper.ashx

Chung, K., & Park, R. C. (2019). Chatbot-based healthcare service with a knowledge base for cloud computing. *Cluster Computing, 22*(S1), 1925–1937. https://doi.org/10.1007/s10586-018-2334-5

Ellis-Brush, K. (2021). Augmenting coaching practice through digital methods. *International Journal of Evidence Based Coaching & Mentoring, 15*, 187–197. DOI: 10.24384/er2p-4857

Joselow, A (2023). Key Chatbot Statistics You Should Follow in 2023. Chatbot.com. www.chat bot.com/blog/chatbot-statistics/

Passmore, J., & Tee, D. (2023a). Can chatbots like GPT-4 replace human coaches: Issues and dilemmas for the coaching profession, coaching clients and for organisations. *The Coaching Psychologist, 19*(1), 47–54. https://doi.org/10.53841/bpstcp.2023.19.1.47

Passmore, J., & Tee, D. (2023b). The Library of Babel: Assessing the powers of artificial intelligence in coaching conversations and knowledge synthesis. *Journal of Work Applied Management.* https://doi.org/10.1108/JWAM-06-2023-0057

Sherman, S., & Freas, A. (2004). The wild west of executive coaching. *Harvard Business Review, 82*(11), 82–93.

Terblanche, N. (2020). A design framework to create artificial intelligence coaches. *International Journal of Evidence Based Coaching & Mentoring, 18*(2), 152–165.

Terblanche, N., & Kidd, M. (2022). Adoption factors and moderating effects of age and gender that influence the intention to use a non-directive reflective coaching chatbot. *Sage Open, 12*(2), 21582440221096136.

Terblanche, N., Molyn, J., De Haan, E., & Nilsson, V. O. (2022a). Coaching at scale: Investigating the efficacy of artificial intelligence coaching. *International Journal of Evidence Based Coaching & Mentoring, 20*(2), 20–36.

Terblanche, N., Molyn, J., De Haan, E., & Nilsson, V. O. (2022b). Comparing artificial intelligence and human coaching goal attainment efficacy. *PloS One, 17*(6), e0270255.

Terblanche, N., Passmore, J., & Myburgh, J. (2021). African organisational coaching practice: Exploring approaches used, and the factors influencing coaches' fees. *South African Journal of Business Management, 52*(1). https://doi.org/10.4102/sajbm.v52i1.2395

Terblanche, N., van Heerden, M., & Hunt, R. (2024). The influence of an artificial intelligence chatbot coach assistant on the human coach-client working alliance. *Journal of Applied Behavioral Science*, Advance online publication 1–18.

Terblanche, N. H. D., Wallis, G. P., & Kidd, M. (2023). Talk or text? The role of communication modalities in the adoption of a non-directive, goal-attainment coaching chatbot. *Interacting with Computers, 35*(4), 511–518. iwad039.

Theeboom, T., Beersma, B., & van Vianen, A. E. M. (2013). Does coaching work? A meta-analysis on the effects of coaching on individual level outcomes in an organizational context. *Journal of Positive Psychology, 9*(1), 1–18. https://doi.org/10.1080/17439760.2013.837499

Chapter 8

Technologies for creativity in coaching

Auriel Majumdar and Stephen Brown

Introduction

Online coaching conversations do not always neatly replicate the in-person experience and while some coaching techniques are straightforward to apply in a digital environment, many are not. For coaches with an interest in working creatively with clients, a significant challenge many will face is how to bring creative coaching practice online and how best to exploit the modern technology available and develop innovative creative approaches.

This chapter first makes the case for creativity in coaching and then explores the ways that digital technology can extend creative coaching practices. It considers the constraints and opportunities that coaches experience when working online and offers insights for any coach wishing to bring their creative selves into their online practice.

Why creativity in coaching?

What exactly is creativity in coaching, and what benefit does a creative approach have over other forms of coaching? Creativity can be defined as the ability to generate innovative ideas, solutions, and possibilities (Runco & Jaeger, 2012), processes that are at the very heart of coaching. In a complex and interconnected world which changes rapidly, without warning, creativity is a necessity so that we can learn and adapt to our turbulent contexts. As Robinson & Lee (2011) noted, we need people who are flexible enough to adapt and find novel solutions to problems old and new. Coaching can be a space that facilitates and develops creative adaptability in both the coach and client. In addition, research has demonstrated the links between the creative arts and health outcomes, and how creativity contributes to our overall well being (Stuckey & Nobel, 2010), increasing positive emotions, improving memory retention, and boosting our immune systems. Encouraging creativity in our clients may therefore have a direct impact on their more general well being beyond the achievement of their goals. Anecdotally this is supported by the number of clients reporting an improved sense of calm and joy resulting from working creatively.

Creative coaching is a broad umbrella term, as broad as the term 'creativity' itself, used to capture a distinct set of processes and approaches. The ICF (International Coaching Federation) identifies two key benefits to creative coaching:

DOI: 10.4324/9781003383741-11

1. As a tool to break unhealthy *(their word)* patterns – instead of being locked into self-fulfilling loops of negative thoughts, emotions and actions, creativity can help envision a desired future state, aligning clients with achievement, creating more self-serving thoughts and behaviours.
2. To identify alternative strategies for existing problems – experimentation with new perspectives to develop successful strategies.

Gash (2016) examined the history, science, and practice of creativity and the practical implications for coaching. She drew a distinction between three diverse ways that creativity might manifest in coaching. First, creative 'doing' where the client is encouraged to engage with a creative activity, perhaps via a physical object or a visual image. Working with postcards, drawing, or writing are all forms of creative doing which can induce a flow state and enable creative insights (p. 85). According to Gash, creative coaching can also mean activating and supporting a client's creativity through facilitating an expansion of ideas and supporting the client to focus and gather 'forward energy' (p. 87). Gash's third category of creative coaching is one in which coaching itself is recognised as a creative process in which, through participation, the client both makes and becomes something 'other' (p. 81).

Palus (2006) suggested that creative coaches "assume that everyone is creative in a significant way and that they can find a foundation for further creativity development if they look in the right places" (p. 263). When a coach provides a safe, creative, and experimental space for their clients then exciting and meaningful things can happen: Clients bring something new into being, whether that be a clear path forward or deeper understanding of themselves (Whitaker, 2010).

Gestalt theory provides insights about the development of self-awareness and creative experimentation. It suggests the role of the Gestalt coach is to be present with the client; to be an instrument in the process of co-creatively raising awareness, for without awareness, no effective action can be conceived, articulated, or taken (Siminovitch & Van Eron, 2006). Practically, Gestalt coaches notice with clients that if they are asked to 'show' a complex situation, say by drawing or selecting a visual image, rather than describe it in words, a deeper sense of knowing becomes accessible to them. As a result, the client may see things in new ways, or gain a fresh perspective. Working with Russian dolls for example, clients can 'map' their complex worlds, take a bird's-eye view of their circumstances and engineer alternative futures by moving the figures into new patterns and relationships (Majumdar, 2020). This takes the coaching encounter beyond a dialogue into a process that Palus (2006) describes as 'World Making' in which the client "explores and develops his or her competency as a world maker...with respect to the transformation of self, relationships, and environments" (p. 265). Sheather (2019) too explores this ability of creative methods to move the coaching encounter beyond dialogue, connecting clients to deeper levels of personal awareness and understanding of their challenges and dilemmas, generating reflection and sense-making that goes beyond words, into the grain of the experience itself (Margulis, 2018). Creative coaching approaches which offer the possibility of 'becoming other' as Gash says, are thus likely to be of interest to coaches wishing to move beyond transactional achievement of short-term goals and instead focus on creating the conditions for the client to make transformational leaps forward.

Creative coaching in the digital world

Creative coaching online can mean simply bringing traditional creative coaching tools and artefacts into an online session. For example, one might draw images on personal notebooks and hold them up to the camera to share or choose a meaningful object and explore its symbolism and relevance to the coaching question. While this might sound simple it does present some challenges for the coach's mindset which are explored below. Creative coaching online can also mean using digital tools to coach creatively, for instance, using a shared digital whiteboard to create visual images or writing poetry or music together using specific software applications, and these present opportunities and challenges of a different sort, both in finding the tools and becoming proficient in their use. This chapter does not recommend specific software for working in this way as the digital world moves fast and tools can have a limited shelf life. Isaacson (2022) offers a wide range of digital coaching resources which could be applied by the coach.

When exploring digital creative coaching, it is important to consider both the perspective of previously creative coaches experiencing constraints in bringing this into their online work, and equally the perspective of coaches who are comfortable using digital technology and want to start creating and adapting digital tools to apply in coaching.

Connection

Coaches commonly complain that working online makes them feel disconnected from their clients. Some describe a sense of being 'trapped in a box' and this interferes both with their capacity to be present and with the fluency with which they can incorporate creative approaches even if they are adept at doing so in person. The virtual world is somehow perceived as less 'real', and this can prove challenging for coaches unused to working in this way. Given research (Passmore, 2021) it is likely that the widespread use of digital channels for coaching is here to stay, and as a result coaches in the 2020s must be adept at coaching online as they are face to face. Fostering an open and supportive environment is critical in any coaching encounter of course, but the importance of creating a safe space where clients can freely express their ideas, thoughts, and emotions without judgement is further emphasised where coach and client want to work creatively. By cultivating an environment of trust, coaches can help clients tap into their creativity, build stronger rapport, and enhance a sense of connection in their work.

Confidence

The impact of Covid-19 across the world in 2020 witnessed a pivot to online learning and coaching. For some coaches this negatively impacted their perception of being able to be creative people. Many lacked the experience and knowledge to use online resources and tools and coach education has done little to address this challenge (Passmore & Woodward, 2023). Previously secure creative coaches may feel that they must develop new skills for virtual working and, consequently, their confidence in their own practice is diminished, as is their confidence to improvise and create.

Clutterbuck in his maturity model has suggested that coaches proceed from an initial reliance on models and processes to more flexible, philosophically informed and system eclectic approaches where tools are 'integrated almost seamlessly into the conversation'. It is striking that the pivot to online working somehow can see experienced coaches step back towards the reassurance of models and processes. Rebuilding the previous confidence takes time, experience and access to the new tools and resources. Allowing ourselves to reflect and re-learn can be a slow and unsettling process. The reality is that while many coaches may be novices in the digital world, they are not novice coaches and have resources and experience to draw on as they navigate the new terrain.

Other coaches report being able to draw on their previous digital experience, for example, in making digital music or visual images and their creative identity has flourished (Turner, 2023). Those coaches that can connect with an existing creative interest seem more easily able to bring this into their online work. Passion and belief are the critical ingredient of creative confidence. Isaacson (2021) suggests the exponential development of technology is however creating a permanent sense of instability, while in equal measure bringing delight and disquiet depending on the technology in particular, our personal preferences, our age, and our background to the global coach community. Whether coaches embrace technology or flee from it will be personal, but what is also certain is that technology will not go away, and will be a growing feature of online coaching.

Skills development

A vital component of working confidently online is possessing the skills to practise effectively in what is, for many, a new coaching environment. The following stages are suggested to developing digital creative coaching skills:

- Become familiar with the online platform being used – whether using Microsoft Teams, Zoom or another alternative platform, coaches need to know their way around screen sharing, sound, handing control to participants or any other features which will enable them to collaborate with the creative tool. Coaches must become well versed with their chosen technology and have a back-up plan if it fails.
- Practice solo – digital devices such as phones, tablets, and laptops are used on a routine basis, and not much additional effort is needed to set aside time to experiment and find out what works. Reframing this time spent trying things as an investment in skills development rather than a distraction or an indulgence can move the emphasis from 'playing' to 'learning'.
- Experiment with others – use online interactions with others playfully, even outside of the coaching process, to hone the coaching approach and gather feedback on its effectiveness. The early lockdown Zoom parties and quizzes helped many people explore the functionality of that platform and similar experimentation will help coaches feel more secure and develop the ability to improvise and create new ways of digitally working in the moment.
- Find coaching role models – coaches significantly benefit from working with and being inspired by other creative coaches. Seeking out those who coach creatively who will have adapted to working online will support learning through watching what they do and how they do it. Coaches report that in some sense their role models give

them 'permission' to work in this way by showing that creativity in coaching is credible and valid.

- Develop networks – there are a growing number of coaches with an interest in creative practice and they often share their knowledge in CPD events. These are also a good place to practise new things with peers and develop skills in a safe and supportive environment. One distinct advantage of online working is that now networks can spread beyond one's immediate locality and be all the richer and more diverse as a result.
- Reflect on practice – skills development does not just arise from amassing coaching hours but also from intentional reflection on that practice. Make sure to set aside dedicated reflection time to assess what has worked well or not so well, what might change and what developmental actions can be taken.
- Engage in supervision – supervision can offer a space for reflection, allowing doubts and vulnerability to be expressed, development needs identified, and new insights to be gained.

Building a digital toolkit

It is true that coaches will approach technology with differing levels of competence and understanding, but this is also the case at the beginning of any coach development journey as coaches become familiar with tools and techniques and develop a repertoire of approaches. Purposefully building familiarity with chosen tools, practising with intent and being evaluative are at the heart of a sound coaching practice and online practice is no different. Many of the tools found and used online are not designed as coaching tools but are ingenious units of web code, sometimes developed for education, as art projects or simply engaging activities to entertain. The challenge is to see how these tools could be adapted for use in coaching but, again, there is no substitute for play, risk-taking and experimentation here. Digital tools are often free, but investing in technology will enhance the coach's offer. A better headset, with a high-fidelity microphone, an upgraded internet router to improve stability and bandwidth or perhaps a premium version of the chosen technology, containing more features. Furthermore, identifying areas of particular interest and using these to drive the search for creative coaching methods to use online seems critical in building a set of digital tools. For some coaches it has been creating poetry and working with visual imagery, for others it is sound and music. If coaches can connect with what motivates them and stirs their creativity, then the search for the right tool becomes more focused and purposeful.

Who does creativity benefit?

In any form of coaching, creative or otherwise, the needs of the client are paramount of course and must inform all the choices made. Practically then, the first question for coaches to consider must be 'how is this in service of the client?' It is easy for coaches to get excited by creativity and want to bring creative methods into every session, but less is more here. Creative methods are useful for helping clients get 'unstuck' or for bringing a change of energy, mood, or tempo but if the client is reflecting well and making progress with a standard coaching approach, then to introduce anything else is superfluous or at worst, gimmicky.

Accessibility

Coaching online certainly allows working beyond the geographical and logistical constraints that apply to face to face delivery. It can also make coaching cheaper and more responsive to client needs. This makes digital coaching more accessible in many ways. Digital tools that enable us to create or choose images or make music or sounds can also improve access for those who find purely dialogue-based coaching challenging, perhaps because of neurodivergence or the sensitivity of the topic they are exploring for instance. These ways of making something tangible, a drawing or poem for instance, which sits in between the coach and client can make the coaching feel safer, less personally intrusive, and more accessible. However, using digital tools, especially when they invite the client to play and experiment, can prove a barrier and a source of interference for some clients who may approach creative 'doing' with a degree of trepidation about their own creative ability. The same doubts coaches may hold about their own proficiency online may also be in the mind of the client and they might not feel confident to try diverse ways of reflecting. Interacting digitally but working remotely can also create barriers for those with impairments affecting motor function, vision, hearing, and physical disabilities. Before engaging in a creative exercise online it would be good practice for the coach to ask whether the client uses any assistive technology which may need to be taken into account and exploring a client's preferences or interests in creative tools. Finally, the coach must create a supportive environment where the pressure to get things 'right' is reduced as much as possible and this applies equally to the coach. Precise contracting is paramount here to ensure that creative approaches do not prove an obstacle to the important work of reflection.

Ethics

The Global Code of Ethics for Coaches, Mentors and Supervisors directs that 'Members will keep, store and dispose of all data and records of their client work including digital files and communications, in a manner that ensures confidentiality, security, and privacy, and complies with all relevant laws and agreements that exist in their client's country regarding data protection and privacy'. By introducing a digital tool during a coaching interaction, coaches should be mindful of basic data protection principles when creating and recording the processes and outputs of creative coaching. When asking clients to share their screen, care must be taken to ensure they do not share any sensitive info in the process of using the creative tool.

Recent research into online behaviour has revealed discrepancies between attitude to data safety and their actual behaviour, the 'privacy paradox' (Barth & De Jong, 2017). For example, typically people do not read all the Terms & Conditions before clicking 'Agree', or always click 'Accept all' when presented with the now standard cookie pop-up message. As part of a duty of care to clients, understanding the data implications of the tools used and raising their awareness of the choices they are making as part of contracting is a critical component of ethical practice, creative or otherwise.

Reflection questions

1. What benefits could clients gain from a creative digital coaching experience?
2. How can coaches use digital creative methods to deepen and extend the coaching encounter?
3. How can coaches develop their competence, confidence and fluency when discovering and using these digital creative methods?

Conclusions

This chapter has explored the benefits of creative coaching and how coaches can bring their creative coaching expertise online. It proposes a set of reflective questions for coaches to consider which will help build confidence and skill in service of clients. The digital genie is well and truly out of the bottle, coaching online is here to stay and if coaches are to realise their creative potential and be fully present in service of clients, they must surely adapt so that they can break out of their virtual boxes and meaningfully connect with each other. Virtual need not be second best. If coaches are willing to meet the challenge, then digital technology can help create a third space in the virtual realm that will support clients in ways previously unimagined. As Jaron Lanier, VR creator noted the point of digital technology is to make the world more "creative, expressive, empathetic and interesting" (2010) which is what creative coaches also aspire to achieve.

References

Barth, S., & De Jong, M. D. (2017). The privacy paradox–Investigating discrepancies between expressed privacy concerns and actual online behaviour–A systematic literature review. *Telematics and Informatics, 34*(7), 1038–1058.

Clutterbuck, D. (2020). An eclectic perspective on coaching supervision. In M. Lucas (Ed.), *101 Coaching supervision techniques, approaches, enquiries and experiments* (pp. 1–122). Abingdon: Routledge.

Garvey, B., Garvey, R., & Stokes, P. (2021). *Coaching and mentoring: Theory and practice.* London: Sage.

Gash, J. (2016). *Coaching creativity: Transforming your practice.* London: Taylor & Francis.

Isaacson, S. (2021). *How to thrive as a coach in a digital world: Coaching with technology.* UK: McGraw-Hill Education.

Isaacson, S. (2022). *Superhuman coaching.* London: Hanwell.

Lanier, J. (2010). *You are not a gadget.* London. Allen Lane.

Majumdar, A. (2020). *Coaching with the Russian Doll technique: Helping clients make sense of their complex worlds.* EMCC Global Conference. Paris, 2020.

Margulis, E. H. (2018). *The psychology of music: A very short introduction.* New York: Oxford University Press.

Palus, C. J. (2006). *Artful coaching. The CCL handbook of coaching: A guide for the leader coach* (pp. 259–285). San Francisco, CA: Jossey-Bass.

Passmore, J. (2021). *Future trends in coaching: Executive report 2021.* Henley-on-Thames: Henley Business School.

Passmore, J., & Woodward, W. (2023). Coaching education: Wake up to the new digital coaching and AI revolution! *International Coaching Psychology Review, 18*(1), 58–72.

Robinson, K., & Lee, J. R. (2011). *Out of our minds.* New York: Tantor Media, Incorporated.

Runco, M. A., & Jaeger, G. J. (2012). The standard definition of creativity. *Creativity Research Journal, 24*(1), 92–96.

Sheather, A. (2019). *Coaching beyond words: Using art to deepen and enrich our conversations.* Abingdon: Routledge.

Siminovitch, D. E., & Van Eron, A. M. (2006). The pragmatics of magic. *OD Practitioner, 38*(1), 51.

Stuckey, H. L., & Nobel, J. (2010). The connection between art, healing, and public health: A review of current literature. *American Journal of Public Health, 100*(2), 254–263.

Turner, A. (2023). *The theory and practice of creative coaching.* London: Anthem Press.

Whitaker, D. (2010). Offering creative choices in mentoring and coaching. In D. Megginson & D. Clutterbuck (Eds.), *Further techniques for coaching and mentoring* (pp. 100–115). Abingdon: Routledge.

Chapter 9

Technologies for systemic coaching

Sam Isaacson

Introduction

Many coaching conversations, particularly within organisations, benefit from taking a systemic lens. Technology can be used to help a client visualise a future plan and explore different perspectives. Coaches can use software already in use by them and their clients, as well as specialist apps to create so-called 'constellations' for exploration. These all offer advantages and challenges compared to physical tools, and range from simple two-dimensional representations to fully-fledged programs built on computer game engines. While some of these immersive environments offer transformative possibilities, their relative unfamiliarity for digital migrants requires careful onboarding and consideration of the client's comfort level. Rapport and psychological safety are essential in effectively using digital coaching tools.

In this chapter we will look at how constellations have been used historically as a tool in coaching, as well as the impact of technology on maintaining rapport in our coaching relationships. We will then spend the majority of the chapter exploring some of the possibilities of using technology to enhance systemic coaching, beginning with the most available tools and moving onto more advanced, specialist technology products. We will conclude the chapter by identifying some areas of caution to pay particular attention to.

Constellations in coaching

The idea of using objects to represent people and concepts that a client is working with in their life is a well-established tool in many coaches' toolkits. Commonly referred to as constellations, objects are arranged in such a way that their (relative) location and visual appearance represent the 'metaphor landscape' (Tompkins & Lawley, 2000) the client has built in their head. This allows them to crystallise what they've been thinking, experiment with different perspectives, and explore what might be possible. Constellation exercises can be profoundly helpful when used well, grappling not only with a symptom that an individual may be able to tactically manage, but with the underlying issue, leading to deeper and more sustainable change (Whittington, 2020). These representations make this a useful tool to aid the coaching process with a diverse range of clients, as they try to navigate the systems they interact with. Constellations can also add value to the coaching engagement as a whole, benefiting the client as well as the many stakeholders they impact through their actions (Hawkins & Turner, 2021).

DOI: 10.4324/9781003383741-12

Working at a systemic level has become increasingly important as the world has become more interconnected, leading some to raise concerns that the systemic approach risks becoming an example of 'pop-science band-wagoning' (Grant, 2015). This shouldn't put us off embracing it, however, because thinking systemically when approaching coaching could be considered a critical ingredient in enhancing its effectiveness when delivered well. Coaching happening inside an organisation is often systemic by design, as coach commissioners seek to address systemic challenges whether this is underrepresentation of specific groups in their workforce or technological change (Lawrence, 2019). Clients too are becoming more aware of this issue as social media brings greater awareness of our interconnectedness.

Coaches report that this is true anecdotally; 'office politics' comes up as a coaching topic regularly. Digital coaching provider EZRA analyses of coaching topics shows that 'Operating in the Matrix' (office politics by another name) is one of the top three most popular topics shared overall across every coaching conversation. The visualisation of a constellation naturally supports systemic coaching through making the client's inner understanding as tangible as possible, allowing for alternative perspectives to be taken. In particular, taking in the system as a whole can bring a new sense of insight. A client might discover that one part of the system simply isn't aware of another, or that the perceptions they've developed aren't helpful to support positive change.

Historically, these tools came from the therapeutic practice of 'family constellations' (Mahr, 1998), in which an individual will select a group of people to each represent someone in their family, positioning them spatially and in a stance that best represents the way they see them within their internal map. This typically takes place with a group of up to 20 people, and so a smaller-scale version evolved that could be used in 1:1 settings.

Physical products designed precisely for this sort of exercise exist. One example would be Coaching Constellations, in which intentionally neutral, smooth, wooden avatars are placed on a circular mat on a table to represent the system. Alternative in-person approaches have included toy characters such as LEGO or Playmobil figures, as well as non-descript items such as buttons, and matryoshka dolls.

Given the value of these insights, there should be no surprise that digital options have emerged, allowing for constellations to be created using technology (Isaacson, 2022). For example, some companies have put up for sale tailored slide backgrounds and packs of icons designed explicitly for use in coaching sessions, to apply to commonly available tools like Microsoft PowerPoint or Google Slides. Research has even shown that digital tools for constellations can lead to particular discoveries and mindset shifts with regard to the most interconnected system we're a part of: the natural world (Disterheft, Pijetlovic & Müller-Christ, 2021).

The importance of the client experience

This history as a physical, highly tactile experience introduces an interesting dynamic when we try to replicate the outcomes using technology. Because the embodied experience is part of what takes the client's mind away from the logical, linear, word-filled conversation and towards something different, there's a risk we'll lose something when moving to a virtual alternative. To counter this somewhat, we might consider three advantages of the technology when compared to the physical products.

First, the objects need to be taken care of; the experience of using an old, faded bag of wooden characters simply isn't as pleasant as using a pristine, new set. Digital products can't get damaged that way, and are often being continuously updated, offering the coach a refreshing experience each time it's accessed. Second, physical items only exist once, needing packing away in-between sessions and risking elements getting lost. Digital products can save their state and exist only in their whole state. As a result, a client can access a constellation in-between sessions at their leisure, for their own continued reflections and an expansion over time in which the same representation can develop as the circumstances and the client's understanding does. Finally, use of digital alternatives allows the client to benefit from the same features that other collaboration products are able to. These more complex coaching experiences can take place from both the coach's and the client's most accessible physical locations, with no additional time or cost needed for travel.

One interesting observation about digital representations of products that were designed as physical items first is that it will either replicate the physical experience as closely as possible, or make it as digitally friendly as possible, but it can't be both. It's not the case that one is better than the other, simply that they're not the same, and coaches ought to therefore think carefully about which will suit them and their clients.

If a coach is familiar with a physical constellation product, they might want to use a digital version of it because it reminds them of their training from the past. For some clients, that will be perfect, while for others the lack of a 'digital-first' mindset might frustrate them. When introducing any technology to a particular coaching session, or to a particular client, the coach should think more broadly than simply whether or not it ticks a series of functional boxes (Isaacson, 2021). Clients need to be able to benefit from using the tool, and each client will respond differently. For one client, the simple act of placing one of a limited selection of shapes on a blank screen will be enough, while another will want to explore a complex landscape with every option available in the product.

Options in two dimensions

The simplest application of systemic constellations as a digital product is to allow a client to represent the system as various shapes in two dimensions. In practical terms, this can take many forms. We will look at two applications here as examples.

Slide deck tools

There are plenty of ways to implement constellations digitally that don't require a specialist tool. This could be applied using an entirely non-directive approach, simply inviting the client to use shapes on a slide as part of a coaching conversation. Or it could take on a more formal structure using a template or specially-designed process model.

The Whole Partnership, for example, presents the following five-step CLEAR method:

• *Clarify* – being clear about the question to be answered, the context, and what a good outcome would look like.

- *Layout* – setting up the constellation visually, slowly introducing one element at a time.
- *Explore* – asking questions about the elements in the constellation and their relationship to one another.
- *Attune* – facilitating the client in becoming fully aware of the constellation.
- *Resolve* – facilitating the client in inserting themselves into the constellation and deciding on actions to take.

Others, such as systemic facilitators Viedma & Hermkens (Viedma & Hermkens, online), offer free templates that load in a slide deck and can be used by a coach, through collaborative software such as Google Slides or Microsoft Office 365, to lead a small selection of pre-designed exercises.

Digital whiteboards

A more flexible tool that allows for more freedom and creativity in its application of this approach is for a coach to create their own top-down view of the physical circular cloth mat, with a selection of icons representing the various objects one would use in a physical experience. These are available to buy as downloads online, and offer a classic example of the digital product having been designed with the physical in mind. Coaches who are experienced with a specific physical product and would like to incorporate more digital experiences into their coaching practice will likely find this a more comfortable shift.

While some of the more popular digital whiteboard tools available are extremely complex, some options are available that intentionally have significantly restricted abilities, such as only allowing the user to add coloured shapes from a pre-populated tray. Once the shapes have been placed onto the canvas they can be resized and rotated, and arrows can be added to represent a variety of systemic connections. The functionality of these are severely restricted, but this is not a criticism. Their simplicity makes them extremely straightforward to use, and they often do what they were designed to do effectively. Those coaches that are looking for a digital-first constellation option that doesn't distract with flashy features will find it here.

The more technologically-comfortable coaches may want to adopt some of the more powerful features in the leading whiteboard products, making best use of interfaces directly into video-conferencing platforms and the more advanced graphical effects. For the right client, this might increase immersion and therefore commitment to the coaching process, but the impact of introducing technology on maintaining rapport should not be underestimated.

Options in three dimensions

A more complex application of systemic constellations is to use the power of technology to represent it in three dimensions. Graphics hardware in computers can now recognise three-dimensional environments and incorporate complex elements such as shadows, movement and 360-degree sound. The most advanced computer game engines, often used for creating three-dimensional spaces and objects, can replicate visual elements that make the representation in many ways indistinguishable from video or photographs.

While adding a layer of complexity to the technology, and therefore potentially in the user experience, this additional opportunity for nuance may make it a more attractive option for some coaches and clients. Again, we will look at two examples here.

Coaching constellation tools

As coaches have started to experiment with technology in their coaching, a handful of products have emerged that could be seen as the most natural next step in the evolution of constellations in coaching. The first step was from using the human body in family constellations to using representative objects in tabletop form. The next step was representing this on a screen in top-down fashion, and these tools use a digital version of the tabletop toolkit in three dimensions.

In some of these tools, such as SystemicVR, the user can select a virtual space within which to set up a table on the screen, such as an office space or a clearing in a forest. A coach and client can simultaneously access the same space remotely, and manipulate the screen to move their perspective around the table. They can replicate, resize and move objects, and zoom in to explore the perspectives of different pieces.

Other tools extend those capabilities in an even more immersive fashion, bringing the user's view down to the level of the objects within entirely virtual environments. In these, it is not simply the case that a virtual generic object represents a person or concept in reality. Instead, the object is itself a meaning-carrying item that builds a more fleshed-out metaphor within the tool. For example, a team exploring a metaphorical 'elephant in the room' might represent that with a literal elephant, which inhabits the virtual space between their avatars, preventing them from seeing one another or an object of importance through the screen, increasing the level of emotional buy-in as part of the process.

The power of this sort of software has been demonstrated in therapy interventions for many years (e.g. van Rijn et al., 2015). Through animated avatars and objects that can change their colour and size, individuals can explore their situations in virtual environments through audio-guided solo experiences, exercises can be facilitated for large groups exploring a topic, and coaches can use the tools in 1:1 and team coaching conversations.

More diverse shapes offer more nuanced coaching conversations, particularly when selected based on common metaphors and established psychodrama concepts. Similarly, customised avatars, when added to the landscape, can much more easily take on the persona of the person represented. In some of these tools, each avatar can be accompanied by a word or phrase to capture what they are saying or thinking. They can take on a variety of sizes and animated stances, and smaller heads and shoulders can be added to float around the avatar giving relevant pieces of advice.

Rethinkly, one example of these tools, is intended to offer more than simply the production of a constellation. It offers two landscapes to build in, one of which is a large, blank arena, and the other of which is designed for more elaborate storytelling. This second landscape incorporates several common turns of phrase as permanent fixtures. There's a crossroads, a fork in the road, a small forest with a calm clearing lit by sunlight, in stark contrast with the rest, which sits in the shadow of an imposing fortress. Drystone walls form small areas of grass, and break at the point where a stream flows, widening under a half-formed bridge until it cascades down a long waterfall beneath an isolated tower. In this landscape, a coach and client can do far more than simply construct a systemic constellation. Exercises such as timelines and digital equivalents of chairwork can be played out through objects placed around the landscape, and its nature as a three-dimensional virtual space allows for playful exploration in much more tangible ways than simply visualising, or looking at bland shapes on a screen.

MUVEs

Perhaps a braver option for some coaches would be the use of mainstream MUVEs (multi-user virtual environments). These games are widely available at affordable prices – or free, in many cases – offering vast, virtual spaces that a user can explore, incorporating a range of game elements depending on the product. The important element for coaching is the user interaction. A lot of media attention has historically been focused on a relatively niche game called Second Life, within which a range of learning interventions have been trialled (e.g. Irwin & Coutts, 2015). Other options would be simple browser-based MUVEs that incorporate private spaces for users, such as Cubic Castles, which encourages interaction with the environment, customisation, and creativity, the wildly popular mining/crafting game cunningly named Minecraft, and the highly competitive, adrenalin-fuelled Fortnite.

The high development budgets available to the developers of some of these products mean that their technical capabilities and the user experience can be expected to be much better, although their design as a game needs careful planning by a coach to incorporate in an appropriate way into a coaching session. When a client is already a user of computer games, they are likely to already have access to one or more of these, and feel comfortable using it, where that's unlikely to be the case for something like SystemicVR or Rethinkly.

Playful use of these games within the right coaching context might produce exciting, creative coaching experiences that offer lasting opportunities for transformation. Some coaches and some clients will find them inappropriate in a coaching context, so they should be considered thoughtfully, but incorporating a gaming element could add a dash of something unique. Using the Minecraft environment to construct a constellation, for example, offers the opportunity for gaming elements (such as roaming computer-controlled enemies or neutral characters open to trade) to add something unexpected to the experience. A skilled coach could facilitate a very different sort of coaching conversation using this sort of tool, with moments influenced by events happening in the game.

Managing with sensitivity

Introduce with caution

The increased computing power and capabilities of some of these tools demonstrate how the greatest strength of something is so often also its greatest weakness. While coaching at its heart is a conversation, using these sorts of technology puts the coach in a position where they must also be wearing the hat of technical support, making it an even greater challenge, and adds a potential additional learning curve for the client, which may not be welcome if they are looking to explore a sensitive issue.

For example, a client producing a constellation in Let's Constellate might accidentally release the mouse button a fraction of a second too early while moving a shape. Most users will immediately notice the error and correct it. In one of the arguably more intense three-dimensional options, the same error may lead to an object being placed far off in the distance, creating a number of stray objects in the environment, potentially increasing the client's stress.

This characteristic makes many of the more complex solutions an unattractive addition to the average coaching session, regardless of the potential power they offer. The relative ease of use and familiarity of a slide deck make it much more preferable to the entirely new user interface, language, keyboard shortcuts, possibilities, and nuances of the more advanced technologies.

The rewards of something like Rethinkly can be transformative for a client. The effect of changing perspective, discovering that what one stakeholder can see is dramatically different from another, is difficult to overstate. But if using the tool itself can become an impediment to new insights, a simpler solution should be preferred.

Exercise patience and discipline

Many complex modern technologies include an extensive tutorial experience before the user is offered freedom to use the product as they wish. Given the time constraints on many coaching conversations, this can feel like a factor that prevents their use. A 10–15 minute onboarding exercise can be a significant portion of a 45-minute session, which may not feel productive for the client. Taking the time out for coaching is already a privilege, and investing some of that solely in order to use a particular piece of technology on this one occasion will not feel justified.

The learning curve with some of these technologies should not be understated. The time taken to get a user comfortable to use it is important. Bypassing a robust onboarding process might feel like the right thing to do in some instances in order to accelerate the benefits of the tool, but taking things slowly is the most prudent course of action. This is particularly true if working with a group or a team, where the entire group should adopt the tool at the speed of the least comfortable participant. Under the right circumstances, these tools can be a delightful enabler for transformative conversations, and a single person using the tool who is less than proficient is unfortunately likely to derail the experience for all involved.

In order to get the most from these tools, contracting clearly at the outset how the tool is to be used will help ensure the conversation remains focused and the technology adds the value it is intended to. It is also important to remain playful at all times when using these tools; when a user's mistake or odd technology quirk offers something out of the ordinary, laughter is often a powerful tool to bat the distraction away and return to the topic at hand. For this reason, some coaches may wish to generally avoid this sort of tool when dealing with certain particularly sensitive topics.

Prioritise rapport

New technologies can sometimes feel chaotic, limiting, and disruptive in unhelpful ways. These characteristics are ones that should be avoided in a coaching session. A level of unpredictability can be positive, when managed well – often, the best learning is at the cusp of not knowing – but this practice of managing the experience well becomes extremely important when a layer of technology sits between coach and client.

Acknowledging this, a good rule for a coach to adopt would be to not introduce something like this to a client for the first time without thinking through the logistics in advance. Setting it up in advance of the coaching session is an absolute must, as is getting comfortable enough with the tool to be confident to respond well when issues occur. And when they do occur, the coach should be prioritising maintaining rapport and acting in a way that empowers the client, rather than doing something that confirms a client's limiting assumptions about their lack of ability.

Implications

Constellations exercises have proven to be highly valuable in systemic coaching. By visually representing a client's internal map through objects and arrangements, constellations allow for a unique and holistic understanding of complex systemic dynamics. This approach facilitates the identification of hidden connections, patterns, and interdependencies that might not be apparent through traditional conversation-based coaching techniques alone. The visual nature of constellations creates a tangible representation of the client's internal perception of reality, providing a powerful tool for exploration and insight.

The emergence of digital alternatives has expanded the possibilities for constellation exercises when working remotely. While physical objects and arrangements have been traditionally used, digital tools now offer accessible and convenient options for coaches and clients. Two-dimensional offerings provide digital platforms that replicate the basic functions of physical constellations, allowing for remote and even asynchronous sessions. Three-dimensional virtual environments take the digital experience to a more immersive level, potentially enhancing engagement and understanding.

However, it is crucial to consider several factors when selecting the appropriate tool. Client preferences and comfort with technology play a significant role in determining the effectiveness of the chosen digital alternative. While some individuals might prefer the tactile and physical nature of constellations work when in person, they may not engage as well when working remotely, and *vice versa* for those clients who embrace the convenience and flexibility of digital options. Coaches should assess the client's technological proficiency and preferences, ensuring that any use of these tools aligns with their comfort level and needs to avoid any potential barriers or frustrations during the coaching process.

In addition, the complexity of certain digital tools requires adequate onboarding and proficiency, which should be taken into consideration by coaches when introducing into a coaching relationship. It's essential to strike a balance between making the most of the advantages of digital tools and ensuring that the client's focus remains on the coaching conversation.

Reflective questions

1. How does integrating constellations into a coaching session impact the client's self-awareness and understanding of a system?

2. What ethical considerations should coaches keep in mind when using digital constellation tools?
3. What potential limitations or challenges might arise from the tools outlined in this chapter, and how should a coach navigate them?

Conclusions

A range of digital tools are available as resources for systemic coaching, which should be used to enhance a coaching engagement where appropriate. The arrangement of virtual shapes, objects, and avatars offers the chance for deeper insights, alternative perspectives, and an exploration of systemic dynamics. While constellations have traditionally been conducted using physical objects, the emergence of digital options has expanded the possibilities for digital coaches. Easily accessible tools provide accessible digital alternatives, while more complex technologies offer more immersive and transformative experiences, although the client's skill level, preferences, and familiarity with technology should be considered when selecting the appropriate tool. Ultimately, maintaining rapport and understanding the client's needs remain essential in leveraging the potential of these tools effectively, and they should not be used at all if these would be negatively affected.

References

Disterheft, A., Pijetlovic, D., & Müller-Christ, G. (2021). On the road of discovery with systemic exploratory constellations: Potentials of online constellation exercises about sustainability transitions. *Sustainability*, 13(9), 5101.

Grant, A. M. (2015). Coaching the brain: Neuro-science or neuro-nonsense? *The Coaching Psychologist*, 11(1), 31–37.

Hawkins, P., & Turner, E. (2021). *Systemic coaching: Delivering value beyond the individual*. London: Routledge.

Irwin, P., & Coutts, R. (2015). A systematic review of the experience of using second life in the education of undergraduate nurses. *Journal of Nursing Education*, 54(10), 572–577.

Isaacson, S. (2021). *How to thrive as a coach in a digital world: Coaching with technology*. Maidenhead: McGraw-Hill – Open University Press.

Isaacson, S. (2022). *Superhuman coaching: Ten technologies that expand coaching beyond what's humanly possible*. London: Hanwell Publishing.

Lawrence, P. (2019). What is systemic coaching? *Philosophy of Coaching: An International Journal*, 4, 35–52.

Mahr, A. (1998). *Ein Plädoyer für's Innehalten—Systemische Familienaufstellungen bei Trennung und Scheidung*.

Tompkins, P., & Lawley, J. (2000). *Metaphors in mind: Transformation through symbolic modelling*. London: Developing Company Press.

van Rijn, B. (2015). Avatar-based therapy within prison settings: Pilot evaluation. *British Journal of Guidance & Counselling*, 45(3), 268–283. https://doi.org/10.1080/03069885.2015.1068273

Viedma & Hermkens. (online). Retrieved on 3 September 2023 from https://onlinefields.net/

Whittington, J. (2020). *Systemic coaching and constellations: An introduction to the principles, practices and application* (3rd ed.). London: Kogan Page.

Chapter 10

Technologies for VR coaching

Andrew Strange and Sam Isaacson

Introduction

The visions of the future created for us (and the technology used to create those visions, for that matter) in films such as Avatar (2009) and Minority Report (2002), are in part realities, but how useful are some of these developments in immersive technology, and how important are they to a coach now and in the near-term future? Short of guaranteeing a one-size-fits-all answer to that question, we can state that as immersive technologies increase in adoption by users and by those developing other technologies, the coach who develops a solid understanding of what constitutes a usable and viable immersive technology toolkit will be better positioned to serve their clients over the longest term. This chapter is intended as an introduction to the current and near-term possibilities for the inclusion of so-called metaverse technologies in coaching. The pace of innovation is constantly ahead of user acceptance and adoption, while the pace of change risks chapters such as this sounding outdated within months.

Definitions

A good place to start will be to define terms like 'collaborative immersive working' and conclude what the media means when it describes the 'metaverse'. This way, we can begin to get an idea about how coaches can take advantage of the virtual worlds available.

The majority of people have not tried using a virtual reality (VR) or mixed reality (MR) headset, but many have at least experienced augmented reality (AR) using a hand-held device such as a smartphone or tablet, in the form of photo filters, for example. All of these approaches form part of the spectrum of immersive technologies, in which the user experiences digital content in a three-dimensional, 360-degree manner, either in addition to (in the case of AR and MR) or entirely separate from (VR) physical reality (see Table 10.1). In using immersive technologies, most people report that the experience of accepting it as real is rapid and compelling, even when cognitively it is clear that it is not. In short, these technologies are true to the concept of 'immersion'.

In more detail, VR is an occluded experience using a headset or wearable device where 3D content is provided separately to each eye creating a depth of vision which conjures up a sense of being immersed in the digital environment. Volumetric sound (surround sound that is projected digitally from locations within the 3D space) which accompanies

DOI: 10.4324/9781003383741-13

Table 10.1 Technology definitions

Virtual reality	VR is the term used for computer-generated 3D environments which are presented using head-worn computer devices that occlude the physical world, enabling the user to explore and interact with the content. True VR is created using two different content streams, one presented to each eye, thus creating depth of perception so that the user has a sense of being immersed in the digital experience. VR content can be 3D generated or filmic, interactive or passive, and can be a personal experience or shared by many users connecting to the same digital environment across a network.
Augmented reality	AR is computer-generated content presented through devices including smart phones, tablets, computers, and head-worn devices as an overlay on top of real-world content accessed through a camera. The capabilities of AR are the same as those of VR, although the lack of occlusion prevents the virtual transportation of users to entirely digital environments.
Mixed reality	MR (sometimes referred to as extended reality, or XR) is a combination of VR and AR presented using head-worn devices, benefiting from the VR occluded experience in which the viewer is in a virtual world, as well as making use of 'pass though' cameras that present the real world in digital form, with the option of AR content being included.

the 3D visual experience completes the feeling of being within the content that is being presented, rather than just looking at it.

AR is the term given to the provision of 3D content to mobile phones and tablets that appears on the user's screen on top of the real world that is already visible through it, in other words reality has been 'augmented'. In this way, AR is a scalable experience immersing the user in possibilities that extend beyond what's real to include the unreal. MR is a hybrid experience of both AR and VR, in which the technology allows a user to access the visuals of the physical world through cameras built into the device.

We will return to talking about wearable immersive devices for 3D content, but for now imagine VR/AR/MR bringing coaches and clients together in a collaborative immersive digital environment in which the coaching conversation takes place as it would in person, but with the added benefits of access to digital content and without the disbenefits that are experienced using video conferencing. The big question to be answered is: Could this be better than meeting face-to-face or via video accompanied by more traditional web and app tools? While in one sense the answer to that question is likely to turn out to be along the lines of 'Not better, but different', anecdotal evidence would suggest that those who have experienced meeting using immersive technologies tend to say that the adoption of collaborative immersive technologies for working is only a matter of time. At the time of writing, certain circumstances act as blockers for adoption, including cost perception, technology interoperability, and social acceptance. The development of consumer devices will accelerate this, as will further development of so-called metaverse platforms alongside increasingly fast connectivity.

The metaverse is sometimes presented in the media as a fully-formed immersive digital wonderland to include virtual locations and digital content, but this is a bit misleading. The metaverse is a term that in reality describes a collection of somewhat diverse platforms and technology which isn't yet integrated or at all seamless. The idea of the metaverse as a parallel digital universe along the lines of a 3D experience of the internet is simply false. While competing technology companies are developing immersive 3D content the metaverse remains nothing more than a concept without the development of a more reliable technology backbone.

But the building blocks of the metaverse are sufficiently in place to provide an appropriate toolkit for the innovative coach. It is now possible to gain access to fast connectivity, wearable devices such as suitable and comfortable headsets and smart-glasses designed for collaborative immersive content, as well as cloud computing and content platforms. These technologies and devices are accessible to those with a desire to use them, with new developments emerging each year.

Science of VR for coaching

An expanding body of research provides evidence for the effectiveness of immersive technologies for enhancing a learning experience in terms of the subjective experience and objective outcomes. Studies demonstrate advantages in learning, recollection, motivation, emotional connection, communication, confidence, and focus when using immersive technologies.

Immersion in VR has been shown to elicit feelings of awe in users, which can in turn lead to increased openness to personal growth and development (Quesnel & Riecke, 2018). VR scenarios deliver highly engaging multi-sensory experiences that capture attention and concentration for learning in a way that books or screens cannot match. Immersive VR scenarios also generate greater emotional intensity which strengthens memory through triggering release of neurotransmitters like dopamine and norepinephrine (Felnhofer et al., 2015).

Particularly against the backdrop of a day-to-day experience of back-to-back video calls, an experience using immersive technologies is much more likely to lead to strong memories. More than that, it's more likely to lead to action. One piece of research, for example, which showed the effects of climate change on coral reefs, increased the likelihood that participants would donate to charity (Nelson et al., 2020).

Research on VR training for skills like public speaking has shown large improvements in factors like memorisation, delivery, and confidence following rehearsal in VR versus traditional methods (Freeman et al., 2017). Practising skills in immersive environments boosts real-world performance more than discussing or visualising an application of it, or even roleplaying the skill in the physical world.

Investigations into the use of VR in coaching have revealed increased levels of non-verbal communication, in particular gesticulation, when compared to video calls (Isaacson, 2021). This helps establish rapport and further cements the likelihood of retained memories; gesticulation positively impacts on learning (Novack & Goldin-Meadow, 2015). VR has even been shown as an effective way to deliver an embodied experience of the empty chair technique (Pugh et al., 2021).

Overall, empirical evidence strongly supports the notion that immersive technologies, in particular VR, offer advantages in activating more of users' mental and emotional capabilities, establishing psychological presence, filling experience gaps, rehearsing realistic scenarios, and enabling new modes of communication and interaction for impactful coaching.

Technological features and capabilities

A range of technological hardware and software features enable uniquely impactful learning and development experiences through immersive technologies. These capabilities combine to create the sense of presence and immersion that makes experiences in immersive technologies resonate at a deeper level than other modalities.

Headsets

To visualise 3D environments, VR headsets feature separate high-resolution displays for each eye with lenses that focus the images and create depth of perception. When accompanied by high refresh rates, users experience smooth, comfortable motion as they move their heads. Headsets rely on extensive technology to accurately track the position and orientation of the user's head in order to render the correct 3D perspective, and range from mobile designs that connect to smartphones or operate using their own connectivity, to tethered designs powered by high-end gaming PCs.

Hand controllers

Natural interaction in VR requires accurate tracking of users' hands and fingers. Advanced controllers feature 6 degrees of freedom allowing precise positioning combined with buttons and triggers for input. Rumble haptic feedback imbues actions like selecting objects with tactile realism, while in some cases hand and finger tracking eliminates the need for controllers entirely, and opens up opportunities for realistic hand gestures and nonverbal communication, including sign language.

Avatars

To give users realistic forms, VR platforms incorporate customisable avatars that the user 'steps into' in the digital environment. With AI-powered generation of natural motion and expressions, connected in some cases to cameras that track the user's own facial expressions, avatars present a believable digital alternative to video, boosting the sense of togetherness and psychological presence between coach and client.

Spatial audio

Positional 3D audio completes the immersive experience by simulating sounds coming from locations around the user in the virtual space. The immersive experience can benefit from large gatherings where participants can connect and speak most clearly to those closest to them, while an administrator maintains the ability to control the volume of their own speech regardless of location.

Content sharing and collaboration

VR platforms enable live content sharing and collaboration, which is most helpful for team coaching. This includes features like voice chat, gestural annotation, virtual whiteboards, file sharing, and screen sharing. Multiple modes of communication and content interaction enhance the ability to co-create, discuss ideas, and share insights within VR coaching sessions.

In summary, current VR systems incorporate a robust set of capabilities and features that enable potent coaching experiences that extend beyond the boundaries of physical reality while maintaining high levels of realism, embodiment, and human connection. These technological foundations will continue advancing to power new possibilities for virtual coaching.

Potential use cases

Immersive technologies open up a diverse range of potential use cases that can enhance coaching engagement, outcomes, and impact. Within the realm of immersive technologies being used as a tool to conduct remote meetings, the business case should already be clear; the practice of coaching should always change in response to changing attitudes towards and adoption of technology (Isaacson, 2021). This is strengthened in the case of team coaching, where the benefits of space, collaborative technologies, focused attention, and breakout groups using spatial audio are all self-evident to any practising team coach who has tried delivering this using video.

There are, however, unique opportunities for coaches to use VR in individual development. Examples of VR coaching use cases with particularly high potential include the following:

Public speaking and high-pressure conversations

Virtual training platforms allow clients to practise high-stakes speeches and presentations with full VR simulations of the actual physical venues, audiences, and environmental conditions. This preparation builds self-efficacy and confidence before actual events, so is helpful in and of itself, and some applications go even further. In addition to a coach providing live support and challenge through feedback and high-quality questions, statistics can be generated to show the user's eye contact and make observations based on language and tone of voice. Immersive simulations in VR also enable clients to safely rehearse and prepare for crucial conversations like contract negotiations, performance reviews, and termination discussions. Realistic practice reduces anxiety and supports the client in preparing for the consequences of their actions.

Perspective taking

VR embodiment experiences let clients literally view situations from someone else's perspective. This can be quite literal, taking on the character of another person while they experience a situation, increasing the likelihood of the client gaining empathy and insights for reducing bias, for example. It can also support in the use case of high-pressure conversations as described above; by taking the place of the character the user has just provided feedback to in a performance review, for example, the client gets to experience themselves, increasing in self-awareness.

In a more abstract sense, a client could create a 'metaphor landscape' and explore it from various different perspectives, increasing their understanding of a situation from different stakeholders' perspectives and gaining the ability to gain, in a very real sense, a bird's-eye view. The advantages of this powerful tool in a coaching setting could include improving cross-cultural communication, resolving conflicts, and enhancing diversity.

Remote meetings

Perhaps the most enticing of all use cases for immersive technologies in coaching is simply as a like-for-like replacement of the video call for remote coaching. Some VR meeting platforms offer a series of different meeting spaces designed to meet specific needs. One might be a basic environment, ideal for 1:1 conversations, while others might include workshop areas with whiteboards and small group areas already set up, others still might lend themselves to presentations, while others have a dozen chairs positioned around a board table.

Within a tool like this, a user can create and customise their own avatar, presenting themselves as a digital version of how they appear in person, offering an opportunity to express their creativity and/or embrace the opportunity of presenting themselves in a way they think might be more widely accepted visually. Some platforms offer capabilities like performing handshakes with tactile feedback ('haptics') through a VR device's controllers.

The sorts of tools typically on offer in these platforms lend themselves well to a technology-enhanced coaching experience. Accessible through a hidden menu (often accessible through a virtual wristwatch or toolbelt), the coach can access the central user interface, including objects like 3D pens, laser pointers and object creators and manipulators. Users can often access sticky notes, files, an in-app camera, and a web browser. Notes and virtual photos can be exported and either used within the 3D space, or attached to emails and file sharing services.

The key characteristics a coach might be looking for in a platform they might want to consider adopting would be the following:

- **Immersive experience:** Step one would be to find a platform that offers a truly immersive experience, allowing a coach and client to feel like they are in the same space together.
- **Customisation:** Many platforms have been designed with specific use cases in mind, such as for casual gaming or formal workplaces. The ideal platform would be one that allows a coach to create virtual spaces and avatars that reflect their personal style and add the most value to a coaching relationship.
- **Multi-platform integration:** With such a wide range of VR systems becoming available, and coaches and clients making use of other technologies such as Microsoft 365, intentionally looking for platforms designed for integration will make it more straightforward to connect with colleagues and clients working across different systems.
- **Collaboration tools:** Some of the key advantages of working in VR come in the form of collaboration tools that make it easy to work together in more creative ways while staying connected. This includes video conferencing, screen sharing, and document sharing.

As these examples illustrate, VR platforms expand possibilities for experiential learning and development in coaching engagements by leveraging embodied cognition, replicating contexts, and producing presence. Creative coaches can identify many additional valuable use cases across individual, team, and organisational relationships.

Implementation challenges

As with any new technology, adopting VR in coaching also poses challenges to effective implementation. While the core technology components are now readily accessible, practical realities around cost, capability, policies, spaces, and perceptions exist. Potential solutions involve starting small, learning rapidly, and communicating benefits.

Pricing

Though consumer VR hardware costs have dropped significantly, the upfront investment and ongoing licensing costs range from hundreds to thousands of dollars per user, particularly at enterprise level. Development of custom VR environments and applications introduces further costs. Starting with small pilot projects and slowly expanding capacity over time can provide a level of control, and as consumer adoption increases, the appetite for VR will likely overtake being put off by price.

Learning curve

While many VR platforms are inherently far more intuitive than the computer keyboard or mouse were when they were first introduced, becoming proficient with this new technology requires training time for both coach and client. Coaches should be prepared to get comfortable using the technology before using it in live situations with a client, so getting prepared before the first request comes through would be wise for many. Starting with simple use cases, allowing practice time, and feeling equipped to provide technical support to the client will help in reducing learning barriers and increasing adoption, as will approaching VR as an ongoing collaborative experiment.

Privacy

The use of any sort of technology introduces concerns around confidentiality, security, and privacy. The sort of data used in VR includes user movement, gestures, and video and audio recordings. Comprehensive data privacy and ethics policies will need to be in place to ensure adherence to regulations, and of course the importance of confidentiality in any coaching context is difficult to overstate. Anonymisation, client consent and control, secure storage, and data destruction protocols will help to mitigate these issues.

Accessibility

While improving, VR use still poses challenges for users with mobility, visual, or other disabilities. As the technology improves, those with additional access needs will be served more fully, but there will always be barriers to universal adoption. Coaches should bear this in mind, putting effort into incorporating appropriate additional hardware and software as required to allow universal access where possible.

Session flow

The technical overhead of donning gear, adjusting settings, and entering/exiting VR can introduce greater levels of disruption in the flow of coaching, whether this happens at the beginning and end of a session or partway through. Preset configurations, quick adjustments, and automation will help to minimise friction, but until these gain wider adoption coaches will need to build in tolerances to compensate for this lost time.

Stigma

Perhaps the biggest blocker at the time of writing is negative stigma or perceptions about VR that might cause reluctance among some clients, and indeed among some coaches. Communicating benefits, ensuring ease of use, and giving clients control can overcome reservations, but the biggest impact is likely to come from positive word-of-mouth recommendations as adoption increases.

Addressing these concerns head-on, starting small to build experience, and iterating on policies and processes, will enable long-term success with the implementation of VR in coaching.

Reflective questions

1. Which clients, coaching topics, or other circumstances would benefit from an immersive experience more than 2D video calling or an in-person experience?
2. What skills does the coach need to develop in order to make these environments work for optimum benefit for their clients?
3. What reasons would a coach have to persuade a client to use immersive technologies in their coaching?

Conclusions

Immersive technologies, in particular VR, offer new potential to increase the impact of coaching engagements by enabling powerful experiential learning experiences, expansive practice environments, and strong psychological presence between coach and client. VR offers measurable improvements in factors like learning, recollection, motivation, focus, communication, confidence, and performance when using VR tools.

Creative application allows coaches to meet a much wider range of learning and development needs through immersive simulations and perspective taking. VR expands possibilities for coaching individuals and teams by transcending distances and physical limitations.

Practical challenges exist that must be proactively identified and managed, especially at larger scales. But early disciplined experimentation and small steps can enable coaches to confidently build VR capabilities and best practices over time.

Thoughtful implementation and use cases tailored to coaching goals will allow immersive VR tools to enhance relationships, deepen experiences, and widen impact. While still a nascent area, VR represents a profoundly transformative platform for the future of coaching. Coaches owe it to their clients to explore and embrace its possibilities.

References

Browning, M., Deca, D., Javitt, D. C., Keshavan, M. S., Sabuncu, M. R., Meyer-Lindenberg, A., Raheja, A., Bergen, K., Salti, M., & Windhorst, U. (2021). Higher cortical activation with virtual reality versus conventional video during fMRI: A systematic review and meta-analysis. *PLOS Biology, 19*(8), e3001220.

Felnhofer, A., Kothgassner, O. D., Schmidt, M., Heinzle, A. K., Beutl, L., Hlavacs, H., & Kryspin-Exner, I. (2015). Is virtual reality emotionally arousing? Investigating five emotion inducing virtual park scenarios. *International Journal of Human-Computer Studies, 82*, 48–56.

Freeman, D., Reeve, S., Robinson, A., Ehlers, A., Clark, D., Spanlang, B., & Slater, M. (2017). Virtual reality in the assessment, understanding, and treatment of mental health disorders. *Psychological Medicine, 47*(14), 2393–2400.

Isaacson, S. (2021). *How to thrive as a coach in a digital world: Coaching with technology.* Maidenhead: McGraw Hill-Open University Press.

Nelson, K. M., Anggraini, E., & Schlüter, A. (2020). Virtual reality as a tool for environmental conservation and fundraising. *PloS One, 15*(4), e0223631.

Novack, M., & Goldin-Meadow, S. (2015). Learning from gesture: How our hands change our minds. *Educational Psychology Review, 27*, 405–412.

Pugh, M., Bell, T., & Dixon, A. (2021). Delivering tele-chairwork: A qualitative survey of expert therapists. *Psychotherapy Research, 31*(7), 843–858.

Quesnel, D., & Riecke, B. E. (2018). Are you awed yet? How virtual reality gives us awe and goose bumps. *Frontiers in Psychology, 9*, 2158.

Chapter 11

Technologies in reflective practice

Clare Beckett-McInroy, Benita Stafford-Smith, and Michelle Lucas

Introduction

Technology pervades almost all elements of our life and work – as a digital coach or supervisor, technology influences and impacts how a client may be assigned, how we connect, the ways we engage, and so forth. Here we consider how technology is currently influencing our reflective practice. The chapter starts with a consideration of why reflective practice is important and we define the range of activities that constitute reflective practice. With coaching supervision being a relatively new field, and an under-researched area in relation to our use of technology, we engaged in a small research study. The research focused on the current experiences of coaches and supervisors in using technology in their reflective practice.

Reflective practice in context?

When working as a coach we enter into a position of privilege, as our clients share with us their successes, challenges, and innermost thoughts. In this way we enable our clients to speak their truth, sometimes for the first time and often for the first time in the presence of another. The coaching relationship is a complex one. Through training we learn how to work in a non-directive manner, allowing the client to create their own solutions. However, if we imagine the coach is without influence, we would be mistaken. Where do our questions come from? What ways do we choose which words to reflect back? What represents listening with neutrality? How can we be sure we are processing our client's words from their map of the world and not ours? Can we genuinely work without having a vested interest in our client's success? What ways do we ensure we are 'fit for purpose'? What ways do we benchmark our practice? The quick answer to these questions is 'we don't know', or at least it is hard to be certain.

This is where reflective practice becomes pertinent. During a single coaching session, the coach receives multiple pieces of information – verbal and non-verbal. Some of this will be held in conscious awareness (that which is chosen to work with or not), some will be located just outside awareness (ingrained habits, preferences and biases), and some will be prompted from unconscious processes (through transference and countertransference). If practitioners are to work in service of clients, their stakeholders, and wider systems, there is a need to slow down, review choice points where decisions on how to act and how to be (or how not do and how not be) were made.

DOI: 10.4324/9781003383741-14

What is reflective practice?

Reflective practice is the art form of slowing down to deliberately contemplate our professional work. It is more than musing, it requires deliberate attention. It has been defined by Butler (2023) as "an iterative, open-ended, creative process, where we take deliberate conscious time to explore and interrogate our practice in a systematic and systemic way. This enables us to adapt what we do and consider how we might develop our future practice, in service of our stakeholders".

Often 'reflective practice' is identified as written journaling or sketching, but it is much more than that. Reflection can be achieved through any of our processing preferences – writing, thinking, speaking, seeing, hearing, touching, imagining, experiencing, through art, poetry, stories, and metaphors… Each practitioner can evolve their own way of doing this creatively, through processes and for positive impact (Beckett-McInroy & Baba, 2022; Lucas, 2023). Reflective practice enables the coach to gain insight into their work by thinking analytically and creatively about any element of it. Reflective practice can be undertaken independently, one-to-one or with others. When it is performed with others the coach enters into the domain of 'supervision'. Supervision is often considered a relatively new aspect of practice and there is a need for wider understanding of it (Joseph, 2016). Supervision can take place with a professionally trained and/or accredited supervisor(s) or it can be done with fellow coaches, or 'peer supervision'. Table 11.1 describes some of the pros and cons of each configuration.

Table 11.1 Pros and cons of different types of reflective practice

Types of reflective practice	Pros	Cons
Independent Reflection ('self-supervision')	• Accessible • Timely • Zero cost	• Easy to de-prioritise • Cannot see one's own blind spots • Self-support and self-challenge may be difficult
Individual Supervision	• More able to explore work In depth • Greater sense of psychological safety • Focus solely on own supervision topics	• Fewer perspectives • May be experienced as intense • Cost implications
Group Supervision	• Increased perspectives • Accelerated learning through working with scenarios from other coaches • Lower cost	• Potentially less depth • Group dynamics need to be managed effectively • Different perspectives from peers may confuse rather than illuminate
Professional Supervision	• More comprehensive • Supports professionalisation of practice (e.g., accreditation or credentialing)	• Price as a potential barrier to entry • Formal commitment
Peer Supervision	• More accessible • Can appear safer • Typically exchange is in time rather than money	• Danger of developmental stagnation • Susceptible to collusion • Possible reluctance to reveal development areas with peers

When considering what reflective practice is, it is tempting to see it as 'reflection', or the act of looking back on something. While 'looking back' is undoubtedly the most well-known type of reflective practice, this is only one lens used in the art of reflective practice. Taking a chronological perspective, the following four types of reflection can be identified:

(1) Reflection for action – preparation and planning for the work. This idea was articulated by Thompson and Thompson (2018) and the phrase 'pre-flection' was coined by Falk (1995).
(2) Reflection in action – considering in the moment, what is occurring and adjusting what to do next, in light of that consideration. This term was first coined by Schön (1983).
(3) Reflection on action – this is what is commonly understood as reflection, reviewing something that has occurred in order to understand it more fully or observe it with more neutrality. This term was also coined by Schön (1983).
(4) Reflection with action – using observations to prompt a change in behaviour and/or to learn alongside others. This term was coined by Ghaye (2010).

For practitioner development, one way to calculate mastery is counting the number of hours of client delivery. However, will the one-hundredth hour of delivery necessarily be any better than the first? What is the breadth and depth of experience? Is practice moving forward with research in the field? Through engaging in reflective practice it is possible to notice over time changes to practise and to self-awareness. Further, through reflective practice with others, practitioners may calibrate performance, sometimes enhanced through 360 'feedforward' (Goldsmith, 2015), using information to positively impact future practice. This can help raise awareness of strengths (that could be taken for granted or reside in unconscious awareness) and development areas (that might have been missed) and in so doing prompt continuous improvement. Our position is that developing a sustainable reflective practice is important for practitioners' growth whatever their discipline, stage of development, and the field they work in.

How does technology influence reflective practice?

Through a series of enquiries (online survey, focus group, and semi-structured interviews) the authors engaged 36 supervisors and coaches to share what they knew about this question through their own and their supervisee's practices. While the sample is small it reflects a cross-section of the global coaching supervision community and therefore offers insight into current practice.

The first insight was the lack of a common language for the use of technology in coaching. We defined CoachTech (see Table 11.2) as "[including] connection tools, digital white boards, art generating tools through artificial intelligence, multisensory enablement, reflection tools such as digital card decks, plus virtual reality options".

Connecting and communicating using coaching technology

The research highlighted a paradox in practitioners' current relationship with technology. For some practices, such as email, communicating with clients via email is such

Table 11.2 What's included in CoachTech

Artificial intelligence: Artificial intelligence (AI) refers to technologies that perform tasks that used to require human intelligence such as autocorrect on mobile phones or navigation applications that can direct people to a certain place. Generative AI creates new content that require creative human-like content including images, audio, code, video or narrative, "in response to... complex and varied prompts (e.g., languages, instructions, questions)" (Lim et al., 2023) based upon what has been previously learnt while affective computing tools can recognise, interpret, and simulate human emotions.

Immersive technologies: Technologies including 3D graphics engines, virtual reality (VR), and augmented reality (AR) all offer approaches that allow a user to interact with a digital environment that is separate from, or overlaid onto, the physical world. VR devices, for example, have been practically used in the medical field and technical settings of business enterprises. Use in supervision remains experimental (Roxo and Brito, 2018) through, for example, seeing landscapes while hearing the supervisor. Immersive tools allow for creative ways to supervise through, for example, sound and vision, which can support self-awareness while enhancing 'future self' exploration (Passarelli, 2015).

Tracking progress: From tracking supervision hours to progress with goals and encouragement in achieving them (Joseph, 2016), there are numerous tools to support such needs allowing access anywhere and anytime such as generic tools (e.g., Slack, Mural Google Docs), and tools designed specifically for coaches (e.g., Coaching.com, Delenta, Paperbell).

Virtual supervision and screen sharing: Shown to be as effective as face-to-face, in relation to coaching research (Welsh, 2019), supervision can take place online live through a number of video-conferencing tools including Microsoft Teams, Zoom, and Google Meet, while presentation software and digital white boards can be shared.

Digital picture cards: Photographic or artwork picture cards can help to inspire meaningful supervision conversations interactively with multiple users to access through, for example, DeckHive where images can be used for reflection metaphorically, where random words can be experimented with, or where models become interactive.

Creative writing and analysis tools: From mind mapping (Buzan and Buzan, 1993) to storyboarding, there are a number of tools to support writing. Applications also exist that can rapidly analyse and highlight significant moments in a coaching or supervision session allowing for learning through deepening self-awareness, identifying ineffective habits and exploring options for future practice.

an embedded practice that it is no longer noticed as 'technology'. While the majority of those surveyed used some kind of video-conferencing software for communication on a regular basis, around a third claimed to 'never' use it. Practitioners highlighted both positives and negative experiences of technology: 'reading signals is more difficult' and 'human connection is reduced', while participants also noticed its environmental and time efficiency benefits.

Those who were reluctant to use technology in their practice saw coaching and supervision as intimate professional relationships, where presence is an essential capacity. They reported concerns that the practitioner's presence would be temporarily lost (managing the technology becomes the focus of attention rather than the dialogue) or, in the extreme, 'given' to the technology (using an app to do something the practitioner has typically done). This perspective is perhaps fed by 2020 media concern with the rise of AI and its possible effect on the profession.

While research is still scant about the user's relationship with artificial intelligence, Terblanche and Cilliers (2020) reveal some interesting findings about trust. Specifically, they found that when looking at usage uptake, trust may not be as important as the perceived usefulness of the chatbot. Three factors were found to be statistically significant determinants of Behavioural Intent (i.e., likelihood of using the chatbot), namely Performance Expectancy, i.e., what they gained from using the chatbot coach, Social Influence, i.e., users care about what other people (whom they know) think about the chatbot, and Attitude, i.e., the positive or negative feelings a user has about using the chatbot coach. While practical security issues such as ensuring firewalls and virus protection is effective and up to date, were identified as important, Terblanche and Cilliers found that these factors may be overlooked by the users when the chatbot is perceived to help them achieve their goals. We wondered if the coach and coach supervisor emphasis on 'presence' may be overstated?

Developments in technology provide new opportunities for understanding the role of, and improving, communication "in the process of building relationships" (Cameron et al., 2015 in Martin et al., 2017). Similarly, coaching technology can also be an aid to supporting brainstorms (Pretorius, 2023) and improving communication. However, the research findings on coaching and chatbots bring forth further questions for supervision. Initial research indicates coaching chatbot sessions work well in simple goal-oriented sessions (Terblanche et al., 2022). Lucas (2017) contrasts the goal-oriented nature of coaching with the more exploratory and open-ended nature of coaching supervision; from this perspective would a chatbot supervisor be as effective?

Our research for this chapter (Beckett-McInroy & Stafford-Smith, 2023) highlighted that how technology is used to facilitate communication has become a matter for contracting. A clear theme emerged around the frustration when clients or supervisees engaged in multi-tasking. This was highlighted by Martin et al. (2017). While greater online working has generally led to a greater tolerance of wider life interruptions (doorbells) and distractions (pets and household members coming into view) agreeing appropriate boundaries and flexibility is needed. Clarifying what constitutes acceptable multi-tasking is a contracting issue. For example, while typing notes on a tablet is ok, surfing the internet is not? Some training applications of video technology track participants' attention level – here, gaining informed consent would be an explicit matter for the contract. The length and use of silences was also noticed by coaches and supervisors. Agreeing ways of working was particularly important for groups, for example, clarifying what is the 'speaking etiquette', i.e., using (or not using) the mute button this extended to other process styles, for example, turn taking.

Reflecting using coaching technology

In a world of 'busy', entering into a state of mind which is optimal for reflection cannot be assumed. Wright (2009) identifies the importance of 'clearing' which she defined as the "useful habit of clearing the chatter in the mind". This is an area where technology could enable 'clearing' prior to reflective practice through the numerous mindfulness apps which are available.

In terms of other technology within supervision, digital whiteboards and shared drives were most frequently cited. The benefits of integrating these coaching technologies into reflective practice included supporting pre-flection, increasing creativity and the value of technology for visual thinkers. Isaacson (2022) also noted that coaching technology could evoke curiosity, specifically that it could "catalyse... new ways of thinking, provoke some experimentation". Participants noticed that working this way can be "modelled in supervision and then the supervisee can use with their clients". There were multiple positive experiences of creative online constellations and of using images of landscapes in group supervision. This is consistent with the finding of Beckett-McInroy and Baba (2022) who report how with groups and with dispersed teams these approaches can help knowledge in our systems emerge.

Our research also highlighted the use of shadow consulting (Schrodee, 1974) where the supervisor supports an individual, pair, or team of consultants to play back parts of their work and 'observe' communication patterns. This can also be done through 'trigger tapes' where snippets of recorded sessions are reviewed independently or shared with a supervisor. This brought into the discussion the value of supervision for consultants as well as coaches, which was also noted by Hawkins, Turner and Passmore (2019), and Birch and de Haan (2021).

The continual developments in technology has meant that it is becoming not only a confusing but also a crowded space. Each new tool requires a practitioner to upskill and then use it on a regular basis to help retain the learning. Constant innovation and change may be contributing to inhibition by coaches and supervisors from integrating coaching technology tools into their reflective practices.

As new coaching technology solutions enter the market most of them acquire new users through complementary or open access versions. But as the technology develops paid options appear with greater functionality. However, this brings social disadvantage (Lim et al., 2023) as not all practitioners in a global community are in a position to purchase these versions. There may also be bias propagation, as AI tools have been shown to reiterate biases present in the dataset (European Union Agency for Fundamental Rights, 2022), potentially reinforcing bias. Care thus needs to be taken in considering ethical aspects of use, as well as functionality.

What do digital coaches reflect upon?

In reflecting on the responses to our research we drew on the three functions of Proctor's Clinical Supervision Model (2008) (see Table 11.3). The Formative/Educative function of supervision is about experiential learning, professional and skills development, and understanding of one's own abilities through reflection. The Restorative/Supportive function of supervision considers the development of supportive relationships with supervisor to help practitioners deal with the emotional impact of their work. The Normative/Managerial function of supervision draws attention to the professional and organisational standards and need for competence and accountability. This function intends to help practitioners meet ethical guidelines, to manage risk and to work with ambiguous challenges.

As supervisors, some of the issues that we anticipated that digital coaches would bring (AI matching; rapport building; shorter more frequent sessions; coach switching) were not mentioned, while other themes were more dominant. However, this is a changing space and themes in early 2020, may change as we progress through the 2020's and different and more AI tools become available.

Table 11.3 What digital coaches bring to supervision, using Proctor's three functions of supervision

Formative/Educative	Restorative/Supportive	Normative/Managerial
• Deepening coaching presence • Working systemically • Identifying parallel processes • Being with not knowing • Resourcing (models, tools, techniques) • Letting go of mentoring habits • Working with a co-team coach	• Reflective practice (including pre-flection) • Imposter syndrome • Objective perspectives on own work • Stepping into authority • Networking • Social/emotional health • Patterns and themes across cases • Addressing conflicting needs of stakeholders • 'Difficult' coaching sessions	• Cleaner contracting • Co-delivering group coaching • Providing feedback • Ethical issues such as confidentiality • When to refer a client to a different type of professional

Reflective questions

1. What inhibits and encourages your adoption of technology into your reflective practice?
2. What similarities and differences do you notice in what digital and 'analogue' coaches bring to supervision and/or reflective practice?
3. What support do you need from professional bodies to ensure you can adopt coaching technology into your reflective practice in an ethical and sustainable way?

Conclusion

Coaching technology has the potential to extend and improve reflective practice. However, despite the normalisation of technology in both professional and domestic lives, in the context of reflective practice, there is currently a noticeable reluctance for the rapid adoption of coaching technology. It is anticipated that the growth of coaching technology will continue to expand during the 2020s and 2030s. Yet, is it possible or even desirable to integrate technology into reflective practice? Lancefield (2019) infers practitioners need to consider whether their adoption of coaching technology is a gimmick or an operational tool in service of our clients. If it is to be the latter, then what do practitioners need to do to navigate this journey with enthusiasm and professionalism?

References

Beckett-McInroy, C. E., & Baba, S. (2022). *Creative reflective practice: Global perspectives for critical reflection on professional experiences.* Bahrain: Beckett-McInroy Publishing.
Beckett-McInroy, C. E., & Stafford-Smith, B. (2023). *CoachTech in coaching supervision.* Unpublished Research.

Birch, D., & De Haan, E. (2021). Supervision for organization consultants and the organizations they work with. *Consulting Psychology Journal, 73*(3), 214–228.

Butler, H. (2023). The territory of reflective practice. In M. Lucas (Ed.), *Creating the reflective habit* (pp. 4–24). Abingdon: Routledge.

Buzan, T., & Buzan, B. (1993). *The mind mapping book: Radiant thinking – The major evolution in human thought.* London: BBC Books.

Cameron, M., Ray, R., & Sabesan, S. (2015). Remote supervision of medical training via video-conference in northern Australia: A qualitative study of perspectives of supervisors and trainees. *BMJ Open, 5*, e006444.

European Union Agency for Fundamental Rights. (2022). *Bias in algorithms – Artificial intelligence and discrimination.* Luxembourg: Office of the European Union.

Falk, D. (1995). Preflection: A strategy for enhancing reflection. *Evaluation/Reflection, 22*, 13. https://digitalcommons.unomaha.edu/slceeval/22

Ghaye, T. (2010). *Teaching and learning through reflective practice: A practical guide.* Abingdon: Routledge.

Goldsmith, M. (2015). Feedforward. In J. Passmore (Ed.), *Leadership in coaching* (2nd ed.). London: Kogan Page.

Hawkins, P., Turner, E., & Passmore, J. (2019). *The manifesto for supervision.* Henley-on-Thames: Henley Business School.

Isaacson, S. (2022). *Superhuman coaching ten technologies that expand coaching beyond what's humanly possible.* Hanwell.

Joseph, S. (2016). A review of research into business coaching supervision. *Coaching: An International Journal of Theory, Research and Practice, 9*(2), 158–168.

Lancefield, D. (2019). How technology is transforming executive coaching. *Harvard Business Review, 3.* Retrieved on 15 July 2023 from https://hbr.org/2019/11/How-Technology-is-Transforming-Executive-Coaching

Lim, W. M., Gunasekara, A., Pallant, J. L., Pallant, J. I., & Pechenkina, E. (2023). Generative AI and the future of education: Ragnarök or reformation? A paradoxical perspective from management educators. *International Journal of Management in Education, 21*(2), Article 100790.

Lucas, M. (2017). From coach to coach supervisor – A shift in mind-set. *International Journal of Evidence Based Coaching and Mentoring, 15*(1), 11–23.

Lucas, M. (2023). *Creating the reflective habit: A practical guide for coaches, mentors and leaders.* Abingdon: Routledge.

Martin, P., Kumar, S., & Lizarondo, L. (2017). Effective use of technology in clinical supervision. *Internet Interventions, 8*, 35–39.

Passarelli, A. (2015). Vision-based coaching: Optimizing resources for leader development. *Frontiers in Psychology, 6*, 412.

Pretorius, L. (2023). Fostering AI literacy: A teaching practice reflection. *Journal of Academic Language & Learning, 17*(1), T1–T8.

Proctor, B. (2008). *Group supervision: A guide to creative practice.* London: Sage.

Roxo, M. T., & Brito, P. Q. (2018). Augmented reality trends to the field of business and economics: A review of 20 years of research. *Asian Journal of Business Research, 8*(2), 94–117.

Schön, D. (1983). *The reflective practitioner: How professionals think in action.* London: Routledge.

Schroder, M. (1974). The Shadow Consultant. *Journal of Applied Behavioral Science, 10*(4), 579–594. DOI: 10.1177/002188637401000408

Terblanche, N., & Cilliers, D. (2020). Factors that influence users' adoption of being coached by an artificial intelligence coach. *Philosophy of Coaching: An International Journal, 5*(1), 61–70.

Terblanche, N. H. D., van Heerden, M. & Hunt, R. (2024). The influence of an artificial intelligence chatbot coach assistant on the human coach-client working alliance. *Coaching: An International Journal of Theory, Research and Practice.* DOI: 10.1080/ 17521882.2024.2304792

Thompson, S., & Thompson, N. (2018). *The critical reflective practitioner*. London: Palgrave.

Welsh, J. (2019). 10 ways technology is changing coaching now and in the future. *Forbes*. www.forbes.com/sites/johnwelsheurope/2019/04/08/10-ways-technology-is-changing-coaching-now-and-in-the-future/

Wright, J. K. (2009). Autoethnography and therapy: Writing on the move. *Qualitative Inquiry*, *15*(4), 623–640.

Part III

Critical factors

Chapter 12

Setting up your online coaching environment

Jonathan Passmore

Introduction

The trend for online coaching has been growing and this trend is likely to continue, with the growth of digital platforms and the advent of AI-enabled coaching. Coaching has moved from the physical environment to the digital environment. This move however requires coaches to do more than simply open their laptops. To provide a professional service to the same standard as coaches working face-to-face with clients, digital coaches should take the same time and trouble to consider the environment in which they are offering coaching and the risks associated with poor set-up and management.

In this chapter we will explore the practical aspects of establishing a suitable online space and the key decisions which coaches should consider as they curate their digital coaching office from background to lighting and from client contracting and data management.

The changing nature of coaching

In many ways this book reflects the changing nature of coaching. Coaching has moved from being a service delivered physically, where more than 90% of coaching conversations in 2014 were delivered face-to-face, to one in 2024 where 90% of coaching conversations take place online (Passmore, 2021).

Coaching will continue to happen in physical spaces: Coaches will still work in outdoor environments (Burn & Passmore, 2022), some clients will request face-to-face meetings at their offices, preferring a more personalised service from their executive coach, and many internal coaches working in the same office location will meet face-to-face. But the emergence of digital coaching platforms, alongside the popularity of digital communications tools such as Zoom, Google Meet and Teams mean that digital coaching has become the de facto medium for most coaches.

This transition, while gradual until 2019, suddenly accelerated during the Covid period of 2020 and 2021, as governments and organisations encouraged people to work from home. As people leapt from face-to-face to online, few people initially thought through the implications of the move from one domain of work to another. Most people can recall examples of people speaking from their bedroom with the unmade bed behind them as if they have just emerged from their duvet, or hearing the noise from the next room as a 6 and 8 year old play out a scene from World Series Wrestling.

DOI: 10.4324/9781003383741-16

But as this emergency arrangement during an extreme health event has become normalised it seems right that coaches should give as much time to considering creating the right image and providing the right context to build the working alliance and facilitate the right outcomes. In addition, coaches should also give detailed consideration to confidentiality, data management, and other aspects of their work as we seek to optimise this new working environment.

Connectivity

A useful place to start might be connectivity. For some people this may seem irrelevant, but for others stable connectivity is a serious challenge and one which needs to be planned. The connectivity challenge can relate to both the stability of the internet connection, and its speed, as well as the supply of electricity to power the digital device and the router.

In terms of connectivity, a number of simple rules can help. First, understand whether the power supply you have connected to is stable. Some parts of the world have scheduled 'dark periods', where the supply is switched off in one area as the grid is unable to meet the demand across the whole region or country. If you live in one of these locations, you may want to explore a back-up generator or a battery system, which charges when power is on and steps in when the grid power is switched off. Or simply schedule your calls for times when the grid is providing power to your area.

Second, connectivity to the internet can also vary widely, even in the US and Europe, with some regions or countries able to offer multi-gigabit speeds, while others languish at less than 1MB. Where we live, on a rural country lane in Southern England, we suffered for years with less than 1Mbps, until working from home made us switch to radio wave signals, and we moved overnight from 1Mbps to 70Mbps. But even with fast signals individual homes can have grey areas, where the speed of the connection drops significantly, as the router struggles to reach that area. To reduce this effect the best advice is to place the router in your office or even better to plug the device into the router. A third option is to install a repeater system which allows your device to plug into any electricity socket and will produce similar outcomes to connecting directly to the router.

A third issue on connectivity is security. First, check the password on the router, some have either no password or have a simple 1-2-3 setting. It's a good idea to create a strong personal password. Using three unconnected words, a symbol and three numbers should prevent unwanted access; for example, Apple1&Pear2&Strawberry9. Alongside this installing VPN (virtual private network) software can ensure the connection is more secure when you are away from home and using public networks.

Lighting, camera positioning and sound

Most people have moved away from static devices to laptops, designed so the screen tilts back when in use. While useful for portability the design creates several ergonomic issues for users. The first of these is neck strain. This can be reduced by following ergonomic advice on setting up the machine; from using a separate keyboard to reduce wrist strain, to raising the height of the machine so the screen is directly opposite the eye line.

For online conversations a second set of issues emerge. This is how the coach's face appears to the client through the laptop camera. When the laptop is placed directly on a desk the screen needs to be tilted back, however this creates a less natural image, as the coach appears to the client to be looking down on them. This problem can be reduced by repositioning the laptop on a stand or box, with the aim of lining the camera to eye level.

If the screen and the camera are too close, such as the recommended distance for typing, the participants' view is restricted to the face. An alternative is to move the screen further back to ensure hands, arms, and shoulders can be seen, as well as face. This more complete picture of the upper half of the body enables greater visibility of non-verbal communication, and while not a full solution, provides useful additional data that coaches can draw upon during the conversation to help clients develop greater self-awareness.

Lighting is a further issue and can be influenced by desk position in relation to natural and artificial sources of light. The optimum position is to sit facing a window, so natural light falls onto the face during daylight, with the option of a ring light being used to increase light to the face during darkness hours. The worst position is for the individual to sit with the window behind them, creating a silhouette effect, reducing the coach or client to a talking dark shape. For those in between these extremes, LED ring lights positioned above the screen can project sufficient light, enhancing the conversation.

A final aspect is sound quality. Different devices have different quality of sound. For some machines it may be helpful to add a sound device to improve sound quality, and test the volume levels before you start, including doing a 'sound check' or equipment check with the client before formally starting the coaching. Some coaches have started to use headsets (headphones) but in my view this reduces the personal nature of the relationship and it is better to find a quiet and private space for the conversation. Of course, if that's not possible for example if you are calling from a café or semi-public space, headphones can reduce the negative impact of background noise from traffic, the coffee machine or people speaking on the next table.

Virtual backgrounds and home office settings

Over the past few years there has been much experimentation with backgrounds, as well as natural environments. Both can work; curating this background to suit the coaches' personal brand and the image they wish to create is as important as the choice of location for a physical coaching conversation. In a physical conversation it would be possible to meet in an open plan office, or a sports bar with a game playing on a large screen in the same room, but most coaches would recognise neither would facilitate a great coaching conversation. The same is true for the choices we make about our backgrounds.

The coach may opt for a digital background. In this case, thinking about the image they want to project and whether regular change (for example a different background each week) or stability (the same background) will facilitate this objective. Over the years I have witnessed scenes from children's movies, coffee shops, fake bedrooms, fake offices, and fake bookshelves. If you prefer a virtual background, aim for one that does not distract, but projects an image where the client can feel relaxed and able to focus on the conversation ahead. Most people seem to prefer a natural background. Once again, I have seen inside peoples' untidy bedrooms, children playing, and people wandering around in the background as well as rooms which suggest the coach themselves needs help planning and managing their apparently chaotic lives. I have also seen good examples, with the individual's books subtly included among the books on their shelves, plain backgrounds with maybe a picture revealing enough about the person to be interesting, but not so much that clients are drawn to ask for too much personal information. In my own case I selected a world map, which almost fills the entire screen and often provokes a short exchange at the start of a coaching relationship, about travel or heritage or future holidays but from then on does not disrupt the conversation. The world map background has not changed in five years and becomes part of the image of a virtual meeting with me, and I hope projects an image of global, big picture-systems thinking and predictability.

Online coaching tools

Many platforms have embedded features such as mute, record, screen share, whiteboards, and breakout rooms (for team coaching). However, the evidence is that coaches are not making maximum use of these tools. This may be that there is anxiety about using them or concern by the coach they will disrupt a session. Yet in face-to-face coaching, coaches were comfortable using a notepad, flip-chart, whiteboard, strengths cards, constellations and other tools. I would argue that coaches simply need to start practising using these tools to build their confidence.

The whiteboard tool can be particularly useful as a replacement for the flipchart, allowing the coach to collaborate with clients, to capture their plan from the session or to jointly work on idea generation. While most platforms, such as Zoom, Teams, and Google Meet offer whiteboards, most have limited functionality compared with specialist products. More specialist tools can provide added features, for example a series of templates which the coach can prepare in advance and draw upon if or when needed in a coaching assignment. Having 10–20 such templates prepared can both project an image of competence and also significantly speed up a project planning or brainstorming activity during a session.

Coaching online also provides the opportunity for recording, for the material to be used in supervision or for personal reflection. This brings with it some ethical questions. The first of these is consent. Some digital coaching companies record conversations as a matter of practice, including reference to this in their terms and conditions. While this may be legal, I would advocate that coaches should not only include this in their legal contractual terms but should also discuss with the client whether they are happy for a recording at the start and confirming this at the end of the session, as the clients opinion may have changed based on the content of the session.

I have proposed a checklist for recording coaching sessions which coaches could use to guide a client conversation (see Box 12.1). One key feature is to include a date for deletion of the data and an agreement to write to the client to confirm the data has been deleted at the end of the agreed period. A period of 40 days seems reasonable, allowing sufficient time for a coach to review the material with their supervisor and to identify learnings from the material.

For coaching platforms and researchers interested in building AI apps, a 40-day period is too short, as they may wish to keep the data for an indeterminate period. In this case personal data should be removed or pseudonymised and the client, coach, and organisation client should all provide written consent for the collection and indefinite retention

---

Box 12.1   Recording checklist

Is this a one-off recording just for this session, or is the agreement for the assignment (Always checks with the client at the start of the session)

Where will the data be stored?

Who will have access to the recording?

How long will the recording be retained by the coach and others (you should state a date when the recording will be deleted, 40 days seems a reasonable period for learning)?

The coach confirms at the end of the period they will email the client to confirm deletion.

On this basis is the client happy to be recorded?

Check with the client at the end of the session, if on the basis of what they said during the conversation, are they still happy with the conversation being held by the coach for the agreed purpose and period?

---

of the data, with access granted to the individual and organisation to audit any data held and retain the right to be forgotten, to ensure personal privacy and organisation confidentiality are protected.

A final aspect to consider is the emergence of VR environments. While these may be less well suited than a physical face-to-face for 1–1 coaching, they are well suited to team coaching. VR can provide the opportunity for a global team to connect from across the world for a quarterly team coaching session, without the production of tonnes of carbon from flights and the impact of jet lag, with whiteboards and other tools available in the app. However, to make best use of these spaces, coaches need to practise and develop the skills of using online spaces, just as they have become skilled at operating in a physical space.

Making appointments

Technology can also help with scheduling meetings. Again, specialist appointment tools like Calendly or "http://cal.com/"Cal.com can enable clients to book slots available in your diary and prevent you from double-booking or forgetting to add an appointment to your schedule.

Coaching relationship

One of the key concerns for many coaches is how the technology may impact on the coaching relationship. There is almost no research into online coaching, although much has been written about its potential over the past few years (Berninger-Schäfer & Meyer, 2018; Kanatouri, 2020; Ribbers & Waringa, 2015). One study (Mitchalik & Schermuly, 2023) however appears to suggest that clients have become acclimated to

---

Box 12.2   Features of the disinhibition effect

Dissociative anonymity
Invisibility
Asynchronicity
Solipsistic introjection
Dissociative imagination
Minimisation of authority

---

online environments and the coach alliance seems as strong online as it is face-to-face. However, what clients find more difficult to do is to repeatedly move between one and the other. It may thus be best to agree with the client what works best for them, and then to stick to an online or a face-to-face relationship throughout the assignment.

In the parallel discipline of counselling, more research has been undertaken and, as might be expected, there are conflicting perspectives (Richards & Vigano, 2013). However, the evidence suggests that, on balance, for most types of therapy, the working alliance is as strong online as it is in face-to-face sessions. A closer examination suggests that for some types of sessions, particularly sessions that are emotionally charged, the 'disinhibition effect' (Suler, 2004) can make clients more likely to be open in their verbal communication as a result of a series of psychological effects, summaries in Box 12.2.

However, to achieve similar outcomes in the coaching relationship to face-to-face coaching, coaches need to pay attention to some of the small details in their set-up. The following three considerations are particularly important: stable secure connection, good quality light and sound, and an appropriate background (environment) to create a sense of order, stability and confidential conversation.

Documentation

Before launching into providing online sessions, coaches should think about creating the appropriate documentation for their practice, such as policies and forms. These will vary depending on the region in which the coach lives and the regions in which they coach. Most coaches use a written agreement with individual clients for the overall assignment. Coaches should review their agreements to reflect the new environment they are working in.

Examples might include amending the contract to reflect a change to the length of each session face-to-face coaching sessions seem to vary between 1–2 hours. Digital coaches seem to have moved closer to the counselling model of the 50-minute hour, allowing time for a comfort break or drink before the next session. Shorter online sessions may also benefit both clients and the coach, reflecting the eye strain of focusing on a screen and a need for movement which may be easier when both people are face-to-face, but is more difficult to manage online.

If you plan to record some sessions this too will need to be agreed with the client, and almost certainly with the client organisation.

It can also be helpful for some clients to provide them with an information sheet. This can describe what coaching is and how the coaching will work at a practical level, such as the length of session and payment terms, but in a digital environment it may be helpful to also include information about the device set-up (sound card, lighting, suggested distance from the screen to allow the face and upper body to be seen) etc., background environment for the call (private), as well as contingency arrangements such as what to do if the connection is lost during the conversation or one or other person can't connect due to a technical issue (for example exchanging emergency contact numbers).

Finally, coaches should give thought to any regulatory implications. This may involve registering with a government body, such as in the UK the Information Commissioner's Office, if they are holding personal data. It may also be worthwhile checking with your insurance company and being clear about the locations of your clients, as some locations may have a culture of litigation, while in other countries professional indemnity cover does not exist.

Reflective questions

1. What arrangements do you need to make before you start coaching using online technologies?
2. What equipment do you need?
3. What might you need to change in your practice?

Conclusion

Moving into the digital environment requires planning and preparation. In this chapter I have explored some of the practical issues of coaching online from setting up the machine, positioning, and environments to documentation. As digital coaching becomes more established, professional coaches should ensure they have in place the appropriate arrangements and create the environment to optimise the value of the coaching work they are delivering.

References

Berninger-Schäfer, E., & Meyer, P. (2018). *Online coaching*. Cham: Springer.

Burn, A., & Passmore, J. (2022). Outdoor coaching: The role of attention restoration theory as a framework for explaining the experience and benefit of eco-psychology coaching. *International Coaching Psychology Review*, 17(1), 21–36. https://doi.org/10.53841/bpsicpr.2022.17.1.21

Kanatouri, S. (2020). *The digital coach*. Abingdon: Routledge.

Mitchalik, N., & Schermuly, C. (2023). Online, offline, or both? The importance of coaching format for side effects in business coaching. *Journal of Managerial Psychology*, ahead-of-print. https://doi.org/10.1108/JMP-01-2023-0068

Passmore, J. (2021). *Future trends in coaching: Executive report 2021*. Henley-on-Thames: Henley Business School. ISBN 978-1-912473-32-8

Ribbers, A., & Waringa, A. (2015). *e-Coaching: Theory and practise for a new online approach to coaching*. Abingdon: Routledge.

Richards, D., & Vigano, N. (2013). Online counseling: A narrative and critical review of the literature. *Journal of Clinical Psychology*, 69(9), 994–1011.

Suler, J. (2004). The online disinhibition effect. Cyberpsychology and behaviour: The impact of the internet. *Multimedia and VR on Behaviour and Society*, 7(3), 321–326. https://doi.org/10.1089/1094931041291295

Building empathy and trust in online environments

Hannes Schilling and Simone Kauffeld

Introduction

Coaching in online environments is getting more common in modern society (Siegrist, 2006). This can be attributed, for example, to the fact that online environments reduce the need for physical interactions and that most people with smartphones can access online environments seamlessly and flexibly from wherever and whenever they want (Xie, 2020). With the emergence of coaching in online environments (Sherpa Coaching, 2012) and the exemplary benefits mentioned before, questions for practitioners arise. One of these questions relates to the success factors of coaching, which are commonly built by face-to-face interactions between coach and client, such as empathy and trust, and how to build these in online environments (Pandolfi, 2020). To answer this question, this chapter takes a deeper look into how empathy and trust are developed in online coaching environments and elaborates on how empathy and trust are relevant to coaching in general.

Empathy and trust as key success factors of coaching

Before diving into the importance of empathy and trust in coaching, it is important to define these concepts. Even though these factors have been explored in the literature, researchers have yet to agree on shared definitions. To break down the discussions on the definitions of both constructs, we adopted Decety and Lamm's (2006, p. 1146) definition of empathy as "the ability to experience and understand what others feel without confusion between oneself and others". As coaching, in general, relies mainly on the interplay between coach and client, we chose to adopt a definition of interpersonal trust from Tagliaferri (2022, p. 3):

> Interpersonal trust is an attitude that an agent a_1 (the trustor) has towards another agent a_2 (the trustee) for a specific purpose ψ. In order for the attitude to qualify as trust, at least two elements are necessary: 1. The trustor must rely on the trustee in order to fulfil purpose ψ. 2. The circumstances in which trust is elicited must contain at least two elements of freedom. Specifically, the trustor must be free to choose whether to rely on the trustee or not; moreover, the trustee must be free to choose to betray the trustor by not contributing to the fulfilment of the purpose which is part of the trusting relationship.

In other words, empathy and trust are both concepts that strongly depend on how people interact with each other. Furthermore, both definitions contain an element of reliance on

DOI: 10.4324/9781003383741-17

the interaction partner. In coaching, this would mean that the coach and the client understand each other and willingly engage in the coaching interaction while simultaneously respecting the freedom of each interaction partner to leave the coaching situation.

As a result of the interaction, described in the definitions of empathy and trust, a relationship between the coach and the client develops over time (Van Coller-Peter & Manzini, 2020). The resulting coaching relationship needs to be perceived as helpful and built on empathy and trust to create a foundation for coaching success (Pandolfi, 2020). Without empathy and trust, the coaching relationship either does not develop at all, or an unstable relationship is created. A stable positive coaching relationship enables the coach to deal with open tasks and goals as well as with the emotional reflections of the client (Haynal, 2022).

As empathy and trust are partly connected to each other but still differing constructs, we first discuss empathy before looking at trust. Regarding empathy, it has been shown that if the coach shows empathy in the communication with the client, the coaching relationships can be built more effectively, and coaching success is achieved more often (Will & Kauffeld, 2018). Furthermore, the communication patterns between the coach and client play a vital role in developing a fruitful coaching relationship and transmitting empathy. Especially practitioners of coaching should focus on empathetic communication patterns to shape the coaching relationship with the client by applying techniques such as active listening, paraphrasing, perspective taking (imagine self and imagine other), or addressing the client's feelings in the coaching session (Diller et al., 2021; Will et al., 2016). Table 13.1 provides practical advice for showing empathy in coaching through these techniques.

Besides the importance of empathy as a building block for the coaching relationship and the relevance for the communication between coach and client, practitioners also need to recognise that empathy is not always interpreted congruently by coach and client (Will & Kauffeld, 2018). For example, Will and Kauffeld (2018) have shown that the empathy self-assessment of coaches can differ from the interpretation of the client, which implies that the coach cannot be sure if they are perceived as empathic in the coaching relationship. Practitioners should, therefore, actively focus on the previously mentioned

Table 13.1 Building empathy in coaching through coaching techniques

Technique	Practical implementation
Active listening	Coaches should demonstrate concern or show non-active behavioural cues like nodding approvingly or keeping eye contact.
Paraphrasing	Coaches should repeat statements of the client in her or his own way to show the client that she or he understands the meaning and depth of the said statements.
Perspective taking (imagine self and imagine other)	Coaches should openly reflect together with the client on how (1) they would feel, behave, and react in the same situation of the client (imagine self) as well as how (2) the client felt, behaved, and reacted in her or his situation (imagine other).
Addressing emotions	Coaches should recognise emotionally loaded statements and directly address the emotional content of said statements.

building blocks of empathy in coaching sessions to increase their chance of being evaluated as empathetic. A practical way for coaches to assess if they are perceived as empathic is by directly asking the client for feedback on their empathetic behaviour.

While empathy is relevant to coaching success, it also functions as a key variable for developing trust in the coaching relationship. Empathy can be used by the coach to create a safe space for the client to open up and develop trust in the coaching relationship and in the coach (Yanchus et al., 2020). Trust, in turn, plays a vital role in fortifying the coaching relationship and enabling an authentic and honest interaction between the coach and the client (Alvey & Barclay, 2007). A trustful interaction can encourage the client to share feelings and emotions, which are necessary for the coaching progress. Furthermore, without trust in the coach, the client struggles more likely to develop a meaningful connection with the coach and is less likely to show vulnerability to the coach (Bluckert, 2005). It is critical in coaching that the clients show vulnerability as it fosters open communication between the coach and the client and facilitates problem identification as well as future planning (Cox, 2012).

A factor that supports the development of trust in coaching is the trustworthiness of the coach (Schiemann et al., 2019). Coaches can describe themselves as trustworthy, yet the client finally determines if she or he perceives the coach as trustworthy. Schiemann et al. (2019) described a variety of possible approaches a coach can use to improve her or his trustworthiness in the eyes of the client and, consequently, the trust in the coaching relationship. These approaches can be clustered into the three pillars of trust established by Burke et al. (2007): ability, benevolence, and integrity. The ability category contains factors directly linked to the interpretation of the coach's abilities, e.g., their preparedness for the coaching session or their responsibility in handling important topics. The benevolence category entails factors directly linked to the intentional expression of the coach, like showing an interest in the topics of the client or actively listening to the coaching goals of the client. Integrity, as the last category, includes similar to the benevolence category factors linked to the personal traits of the coach, e.g., is the coach authentic, honest, accepting, or personal? Integrity can be shown by coaches by keeping promises and acting according to their words. Even if the coach actively engages in such trust-nurturing approaches and the client interprets the coach as trustworthy, another factor influences trust in the coaching relationship. This factor is the situation in which the coaching takes place. For example, it can make a difference whether the client wants a coach, or if the client is self-funding, or if they have been instructed to engage in the coaching process by their employer. Situation-specific trust can also include the environment in which coaching is performed: For example, a client can have higher trust in the coach, while in-person 1-on-1 coaching takes place, but less in group coaching settings in online environments (Jackson & Bourne, 2020). For this reason and due to the increase in coaching conducted in online environments (Sherpa Coaching, 2012), the following section elaborates on the challenges of building empathy and trust in online environments (Van Dyke, 2014).

The challenges of conveying empathy and developing trust in online coaching environments

As outlined before, empathy and trust are important for coaching success. Thus, it is needed to reflect on how empathy and trust are conveyed in a digital setting and why this can be challenging for coaches. Although the popularity of coaching in online environments has increased (Passmore, 2021; Van Dyke, 2014) and, accordingly, more research focused on coaching in online environments (Wen & Wang, 2022), in contrast, the literature on empathy and trust in online coaching environments is still scarce and often dates back to the 2000s and 2010s.

Literature concerning online coaching states that online coaching can take place in a variety of settings (Van Dyke, 2014). While some online coaching environments only use text-based interactions between coach and client, others rely on virtual, audio, or video contact. Examples of text-based online environments for coaching are chats or blogs, while virtual, audio, or video-based coaching is conducted via Zoom, Skype, or other telecommunication software (Wen & Wang, 2022).

According to the media richness theory (Ishii et al., 2019), online environments should strive to transmit as much verbal and non-verbal information as possible to increase the clarity of communication between, for example, coach and client (D'Urso & Rains, 2008). Online environments which only use text-based communication are on the lower end of the verbal and non-verbal information continuum, whereas, for example, video-based online environments approach the higher end of the continuum. To gain a better overview of the media richness theory, we extended and transformed a graph by Reichwald et al. (1998) into Table 13.2.

The choice of the online coaching environment is of practical relevance for establishing empathy and trust, as online environments which are on the lower end of the continuum could potentially lead to greater challenges in conveying empathy and trust. For example, Bos et al. (2002) showed that online environments that used text-based interactions had lower trust ratings than online environments, like virtual or video contact, where non-verbal cues could be identified. Moreover, even if the interaction partners recognized non-verbal cues through virtual or video contact, it took them longer to create trust compared to face-to-face settings. The study also showed that the created trust in virtual and video contact is less resilient than in face-to-face settings: As trust is an important building block of the coach–client relationship, the relationship might be more vulnerable to negatively altering in online environments.

Similar to trust, the online environment in which coaching takes place can also influence the perception of empathy. Verbal communication between interaction partners is important for conveying empathy in online environments as tone, intensity,

Table 13.2 Media richness theory

Medium for coaching	Media richness continuum	Verbal and non-verbal information transmission continuum	Complexity of the communication continuum
In-person meeting	Highest	Verbal and non-verbal	Most complex
Video meeting	Higher	Verbal and non-verbal	More complex
Telephone meeting	High	Verbal and non-verbal	Complex
Voice mail	Moderate	Verbal	Medium
Chat meetings	Moderate	Verbal	Medium
Telefax	Low	Verbal	Simple
Email	Lower	Verbal	More simple
Letters	Lowest	Verbal	Most simple

and sound of voice are, besides the actual meaning of the spoken word, critical components of being perceived as empathic (Grondin et al., 2019). Therefore, online coaching environments like chats and blogs lack critical components compared to voice-transmitting online environments in creating empathy between interaction partners. Equally important to verbal cues in conveying empathy are visual and non-verbal cues like gestures, eye contact, and other bodily movements (Prochazkova & Kret, 2017). These types of cues enable interaction partners to mimic each other's behaviour and emotions, creating stronger empathic contagion (Prochazkova & Kret, 2017). From this, online coaching environments, which enable visual contact through, for example, video-based communication, should consequently achieve empathic communication easier than online environments in which visual and verbal cues are not identifiable. Furthermore, the decision between synchronous and asynchronous coaching communication is important for choosing an online coaching environment, as asynchronous online environments lack non-direct feedback loops that are important in creating empathy (Grondin et al., 2019).

Grondin et al. (2019) also highlight the importance of technical requirements in online environments, as poor signal quality or internet problems hinder seamless and clear communication between coach and client. In turn, poor signal quality or internet problems might harm the creation of empathy and trust. Dependent on the chosen online coaching environment, also other technical requirements are important for creating empathy and trust, like a functioning microphone or video camera (Van Coller-Peter & Manzini, 2020). If the microphone is broken or changes the voice of one of the interaction partners, the other interaction partner can perceive the communicated statements as less empathetic and, in turn, might assess the interaction partner as less trustworthy. Similarly, a broken or bad video connection hinders the identification of non-verbal and visual cues, complicating the process of trust and empathy creation.

While the challenges of building empathy and trust in online coaching environments are complex, the next section of this chapter outlines how these hurdles can be mitigated. Therefore, insights from face-to-face coaching settings will be combined with the findings from research in online coaching environments.

Building empathy and trust in online coaching

In the last section, a variety of challenges for creating empathy and trust in online environments were pointed out, yet these challenges can be tackled. For example, techniques that facilitate building trust and empathy in face-to-face coaching sessions can be transferred to online coaching settings, such as active listening. Combining the finding from the media richness theory (D'Urso & Rains, 2008) and the study of Bos et al. (2002), empathy and trust are best built in online coaching environments which allow the use of video and audio contact as these online environments ensure proper identification of verbal and non-verbal information between coach and client. Using video and audio in online environments, techniques like holding eye contact and nodding approvingly can be utilised to create empathy (Will et al., 2016). Furthermore, if the audio and video contact takes place in a synchronous online environment, with minimal latency, the coach can give direct feedback and paraphrase the client's statements, ensuring that the communication patterns are perceived as empathetic (Grondin et al., 2019; Will et al., 2016).

Moreover, online coaching environments also enable new coaching techniques like shadowing, which could foster trust building by providing direct feedback to the client via communication technologies between online sessions.

Van Coller-Peter and Manzini (2020) argue that the coach needs to ensure that the online environment is not only compatible with their own needs but also with the client's needs. Thus, the coach and client should decide jointly on the online coaching environment to enable a comfortable technical surrounding for both interaction partners. Furthermore, ensuring that the online environment is suitable for fluent and seamless communication between coach and client and that the internet connection is stable can help to increase the perceived trustworthiness of the coach as these preparations before the coaching session provide insights into the abilities of the coach (Grondin et al., 2019; Schiemann et al., 2019; Van Coller-Peter & Manzini, 2020).

As stated before, high-quality sound and video, with a fast and reliable internet connection is a prerequisite for empathy and trust building in online environments (Grondin et al., 2019; Van Coller-Peter & Manzini, 2020). This is also important for online coaching environments as the correct adjustment of the camera can enable a better perception of non-verbal interactions (Nguyen & Canny, 2009). Furthermore, a quality microphone can ensure clear and natural voice perception, which supports delivering coaching techniques like paraphrasing and, in turn, fosters empathy and trust building (Schiemann et al., 2019; Van Coller-Peter & Manzini, 2020; Will et al., 2016).

As pointed out previously, the ratings of empathetic communication and being a trustworthy coach do not always match between coach and client (Schiemann et al., 2019; Will & Kauffeld, 2018). This discrepancy can be reduced in physical and online coaching environments by techniques like self-reflection or transparency of the coach. Following Schiemann et al. (2019), these techniques refer to the ability category of being perceived as trustworthy by the client. Coaches can use transparency and self-reflection in online environments to reflect on how empathetic or trusting the rapport is between them and their client to adjust their behaviour, fostering, in turn, the creation of enhanced rapport (Van Coller-Peter & Manzini, 2020). Checking in and giving feedback is a useful way for coaches to increase their empathic communication and allow clients to provide feedback on the relationship and their experience of the coach's empathy and wider communications. Participants in the study of Van Coller-Peter and Manzini (2020) highlighted the importance of checking in as a coach to correct beliefs and information while coaching in online environments. Simultaneously the coach can also provide feedback to the client to foster empathic and trusting rapport building. Providing direct feedback was also identified by Grondin et al. (2019) and Schiemann et al. (2019) as a powerful technique for building empathy and trust in coaching environments.

Studies on trust building in online environments revealed that mixing face-to-face interactions and online interactions works best for establishing a trusting relationship in online coaching, especially if the face-to-face interaction precedes the interaction via online environments (Jarvenpaa et al., 2000; Maznevski & Chudoba, 2000). For example, a face-to-face session can be included in the online coaching by adding a brief and initial face-to-face 'get-to-know' session. Another way for coaches to build empathy and trust in online coaching environments is through perspective taking (Tóth & Reinhardt, 2019).

Perspective taking can be used to demonstrate concern when the coach actively listens to statements made by the client (Will et al., 2016).

At the beginning of this chapter, it was mentioned that empathy and trust in coaching strongly influence the relationship between coach and client (Pandolfi, 2020). A stable and positive relationship, built on empathy and trust, is relevant to coaching success. Thus, it is important to establish rapport in online coaching environments to nurture building empathy and trust between the coach and client. Van Coller-Peter and Manzini (2020) outlined multiple techniques for building a fruitful rapport between coach and client in online environments. One of these techniques is that the coach and client are authentic and honest with each other in the way that both interaction partners can be themselves. This is especially challenging in non-visual online environments, as authenticity and honesty rely considerably on visual social signals (Van Coller-Peter & Manzini, 2020). Therefore, authenticity and honesty can be utilised in the best way to build empathy and trust in online coaching environments if both coach and client use a video camera. This online rapport-building strategy goes along with the findings of Schiemann et al. (2019) that an honest and authentic coach is perceived as more trustworthy in their face-to-face coaching settings. Furthermore, establishing clear guidelines for the coaching and developing a joint understanding of expectations and boundaries supports building a positive relationship between the coach and the client (Van Coller-Peter & Manzini, 2020). This is especially important in online coaching environments, as the coach can be perceived as easily available at all times (Anthony & Nagel, 2021). If this perceived availability does not hold up, trust in the coach can suffer as a result. Initiating this expectation management between the interaction partners is part of the coach's responsibility and can help the coach to convey their trustworthiness (Schiemann et al., 2019).

Most factors mentioned in this chapter to build empathy and trust in online coaching environments are based on findings concerning 1-on-1 coaching settings. Furthermore, these 1-on-1 coaching settings often apply to business or clinical contexts (Grondin et al., 2019; Pandolfi, 2020; Schiemann et al., 2019). In addition, while 1-on-1 coaching primarily focuses on the goals of the individual, group coaching can foster the goal achievement of multiple clients at the same time (Thornton, 2010; Van Dyke, 2014). Thus, building empathy and trust in online coaching environments must also be understood in settings and contexts besides 1-on-1 coaching in business and clinical contexts. In particular, group coaching settings and online group coaching settings are to be illuminated as these have been shown to be effective tools in other contexts (Jordan et al., 2016; Stein et al., 2013). Furthermore, group coaching in online environments allows practitioners to deliver coaching across a wider geographical area. Jackson and Bourne (2020) found that trust was built in online group coaching settings through the safety of the client's environment. In online group coaching environments, the clients can choose their own environment where they feel most comfortable building trust and where they want to participate in the group coaching. Moreover, online group coaching settings could lead to a disinhibition effect (Suler, 2004) as their trust in their anonymity increases, explaining, for example, why clients share more information in online environments than in face-to-face settings. Such effects were exemplarily described by Martin (2013), who investigated online group discussions. Furthermore, Jackson and Bourne (2020) found that, similarly to 1-on-1 online coaching environments, the camera and video were important for building trust as such technologies enabled the identification of facial expressions.

As the literature on online group coaching settings needs to further explore the empathy and trust-building process, the next section of this chapter explores the implementation of the identified empathy and trust-building factors from this chapter in a real-world example outside the business and clinical context.

Building empathy and trust for coaching in online environments: Case study

Translating theoretical knowledge and scientific findings into the practical field can be challenging. Therefore, this section focuses on a practical example of how empathy and trust can be built in an online peer-to-peer group coaching environment. The project D1RECTIONS at Technische Universität Braunschweig, Germany, trained students from higher years to coach new students using a peer-coaching model on topics like student success strategies or first steps in the university. The peer coaching consisted of seven sessions and was conceptualised as group coaching that could be conducted either face-to-face, online, or a mix of both. The peer coaching was been transferred into an online environment following the insights from digital group-coaching sessions of a preceding project (Wittner et al., 2021). All coaches in the peer-coaching groups were trained and advised to follow specific empathy and trust-building strategies in their online coaching environments.

First, coaches were trained in the online environment BigBlueButton, a virtual classroom and online conference software. In their training, the coaches were advised to use this online environment or a similar one with their coaching groups as online environments, which include video and audio contact, foster empathy and trust building better than environments that only use text-based interactions (Bos et al., 2002; D'Urso & Rains, 2008). In addition, coaches were briefed on the importance of the equipment (camera and microphone) and connectivity which could hinder the development of the coaching relationship aspects such as empathy or trustworthiness (Grondin et al., 2019; Schiemann et al., 2019; Van Coller-Peter & Manzini, 2020).

Before the first peer-coaching session, a kick-off meeting took place in which the coach and clients had the opportunity to get to know each other. The kick-off meeting took place either in a face-to-face setting or in an online environment and was designed to help the coach and client to build an empathetic and trusting relationship for the following online coaching sessions (Jarvenpaa et al., 2000; Maznevski & Chudoba, 2000; Van Coller-Peter & Manzini, 2020). Furthermore, clients had the opportunity to create additional chat-based online environments in which the coach and the clients could interact more privately. Thus, building empathy and trust among each other was enabled by intimacy. In the online coaching environment, the coaches were encouraged to use various techniques to build empathy and trust with the clients, such as paraphrasing and active listening (Will et al., 2016). While these techniques contributed to the development of trust and feelings of empathy, they also facilitated a positive relationship by creating a safe space for clients and increasing confidentiality (Van Coller-Peter & Manzini, 2020). Coaches and clients maintained an open feedback culture in the online coaching sessions allowing both interaction partners to be their authentic and honest selves, fostering empathy and trust between them (Schiemann et al., 2019; Van Coller-Peter & Manzini, 2020). The last coaching session in the online environment ended with feedback rounds between the coach and clients concerning coaching goal attainment.

Implications for practice

This chapter contains a variety of implications for coaching in online environments and especially for building empathy and trust in online coaching environments. One of these implications is that the coach's decision on a specific online environment already has consequences on the development of empathy and trust. Digital coaches are advised to choose an online environment that is rich in verbal and non-verbal cue transmission, like, for example, video- and audio-enabled online environments. Empathy and trust can be built more easily in such online environments compared to only text-based environments, as the client can identify verbal and non-verbal cues (Bos et al., 2002; D'Urso & Rains, 2008). Moreover, the decision on the specific online environment should be made jointly with the client to ensure that the chosen online environment provides the technical requirements with which both are comfortable. This shared decision strengthens the empathetic and trusting rapport building between the coach and client (Van Coller-Peter & Manzini, 2020). While preparing for coaching in online environments, the coach is urged to review their technical equipment (microphone and camera) because these can hinder building empathy and trust (Grondin et al., 2019; Van Coller-Peter & Manzini, 2020). Possible ways in which the coach can test if verbal and non-verbal cues are transmitted clearly through the technical equipment is through holding test coaching sessions with other coaches. In these artificial online coaching sessions, the coach can also test if tone, sound, and voice are perceived as empathetic and trustworthy (Grondin et al., 2019).

Furthermore, coaches should try to execute the first coaching session in a face-to-face setting before changing to coaching in online environments or having an in-person 'get-to-know' session, as it has been shown to simplify and speed up the building of empathy and trust in online coaching environments (Jarvenpaa et al., 2000; Maznevski & Chudoba, 2000). Moreover, the planning of online coaching sessions and the technical preparations are important parts of building empathy and trust between the coach and client, as these activities provide insight into the coach's skills for the client. Digital coaches should be well prepared for coaching in online environments, as clients can attribute good preparation and planning to their professional abilities as a coach. In turn, coaches, who are well-prepared and good at planning are more likely to be perceived as trustworthy (Schiemann et al., 2019). Further, coaches should use techniques like paraphrasing, active listening, and addressing the client's feelings in the online coaching session, more frequently than face to face, to foster empathetic communication (Will et al., 2016). In combination with these techniques, the digital coach needs to be authentic and honest with the client, as authenticity and honesty foster empathetic and trusting rapport building in online environments as well as being perceived as a trustworthy coach (Schiemann et al., 2019; Van Coller-Peter & Manzini, 2020).

Reflective questions

1. Do I pay attention to empathy and trust in online coaching environments?

2. Do I use empathy- and trust-building techniques like paraphrasing, active listening, and perspective taking?
3. Is my technical equipment up to date to deliver high-quality online coaching?

Conclusion

The main objective of this chapter was to outline the factors which facilitate and enable building empathy and trust in online environments. After the importance of empathy and trust for coaching was described and the challenges of building empathy and trust in online environments were depicted, the building blocks of developing empathy and trust in online coaching environments were illuminated. Digital coaches can take away from this chapter that a variety of factors need to come together to establish empathy and trust in online coaching environments. The online environment itself needs to be wisely chosen in cooperation with the client, the technical requirements need to be met and checked repeatedly, and the coach needs to pay attention to her or his own behaviour in the online coaching environment. Future research needs to unveil more aspects that are important for building empathy and trust in online coaching environments and thus extend the knowledge summarised in this chapter.

References

Alvey, S., & Barclay, K. (2007). The characteristics of dyadic trust in executive coaching. *Journal of Leadership Studies, 1*(1), 18–27.

Anthony, K., & Nagel, D. M. (2021). *Coaching online: A practical guide.* London: Routledge.

Bluckert, P. (2005). Critical factors in executive coaching – the coaching relationship. Industrial *and Commercial Training, 37*(7), 336–340. https://doi.org/10.1108/00197850510626785

Bos, N., Olson, J., Gergle, D., Olson, G., & Wright, Z. (2002, April). Effects of fourcomputer-mediated communications channels on trust development. In Dennis Wixon (ed.), *Proceedings of the SIGCHI conference on human factors in computing systems* (pp. 135–140). New York, NY, United States: Association for Computing Machinery.

Burke, C. S., Sims, D. E., Lazzara, E. H., & Salas, E. (2007). Trust in leadership: A multi-level review and integration. *The Leadership Quarterly, 18*(6), 606–632.

Cox, E. (2012). Individual and organizational trust in a reciprocal peer coaching context. *Mentoring & Tutoring: Partnership in Learning, 20*(3), 427–443.

Decety, J., & Lamm, C. (2006). Human empathy through the lens of social neuroscience. *Scientific World Journal, 6,* 1146–1163.

Diller, S. J., Mühlberger, C., Löhlau, N., & Jonas, E. (2021). How to show empathy as a coach: The effects of coaches' imagine-self versus imagine-other empathy on the client's self-change and coaching outcome. *Current Psychology, 42,* 1–19.

D'Urso, S. C., & Rains, S. A. (2008). Examining the scope of channel expansion: A test of channel expansion theory with new and traditional communication media. *Management Communication Quarterly, 21*(4), 486–507. https://doi.org/10.1177/0893318907313712

Grondin, F., Lomanowska, A. M., & Jackson, P. L. (2019). Empathy in computer-mediated interactions: A conceptual framework for research and clinical practice. *ClinicalPsychology: Science and Practice, 26*(4), e12298.

Haynal, V. (2022). The coaching relationship. In Veronique Haynal & René Chioléro (eds.), *Coaching physicians and healthcare professionals* (pp. 30–56). New York: Routledge.

Ishii, K., Lyons, M. M., & Carr, S. A. (2019). Revisiting media richness theory for today and future. *Human Behavior and Emerging Technologies, 1*(2), 124–131.

Jackson, S., & Bourne, D. J. (2020). Can an online coaching programme facilitate behavioural change in women working in STEM fields. *International Coaching Psychology Review, 15*(1), 20–36.

Jarvenpaa, S. L., Tractinsky, N., & Vitale, M. (2000). Consumer trust in an internet store. *Information Technology and Management, 1*(1–2), 45–71.

Jordan, S., Gessnitzer, S., & Kauffeld, S. (2016). Effects of a group coaching for the vocational orientation of secondary school pupils. *Coaching: An International Journal of Theory, Research and Practice, 9*(2), 143–157.

Martin, K. H. (2013). Leveraging disinhibition to increase student authority in asynchronous online discussion. *Journal of Asynchronous Learning Networks, 17*(3), 149–164.

Maznevski, M. L., & Chudoba, K. M. (2000). Bridging space over time: Global virtual team-dynamics and effectiveness. *Organization Science, 11*(5), 473–492. https://doi.org/10.1287/orsc.11.5.473.15200

Nguyen, D. T., & Canny, J. (2009). More than face-to-face: Empathy effects of videoframing. In Dan R. Olsen Jr., Richard B. Arthur, Ken Hinckley, Meredith Ringel Morris, Scott E. Hudson, Saul Greenberg (eds.), *Proceedings of the 27th international conference on human factors in computing systems*. Boston, MA: ACM press. https://doi.org/10.1145/1518701.1518770

Pandolfi, C. (2020). Active ingredients in executive coaching: A systematic literature review. *International Coaching Psychology Review, 15*(2), 6–30.

Passmore, J. (2021). *Future trends in coaching: Executive report 2021*. Henley-on-Thames: Henley Business School. ISBN 978-1-912473-32-8

Prochazkova, E., & Kret, M. E. (2017). Connecting minds and sharing emotions throughmimicry: A neurocognitive model of emotional contagion. *Neuroscience & Biobehavioral Reviews, 80*, 99–114.

Reichwald, R., Möslein, K., Sachenbacher, H., & Englberger, H. (1998). *Telekooperation – verteilte Arbeits- und Organisationsformen*. Berlin: Springer.

Schiemann, S. J., Mühlberger, C., Schoorman, F. D., & Jonas, E. (2019). Trust me, I am acaring coach: The benefits of establishing trustworthiness during coaching bycommunicating benevolence. *Journal of Trust Research, 9*(2), 164–184.

Sherpa Coaching. (2012). *Sherpa Coaching Seventh Annual Executive Coaching Summary*. Cincinnati, OH. Retrieved from: http://sherpacoaching.com/survey.html

Siegrist, R. (2006). Online-coaching. In E. Lippmann (Ed.), *Coaching* (pp. 304–314). Berlin, Heidelberg: Springer.

Stein, D. S., Wanstreet, C. E., Slagle, P., Trinko, L. A., & Lutz, M. (2013). From 'hello' to higher order thinking: The effect of coaching and feedback on online chats. *The Internet and Higher Education, 16*, 78–84.

Suler, J. (2004). The online disinhibition effect. *CyberPsychology & Behavior, 7*(3), 321–326. https://doi.org/10.1089/1094931041291295

Tagliaferri, M. (2022). Reviewing the case of online interpersonal trust. *Foundations of Science, 28*, 1–30.

Thornton, C. (2010). *Group and team coaching: The essential guide*. New York: Routledge.

Tóth, L., & Reinhardt, M. (2019). Factors underlying the coach-athlete relationship: The importance of empathy as a trait in coaching. In P. Buchwald, K. Kaniasty, K. A. Moore, & P. Arenas-Landgrave (Eds.), *Stress and Anxiety* (vol. 28). Logos Verlag: Berlin.

Van Coller-Peter, S., & Manzini, L. (2020). Strategies to establish rapport during onlinemanagement coaching. *SA Journal of Human Resource Management, 18*, 9. https://doi.org/10.4102/sajhrm.v18i0.1298

Van Dyke, P. R. (2014). Virtual group coaching: A curriculum for coaches and educators. *Journal of Psychological Issues in Organizational Culture, 5*(2), 72–86.

Wen, L., & Wang, Y. (2022). Applying an interactive learning approach provided by an academic coach in a graduate-level accounting course. *Higher Education, Skills and Work-Based Learning, 12*(5), 928–943.

Will, T., Gessnitzer, S., & Kauffeld, S. (2016). You think you are an empathic coach? Maybeyou should think again. The difference between perceptions of empathy vs. empathic behaviour after a person-centred coaching training. *Coaching: An International Journal of Theory, Research and Practice, 9*(1), 53–68.

Will, T., & Kauffeld, S. (2018). Relevanz von Empathie für dyadische Beziehungen–Über einunterschätztes Konstrukt in der Coach-Klienten-Interaktion. *Coaching| Theorie & Praxis, 4*(1), 45–54.

Wittner, B., Jantzen, M., Powazny, S., Klauke, F., & Kauffeld, S. (2021). CHO1CE+ – first-generation-studierende auf ihrem bildungsweg in präsenzcoachings, trainings unddigital unterstützen und begleiten. *Diversität, Partizipation Und Benachteiligung Im Hochschulsystem* (pp. 133–160). Verlag Barbara BudrichLeverkusen. https://doi.org/10.2307/j.ctv2114fsp.9

Xie, J. (2020). On the exploration of a mobile executive functioning coaching solution for students with and without disabilities in post-secondary STEM education. *International Journal of Mobile Learning and Organisation, 14*(2), 136–160.

Yanchus, N. J., Muhs, S., & Osatuke, K. (2020). Academic background and executive coachtraining. *Professional Psychology: Research and Practice, 51*(4), 390.

Chapter 14

Relational factors in digital coaching

Harald Geißler and Stefanie Rödel

Introduction

The quality of the coach–client relationship is an essential coaching success factor (Behrendt, 2019; Behrendt & Greif, 2022; Greif, 2015). Therefore, the question arises of what are the key ingredients that nurture a fruitful relationship in coaching. This is even more important considering the advent of digital coaching. Many coaches have questioned the potential effectiveness of digital coaching and the ability for the coaches to form an effective alliance online (Heller et al., 2018). In this chapter we aim to provide a broad perspective of relationships in coaching drawing on philosophical and neuro-psychological insights. Moreover, we will discuss how digital coaching can be used to nurture an effective coach–client relationship and how coaches can select and use coaching media to enhance the coaching experience.

Beyond the working alliance

A relationship is "a situation in which two people's feelings, thoughts, and behaviours are mutually and causally interdependent" (Jowett et al., 2010, p. 20). To better understand the key elements that form relationships in coaching and how they interact, it is reasonable to differentiate relationships into different aspects, so-called *reference domains*. For example, the *coach* and *client* build a distinct *reference domain*. As the coach and client interact by communicating and the client's self-reflection can be understood as inner dialogue, it is further reasonable to differentiate between relational and content-related aspects of relationships (cf. communication theory, Watzlawick et al., 1967). Thus, the coaching content is another *reference domain*. These considerations are supported by the finding that the *task* and *goals* aspect of the working alliance seems to be more important than the *bond* aspect to coaching success (Mannhardt & de Haan, 2022). The coaching content itself is defined by two interdependent aspects that need to be reflected in the context of the client's life: the coach's and client's perspectives on the *client's problems* (Schreyögg, 2022) and *potential solutions*. An example of why the *client's problems* and *potential solutions* need to be considered differently but as interconnected is the finding that at the beginning of a coaching process, the client's goals are often part of their problems (Eidenschink, 2015).

In summary, the quality of the coach–client relationship needs to be considered in four different *reference domain*s that are embedded in a certain context (Figure 14.1): the coach, the client, and their perspective on the *client's problems* and *potential solutions*.

DOI: 10.4324/9781003383741-18

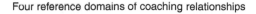

Four reference domains of coaching relationships

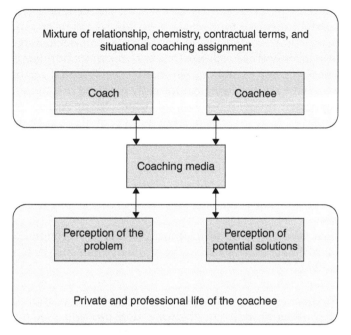

Figure 14.1 Coaching mediates between the reference domains of coaching relationships.

The relational aspect of the coach–client relationship is defined by a mixture of relationship 'chemistry' between coach and client, the contractual terms (Kruger & Terblanche, 2022), and the situational coaching assignment. The content-related aspect of the coach–client relationship is defined by the coach's and client's perspectives on the *client's problems* (Schreyögg, 2022) and *potential solutions*.

To mediate between the *reference domain*s and, therefore, shape the relationship, coaching media can be used. Coaching media can be either used to enable or facilitate communication and problem-solving (Geißler et al., 2022; Geißler & Rödel, 2023). Therefore, coaching media is divided into *communication media* and *problem-solving media*. Both can be either in a natural or digital form. While *communication media* (face-to-face or digital communication via synchronous and asynchronous video, audio, and text tools; Armutat et al., 2015) is only used to enable the interaction of coach and client, *problem-solving media* aspires to trigger specific psychological processes to shape the clients' relationship with their problem and potential solutions (Geißler et al., 2022; Geißler & Rödel, 2023). Thus, coaching media have an impact on all relational factors in coaching. Coaching media need to be *methodically configured* and embedded in the coaching process to effectively mediate between the different *reference domains* and, thus, contribute to coaching success (Geißler & Rödel, 2023).

Furthermore, it is important that coaches understand that, from a philosophical point of view (cf., Heidegger, 1967; Buber, 2008), people can only have two types of relationships with the outside and their inner world, so-called *relational modalities*: object-referential and subject-referential relationships (Geißler, 2000). Object-referential relationships are characterised by the understanding that something can be measured, controlled, and utilised for a specific purpose. Or in other words, people take a bird's-eye perspective and create a certain distance to evaluate a certain situation or aspect. Thus, this perspective emphasises a more analytical and instrumental approach. Subject-referential relationships can be understood as lived experiences that cannot be quantified and have a meaning and purpose for our existence. Thus, subject-referential relationships are characterised by a personal view and being emotionally involved in a situation.

These considerations are supported by neuropsychology (Kuhl, 2010; Puspa, 2022; Schmidt, 2004; Ryba & Roth, 2019), showing that psychological activities can be associated with two different brain regions and, thus, two distinct psychological processes (Engel & Kuhl, 2022; Kuhl, 2010; Schmidt, 2004):

1. *Consciously rational activities* enable *self-regulation* and the development of *object-referential relationships*. They are located in the cerebral cortex and are, in evolutionary terms, relatively new.
2. *Unconsciously emotional activities* enable the development of subject-referential relationships and are evolutionarily older and located in the reptilian brain and the limbic system (Kuhl, 2010; Puspa, 2022).

In summary, coaches need to develop a new perspective on coaching relationships beyond the working alliance, considering different *reference domains* and *modalities*. Furthermore, coaches need to use *methodically configured* coaching media to mediate between the four *reference domains* and stimulate either *conscious, rational activities* or unconscious *emotional activities*, depending on the client's needs. But how can coaches methodically configure coaching media to stimulate specific *relational modalities* and mediate between the *reference domains*?

Successful configuration and use of digital coaching media

In general, coaching media needs to be capable of triggering *psychological processes* (Scholl & Schmidt-Lellek, 2022) to nurture a successful coach–client relationship (Geißler & Rödel, 2023). However, different coaching media have different impacts: for example, questions and reflections are more helpful for the coach, whereas factual information and self-disclosure are more beneficial for clients (Geißler, 2017; Myers, 2017). Thus, different types of coaching media are likely better suited to mediate between specific *reference domains* or activate *specific psychological processes* than others.

To evaluate which coaching media are most suitable for mediating between different *reference domains* in a digital environment, their opportunities and limitations must be considered based on their physical characteristics. *Physical characteristics* or *media configuration components* of digital coaching media are defined by the provided acoustic, visual, tactile, and olfactory sense data and whether the interaction can take place in real-time (synchronously) or with a time delay (asynchronously). The variety and form of these *physical characteristics* impact what *psychological processes* are activated (e.g., digital images can activate *emotional thinking*, text-based tools can activate *rational thinking*). Thus, the potential impact of *communication* and *problem-solving media* needs to be considered in light of the *psychological processes* that can be activated based on the available *media configuration components*.

Methodically configured and implemented *communication media* can facilitate the activation of specific psychological processes, e.g., memorising stressful experiences, perceiving one's own motivation, and reflecting on the root cause of the coaching problem. By activating psychological processes, the *communication media* contributes to how relationships between coaches and clients and their perception of the clients' problems and potential solutions evolve (see exemplary, Table 14.1). Nevertheless, the *communication media* takes only a mediating role.

Furthermore, methodically embedded *communication media* can be combined with analogue and digital *problem-solving media* (Geißler, 2022; Kanatouri & Geißler, 2017). Coaching *problem-solving media* are primarily designed to shape the relationship between clients and their problems and potential solutions. Thus, these tools can also be used for *self-coaching* (Geißler et al., 2007). There are four types of digital *problem-solving media*:

1. Digital text- and character-based coaching tools, e.g., Miro (2023) or Virtual Goal Attainment Coaching (Geißler & Rödel, 2023)
2. Digital images, e.g., ZRM® (2023)
3. 2D visual tools, e.g., Coachingspace's Inner Team (2023)
4. 3D tools with virtual worlds and avatars, e.g., ProReal (2023).

Table 14.1 Communication media can be configured methodically to transmit sense data to activate psychological processes and mediate between reference domains

Methodically configured communication media transmitted (sense) data	Activated psychological processes	Mediation between reference domains, forming the relationship
Coach question: It's nice that we now also meet in person. Why are you here?	Memory of mentally stressful experiences	Coach–client
Factual information from the client: My boss is putting pressure on me because I have not been able to cope with my work lately and I am making more and more mistakes.		Client problem/status quo
Coach question: What do you think should change for the better?	Perceiving one's own motivation	Coach–client problem/ goal
Self-revelation of the client: My most urgent wish is that my boss finally sees my work overload and reduces it.		Client problem/goal
Coach question: Have you ever talked to your boss about this? Because talking to each other is usually a good problem-solving strategy.	Examination of own problem-solving activities	Coach–client problem/ goal solution
Factual information from the client: No, you can't talk to him. He is not interested in such things.	Reflection on own problem-solving activities	Client problem/goal solution

Table 14.2 Physical characteristics of selected digital coaching problem-solving media and the mental processes they activate

Digital problem-solving media	Physical properties and possible uses	Activation of psychological processes
Virtual Goal Attainment Coaching (VGA, 2023)	• Written questions, divided into six groups • Client reflects and answers the questions in a written form • Suitable for self-coaching • Option to illustrate answers with images	• Focus on details and contextual information • Visualisation activates feelings and intuitive thinking
Zurich Ressources Model (ZRM) (2023)	• Meaningful images • Visualisation of written coaching goals • Relates to the client's emotional attitude or position • Definition of a motto goal	• Visualisation activates feelings • Motto goal stimulates intuitive thinking
'Inner Team' by Coachingspace (2023)	• Enables clients to capture the inner voices • Drawings that depict faces in different moods • Speech bubbles can be added and edited	• Visual-auditive simulation activate situation-specific feelings and motivational impulses
ProReal (2023)	• Multifaceted virtual world with avatars • Location can be selected • Simulation of functional units or parts of one's own personality • Speech bubbles can be added and edited • Avatars can express feelings and show gestures	• Visual-auditive simulation with paralingual information activate situation-specific feelings towards other or oneself • Motivational impulses

Digital *problem-solving media* use the inherent *physical characteristics* that serve as *media configuration components* to stimulate specific mental problem-solving activities. Thus, they act as *relational factors* shaping the relationship between *reference domains*: the coach, the client, and their perception of the client's problems and potential solutions. Therefore, they contribute to nurturing the coach–client relationship. For example, tools with pre-written coaching questions (e.g., Virtual Goal Attainment Coaching, VGA, 2023) enable clients to reflect on 'why' they have engaged in coaching. Furthermore, additional visualisation activates feelings and intuitive thinking. How *digital problem-solving media* can stimulate mental problem-solving activities is exemplarily illustrated in Table 14.2.

Digital problem-solving media and the two relational modalities

Based on the *methodical configuration of the media components*, *digital problem-solving media* can be used to activate either *object-referential* or *subject-referential mental processes*.

Table 14.3 Exemplary components of the 'virtual coaching needs assessment' 1 = (10 = extremely important/specific)

Topic	Exemplary questions to be answered in writing by the client
What do I ultimately want? (outcome goal)	What is the outcome goal of my coaching, meaning what positive changes should occur in my life through coaching, and by when?
Importance, difficulty, and pressure	How important, on a scale of 0 to 10, is the mentioned change?
Solution ideas	How specifically, on a scale of 0 to 10, do I know what I no longer want to tolerate/do?
Solution activities	How specifically, on a scale of 0 to 10, do I know exactly what I would need to do to achieve my outcome goal?
Desire	How important/unimportant, on a scale of 0 to 10, is it for me to have a coach who helps me clarify my ideas and critically examine my thoughts?
Indicators of success	How can I clearly recognise that my (self)coaching has been successful?

To develop object-referential relationships, *digital coaching problem-solving tools* need to be designed in a way that they can stimulate processes that identify and analyse data in small, precisely controlled steps. Therefore, digital text-based coaching problem-solving media seem to be beneficial for stimulating these processes and, in turn, nurturing the coach–client relationship as a rational factor. An exemplary tool that is based on behaviouristic (Eldridge & Dembkowski, 2013), cognitive (Auerbach, 2006), and systemic (Kriz, 2022) coaching theories that can stimulate object-referential processes is the 'virtual coaching needs assessment' (Table 14.3). Stimulating the development of object-referential relationships is associated with the goals and tasks aspect of the working alliance.

Although the tasks and goals aspect seems to be especially important, *unconscious psychological processes* that enable the development of subject-referential relationships, nurturing the bonds aspect of the working alliance, are important for coaching. For instance, unconscious mental activities enable parallel processing of large amounts of data from various experiences at high speed, fast and intuitive assessments of reality, and decision-making. Moreover, they allow clients to explore their feelings, emotions, and deeper subjective experiences. Thus, they enable them to gain insights into their own values, beliefs, and motivations and facilitate self-awareness and personal growth. These considerations are rooted in humanistic psychology (Stober, 2006), positive psychology (Freire, 2013), the narrative approach (Stelter, 2013), Gestalt therapy (Bachmann, 2022), and depth psychology (Allcorn, 2006). The prerequisite for intuitive interactions with oneself and the world is an associative connectedness that excludes mental distancing and reflection (Kuhl, 2010; Puspa, 2022). Thus, *digital coaching problem-solving tools* need to stimulate creativity and associations to activate subject-referential brain processes. Image tools, such as the Zurich Resources Model, or 3D visual world with avatars, like ProReal, can effectively support the clients to interact with themselves and the world intuitively.

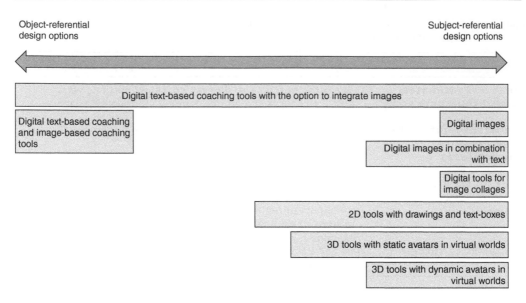

Object-referential
design options

Subject-referential
design options

Digital text-based coaching tools with the option to integrate images

Digital text-based coaching
and image-based coaching
tools

Digital images

Digital images in combination
with text

Digital tools for
image collages

2D tools with drawings and text-boxes

3D tools with static avatars in virtual worlds

3D tools with dynamic avatars in
virtual worlds

Figure 14.2 Based on the configuration of the media components, digital problem-solving media can stimulate object-referential or subject-referential mental processes.

In summary, the above mentioned digital *problem-solving media* can be used to activate object-referential or subject-referential mental processes based on the *configuration of the media components* (Figure 14.2).

The provided overview assumes that there are different *communication media components* (Geißler, 2022; Schütz & Kaul, 2022) that can be configured to either activate object-referential or subject-referential mental processes. *Communication media components* can be understood as configuration modalities. *Illocutionary speech acts* and *propositional communication content* can stimulate either object-referential or subject-referential mental processes based on their configuration. An *illocutionary speech act* refers to the intentional impact of a speaker on the listener, while the *propositional communication content* refers only to the message itself without intentions. All other *communication media configuration components*, like *paralinguistic expressions* (e.g., non-verbal body expressions, gestures, eye and facial expressions, tone, and pitch of voice), *external appearance*, and *spatial context,* are more suitable to activate subject-referential mental processes.

As not all *communication media* (e.g., face-to-face, video conferences, etc.) are suitable for applying the different *communication media configuration components* due to their *physical characteristics* (e.g., paralinguistic expressions cannot be perceived in telephone coaching), coaches should proceed as follows:

- Select the appropriate coaching tools according to the specific needs.
- Combine them into meaningful tool clusters or sequences.
- Integrate them into suitable digital communication media.

Facilitating coaching success by specific coach behaviours

Coaches can use coaching media to nurture all aspects (bonds, tasks, and goals) of the working alliance. Nevertheless, more coaching success factors have been identified (e.g., Behrendt, 2019; Geißler, 2002; Greif, 2010, 2021; Schreyögg, 2015) that can be linked to the coach's behaviour and affect the relational factors. As all frameworks for coaching success have been developed in light of in-person face-to-face coaching (cf., Behrendt, 2019; Geißler, 2002), the question arises of how they can be transferred into a digital environment. Therefore, the seven coaching success factors (Figure 14.3; Greif, 2021) have been translated into 15 practices that consider the physical and psychological characteristics of digital problem-solving media and that outline how coaches can be successful in online environments (see Table 14.4, Geißler et al., 2023).

Furthermore, coaches can adopt 11 different roles to develop and nurture a fruitful working alliance (Geißler, 2002; Schreyögg, 2015), providing stimulation for object-referential and subject-referential reasoning. Each role facilitates the client to develop one or more relational factors and, therefore, helps to establish a successful coach–client relationship. Table 14.5 provides an overview of the 11 roles and concrete examples of how coaches can adopt these roles.

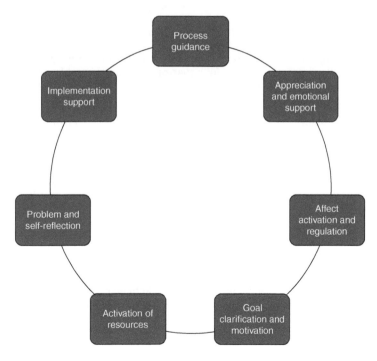

Figure 14.3 Seven coaching success factors.

Source: Greif, (2021).

Table 14.4 Mapping of in-person coaching success factors according to (Greif, 2021)[1] and success factors of digital coaching, including coach behaviour examples (Geißler et al., 2023)

Success factors	Success factors in digital coaching	and exemplary coach behaviours
Process guidance	Technical-organisational guidance	The coach demonstrates how to use a specific digital coaching tool.
	Conceptual configuration of 2D/3D tools	The coach introduces the concept of, e.g., the Inner Team and explains how to utilise it for constellation work.
	Needs-based process structuring	The coach identifies the coaching needs and suggests using specific coaching tools in a certain combination.
Appreciation and emotional support	Client-centered storytelling activation	The coach encourages the client to recall and narrate a specific experience with or without specific coaching tools.
	Emotional awareness and somatic work	During immersive image viewing or constellation work with avatars in virtual worlds, the coach aks the client to feel their body and perceive their current feelings.
Affect activation and regulation	Emotional awareness and somatic work	During immersive image viewing or constellation work with avatars in virtual worlds, the coach aks the client to feel their body and perceive their past feelings.
	Success imagination and recall	The coach encourages the client to imagine a successful situation and use a suitable digital coaching tool to visualize their own actions in that situation, as if in a film-like experience.
Goal clarification and motivation	Immersive image work	The coach asks the client to immerse himself imaginatively in a self-selected digital image.
Activation of resources	Client-centred storytelling activation	The coach encourages the client to recall and narrate a specific positive experience with or without specific coaching tools.
	Immersive image work	The coach asks the client to immerse himself imaginatively in a self-selected digital image, representing a positive experience.
	Interactive process enactment	In immersive image viewing or constellation work with avatars in virtual worlds, the coach addresses a particular aspect of the client's personality as if he were talking to a conversational partner.

Table 14.4 (Continued)

Success factors	Success factors in digital coaching	and exemplary coach behaviours	
Problem and self-reflection	Moderating self-reflections without coaching tools	The coach communicates synchronously or asynchronously in a digital environment with the client and ...	... moderates self-reflection without using digital coaching tools.
	Stimulating self-reflections without coaching tools		... intentionally provides impulses, e.g., in the form of hypotheses, without using digital coaching tools.
	Moderating text-based self-reflections		... moderates self-reflection with digital text-based coaching tools.
	Stimulating text-based self-reflections		... provides focused self-reflection impulses using digital, text-based coaching tools, e.g., raising hypotheses.
	Moderating 2D/3D tool-based self-reflections		... moderates the self-reflection with digital 2D/3D coaching tools.
	Stimulating 2D/3D tool-based self-reflections		... provides concrete impulses for self-reflection with 3D tools based on the visualisation of the client's coaching topic; suitable for constellation work.
Implementation support	Success imagination and recall	The coach encourages the client to imagine the goal status and associated feelings.	
	Emotional-motivational implementation support and action stimulation	The coach praises the client's recent successes, jointly develops implications of future actions, and documents them in a digital, text-based coaching tool.	

Insights

Relationships are at the heart of all coaching. Thus, nurturing fruitful relationships is a central success factor in coaching. Beyond the 'chemistry' between coach and client, the bond aspect of the working alliance, it is important to enable the clients to develop a fruitful relationship with their problems and potential solutions, the tasks and goals aspect of the working alliance.

Relationships are developed by two different mental processes, a conscious rational process and an unconscious emotional and intuitive one. The conscious rational process enables coaches to build object-referential relationships that are associated with the tasks and goals aspect of the working alliance. The unconscious emotional and intuitive process facilitates the development of subject-referential relationships that are associated

Table 14.5 Eleven roles of a coach that facilitate a fruitful working alliance

Role	Coach behaviour
Professional and ethical designer	• Explain the coaching concept to the client in a manner so suits their understanding. • Explain why and how digital coaching tools are used to provide a clear and customised structure to the coaching process. • Explain the process design and the reasons for using and methodically designing digital coaching problem-solving media.
Safe space designer and resource-support	• Explain when and why specific (digital) coaching tools are used and the level of data security they provide. • Suggest disabling the video camera when using digital coaching tools to optimise their resources. • Provide the client with the opportunity to communicate current events or problems in a timely manner between coaching sessions using digital media (e.g., email).
Task-oriented service provider	• Prior to the coaching, conduct a face-to-face conversation or video call with the client to evaluate the personal compatibility and agree on the financial, technical, and organisational coaching conditions. • Define the coaching needs for each session at the beginning with the client. • Clarify with the client the extent to which the current coaching needs were met at the end of each session.
Reflective catalyst	• Positively and critically scrutinise client's statements and their interaction with the used digital coaching tools concerning their coaching problem and potential solutions. • Develop hypotheses that help clients to specify problems and confront clients in a respectful manner.
Guiding advisor	• Provide personal experience, professional guidance, and learning journeys how digital communication and problem-solving tools can help clients to shape their problems perception and propose tailored actions.
Critical learning partner	• Exploratory discussions with clients regarding their digital tool-based self-coaching exercises before and during coaching sessions. • Explore with the client the reasons, topics, and initial conditions of the coaching and encourage them to document these in an appropriate electronic text-based coaching tool. • Continuously monitor how clients interact with digital coaching resources provided, paying particular attention to potential problems and resistance.
Learning-stimulating feedback provider	• Discuss the client's progress that is based on their self-coaching exercises with digital coaching tools during the session and provide constructive proposals to nurture their development. • Provide feedback on (1) the client's interaction behaviour and media utilisation in the coaching process, (2) the available mental problem-solving resources, and (3) the level of goal attainment.
Creativity-stimulating provocateur	• Engage with the digital coaching tools that clients use to • respectfully examine the meaningfulness of the defined coaching goal, • provide hypothesis-driven alternative perspectives, • motivate clients to engage in interactive processes in which they can emotionally empathise with others or specific aspects of their personality.

Table 14.5 (Continued)

Role	Coach behaviour

Energising activator	• Select appropriate digital coaching tools and methodically configure them to
	   • motivate clients to be open to alternative perspectives,
	   • encourage clients to explore alternative courses of action,
	   • celebrate (partial) successes,
	   • motivate clients to engage in interactive processes in which they can emotionally empathise with others or specific aspects of their personality.

Trust- building stabiliser	• Explain the practical usage of digital tools used and data security to ensure a sense of trust before using them. • Develop a profound and transparent conversational framework and process structure for selecting and methodologically designing digital coaching tools. • Utilise email communication at the end of the coaching process to assist clients in implementing actions effectively.
Empathetic companion	• Listen actively, demonstrate attention with paralingual expressions, and provide concise summaries of the client's key statements and underlying emotions. • Be sensitive to the client's feelings and mirror them appreciatively, using tools that make inner-psychic processes more tangible through visualisations. • Guide clients in viewing digital images in an empathetic and exploratory way by encouraging them to immersively engage with the images through a specific question or task.

Source: Geißler (2002); Schreyögg (2015).

with the bond aspect of the working alliance. Coaching is most successful when it is well-balanced in terms of object-referential and subject-referential aspects.

The coach needs to apply communication media configuration components, such as *illocutions* (e.g., summarising, questions) and *propositional communication content*, methodically to stimulate the two different mental processes. Media configuration components that refer to the *linguistic language system* are relational factors of high importance because they can shape the relationships between the coach, the client, the coaching problem, and potential solutions object-referentially and subject-referentially. Besides digital communication media, which can be used to apply the linguistic language system as a relational factor, the coach can use *problem-solving media* to activate these mental processes. Based on their physical characteristics, some digital media or tools are more suitable for specific processes than others. Thus, the so-called media richness (Geißler & Rödel, 2024) needs to be considered when selecting, configuring, and implementing technology methodically in the coaching process. For example, digital text-based *problem-solving media* can be used methodically to stimulate conscious rational processes, while more visual tools, such as digital images, 2D tools including drawings, and 3D worlds with avatars, are well configured to nurture unconscious emotional and intuitive processes.

Furthermore, there are more success factors in coaching (e.g., Behrendt, 2019; Geißler, 2002; Greif, 2010, 2021; Schreyögg, 2015) that impact the relational factors and the quality of the coaching relationship. In general, 15 success factors have been identified for digital coaching (Geißler et al., 2023) that are based on established frameworks (Greif, 2021). Moreover, coaches can take 11 different roles and use digital media methodically to develop and nurture a fruitful working alliance (Geißler, 2002; Schreyögg, 2015).

Reflective questions

1. How do I stimulate conscious, object-referential thought processes?
2. How do I stimulate unconscious, subject-referential processes?
3. Am I capable of nurturing fruitful coach–client relationships in a digital coaching setting?

Conclusion

While the working alliance is an important success factor in coaching, there are more relationships that are critical to coaching success. In particular, the relationship of clients to their problems and potential solutions plays a crucial role (Graßmann, 2022). In accordance with these considerations, it is unsurprising that the tasks and goals aspect of the working alliance seems to be more important for coaching than the bond aspect (Mannhardt & de Haan, 2022). In general, relationships can be developed by using two different mental modalities, conscious rational processes are especially important for the tasks and goals aspect of the working alliance, while unconscious emotional and intuitive processes are particularly important for the bond aspect. Furthermore, coaches can use different communication media configuration components, such as linguistic language, to activate specific problem-solving activities. These communication media components can be transmitted through digital communication media (e.g., video conferences). Moreover, digital problem-solving media can be methodically implemented to stimulate either rational or emotional, intuitive mental processes. Based on their physical characteristics, different digital problem-solving media can be more or less suitable to activate certain mental processes.

Finally, there are more success factors in (digital) coaching (Geißler et al., 2023) that affect the relational factors and, in turn, the quality of the relationship in coaching: coaches can show specific behaviours (cf. Geißler et al., 2023) to address success factors. Furthermore, coaches can take on different roles to nurture-specific relational aspects. As this is a conceptual framework for developing fruitful relationships in digital environments, further research is needed.

References

Allcorn, S. (2006). Psychoanalytically informed executive coaching. In D. R. Stober & A. M. Grant (Eds.), *Evidence Based Coaching Handbook* (pp. 129–149). Hoboken, NJ: Wiley.

Armutat, S. et al. (2015). *Virtuelles Coaching – Bilanz und Orientierungshilfe*. DGFP-Praxispapiere, Leitfaden 08/2015.

Auerbach, J. E. (2006). Cognitive coaching. In D. R. Stober & A. M. Grant (Eds.), *Evidence Based Coaching Handbook* (pp. 103–128). Hoboken, NJ: Wiley.

Bachmann, T. (2022). The forms of contact: An approach to theme, process, state, and methods in coaching. In S. Greif, H. Möller, W. Scholl, J. Passmore, & F. Müller (Eds.), *International Handbook of Evidence-Based Coaching* (pp. 349–368). Cham: Springer.

Behrendt, P. (2019). *Successful Behavior in Coaching, Career Counseling, and Leadership.* (Doctoral dissertation). University of Freiburg im Breisgau.

Behrendt, P., & Greif, S. (2022). Success factors in the coaching process. In S. Greif, H. Möller, W. Scholl, J. Passmore, & F. Müller (Eds.), *International Handbook of Evidence-Based Coaching* (pp. 877–888). Cham: Springer.

Berry, M. R. (2005). *A comparison of face-to-face and distance coaching practices: The role of the working alliance in problem resolution.* (Unpublished doctoral dissertation). Georgia State University, Atlanta, GA.

Berry, R. M., Ashby, J. S., Gnilka, P. B., & Matheny, K. B. (2011). A comparison of face-to-face and distance coaching practices: Coaches' perception of the role of the working alliance in problem resolution. *Consulting Psychology Journal: Practice and Research, 63*, 243–253.

Bordin, E. S. (1979). The generalizability of the psychoanalytic concept of the working alliance. *Psychotherapy: Theory, Research & Practice, 16*(3), 252–260.

Buber, M. (2008). *Ich und Du*. Stuttgart: Reclam.

Charbonneau, A. M. (2002). *Participant self-perception about the cause of behavior change from a program of executive coaching.* (Unpublished doctoral dissertation). Alliant International University, Los Angeles, CA.

Csikszentmihalyi, M. (1975). *Beyond Boredom and Anxiety: The Experience of Play in Work and Games.* San Francisco, CA: Jossey-Bass.

de Haan, E., Grant, A. M., Burger, Y., & Eriksson, P. (2016). A large-scale study of executive and workplace coaching: The relative contributions of relationship, personality match, and self-efficacy. *Consulting Psychology Journal: Practice & Research, 68*(3), 189–207.

Deniers, C. (2019). Experience of receiving career coaching via Skype: An interpretive phenomenological analysis. *International Journal of Evidence-Based Coaching and Mentoring, 17*(1), 72–81.

Diller, S. J., Brantl, M., & Jonas, E. (2022). More than working alliance: Exploring the relationship in entrepreneurial coaching. *Coaching Theorie & Praxis, 8*, 59–75.

Eidenschink, K. (2015). Der einäugige Riese: "Lösungsorientiertes Coaching". Vom Unsinn einer problematischen Fokussierung. In A. Schreyögg & C. Schmidt-Lellek (Eds.), *Die Professionalisierung von Coaching* (pp. 309–223). Wiesbaden: Springer.

Eldridge, F., & Dembkowski, S. (2013). Behavioral coaching. In J. Passmore, D. Peterson, & T. Freire (Eds.), *The Wiley Blackwell Handbook of the Psychology of Coaching and Mentoring* (pp. 298–318). Chichester: Wiley-Blackwell.

Engel, A. M., & Kuhl, J. (2022). Affective change for action control and Selbst-growth in coaching. In S. Greif, H. Möller, W. Scholl, J. Passmore, & F. Müller (Eds.), *International Handbook of Evidence-Based Coaching* (pp. 27–38). Cham: Springer.

Frazee, V. R. (2008). *E-coaching in organizations: A study of features, practices, and determinants of use.* (Unpublished doctoral dissertation). University of San Diego University.

Freire, T. (2013). Positive psychology approaches. In J. Passmore, D. Peterson, & T. Freire (Eds.), *The Wiley Blackwell Handbook of the Psychology of Coaching and Mentoring* (pp. 426–442). Chichester: Wiley-Blackwell.

Geißler, H. (2000). *Organisationspädagogik*. München: Vahlen.

Geißler, H. (2002). Das Konzept: Führung als organisationale Ausbalancierung. In H. Geißler (Ed.), *Balanced Organization* (pp. 1–14). Neuwied: Luchterhand.

Geißler, H. (2017). *Die Grammatik des Coachens*. Wiesbaden: Springer.

Geißler, H. (2022). E-Coaching: An Overview. In S. Greif, H. Möller, W. Scholl, J. Passmore, & F. Müller (Eds.), *International Handbook of Evidence-Based Coaching* (pp. 269–281). Cham: Springer.

Geißler, H., Broszio, A., Fritsch, M., Naumann, V., & Sadowski, V. (2022). *Bedeutsame Momente und Erfolgsfaktoren im Online-Coaching*. Wiesbaden: Springer.

Geißler, H., Hasenbein, M., Kanatouri, S., & Wegener, R. (2014). E-coaching: Concept and empirical findings of a virtual coaching program. *International Journal for Evidence-Based Coaching and Mentoring, 12*(2), 165–187.

Geißler, H., Helm, M., & Nolze, A. (2007). Virtuelles Selbstcoaching – Konzept und erste Erfahrungen. *OSC Organisationsberatung, Supervision, Coaching,* 1/2007, 81–93.

Geißler, H., & Rödel, S. (2023). *Praxishandbuch professionelles Online-Coaching*. Weinheim, Basel: Beltz.

Geißler, H., & Rödel, S. (2024). Media richness. In J. Passmore, S. Diller, & M. Brantl (Eds.), *The Digital & AI Coaches' Handbook*. Abingdon: Routledge.

Geißler, H., Rödel, S., Metz, M., & Bosse, M. (2023). Erfolgsfaktoren im Online-Coaching. *OSC Organisationsberatung, Supervision, Coaching, 30*, 7–25.

Gessnitzer, S., & Kauffeld, S. (2015). The working alliance in coaching: Why behavior is the key to success. *Journal of Applied Behavioral Science, 51*, 177–197.

Ghods, N. (2009). *Distance coaching: The relationship between coach-client relationship, client satisfaction, and coaching outcomes.* (Unpublished doctoral dissertation). University of San Diego.

Graßmann, C. (2022). Die Arbeitsbeziehung im Coaching: Ein Forschungsüberblick und Handlungsempfehlungen für die Praxis. *OSC Organisationsberatung, Supervision, Coaching, 29*, 331–346.

Graßmann, C., Schömerich, F., & Schermuly, C. (2020). The relationship between working alliance and client outcomes in coaching: A meta-analysis. *Human Relations, 73*, 35–58.

Greif, S. (2015). Allgemeine Wirkfaktoren im Coachingprozess. Verhaltensbeobachtungen mit einem Ratingverfahren. In H. Geißler & R. Wegener (Eds.), *Bewertung von Coachingprozessen* (pp. 51–80). Wiesbaden: Springer.

Greif, S. (2021). *Was ist Coaching? Wissenschaftliche Grundlagen und praktische Methoden.* Osnabrück: Amazon.

Greif, S., Schmidt, R., & Thamm, A. (2010). *The Rating of Seven Coaching Success Factors – Observation Manual. Osnabrück*: Unpublished manuscript.

Heidegger, M. (1967). *Sein und* Zeit (11th ed.). Tübingen: Max Niemeyer Verlag.

Heller, J., Triebel, C., Hauser, B., & Koch, A. (2018). *Digitale Medien im Coaching*. Berlin, Heidelberg: Springer.

Horvath, A. O., & Greenberg, L. S. (1989). The development and validation of the Working Alliance Inventory. *Journal of Counseling Psychology, 36*, 223–233.

Jowett, S., O'Broin, A., & Palmer, S. (2010). On understanding the role and significance of a key two-person relationship in sport and executive coaching. *Sport & Exercise Psychology Review, 6*(2), 19–30.

Kanatouri, S., & Geißler, H. (2017). Adapting to working with new technologies. In T. Bachkirova, G. Spence, & D. Drake (Eds.), *The Sage Handbook of Coaching* (pp. 713–728). London, UK: Sage.

Kriz, J. (2022). Systems theories as a basis for coaching. In S. Greif, H. Möller, W. Scholl, J. Passmore, & F. Müller (Eds.), *International Handbook of Evidence-Based Coaching* (pp. 889–900). Cham, Switzerland: Springer.

Kruger, F., & Terblanche, N. H. D. (2022). Working alliance theory in workplace coaching: A pilot study exploring the missing role of the organization. *Journal of Applied Behavioral Science.* https://doi.org/10.1177/0021886322113612

Kuhl, J. (2010). *Lehrbuch der Persönlichkeitspsychologie*. Göttingen, Germany: Hogrefe.

Mannhardt, S. M., & de Haan, E. (2022). The coaching relationship. In S. Greif, H. Möller, W. Scholl, J. Passmore, & F. Müller (Eds.), *International Handbook of Evidence-Based Coaching* (pp. 173–186). Cham, Switzerland: Springer.

Myers, A. (2017). Researching the coaching process. In T. Bachkirova, G. Spence, & D. Drake (Eds.), *The Sage Handbook of Coaching* (pp. 589–609). London, UK: Sage.

Passarelli, A., Trinh, M. P., Van Oosten, E. B., & Varley, M. (2020). Can you hear me now? The influence of perceived media richness on executive coaching relationships. *Academy of Management Proceedings, 2020*(1), 13211.

Passarelli, A. M., Trinh, M. P., van Oosten, E. B., & Varley, A. (2023). Communication quality and relational self-expansion: The path to leadership coaching effectiveness. *Human Resource Management, 62,* 661–680.

Puspa, L. (2022). Brain-focused coaching. In S. Greif, H. Möller, W. Scholl, J. Passmore, & F. Müller (Eds.), *International Handbook of Evidence-Based Coaching* (pp. 77–97). Cham, Switzerland: Springer.

Ryba, A., & Roth, G. (2019). *Coaching und Beratung in der Praxis: Ein neurowissenschaftlich fundiertes Integrationsmodell.* Stuttgart, Germany: Klett-Cotta.

Schmidt, G. (2004). *Liebesaffären zwischen Problem und Lösung.* Heidelberg, Germany: Carl-Auer.

Scholl, W., & Schmidt-Lellek, C. (2022). Understanding in coaching: An intersubjective process. In S. Greif, H. Möller, W. Scholl, J. Passmore, & F. Müller (Eds.), *International Handbook of Evidence-Based Coaching* (pp. 949–958). Cham, Switzerland: Springer.

Schreyögg, A. (2015). Die potenzielle Rollenvielfalt des Coachs. In A. Schreyögg & C. Schmidt-Lellek (Eds.), *Die Professionalisierung von Coaching* (pp. 245–256). Wiesbaden, Germany: Springer.

Schreyögg, A. (2022). The organizational context in coaching. In S. Greif, H. Möller, W. Scholl, J. Passmore, & F. Müller (Eds.), *International Handbook of Evidence-Based Coaching* (pp. 681–690). Cham, Switzerland: Springer.

Schütz, A., & Kaul, C. (2022). Means of verbal and non-verbal communication in coaching. In S. Greif, H. Möller, W. Scholl, J. Passmore, & F. Müller (Eds.), *International Handbook of Evidence-Based Coaching* (pp. 565–576). Cham, Switzerland: Springer.

Stelter, R. (2013). Narrative approaches. In J. Passmore, D. Peterson, & T. Freire (Eds.), *The Wiley Blackwell Handbook of the Psychology of Coaching and Mentoring* (pp. 407–425). Chichester, UK: Wiley-Blackwell.

Stober, D. R. (2006). Coaching from the humanistic perspective. In D. R. Stober & A. M. Grant (Eds.), *International Handbook of Evidence-Based Coaching* (pp. 17–50). Hoboken, NJ: Wiley.

Watzlawick, P., Beavin, J. H., & Jackson, D. D. (1967). *Pragmatics of Human Communication.* New York: W.W. Norton.

Chapter 15

Creating media rich environments for digital coaching

Harald Geißler and Stefanie Rödel

Introduction

The media used to support the process of coaching is a key feature of coaching. Media richness, refers to those media conditions that offer a relevant problem-solving benefit. To make practical use of these potentials, it is necessary to shape them in a methodologically target-oriented way. Furthermore, we must also consider that the use of media is not only associated with potential benefits but also with certain costs and burdens. This difference defines the *media value*.

In order to clarify how media richness in online coaching can be appropriately captured, first, an overview of the most important digital coaching media will be given. On this basis, a discussion of the conceptual fundamental principles of the media richness theory (Daft & Lengel 1984, 1986; Dennis & Valacich, 1999) will follow in order to contribute to the development of a media theory of coaching.

Media richness of digital coaching

Conceptual preliminary notes

In contrast to the tradition of defining media only as technical tools (McLuhan, 1964), we propose a conceptually broader understanding of media. As we will explain later in detail, there are many arguments to conceptualise coaching media not only with reference to technical coaching conditions but also to the corresponding psychological activities, which are essential for solid problem-solving processes (Geißler et al., 2022; Geißler & Rödel, 2023).

Therefore, coaching media have a similar function to musical instruments when making music. A violin, for example, can produce completely different sounds than a xylophone or a kettledrum. In other words, the tonal potentiality of each musical instrument has a specific characteristic. With reference to coaching, the media richness of different coaching media can therefore be understood as equivalent to the tonal potentiality of different musical instruments. For example, video conferencing provides completely different communication options than emailing does. Furthermore, it makes a difference whether audio communication is combined with written questionnaires or with 3D tools offering virtual worlds with avatars (Geißler & Rödel, 2023; Geißler et al., 2023). Therefore, the central question which every coach faces is: Which coaching media should I use in my coaching in order to 'orchestrate' it in a meaningful way (Berninger-Schäfer,

DOI: 10.4324/9781003383741-19

2018; Geißler et al., 2022)? Moreover, the next question must be: How should I design the selected media methodologically to get the right 'sound' and to make coaching a co-creative work of art (Geißler & Rödel, 2023).

For this purpose, coaches must dispose of comprehensive conceptual knowledge, solid filigree craftsmanship, and aesthetically sensitised creativity and creative power, which enables them to integrate this knowledge and skills into their own personality. In this sense, one could discuss the further question of whether the personality of the coach also influences or acts as a distinct coaching medium.

Digital coaching media and its media richness

The field of coaching media is divided into two major areas (Geißler, 2022; Geißler & Rödel, 2023). The first covers the media serving the communication between coach and client. It can therefore be called *coaching communication media*. The second covers the media, which are used to guide problem-solving processes. They can also be used for self-coaching. These are referred to as *coaching problem-solving media* (Geißler, 2022; Geißler & Rödel, 2023).

Media richness of the different coaching communication media

For online-coaching sessions there are synchronous and asynchronous options for video, audio, and text communication. Based on the theory of Daft and Lengel (1984, 1986) and its further development (Dennis & Valacich, 1999), the coaching media richness can be rated with reference to four characteristics: symbol variety, immediacy of feedback, rehearsability, and reprocessability.

At first sight, the most important characteristic seems to be *symbol variety*, i.e., the variety of (acoustically, visually, or tactilely) perceivable sense data that a communication medium can convey. In this way, the media richness of the different coaching communication media can be profiled as illustrated in Table 15.1.

The second media richness characteristic refers to the *immediacy of feedback*. This means the temporal transmission of auditory or visual sense data. In order words, it refers to whether the sense data is transmitted synchronously (at the same time) or

Table 15.1 Rating of the multiplicity of the auditive, visual, and tactile features of the coaching communication media

Communication media	Multiplicity of the perceivable sense data		
	auditive	*visual*	*tactile*
Face-to-Face Comm.	comprehensive	comprehensive	comprehensive
Synchronous Video Comm.	comprehensive	partly limited	---
Asynchronous Video Comm.	comprehensive	partly limited	---
Synchronous Audio Comm.	comprehensive	---	---
Asynchronous Audio Comm.	comprehensive	---	---
Synchronous Text Comm.	---	---	---
Asynchronous Text Comm.	---	---	---

Source: Geißler (2022); Passarelli et al. (2022).

asynchronously (with a time delay). According to Daft and Lengel (1984, 1986), a high media richness is given if a high symbol variety is combined with immediacy of feedback. This is the case, particularly in face-to-face communication and synchronous video communication, even though the latter is partially reduced. Correspondingly, media richness is rated extremely low in email coaching because the symbol variety is comparably low, and it is not possible to provide or receive immediate feedback.

This view is contradicted by the reduced social cues approach (Kiesler et al., 1984; Sproull & Kiesler, 1986) with the argument that the lack of immediate feedback can also be beneficial for problem-solving processes. This is because it generates a protective and developmental space for independent thought processes. This argument is supported by the findings of the channel expansion theory (Carlson & Zmud, 1999), the hyperpersonal perspective theory (Walther, 1996, 2007), and the findings of Clutterbuck (2010, p. 16f.), which refer to digital coaching. Therefore, it is reasonable to consider the provision or enabling of *protective and developmental spaces for independent thinking* as a further media richness characteristic.

Furthermore, drawing on Dennis and Valacich (1999), two more characteristics relevant to coaching can be added, namely, as follows:

- *Rehearsability*, describing "the extent to which the media enables the sender to rehearse or fine tune the message before sending" (Dennis & Valacich, 1999, p. 2).
- *Reprocessability*, referring to "the extent to which a message can be re-examined or processed again within the context of communication event" (Dennis & Valacich, 1999, p. 3).

In addition, the advantage that coaches and coachees have with online coaching by location independence must also be considered. Online coaching saves time and money, protects the environment, and integrates disabled people. However, as presence is a central success factor in coaching and coach and client are spatially separated in online coaching, telepresence is another important characteristic of coaching media richness.

These considerations lead to the following profile of communication media, outlined in Table 15.2.

With regard to these characteristics, the media richness of the different coaching communication media can be rated as follows in Figure 15.1 (cf., Armutat et al., 2015).

Table 15.2 Rating of the media richness

	Immediacy of feedback	Protective and developmental space	Rehearsability	Reprocess - ability	Telepresence
Face-to-Face Comm.	X	—	—	—	—
Synchronous Video Comm.	X	—	—	X	X
Asynchronous Video Comm.	—	X	X	X	X
Synchronous Audio Comm.	X	—	—	X	X
Asynchronous Audio Comm.	—	X	X	X	X
Synchronous Text- Comm.	X	—	—	X	X
Asynchronous Text Comm.	—	X	X	X	X

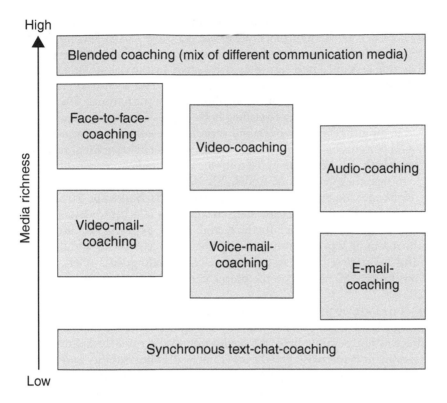

Figure 15.1 Rating of the media richness of the different coaching communication media.

Blended coaching is at the top of the ranking. In this format, face-to-face communication is sequentially combined with the digital formats of synchronous and asynchronous video, audio, and text communication. The formats need to be chosen according to the situation and the client's needs (Mundelsee, 2022). Taking into consideration the partially quality-limiting conditions of immediacy of feedback, it is to be expected that the synchronous modalities of face-to-face, video, and audio communication will predominate in this media mix. On the other hand, with sufficient format competence (Berninger-Schäfer et al., 2018), the formats of asynchronous video, audio, and text communication can be used to offer the clients protected spaces for reflection (Clutterbuck, 2010). In addition, they can be used to offer support in difficult situations between the coaching sessions when coach and client do not meet personally or virtually.

Face-to-face coaching is in second place in this ranking. This evaluation is mainly based on the fact that all sensory data can be conveyed synchronously and that the spatio-temporal presence is particularly important for the interpersonal relationship (Geißler & Rödel, 2024). However, this positive assessment is partly diminished by three aspects:

• The temporal, financial, and possibly ecological expenses of travelling.
• The problem of the possible exclusion of disabled persons.
• The lack of reprocessability and rehearsability.

These weaknesses of face-to-face coaching draw attention to the key strengths of *video coaching* (Deniers, 2017). In the first place, there are no travel costs. Second, it is possible to make low-threshold video recordings that support the client in the follow-up process to the coaching session. These advantages are offset by the risk of internet disruptions or other technical disturbances, possible license fees for data-secure communication technology, and above all, the partly reduced symbol variety (Kanatouri, 2020). This is because in video coaching, sensory data regarding body expressions and personal appearance are conveyed in a quite limited manner, and veritable eye contact is also not possible (Geißler, 2022). And perhaps most serious is the fragility of the interpersonal relationship due to the fact that coach and client are in different locations and can interrupt their contact with a single mouse click (Geißler & Rödel, 2023).

In contrast, *telephone coaching* (Berry et al., 2011; Charbonneau, 2002; Ghods, 2009) does not use visual communication data at all. This is a disadvantage because diagnostically important data, especially face and body expressions, are missing. However, this shortcoming can be compensated. Therefore, the coach should be well-trained in mindful awareness and careful analysis of paralinguistic client behavior. Furthermore, invisibility while being on the phone can also serve as a protective space (McLaughlin, 2013).

The next step is to look at the asynchronous formats of *video mail, voice mail, and email coaching* (e.g., Poepsel, 2011; Ribbers & Waringa, 2015). Due to the fact that immediate feedback is not possible here, the media richness is rated comparatively low. However, this assessment is relativised by the advantages of rehearsability and reprocessability as well as by the fact that the asynchrony of these media also provides protective spaces for independent thinking (Clutterbuck, 2010; Richter & Schindler, 2018). This possibility can be particularly valuable in the final phase of a coaching process.

Finally, the lowest position in the ranking is occupied by synchronous chat coaching, mainly because the symbol variety of this medium is very low. This shortcoming cannot be sufficiently compensated by the immediacy of feedback. For this reason, chat coaching is only used extremely rarely in coaching practice.

Overview of the most important digital coaching problem-solving media

Some of the coaching communication media discussed can be combined with various natural and digital coaching problem-solving media. In this chapter, the focus is on digital coaching problem-solving media, namely, as follows:

- Coaching tools for free writing, drawing or painting.
- Coaching tools with pre-prepared written questions.
- Electronic 2D-visual image-based tools.
- Electronic drawings to be filled with texts.
- Tools providing 3D-visual worlds for constellation work with avatars.
- Online journal as a problem-solving mega tool.

Coaching tools for free writing, drawing, or painting, such as the whiteboard or simple Word processing and/or presentation tools, can simulate a canvas, similar to the flipchart.

They can be used for documentation or, for example, creative visualisation of scaling or timeline work. The most important composition elements are text fields, shapes, arrows, lines, or symbols. Examples of online tools are Lucidspark (2023) or Mural (2023), as well as the whiteboards in video communication platforms such as Zoom (2023) (Geißler & Rödel, 2023).

Coaching tools with pre-prepared written questions support the effective clarification of needs and objectives (Geißler et al., 2014). The answers can be illustrated with the help of electronic images. One application that has been empirically evaluated for its effectiveness is the web-based coaching programme 'Virtual Goal Attainment Coaching (VGC)' (Geißler et al., 2014; case study in Geißler & Rödel, 2023, pp. 188–195). In later phases of the coaching process, it can be helpful to use the text-based coaching tool '7-Fields-Scheme' to reconstruct relations of cause and effect and to track down the difference between the coaching concern and the client's reality (Geißler, 2022; case study in Geißler & Rödel, 2023, pp. 207–213).

Electronical 2D-visual image-based tools effectively support the client in getting access to emotions and to unconscious processes (Berninger-Schäfer, 2018; Geißler et al., 2022; Geißler & Rödel, 2023). This is especially true when the creative methods of image work are linked to embodiment, i.e., the perception of body signals and feelings (somatic markers) (Messerschmidt, 2015; Kuhl & Strehlau, 2009; Geißler & Rödel, 2023, pp. 222–223). Freely selected images from an own or online image pool (e.g., Pixabay 2023) can be commented by text or assembled into collages. The image-based ZRM® online tool (2023) is also a well-researched tool in practice (Krause & Storch, 2010). The 2D-visual Inner Team of the Coachingspace (2023) platform provides stylised faces with different facial expressions on a whiteboard. Here, lines can be connected and text can be added (e.g., speech bubbles, names). Further examples are Whole Partnership (2023), or Online Fields (2023). At the same time, it is useful to develop tool-independent templates for interventions such as the sociogram, wheel of life, or tetralemma (Geißler & Rödel, 2023) or to create one's own personalised collection of templates for organisational charts and diagrams (e.g., Canva, 2023; Slidehunter, 2023).

Avatars in 3D-visual tools are visualised representatives of different groups, persons, organisations, ideas, or parts of the personality (Geißler & Rödel, 2023, pp. 230–264). With the help of these constellations, dynamics of relationships and conflicts, the client's role and options for action can be elaborated (Krause, 2018). Through different perspective settings in the tool, the scenery can be viewed from above or through the eyes of a specific avatar, which enhances immersion (Geißler & Rödel, 2023; Tawadros et al., 2018).

Coachingspace (2023) is a platform that offers a 3D-visual constellation board on which digitally converted, inscribable wooden figures or animals can be placed, for example, for system or problem constellations. Various virtual consultation spaces (e.g., office or natural settings such as beach or mountain landscapes) are available (Geißler & Rödel, 2023, pp. 246–247).

CoSpaces (2023) offers several virtual worlds with static avatars in the shape of people, animals, plants, and objects that can be used to visualise social structures and/or the clients' inner team. The avatars can be visually configured and labeled with a name and speech bubbles and thus can be used for communication with each other (Geißler & Rödel, 2023, pp. 234–235; Krause, 2018).

ProReal (2023) is a 3D-visual Internet application with a mystical-looking world and stylised, human-like gender- and faceless avatars. They can show emotions with the help of expressive body movements, walk through the landscape, and communicate with each other via speech bubbles. The scenery can also be enriched with metaphorically charged symbolic objects (props), such as a clock, a treasure chest, or a roadblock (Geißler & Rödel, 2023, pp. 235–237; Tawadros et al., 2018).

Last but not least, an *online journal*, for example, can be used in the form of a shared digital drive presentation. This can be seen as a problem-solving mega-tool by which the co-creation process of the co-creative aesthetic artwork can be traced and designed. It serves to document the coaching content worked on (e.g., by inserting screenshots from the aforementioned tools or links to video recordings of coaching sessions). Furthermore, the client can work in it asynchronously when answering text-based question sets or processing transfer tasks. Finally, it can be used synchronously in the coaching session as a whiteboard (Geißler & Rödel 2023, pp. 272–284).

Media richness of the coaching communication media, amplified through coaching problem-solving media

In the following, the focus will be set on the media richness that arises when certain coaching communication media are associated with specific coaching problem-solving media (Berninger-Schäfer, 2018; Geißler, 2018, 2022; Geißler & Metz, 2012; Geißler & Rödel, 2023; Kanatouri, 2020; Kanatouri, & Geißler 2016).

Looking at the coaching problem-solving media presented in the previous section, it becomes clear that all of them reduce the media richness characteristics of rehearsability and reprocessability in different ways. Furthermore, they are characterised by a symbol variety that is limited to visual sense data. Therefore, in order not to overload the visual communication channel, it is recommended to combine them primarily with synchronous audio communication. In addition, a connection with video messages is also possible in many cases.

The situation is a bit different with regard to *text-based coaching tools*. For these, it seems reasonable to decide together with the client with regards to the specific situation whether the video camera should be switched on or off when working with these tools in order to offer a personal space for protection and development.

On this basis, the media richness rating shown in Figure 15.2 refers to the following combinations of coaching communication media and coaching-problem-solving media:

- synchronous video or audio communication enriched with digital text-based coaching tools;
- synchronous audio communication enriched with digital text-based or image-based coaching tools;
- synchronous audio communication enriched with text-based and 2D-visual problem-solving-tools;
- synchronous audio communication enriched with text-based and 3D-visual problem-solving-tools;
- mix of digital coaching communication tools enriched with digital text-based and image-based as well as 2D- and 3D-visual problem-solving-tools (including online journal).

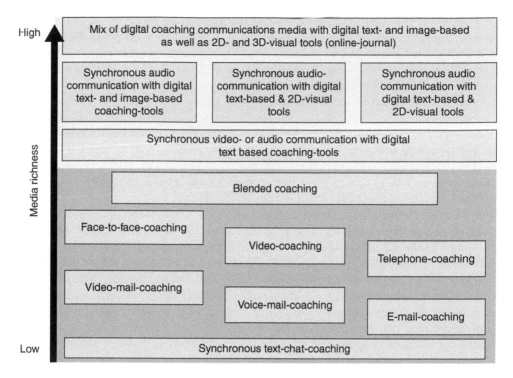

Figure 15.2 Evolvement of the media richness evaluation based on combining different coaching communication media with different digital coaching tools.

This selection of different digital coaching tools is based on the understanding that text-based coaching tools are central to the media richness of coaching (Geißler et al., 2023) and that combining them with other coaching tools is appropriate.

While evaluating the media richness of these media combinations, it becomes reasonable that the media richness characteristic of symbol variety must be modified into *symbol value*, i.e., the value a medium's sense data can generate for valuable problem-solving activities. As shown later on in detail, these are as follows:

- the clients' rational and intuitive thinking,
- their rational and intuitive action control,
- and their self-efficacy experiences as well as their emotional and body perceptions.

On this basis, the evaluation provides two basic insights:

- Combining digital communication media with digital coaching problem-solving media results in a media richness higher than the media richness of digital coaching sessions in which no additional coaching tools are used.
- The media richness can be increased even further by combining digital text-based tools with other digital tools.

At a high level, the relatively lowest media richness can be found in coaching sessions in which digital audio or video communication is enriched with tools for open writing, drawing and/or painting in order to record the most important steps and results of the coaching process in writing (Berninger-Schäfer, 2018). As described above, a whiteboard alternative of video communication technology, for example, Word or PowerPoint documents, visually made accessible to the client via screen sharing, is suitable for this purpose.

Moreover, the coaching media richness is comparatively much higher when working with pre-prepared coaching questions that have to be answered in writing by the clients. They primarily stimulate *rational thinking* (Geißler, 2018). Furthermore, they pre-structure the coaching process and thus respond to a central coaching success factor (Behrendt, 2019; Geißler et al., 2023; Greif, 2015, 2021).

The overall relatively high media richness of digital text-based coaching tools can be further increased by combining them with digital images or with image-based coaching tools – such as the ZRM® (2023). As described above, these tools usually also offer text-based media components. The great advantage of such a connection is that the immersive contemplation of images stimulates *intuitive thinking* (Messerschmidt, 2015) and is thus an important supplement to the comparatively rationally designed work with texts.

An alternative to this, roughly equivalent in terms of media richness, is to combine digital text-based coaching tools with different kinds of 2D visual design tools. It is valuable for the coaching process that the clients themselves have to shape them (i.e., by entering figures, text, etc.) in a solution-oriented and problem-solving-oriented way to stimulate their own *intuitive action control* (Berninger-Schäfer, 2018; Krause, 2018; Tawadros et al., 2018). These characteristics by themselves already establish a high media richness. This can be further enhanced by recording the gained insights in written form. For this reason, the conjunction of 2D tools with digital text-based tools is important.

The alternative to this is the use of 3D visual coaching tools. Their central feature is to provide avatars, i.e., digitally generated figures in the shape of people, animals, plants, and objects, as well as mythical creatures, which can be set up in virtual worlds (Tawadros et al., 2018). ProReal, in particular, offering avatars that can be configured, walk and express feelings by postures, displays a relatively high media richness. This is because of its high symbol variety and its fruitful opportunities to stimulate problem-solving *intuitive thinking and action control* (Geißler & Rödel, 2023). In addition, it can be perfectly combined with *embodiment work* (Storch & Weber, 2022). Just like the 2D-visual design tools, they already have a high media richness in themselves and this can be increased even more when the client's insights are written down in text-based tools (Geißler et al., 2014).

Finally, the highest media richness is given in coaching sessions in which the digital coaching formats presented above are connected sequentially and when the most important results of the coaching process are documented in an *online journal*.

Open questions

The dilemma of empirical coaching research

In the following section, the empirical study of Passarelli et al. (2020) will be discussed to reflect the research problem that coaching media richness cannot be empirically tested,

Table 15.3 Media richness of phone, video, and face-to-face communication

Richness feature	Phone	Video	Face-to-face
Nonverbal communication			
• body language	Low	Medium	High
• facial expression	Low	High	High
• posture	Low	Medium	High
• gesture	Low	Medium	High
• eye gaze	Low	Medium	High
• paralanguage (volume, pitch, inflection etc.	High	High	High
• touch	Low	Low	High
Immediate feedback	Medium	Medium	High
Natural language use	High	High	Highest
Personalisation	High	High	Highest

Source: Passarelli et al. (2022, p. 34).

because, in coaching practice, it never appears in isolation, but always as a methodically designed media richness.

Passarelli et al. (2020) rely on the concept of media richness developed by Daft and Lengel (1984, 1986) and show how this concept can be applied to evaluate the media richness of face-to-face, video, and audio coaching and to compare their effectiveness in achieving success.

The first step of the study was to identify the media richness features, which are important to assess the media richness profile of face-to-face, video, and audio coaching and to have it checked by test persons (see Table 15.3).

On this basis, it was expected that the differences in media richness of face-to-face, video, and audio coaching would correlate with a correspondingly different coaching effectiveness. However, this could not be proven. In the following, it will be shown that these research results reflect a deeper problem. To understand it, it is necessary to clarify the conceptual foundations of Daft and Lengel's (1984, 1986) media richness theory.

The conceptual basics of the media richness theory

The concept of media richness was originally developed by Daft and Lengel (1984, 1986) in order to clarify with reference to the criterion of an optimal *cost-benefit ratio* the following question: *Which communication media should be used in organisations for which purposes?*

To answer this question, Daft and Lengel refer to two basic tasks of any organisation: The first is to provide the knowledge which is necessary for the value creation process (*Uncertainty Problem*). The second task is to ensure that the available knowledge is interpreted and used in a consistent manner (*Equivocality Problem*).

At the time of publishing their paper in 1986, the following *communication media* were available to solve these two tasks or problems, each with a different media richness: (1) face-to-face communication, (2) telephone calls, (3) personal documents such as letters or memos, (4) impersonal circulars, and (5) number tables (Daft & Lengel 1986, p. 560). This list has been enriched by Passarelli et al. (2020) by adding video communication and determining its media richness between face-to-face and audio communication. This can be seen as a meaningful update and continuation of this approach. In order to determine the media richness of the specific communication media, Daft and Lengel refer to three different aspects:

- the different *physical characteristics* of the respective communication channel,
- the sense data that can be conveyed with their help,
- and the *mental conditions, to understand* the information that is covered in these sense data.

In this way, they conceptually tie *media richness* to *information richness*, especially with regard to the equivocality problem (Daft & Lengel, 1986, p. 560). Taking this into consideration, it becomes clear that Daft and Lengel establish their concept of media richness on the *structural coupling* of physical media characteristics with the corresponding mental activities, which are essential for understanding the information conveyed with the sense data of the communication channel.

The importance of this structural coupling has not been sufficiently taken into account in the reception of their theory (Boos & Jonas, 2008, pp. 206–207; Dennis & Kinney, 1998; Dennis & Valacich, 1999; El-Shinnawy & Markus, 1992; Kinney & Watson, 1992; Rice & Shook, 1990). In the same sense, Passarelli et al. (2020) relate the concept of media richness relatively unilaterally to the physical conditions of the communication channel and the sense data conveyed by it. This becomes tangible as they concretised media richness with the help of *media richness features*, which – with the exception of 'personalisation' – relate to the following physical communication characteristics:

- non-verbal communication, i.e., body language, facial expression, posture, gesture, eye gaze, and paralanguage,
- natural use of language,
- the immediacy of feedback.

The first two of these three features have been summarised by Dennis and Valacich (1999, p. 2) in their reception of the media richness theory in the characteristic of *symbol variety*. It can therefore be stated that the attempt made by Passarelli et al. (2020) to make Daft and Lengel's media richness theory fruitful for coaching has, on the one hand, provided valuable impulses to the coaching discourse. But, on the other hand, it stands in a reception history of this theory which is based on a unilateral view. This is characterised by the fact that the media richness of communication media is only bound to the physical conditions of their communication channel and the sense data conveyed by them. In this way, media richness theory comes close to the *reduced social cues approach* (e.g., Sproull & Kiesler, 1986).

This limitation can be overcome by clarifying how important the various sensorially perceptible characteristics of the different coaching communication media are for the development of solid problem-solving practice.

The discussion of the question later in the paper shows that the differences in the media richness of face-to-face, video, and audio coaching are probably a bit lower than Passarelli et al. (2020) assume. This is because these three coaching formats do not show any differences with regard to the two richness features that are of crucial importance for coaching, namely *natural language* and *paralanguage*.

Furthermore, there is a tension between the small differences in the media richness of face-to-face, video, and audio coaching and the empirical finding that their effectiveness is quite similar. The reason for this difference seems to be that Passarelli et al. (2020) eval-uated only the effectiveness of the methodologically designed communication media and not the effectiveness of the communication media itself. In other words, it can be assumed that the examined coaches compensated for specific weaknesses of the used coaching media. This argument could explain the research findings that higher media richness does not correlate with better communication successes (Dennis & Kinney, 1998; Kinney & Watson, 1992; Valacich et al., 1994).

Proposal for further development

The media components of the coaching communication media and its media richness

With regard to the problems just described, it makes sense to define the media richness characteristic of symbol variety a bit differently from Passarelli et al. (2020) and to dis-tinguish between the following media components (Geißler, 2022):

- the linguistic system of the language with the two components of

  - the illocutionary speech acts that regulate the relationship between coach and client
  - and the propositions, i.e., the communicated contents

- the paralinguistic communication behaviour (speech speed, loudness, articulation, intonation of single words, etc.)
- eye expressions (expression, movement of the gaze direction and mutual eye gaze)
- non-verbal body expressions (facial expressions, gestures, body movement and posture)
- outer appearance (gender, age, body characteristics such as height and weight, dress-ing, haircut, jewellery and many more)
- touch (especially shaking hands during welcoming and farewell in face-to-face coaching)
- coaching context (virtual or spatio-temporal presence, in the office of the coach or during a walk in the forest with the client)

Compared to the media richness features identified by Passarelli et al. (2020), the follow-ing changes are made:

- Natural language is extremely important for coaching – and probably also for business communication (Spears et al., 2001, p. 616f.). For this reason, it makes sense to list its two main components, i.e., illocutions and propositions separately.
- On the other hand, the media richness features of 'facial expressions', 'posture', and 'gestures' are relatively close to each other so that they can be summarised by means of the media components of 'nonverbal body expressions' (Schütz & Kaul, 2022).
- Furthermore, context is an important media component and should be added to the compilation of Passarelli et al. (2020). In video communication, it is important whether the coach allows the client a view into his office, blurs the background, or chooses a virtual background conveying a certain mood or atmosphere (Geißler, 2022).

Accordingly, the media components justified in this way are assessed as follows in terms of their significance for coaching success.

Table 15.4 The components of the coaching communication media and its symbol value

Media components	Symbol value
illocutionary speech	highest
propositional communication contents	highest
paralinguistic communication behaviour	high
eye expressions	high
body expressions	medium
outer appearance	low
touch	low
coaching context	low – high

Table 15.4 shows the components of the coaching communication media and its symbol value.

The sense data of the communication channel, which provide information about the linguistic *system of language*, contain information about the *illocutionary speech acts* (Austin, 1962; Searle, 1969), by which the communication partners perform rational and intuitive action control in the coaching process. Therefore, this media component has an extremely *high value* for the problem-solving process of coaching (Geißler, 2017).

This assumption also applies to the second essential aspect of the linguistic language system, the *propositions*. They consist of the communication contents being indispensable for problem-solving in coaching and which are developed with the help of rational and intuitive thought processes (Geißler, 2017). For this reason, this media component has an *extremely high symbol value*.

The *paralinguistic sensory data* have a bit lower but still *very high value* for the problem-solving process. The reason is that they establish feeling and bodily experiences in the recipients and in this way specify the executed and stimulated illocutions and transmitted communication contents (Geißler, 2022; Schütz & Kaul, 2022).

The sense data containing information of the *eye expressions* serves two purposes. The reciprocal eye contact serves the intuitive action control of the communication partners, in particular, by indicating with eye contact when one wants to make a speech contribution (Chen et al., 2013). However, this action control can, in principle, also be taken over by illocutionary speech acts. Similarly, emotions are reflected unaltered in the eyes of communication partners and trigger emotional and bodily perceptions in the receiver (Roth, 2021). Thus, they can also be compensated by the sense data with which paralinguistic information is conveyed (Geißler, 2022). Due to these compensation possibilities, they again have a *bit lower, but still high value* for the problem-solving process of coaching.

In contrast, the sense data providing information about *body expressions* only have a *moderately high value*. This is because the intuitive thought processes and emotional and bodily experiences they stimulate are *significantly less valuable* than the *paralinguistic sense data and eye expressions* (Schütz & Kaul, 2022).

In contrast, the sense data providing information about the *external appearance* of the communication partners have only a *low value*. This is because it is sense data that can stimulate intuitive thinking and intuitive action control not only positively, but possibly also negatively, by stimulating prejudices and problematic affects (McLaughlin, 2013).

Likewise, *physical touch* has only a low value, which in face-to-face coaching is usually limited to shaking hands during greetings and farewells (Schütz & Kaul, 2022).

In contrast to this, sense data referring to the *coaching context* have an ambivalent value. For the problem-solving process, i.e., for the task and goal aspect of the working alliance, the value is rather *low* (Graßmann, 2022) but for the intuitive action control of the interpersonal relationship between coach and client, i.e., for the bond aspect of their Working Alliance, it is rather *high* (Graßmann, 2022).

From the symbol variety to the symbol value

The previous considerations have shown that the value of coaching media is not directly determined by the symbol variety (i.e., by the variety of sensory perceptions, which are made possible using a certain coaching medium). Accordingly, it makes sense to follow the reception of the media richness theory proposed by Dennis and Kinney (1998), because they tie media richness to the 'multiplicity of information cues'. This focus on the information contained in the communicated sense data draws attention to the *structural coupling that exists between the physical and the mental communication conditions.* Therefore, it needs to be clarified, which mental client activities are stimulated by the media richness features of natural language use and non-verbal communication (body language, facial expression, posture, gesture, eye gaze, paralanguage, touch). Furthermore, in the next step, these mental activities must be clustered in a meaningful way.

This leads to the recognition that coaching processes have different objectives, i.e., intersubjectively perceivable outside and mental ones in the inside. The latter is determined by the inner dialogues that the clients have to conduct in order to mediate the primarily rationally controlled personality parts that support them in achieving their coaching goals (Schmidt, 2004) with the primarily emotionally and effectively controlled personality parts that have so far hindered them in doing so (Schmidt, 2004). Julius Kuhl (Kuhl & Strehlau, 2009; Kuhl, 2010, pp. 378–427) calls the first personality part the rational 'I' and the latter the emotional 'SELF'. These two parts of our personality determine how we can think, act, and make experiences (Geißler & Rödel, 2023, pp. 82–86). Therefore, the media richness of a particular coaching medium is also defined by the media conditions that activate

- the clients' rational and intuitive thinking,
- their rational and intuitive action control,
- and their self-efficacy experiences as well as their emotional and body perceptions.

As these mental conditions are basic for the problem-solving process, they are called mental problem-solving media as shown in Table 15.5.

Table 15.5 The mental problem-solving coaching media

Rationally controlled mental activities	Emotionally controlled mental activities
rational thinking	intuitive thinking
rational action control	intuitive action control
self-efficacy experiences	emotional and body perceptions

The media richness of coaching media, mainly serves the rational self-control

For the stimulation of *rational thinking* (Geißler, 2017, pp. 224–251), coaches should reflect, which coaching medium is good or best suited to stimulate or guide the client in order to

- identify coaching relevant details,
- combine these details into groups of different size,
- recognise their similarities and differences,
- recognise causal relationships that may exist between the identified details and/or the groups of details,
- recognise meanings and normative connections that may exist between the identified details and/or the groups of details,
- and on this basis finally to evaluate, on the one hand, the present and, on the other hand, certain imaginable coaching conditions.

These processes can be enabled primarily by text-based coaching problem-solving with pre-prepared written coaching questions (Geißler et al., 2014; Geißler, 2022; Geißler & Rödel, 2023, pp. 188–195).

Regarding the client's *rational action control* coaches should analyse which coaching medium is good or best suited to stimulate or guide the client to

- identify possible goals for action with regard to his or her professional or private life practice,
- to examine their value,
- develop suitable action goals, appropriate relationships between purpose and means,
- draft alternative plans with stage goals and goal-oriented activities on the basis of the above-mentioned relationships of purpose and means,
- prepare a cost-benefit analysis for these plans and,
- correct these plans on the basis of implementation experience.

These processes can be enabled primarily using open writing and drawing coaching tools, as well as using the text-based coaching tools mentioned above.

For the stimulation of *rational handling of self-efficacy experiences* coaches should reflect which coaching medium is good or best suited to stimulate or guide the client to

- rationally deal with experiences of their professional and/or private life practice in which they experienced themselves as an object of adverse circumstances,
- deal rationally with experiences of coaching practice in which the clients have experienced being controlled, at least to some extent, against their will by the coach,
- rationally deal with experiences of their professional and/or private life practice in which they succeed or have succeeded in controlling themselves and their world the way they want to,
- rationally confront experiences in their coaching practice in which they succeed or have succeeded in steering the coaching process the way they want it.

These processes can be enabled by coaching tools that have a high creativity potential for the clients, e.g., 3D tools with virtual worlds in which avatars can be set up.

The media richness of the coaching media mainly serves emotional self-control

For the stimulation of *emotional thinking* (Nohl, 2023), coaches should consider which coaching medium is good or best suited to stimulate or guide the client to

- recall past experiences and relive them scenically with all feelings,
- sensitively direct one's own attention to certain aspects of past experiences,
- open oneself for spontaneous associations and fantasies,
- imagine unrealised possibilities of action and experience of the past,
- scenically imagine positive possibilities for action and experience in the future,
- sensitively direct one's own attention to certain aspects of these imaginings,
- pursue the existential meaning of certain experiences and living conditions.

These processes can be enabled by coaching tools that offer digital images and 3D tools with virtual worlds and avatars.

The coach must proceed in a very similar way when it comes to the conditions of the *emotional action control* of the clients. Here, too, the question is which coaching medium is good or best suited to stimulate or guide the client to

- align one's own actions and planning with a self-congruent meaning,
- react intuitively and to act intuitively in the coaching situation, and
- intuitively evaluate possible actions and decisions.

These processes can be enabled with the help of 3D tools with virtual worlds and avatars.

For the stimulation of the *emotional and affective handling of emotional and body perceptions* (Schmidt, 2004), the coach should reflect which coaching medium is good or best suited to stimulate or guide the client to

- remember one's own feelings and body perceptions of earlier experiences and to relive them scenically with all feelings,
- sensitively direct one's own attention to certain feelings and body perceptions,
- try out different body postures and movements and to perceive the feelings associated with them, and
- give voice to the feelings and body perceptions perceived.

These processes can also be enabled with the help of the 3D tools with virtual worlds and avatars just mentioned.

Key implications

Our discussion has shown that the different coaching communication and problem-solving media offer specific benefits for solid problem-solving processes. These benefits determine media richness, on the one hand, by the specific physical characteristics of the different media, and, on the other hand, by the mental activities which are triggered by them. On this basis we could demonstrate that media richness of digital coaching media is made up of several factors: A first, very obvious benefit that all digital coaching communication media provide is the *savings of travel costs* or the *spatial delimitation*. The second and undoubtedly most important benefit factor refers to the characteristic that traditionally is called *symbol variety*. The discussion has shown that this characteristic should be modified into *symbol value*, because media richness is determined not only by the physical characteristics of the coaching media, but also by the mental problem-solving activities, which can be triggered by different media. This value is especially high when appropriate coaching communication media are combined with various coaching problem-solving media especially when text-based coaching tools are central to this process.

Another media richness feature is the *reprocessability* that characterises all digital coaching communication media and problem-solving media. This is because they all offer the possibility of electronically documenting coaching processes and work results in a low-threshold manner and to make them available as often as desired.

In addition, all asynchronous coaching communication media and all digital coaching tools are characterised by the useful characteristic of *rehearsability*. This is because they offer the possibility of trying out alternative methodological approaches.

Finally, another benefit factor is the *immediacy of feedback* and the *provision of protective and developmental spaces* for independent thinking.

As illustrated in Figure 15.3 the potential benefits of coaching media reflect only one side of the *media value*. The other side are the *financial and psychological costs or burdens* (see also Clark & Brennan, 1991, p. 142ff.). Particularly noticeable here are travel

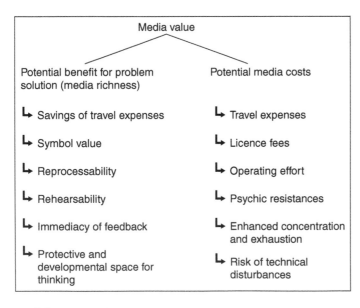

Figure 15.3 Media value.

costs, which, however, only apply to face-to-face coaching. If we look at the costs and burdens in online coaching, first of all, *license fees* need to be mentioned due to the use of data-secure communication technologies and certain coaching tools such as ProReal. In addition to these financial burdens, there are also psychological burdens in the use of digital coaching tools such as *the effort of using the technical devices and programmes.*

A completely different issue arises when the use of digital media encounters *psychological resistance* because it is *something new or unfamiliar.* Another stress factor is the fact that the use of digital communication media requires *increased attention and effort* (Bailenson, 2021). This is especially true for the use of 3D tools with configurable avatars.

And last but not least, there is also the *risk of technical disruptions* and the *provision of possible exit strategies,* e.g., exchanging telephone numbers for the case of a breakdown of video communication due to an internet disruption.

Reflective questions

1. How can I best combine the communication and problem-solving media used in digital coaching in order to work on the present coaching issue?
2. Which of the tools that I use typically are most suitable to stimulate which mental conditions and possibilities in the clients?
3. Where do I see the greatest need for development with regard to the selection, combination, and practical use of digital coaching media in my practice?

Conclusion

Digital coaching media are characterised by their inherent physical, financial, ecological, and mental conditions that have benefits and costs, with regard to the development of solid problem solutions. This potential determines the coaching media value. However, high media value does not lead directly to a high coaching effectiveness. This is because coaching media can only generate a concrete benefit, i.e. coaching success, if they are *methodically configured in a certain way.* This methodological design must appropriately take into account the *contextual conditions* of the coaching case, namely above all the *specific aspects of the coaching problem* and the *current coaching phase* as well as the *technical media familiarity* of the clients and, last but not least, the *qualification of the coach* in using digital media professionally. These interrelations make it nearly impossible to isolate the media richness of coaching media in order to examine the effects that emanate from it. Thus, it is hardly possible to empirically prove the significance of different media richness for the effectiveness of coaching. For this reason, it makes sense to distinguish categorically between a *potential media richness* and a *methodologically configured media richness.* With the help of this distinction, it can be explained that in the study by Passarelli et al. (2020) the participants rated the potential media richness of face-to-face, video and audio coaching differently, but that at the same time the corresponding coaching sessions were similarly successful. This is because it can be assumed that the examined coaches compensated the differences in *potential media richness* by correspondingly different *methodological configurations,* so that the methodologically designed media richness of their coaching sessions was almost identical.

References

Armutat, S. et al. (2015). *Virtuelles Coaching – Bilanz und Orientierungshilfe*. DGFP- Praxispapiere, Leitfaden 08/2015.

Austin, J. L. (1962). *How to do things with words*. Cambridge: Harvard University Press.

Baecker, D. (2016). Unruhe stiften: Coaching als Medium und Form. In R. Wegener, M. Loebbert, & A. Fritze (Eds.), *Coaching und Gesellschaft* . Wiesbaden: Springer.

Bailenson, N. (2021). Nonverbal overload: A theoretical argument for the causes of zoom fatigue. *Technology, Mind, and Behavior*, 2(1). https://tmb.apaopen.org/pub/nonverbal-overload/release/2

Behrendt, P. (2019). *Successful behavior in coaching, career counseling, and leadership*. Diss. Freiburg im Breisgau.

Berninger-Schäfer, E. (2018). *Online-coaching*. Wiesbaden: Springer.

Berninger-Schäfer, E., & Kineselassie, E. (2018). Formatkompetenz von Coaches. In R. Wegener, S. Deplazes, M. Hänseler, H. Künzli, St. Neumann, A. Ryter, & W. Widulle (Eds.), *Wirkung im Coaching* (pp. 163–175). Göttingen: Vandenhoek & Ruprecht.

Berry, R. A., Ashby, J. S., Gnilka, P. B., & Matheny, K. B. (2011). A comparison of face-to-face and distance coaching practices: Coaches' perceptions of the role of the working alliance in problem resolution. *Consulting Psychology Journal: Practice and Research*, 63(4), 243–253.

Boos, M., & Jonas, K. J. (2008). Medienvermittelte Kommunikation. In B. Batinic & M. Appel (Eds.), *Medienpsychologie* (pp. 197–217). Wiesbaden: Springer.

Carlson, J. R., & Zmud, R. W. (1999). Channel expansion theory and the experiential nature of media richness perceptions. *Academy of Management Journal*, 42(2), 153–170.

Charbonneau, A. M. (2002). *Participant self-perception about the cause of behavior change from a program of executive coaching*. Unpublished doctoral dissertation, Alliant International University, Los Angeles, CA.

Chen, F. S., Minson, J. A., Schöne, M., & Hinrichs, M. (2013). In the eye of the beholder: Eye contact increases resistance in persuasion. *Psychological Science*, 24(11), 2254–2261.

Clark, H. H., & Brennan, S. E. (1991). Grounding in communication. In L. B. Resnick, J. M. Levine, & S. D. Teasley (Eds.), *Perspectives on socially shared cognition* (pp. 127–149). Washington, DC: American Psychology Association.

Clutterbuck, D. (2010). Welcome to the world of virtual coaching and mentoring. In D. Clutterbuck & Z. Hussain (Eds.), *Virtual Coach, virtual mentor* (S. 3–30). Charlotte, NC: Information Age Publishing.

Daft, R. L., & Lengel, R. H. (1984). Information richness: A new approach to managerial behavior and organization design. In B. Staw & L. L. Cummings (Hrsg.), *Research in Organizational Behavior* (vol. 6, S. 191–233). Greenwich: JAI.

Daft, R. L., & Lengel, R. H. (1986). Organizational information requirements, media richness and structural design. *Management Science*, 32, 554–571.

Deniers, C. (2017). *'This is the virtual world and you can only see via this camera' – Experiences of receiving career coaching via Skype: An interpretative phenomenological analysis*. Master's thesis, Birkbeck College, University of London.

Dennis, A. R., & Kinney, S. T. (1998). Testing media richness theory in the new media: The effects of cues, feedback, and task equivocality. *Information Systems Research*, 9(3), 256–274.

Dennis, A. R., & Valacich, J. S. (1999). Rethinking media richness: Towards a theory of media synchronicity. *Proceedings of the 32nd Hawaii International Conference of System Sciences* (S. 1–10).

El-Shinnawy, M. N., & Markus, M. I. (1992). Media richness theory and new communication media. A study of voice mail and electronic mail. *Proceedings of ICIS* (S. 91–105), Dallas, TX.

Engel, A. M., & Kuhl, J. (2022). Affective change for action control and self-growth in coaching. In S. Greif, H. Möller, W. Scholl, J. Passmore, & F. Müller (Eds.), *International handbook of evidence-based coaching* (pp. 27–38). Cham: Springer Nature Switzerland.

Geißler, H. (2017). *Die Grammatik des Coachens*. Wiesbaden: Springer.

Geißler, H. (2018). Virtuelles Coaching (VC) und das in ihm enthaltene Professionswissen. In J. Heller, C. Triebel, B. Hauser, & A. Koch (Hrsg.), *Digitale Medien im Coaching* (S. 91–102). Wiesbaden: Springer.

Geißler, H. (2022). E-coaching: An overview. In S. Greif, H. Möller, W. Scholl, J. Passmore, & F. Müller (Hrsg.), *International handbook of evidence-based coaching* (pp. 269–280). Cham: Springer Nature Switzerland.

Geißler, H., Broszio, A., Fritsch, M., Naumann, V., & Sadowski, V. (2022). *Bedeutsame Momente und Erfolgsfaktoren im Online-Coaching*. Wiesbaden: Springer.

Geißler, H., Hasenbein, M., Kanatouri, S., & Wegener, R. (2014). E-coaching: Concept and empirical findings of a virtual coaching programme. *International Journal for Evidence Based Coaching and Mentoring, 12*(2), 165–187.

Geißler, H., & Metz, M. (2012). *E-Coaching und Online-Beratung*. Wiesbaden: Springer.

Geißler, H., & Rödel, S. (2023). *Praxishandbuch professionelles Online-Coaching*. Weinheim, Basel: Beltz.

Geißler, H., & Rödel, S. (2024). Relational modalities and factors in digital coaching. In J. Passmore, S. Diller, & M. Brantl (Eds.), *The digital coaches' handbook*.

Geißler, H., Rödel, S., Metz. M., & Bosse, M. (2023). Erfolgsfaktoren im Online-Coaching. *Organisationsberatung, Supervision, Coaching, 30*, 7–25.

Ghods, N. (2009). *Distance coaching: The relationship between coach-client relationship, client satisfaction, and coaching outcomes*. Unpublished doctoral dissertation. San Diego University, CA.

Graßmann, C. (2022). Die Arbeitsbeziehung im Coaching: Ein Forschungsüberblick und Handlungsempfehlungen für die Praxis. *Organisationsberatung Supervision Coaching, 29*, 331–346.

Greif, S. (2015). Allgemeine Wirkfaktoren im Coachingprozess. Verhaltensbeobachtungen mit einem Ratingverfahren. In H. Geißler & R. Wegener (Hrsg.), *Bewertung von Coachingprozessen* (S. 51–80). Wiesbaden: Springer.

Greif, S. (2021). *Was ist Coaching? Wissenschaftliche Grundlagen und praktische Methoden*. Osnabrück: Amazon.

Kanatouri, S. (2020). *The digital coach*. Abingdon: Routledge.

Kanatouri, S. (2021). Digital coaching in Rauen Handbuch coaching. In C. Rauen (Ed.), *Handbuch Coaching* (pp. 131–163). Hogrefe: Gottingen.

Kanatouri, St., & Geißler, H. (2016). Adapting to working with new technologies. In T. Bachkirova, G. Spence, & D. Drake (Hrsg.), *The Sage handbook of coaching* (S. 713–738). Los Angeles, CA: Sage.

Kiesler, S., Siegel, J., & McGuire, T. (1984). Group and computer-mediated discussion effects in risk decision making. *Journal of Personality and Social Psychology, 52*(5), 917–930.

Kinney, S. T., & Watson, R. (1992). The effect of medium and task on dyadic communication. *Proceedings of International Conference on Information Systems* (S. 107–117), Dallas, TX.

Krause, S. (2018). Online-Aufstellungen und virtuelle Coaching-Landkarten. In J. Heller, C. Triebel, B. Hauser, & A. Koch (Hrsg.), *Digitale Medien im Coaching* (S. 117–127). Wiesbaden: Springer.

Krause, F., & Storch, M. (2010). *Ressourcen aktivieren mit dem Unbewussten*. Bern: Huber.

Kuhl, J. (2010). *Lehrbuch der Persönlichkeitspsychologie*. Göttingen u.a.: Hogrefe.

Kuhl, J., & Strehlau, A. (2009). Handlungspsychologische Grundlagen des Coachings. In B. Birgmeier (Hrsg.), *Coachingwissen – Denn sie wissen nicht, was sie tun?* (S. 171–182). Wiesbaden: VS Verlag.

McLaughlin, M. (2013). Less is more: The executive coach's experience of working on the telephone. *International Journal of Evidence Based Coaching and Mentoring, 7*, S 1–13.

McLuhan, M. (1964). *Understanding media: The extensions of man*. New York: McGraw-Hill.

Messerschmidt, J. (2015). *Das Selbst im Bild*. Frankfurt/M. u.a.: Peter Lang Verlag.

Mundelsee, L. (2022). Die Zukunft des Coachings? Sehr wahrscheinlich wird sie blende(n)d! In F. Strikker & U. Böning (Eds.), *Zur Zukunft des Business Coachings* (pp. 244–250). Hannover: ibidem Verlag.

Nohl, M. (2023). *Intuition für Coachs: Arbeit mit dem Unbewussten verstehen, entwickeln und im Coaching einsetzen.* Bonn: Manager Seminare.

Passarelli, A., Trinh, M. P., Van Oosten, E. B., & Varley, M. (2020). Can you hear me now? The influence of perceived media richness on executive coaching relationships. *Academy of Management Proceedings, 2020*(1), 13211.

Passarelli, A., Trinh, M. P., Van Oosten, E. B., & Varley, M. (2022). Communication quality and relational self-expansion: The path to leadership coaching effectiveness. *Human Resource Management, 2022*, 1–20.

Poepsel, M. (2011). *The impact of an online evidence-based coaching program on goal striving, subjective well-being, and level of hope.* Doctoral dissertation, Capella University.

Ribbers, A., & Waringa, A. (2015). *E-coaching: Theory and practice for a new online approach to coaching.* London: Routledge.

Rice, R. E., & Shook, D. (1990). Relationships of job categories and organizational levels to use communication channels, including electronic mail: A meta-analysis and extension. *Journal of Management Studies, 27*, S. 195–229.

Richter, S. D., & Schindler, W. (2018). "Schreiben befreit" – Asynchrones textbasiertes Online-Coaching. In J. Heller, C. Triebel, B. Hauser, & A. Koch (Hrsg.), *Digitale Medien im Coaching* (pp. 49–60). Wiesbaden: Springer.

Roth, G. (2021). *Bildung braucht Persönlichkeit.* Stuttgart: Klett-Cotta.

Schmidt, G. (2004). *Liebesaffären zwischen Problem und Lösung.* Heidelberg: Carl-Auer.

Schütz, A., & Kaul, C. (2022). Means of verbal and non-verbal communication in coaching. In S. Greif, H. Möller, W. Scholl, J. Passmore, & F. Müller (Eds.), *International handbook of evidence-based coaching* (pp. 565–576). Cham: Springer.

Searle, J. R. (1969). *Speech acts.* Cambridge: Cambridge University Press.

Spears, R., Lea, M., & Postmes, T. (2001). Social psychological theories of computer-mediated communication: Social pain or social gain. In P. Robinson & H. Giles (Eds.), *The new handbook of language and social psychology* (pp. 601–623). Chichester: John Wiley & Sons.

Sproull, L., & Kiesler, S. (1986). Reducing social context cues: Electronic mail in orgnizational communication. *Organizational Behavior and Human Decision Processes, 37*, 157–187.

Storch, M., & Weber, J. (2022). Embodiment and its importance for coaching. In S. Greif, H. Möller, W. Scholl, J. Passmore, & F. Müller (Eds.), *International handbook of evidence-based coaching* (pp. 281–292). Cham: Springer Nature Switzerland.

Tawadros, T., Tinker, D., & Jackson, A. H. (2018). Coaching in a virtual world – Your avatar will see you now. In J. Heller, C. Triebel, B. Hauser, & A. Koch (Hrsg.), *Digitale Medien im Coaching* (S. 129–137). Wiesbaden: Springer.

Valacich, J. S., Mennecke, B. E., Wachter, R. M., & Wheeler, B. C. (1994). Extensions to media richness theory: A test of the task-media fit hypothesis. *Proceedings of the Twenty-Seventh Hawaiian International Conference on Systems Sciences* (S. 11–20). Maui: Hawaii.

Walther, J. B. (1992). Interpersonal effects in computer-mediates interaction: A relational perspective. *Communication Research, 19*(1), S. 52–90.

Walther, J. B. (1996). Computer-mediated communication: Impersonal, interpersonal, and hyperpersonal interaction. *Communication Research, 23*, S. 3–43.

Walther, J. B. (2007). Selective self-presentation in computer-mediated communication: Hyperpersonal dimensions of technology, language, and cognition. *Computers in Human Behavior, 23*, 2538–2557.

Chapter 16

Managing cybersecurity

Alexandra J.S. Fouracres

Introduction

Cybersecurity features across all digital practice. Without security applied to hardware, software and content, individuals and organisations risk both exposure to legal, financial, reputational, and ethical challenges. This chapter covers a broad overview of the importance of cybersecurity in digital coaching. It outlines how just as we should view digitalisation and AI as a partner to our coaching (Hawkins & Turner, 2020), we also need to see cybersecurity as a partner to keeping everything we do, say, and store – safe. The implications of not having security in place are discussed, alongside applied examples. Finally, a model is provided, that can be used alone or in groups to reflect on why it is important to start on a journey of embedding cybersecurity into your practice – or to improve upon what you already have in place.

Cybersecurity goals

Coaches and their clients are at risk from a variety of cyber-related crime. These include scams aimed at a coach or their practice, financial fraud techniques which elicit payments the victim believes are genuine (through spoofed invoices or emails), and cyber-dependent crime (examples: video call hacking, malware, ransomware) (Fouracres, 2022).

Upskilling on cybersecurity is essential for any person working digitally, particularly someone working with confidential and sensitive data. It is rare today that a coach has nothing related to their practice and clients on a device which is connected to the internet. Calendar meetings, client logs, contact information, invoices, emails, supervision records, and other sources of information containing information about clients are continuously at risk from cyber threats. All data can be intercepted or exfiltrated over the internet whether it is held *at rest* on your computer (stored), *in transit* (over email or via other means), or *in use* (being read or updated). Additionally, as digital coaches, we may be making use of video conferencing and other software to work with our clients or operating over digital coaching platforms. Cyber threat actors that gain unauthorised access to networks or devices (via security weaknesses) may gain the ability to join your calls in the background and they may patiently over time capture your log-in credentials to the different tools you use, eventually exploiting what they may find on such platforms as well as what they find on your device (Biju et al., 2019; Okereafor & Manny, 2020).

DOI: 10.4324/9781003383741-20

Reality

Many sources of statistics on cybercrime exist. It is estimated that by 2027, global cyber-crime costs could exceed $23 trillion US dollars (Fleck, 2022). To give a sense of how rapidly these costs are rising, but how unpredictable they also have been, in 2020, it was predicted previously that by 2025, cybercrime costs would exceed $10.5 trillion US dollars (Morgan, 2020) – but at the end of 2022, $8.44 trillion was estimated to be lost already, with $11.50 trillion in losses predicted, at the time of writing, for the end of 2023 (Fleck, 2022). On the other side, which feeds this crime – data – is growing too. Our appetite for the amount of data we create, store, and use is estimated as having totalled roughly 74 zettabytes (that's 21 zeros after the last number) in 2021 and expected to rise to an estimated 149 zettabytes in 2024 (Andre, 2023).

Cybersecurity is not about disrupting the advancement of digitalisation, rather it is about optimising our ability to operate safely. This improves a practice's ability to keep any data and conversations pertaining to clients as secure as possible, further improving the ability to provide uninterrupted services using tools that securely serve a client's needs and situation optimally. Time spent ensuring a practice is as secure as possible reduces the likelihood of a cyber incident occurring which in turn aids the digital coach to operate 'business as usual' and achieve their mission, strategy, and goals. Our approach to security can make the difference between securing our use of the digital space and becoming a victim of cybercrime with our data taken through unauthorised access by malicious threat actors and put in the wrong hands.

Options

Cyber threat actors today have many ways they can join your client conversations or find a way into your client data. They seek the weakest point to deploy malicious software (malware) that is used to gain unauthorised access. Malware can be transmitted today in many ways and not just via links that we have learned to take care when clicking on. It can be transmitted via files, attachments, websites, images, links, code, or other. You are susceptible to malware when using an insecure network or using a device or software you haven't run updates on. Other risks come from video-conferencing software that isn't continuously kept up to date with new security risks by the software company or where you skip the security options the conferencing software comes with. Sharing a computer with others – you are as safe as the behaviours and actions of the others using the device. Use of public WiFi (even with VPN), lack of security software, use of old software, use of insecure chat channels, not using secure log-in credentials all put you at risk of attacks. Other vulnerabilities include IoT devices attached to your WiFi, for example washing machines, games consoles, fitness apps can be accessed by threat actors and used as a way to transmit malware across the network (Baltazar, 2022).

Added to this, the sophistication of online attacks has reached a level that it is difficult for us to discern what is fake from what is real (Vayansky & Kumar, 2018), we can all find ourselves believing something is genuine only to find out it was not. When a weakness opens a door for an attacker to implement malware into our networks or devices – it's the other layers of defence we have set up that may stop anything further from happening. This is why most cybersecurity professionals will recommend you set up layered defences.

Technology defence layers include elements such as using best-in-class security software, making use of security settings on products we use, using secure and updated devices and products, operating best practices with log-in credentials, securing our networks, router – and much more. Equally of importance is training ourselves to operate safely online, adopting cyber secure behaviours, learning to spot threats and red flags – evoking in us a sense not to respond to any form of request asking for something unusual (NCSC, 2022). Finally, if something still activates, it is our response and our first steps reacting to anything abnormal happening, as well as eventually recovering from it, that can be key.

Another way to motivate action is to understand: we actively 'help' a threat actor through our vulnerabilities (as noted above) or by accessing something containing malicious software, we also passively 'help' by not implementing cybersecurity. This applies also to our personal/private use of cyberspace. The good news is starting on, or improving on, all of the areas of defence noted above is very doable for any coach (Fouracres, 2022).

Way forward

Cyberattacks can lead to business interruption, legal costs, recovery costs, and brand damage – this is the surface impact. Legal cases can drag out, reputational damage takes time to reverse, and being a victim of cybercrime can be psychologically impactful (Palassis et al., 2021; Pattnaik, 2023). Cybercrime can affect both your practice and also your clients whose information and data can be exfiltrated and exposed. Each person affected will have their own unique aftermath to deal with.

It is important for coaches to recognise that the psychological impact starts from the moment someone has knowledge that something about them might be 'out there'. Research with victims of hacking and cybercrime has documented participants' fear and perceived risk linked to the deep uncertainty experienced around what has happened and what might happen with the information which has been accessed (Gibson & Harfield, 2022, Palassis et al., 2021). Meaning, whether the person will be identified or connected to the data or not, at that point – and even if they never are – is not the bottom line here. Knowing that personal information has been revealed outside of the trusted environment they shared can be the start of psychological harm (Gibson & Harfield, 2022; Ralston, 2020; 2021). The case of Vaastamo in Finland, a psychotherapy company where records on their platform were breached also led to a number of vivid reports that covered the psychological impact reported by victims, even where they were not sure if their information would be published (Ralston, 2021; WithSecure, 2022).

This reaction to being a victim of cybercrime (see Box 16.1) is not one to downplay from another view: exposure of information on the darkweb (one of the ways cyber criminals sell data) has the potential to be permanent. What is perceived harmful exposure may differ for person-to-person, but once anything is on the darkweb it is extremely difficult – often impossible – to remove. Moreover, it may be copied and redistributed and bought by other parties (ID Agent, n.d).

Our role in preventing harm

Research indicates some people may disassociate their online from real-life activities (Suler, 2004; Lin et al., 2018), leading us to be potentially more likely to engage in risky

---

Box 16.1   Perspectives of being a cybercrime victim

Operational impact of cyberattacks for the coach
A cyberattack can result in business downtime, data loss, and financial loss during recovery. Any resulting breach can cause financial and reputational harm and affect the "operability of the data holding entity" (Gibson & Harfield, 2022, p.18) – i.e. of the coach, coaching company, or digital platform. Depending on the laws and regulations in the country of operation of the coach, other impacts of attacks include legal and regulatory implications which can go on for many years after an attack.

Immediate impact for the client
The harms a person can experience may come from a sense of loss of control over their identity and can be categorised as material (including financial impacts), medical (for example, psychological distress or even psychological illness), and moral (from impact on autonomy) (Gibson & Harfield, 2022). Each victim will need to assess damage of any exposed data pertaining to their identity and review what they have control over changing.

Coach and client – impact of being a victim
Both coach and client may feel associated psychological and emotional harms. The impacts of which should not be underplayed (Jansen & Leukfeldt, 2017). Victims of hacking portray emotional impacts such as anxiety, depressive symptoms, frustration, and anger, feel more vulnerable and a sense of violation (Palassis et al., 2021; Pattnaik et al., 2023). Secondary effects such as time loss, impact on social relationships can occur and linger (Button et al., 2014, Palassis et al., 2021). Some victims of cybercrime appear to form problem-focused coping strategies that involve them modifying their behaviour to be more careful in cyberspace (Palassis et al., 2021).

---

behaviour online than offline (online disinhibition effect; Agustina, 2015; Suler, 2004). As practitioners, we need to keep this in mind and do the opposite. The conversations we have with our clients involve their innermost worlds.

When someone is a victim of cybercrime, there can be a ripple effect to their systems and connections. Consider a client you have currently that has revealed a number of very personal things about themselves that may come up in your logs, shared conversations, or in any correspondence to you. If that was released publicly, how would that impact the client but also the connected parties, companies they work for, decisions they are making, business deals they've been part of? How might that ripple out further?

When we commit to keeping everything confidential and state that to clients, that means we are committing to keeping every conversation safe online, every document we have, every data point. That means understanding what puts our use of the digital space at risk. Only then can we uphold the ethics guidelines we state adherence to, in terms of confidentiality and data integrity, through implementing security measures, secure behaviours and practices that actually do protect that information (Fouracres, 2022).

Starting a cybersecurity journey

As coaches we often will use models and techniques to help our clients unlock solutions. Consider which coaching model you would use with yourself on this topic to enable you to move to a place of not seeing the challenging side of this, but rather the opportunities and reframe this as a positive challenge or addition to your continued professional development. Building competencies in protecting your practice and client data and preparing yourself to react if something happens, will also transfer towards better protecting also your own private, home use of the digital space. Meaning, time invested in this topic can go a long way (see Box 16.2).

RISE – a Starter Reflective Model of Cybersecurity for Practitioners

The RISE reflective model of cybersecurity compacts some of the insights and implications of this chapter to encourage someone new to cybersecurity concepts to start reflecting on their first intentional steps. The model only covers a very limited number of topics and does not replace the need for practitioners to consider cybersecurity more comprehensively including layered technological defences, processes, practices, and behaviours. For example, the model does not cover use of devices and software or secure credentials amongst a variety of other topics (for these see Fouracres, 2022). The model however provides an introduction to encourage reflection and get you started. Four steps are proposed (see Table 16.1).

Review – take some honest reflection on what you do today.
Identify – map out changes you need to make.
Secure – implement and improve through action.
Evolve – consider how to further develop and embed your learning over time.

Box 16.2 Security review

1. How often do you review your security?
2. When did you last notice an update on your computer? Did you run it straight away?
3. When you download a new tool, programme, app or other – have you considered and researched the security of it prior to doing so?
4. Do you spend time checking the security options of any software before you use it?
5. When was the last time you asked yourself (about anything): "is this secure?"

Note: Implementing cybersecurity extends far beyond these few points above to many more areas, but this list is constructed of some of the actions you can already review your mindset against.

Table 16.1 RISE

REVIEW	IDENTIFY	SECURE	EVOLVE
Review the technological defences you have today.	What has this chapter inspired you to do next? What are the layers of defence you think you have in place – list them. Identify resources to assess the technological defences you need to put in place.	Research and implement any new defences. Improve existing defences.	Next time information arrives from authorities/banks or comes up in the media – how can you take note and absorb it differently to how you do today? How will it keep you informed on how you protect your practice? How will you be more active going forward in terms of your cyber defences? What can you do next?
Review your digital coaching behaviours and response capability.	Identify areas you could be more secure. Where are you vigilant and where are you too relaxed to red flags? What needs to change? If something happens tomorrow, how will you react?	Implement safer digital coaching behaviours and practices. How will you keep yourself accountable to your new ways? Embed this. Research and implement new practices around how you would respond to a cyber incident.	Going forward how will you continue to build up your awareness to keep you on track with secure behaviours? Walk through your response strategy with others or create a test scenario to review its efficacy.
Review your processes around client data.	Identify ways to inform your clients about the risks and what you do to mitigate them. Identify where you share information with others but are not informing your clients. Clients need to know where their information is exposed (with or without their names).	Inform clients about cyber risks, ensure they are also aware of their own role in keeping data and conversations you have with them secure. Inform your client of every situation you share – with or without their original name. That is true respect and attention to data privacy.	Going forward how will you balance keeping the data you need: secure and the data you don't: deleted? What will you learn next when it comes to data privacy, protection, and security? How will you in the future further review how you store, transmit, use and delete data?

How to use the model:

Individual practitioners: use the model to raise your cybersecurity via reflection and actions that you commit to. The journey should be seen as continuous from this starting point – always consider what will you do next?

Supervision groups, learning groups or peer-practice groups: use the model to raise your cybersecurity through reflective discussion – including on the ethical issues that security topics can bring up. Create accountability together on actions you will commit to. An activity to consider may also be having each member research a different cybersecurity topic related to what comes up for the group using the model and present back to the group.

Company owners (whether a coaching business, platform, or other coaching service): the chapter should have raised or added to your awareness on the importance of protecting client data and the impact of cybercrime. Revise if you are involved enough in knowing how your company is protecting clients, itself, and staff. What are the defence and response strategies in place and are they adequate for the level of sensitivity of the data? Reflect on the systemic ripple effect of the harm resulting from cyber breaches (Pattnaik et al., 2023).

Implications

This chapter has aimed to raise awareness of the need for cybersecurity for anyone coaching others. Each practitioner should have gained a sense of the need for a mindset of: "I am responsible for ensuring that my practice, clients and client data are as protected as possible from cyber risks".

Cybersecurity is a form of positive strategy. It may take coaches longer to establish trust when coaching clients online (Kirkman et al., 2002) – being able to add to your contracting information about how you secure your use of the digital space (including conversations as well as any and all written data) may be something a practitioner can do towards building that trust. Being honest with clients that there will always remain a small risk due to the sophistication of cyberattacks today is also important, along with preparing how to react and respond if something does happen (Fouracres, 2024).

A positive mindset on cybersecurity will keep us adjusting and resilient in the face of what is an extensive cyber threat landscape. If you were a client at your practice, how would you want to feel about the security of the conversations you have, and data held? Cybercrime is evolving. It's crucial that we are actively improving our cybersecurity practices on an ongoing basis.

Reflective questions

1. What has been your biggest learning from this chapter?
2. Is there a way you can share that learning with others?

3. Which topics have you found most challenging and will make a commitment to research more on? Coach yourself: how will you stay on track and ensure you commit to these actions?

Conclusion

Working digitally has become a fantastic, integral part for our coaching practices. It has opened many opportunities to provide a wide range of options and services to our clients. All the digital connect points, and data, that we exchange over cyberspace have a very different means to an end for a cyber threat actor though. An intercepted phone call, list of your clients, list of demographics, payment records, logs or any other client data, is very attractive to those experienced in selling such data for financial gain or to achieve a goal to cause disruption.

We need to stop thinking that is *not* a problem for us: data protection legislation and ethics guidelines make it clear we are responsible for (amongst other things) confidentiality and creating a safe space. Meaning, all coaches need to be cybersecurity capable – delaying this just leaves us, and our clients, at risk. Finally, cybersecurity is not difficult. Every coach can do it. You just need to hit *go*.

References

Agustina, J. R. (2015). Understanding cyber victimization: Digital architectures and the disinhibition effect. *International Journal of Cyber Criminology, 9*(1), 35–54. https://doi.org/10.5281/zenodo.22239

Andre, L. (2023, January 07). Finances online. *53 Important Statistics About How Much Data Is Created Every Day.* https://financesonline.com/how-much-data-is-created-every-day/

Baltazar, P. (2022). How and where do hackers hide malware? 6 September 2022. *MalwareFox.* Retrieved July 23, 2023 from www.malwarefox.com/how-and-where-do-hackers-hide-malware/

Biju, J. M., Gopal, N., & Prakash, A. J. (2019). Cyber-attacks and its different types. *International Research Journal of Engineering and Technology, 6*(3), 4849–4852.

Borwell, J., Jansen, J., & Stol, W. (2021). Comparing the victimization impact of cybercrime and traditional crime: Literature review and future research directions. *Journal of Digital Social Research, 3*(3), 85–110. https://doi.org/10.33621/jdsr.v3i3.66

Button, M., Lewis, C., & Tapley, J. (2014). Not a victimless crime: The impact of fraud on individual victims and their families. *Security Journal, 27*(1), 36–54. https://doi.org/10.1057/sj.2012.11

Cartwright, A., Cartwright, E., Xue, L., & Hernandez-Castro, J. (2023). An investigation of individual willingness to pay ransomware. *Journal of Financial Crime, 30*(3), 728–741. https://doi.org/10.1108/JFC-02-2022-0055

Fleck, A. (2022, December 2). Statistica. *Cybercrime Expected to Skyrocket in Coming Years.* Retrieved July 16, 2023 from www.statista.com/chart/28878/expected-cost-of-cybercrime-until-2027/

Fouracres, A. J. S. (2022). *Cybersecurity for coaches and therapists: A practical guide for protecting client data.* Routledge.

Fouracres, A. J. S. (2024). Handing a data breach out of your control. In W. A. Smith, D. Magadlela, E. Hirsch Pontes, & D. Clutterbuck (Eds.). *Ethical case studies for coach development and practice: A coach's companion.* Routledge.

Gibson, D., & Harfield, C. (2022). Amplifying victim vulnerability: Unanticipated harm and consequence in data breach notification policy. *International Review of Victimology.* https://doi.org/10.1177/02697580221107683

Hawkins, P., & *Turner, E. (2020). Systemic coaching: Delivering value beyond the individual.* Routledge/Taylor & Francis Group.

ID Agent. (n.d.). *If your personal data is found on the dark web, can it be removed?* Retrieved July 16, 2023 from https://support.idagent.com/hc/en-us/articles/360035024992-If-your-perso nal-data-is-found-on-the-dark-web-can-it-be-removed-

Jansen, J., & Leukfeldt, R. (2017). Coping with cybercrime victimization: An exploratory study into the impact and change. *Journal of Qualitative Criminal Justice & Criminology.* https://doi. org/10.21428/88de04a1.976bcaf6

Kirkman, B. L., Rosen, B., Gibson, C. B., Tesluk, P. E., & McPherson, S. O. (2002). Five challenges to virtual team success: Lessons from Sabre, Inc. *Academy of Management Perspectives, 16*(3), 67–79. https://doi.org/10.5465/ame.2002.8540322

Lin, X., Su, W., & Potenza, M. N. (2018). Development of an online and offline integration hypoth esis for healthy internet use: Theory and preliminary evidence. *Frontiers in Psychology, 9,* 492. https://doi.org/10.3389/fpsyg.2018.00492

Morgan, S. (2020, November 13). *Cybersecurity ventures.* Retrieved July 16, 2023 from https:// cybersecurityventures.com/hackerpocalypse-cybercrime-report-2016 /

NCSC. (2022, December 20). *Telling users to 'avoid clicking bad links' still isn't working.* www. ncsc.gov.uk/blog-post/telling-users-to-avoid-clicking-bad-links-still-isnt-working

Okereafor, K., & Manny, P. (2020). Understanding cybersecurity challenges of telecommuting and video conferencing applications in the Covid-19 pandemic. *International Journal in IT & Engineering, 8*(6), 13–23. http://doi.org/10.6084/m9.figshare.12421049

Palassis, A., Speelman, C. P., & Pooley, J. A. (2021). An exploration of the psychological impact of hacking victimization. *Sage Open, 11*(4), 21582440211061556

Pattnaik, N., Nurse, J. R., Turner, S., Mott, G., MacColl, J., Huesch, P., & Sullivan, J. (2023). It's more than just money: The real-world harms from ransomware attacks. *17th International Symposium on Human Aspects of Information Security & Assurance (HAISA 2023).* Canterbury, Kent, United Kingdom. https://doi.org/10.48550/arXiv.2307.02855

Peachey, K. (2020, December 23). Brazen fraudsters offer crime subscription service. *BBC News.* Retrieved July 16, 2023 from www.bbc.com/news/business-55424091

Ralston, W. (2020, December, 09). A dying man, a therapist and the ransom raid that shook the world. *Wired.* Retrieved July 16, 2023 from www.wired.co.uk/article/finland-mental-health-data-breach-vastaamo

Ralston, W. (2021, May, 04). They told their therapists everything – Hackers leaked it all. *Wired.* Retrieved July 16, 2023 from www.wired.com/story/vastaamo-psychotherapy-patients-hack-data-breach/

Suler, J. (2004). The online disinhibition effect. *CyberPsychology & Behavior, 7*(3), 321–326. http://doi.org/10.1089/1094931041291295

Taylor, P. (2022, September 08). Amount of data created, consumed, and stored 2010-2020, with forecasts to 2025. *Statistica.* Retrieved July 21, 2023 from www.statista.com/statistics/871513/worldwide-data-created/

Vayansky, I., & Kumar, S. (2018). Phishing-challenges and solutions. *Computer Fraud & Security, 2018*(1), 15–20. https://doi.org/10.1016/S1361-3723(18)30007-1

Wall, D. S. (August 19, 2021). The transnational cybercrime extortion landscape and the pan demic: Changes in ransomware offender tactics, attack scalability and the organisation of offend ing. *European Law Enforcement Research Bulletin 2021.* Available at SSRN: https://ssrn.com/abstract=3908159

WithSecure. (2022, November 9). *Cyber Security Sauna: Breaking Views – The Vastaamo case.* [Video] YouTube. https://youtu.be/2qqKcke20cM

Chapter 17

Managing ethics online

Rachel Hawley, Eve Turner, and Ioanna Iordanou

Introduction

The purpose of this chapter is to contribute to the understanding and practice of managing ethics when coaching in digital environments. In contrast to earlier writings, where the focus has been cast on issues such as artificial intelligence (AI), we place emphasis on the relational perspective, to explore ethical issues for managing ethics in these digital online environments. Given the limited research available in this area, the chapter is informed by findings from research conducted with coaches and coach supervisors as part of the work for this chapter. The organisation of our discussion is framed around the following areas: the ethics of preparation, the ethics of process, the ethics of relations, and the ethics of diversity and inclusion in a global context.

The changing nature of coaching

Over the last decade, discussion about the ethics of the digital world has increased, generating a variety of research questions (cf., Bürgi et al., 2023; Turner & Goldvarg, 2021). The term 'coaching online' encompasses coaching, supervision, and training undertaken in virtual settings. Despite the growth in this type of coaching online (Clutterbuck, 2023; SHERPA, 2020), there has been relatively little research on managing ethics when coaching online. Much that is available relates to process and alternatives to face-to-face coaching, including (see, for example, Passmore & Tee, 2023). For this reason, this chapter also reflects original research to consider key ethical issues (see participant acknowledgements), with a particular focus on the relational perspective (see, for example, Lewis, 2020).

The Covid-19 pandemic, which started in early 2020, arguably brought virtual working into greater focus, not only for coaches but for mentors, psychologists, therapists, and their supervisors. Therefore, perspectives of experienced coaches and coach supervisors who moved to virtual coaching during this turbulent time, as well as those already seasoned in virtual working in diverse contexts globally are included. As a result, several ethical issues were identified. These are discussed together with findings from the literature.

The literature encourages coaches to be 'ethical coaches', to have ethics at the fore, and to constantly consider ethics (Iordanou et al., 2017; Smith et al., 2023). However, the experience of navigating coaching ethics – online and offline – suggests it is more complex in practice. This raises the question of whether it is even possible to enable coaches

DOI: 10.4324/9781003383741-21

to be ethically aware. Ethical issues are, by nature, unpredictable, complex, and messy. Becoming – and being – ethically aware requires us to have these kinds of conversations, practising reflexively (see, for example, Iordanou et al., 2017). We may never get to the point of ethical completeness.

The ethics of preparation

When conducting coaching sessions using digital communications, some of the most poignant practical aspects of the preparation in advance of the coaching carry ethical implications that are significant for the development of an ethically grounded coaching practice. It is critical to develop awareness about their significance for an ethical coaching practice, focusing specifically on personal preparation, technology preparation, and visual preparation.

Personal preparation

Several ethical considerations can influence the preparation of a coach prior to, during, and after a virtual coaching engagement. Effective time management is one that is widely encountered among practitioners. More specifically, effective time management before, during, and after virtual coaching sessions is deemed paramount in order to allow for self-care and reflection that can enhance the quality of the coaching relationship (see, for example, Meyer, 2023). Indeed, while the time saving that ensues from minimising physical travel was hailed as a positive aspect of virtual engagements, it can offer the delusion of substantial extra time, which can backfire. This is because it becomes a lot easier to ignore building-in essential breaks between virtual sessions. The trap of back-to-back meetings is inescapable. To mitigate this risk, coaches can consider creating a transition space, which can help coaches to pause, breath, and mentally prepare for the following session. The need for preparation and downtime is highlighted as paramount in online coaching (Meyer, 2023). It is especially important because virtual coaching sessions might demand more intense attention on the part of the coach, since, due to the physical distance, tonal shifts are more difficult to discern in virtual communication (Kanatouri & Geissler, 2017). The impact of the brain having to work harder when coaching online is something that Huberman (2021) terms 'brain concussion'.

Aside from effective time management before and after online-coaching sessions, coaches are encouraged to actively consider ways to create a safe space for the coaching to take place in, which is crucial for establishing and maintaining a respectful coaching relationship in digital environments. This means minimising potential distractions as much as possible. Here, a coach needs to consider whether other people (or pets) in the vicinity might interfere with the flow of the session. Other distractions, such as post or shopping deliveries, should also be considered, as well as something as simple as an audible email notification received by the coach during the coaching, which could interfere with the flow of communication (Ribbers & Waringa, 2015). To reiterate the significance of creating a safe space for the client, coaches can actively reflect on what a client needs in order to feel safe. To answer this question, the nature of the technology used needs to be considered (Meyer, 2023; Van Coller-Peter & Manzini, 2020).

Technological preparation

Beyond preparing themselves for the online coaching, coaches can consider using their professional experience to support and prepare clients for this process. The first ethical consideration here is the use of technology. While this will be discussed in detail further down, here it is important for both coach and client to be mentally prepared for potential technology failures, such as freezing or blurring image and out-of-sync audio. These issues can interfere with the flow of the coaching session and the potential for building rapport in the coaching relationship (Van Coller-Peter & Manzini, 2020). While some individuals might accept such mishaps as an inexorable consequence of virtual communication, others might experience a level of frustration or disillusionment that is not conducive to the coaching process or the coaching relationship. For this reason, when possible coaches might ask clients to send meeting invites directly to them, using their preferred software. Ultimately, success of the coaching process is a shared endeavour and signals the importance of contracting, specifically for the purpose of online working to take the contextual nuances into account (Meyer, 2023).

Visual preparation

The final ethical consideration in terms of preparation, is visual preparation. Here, a great deal of consideration needs to be placed on the background of the coaching dyad, as it could interfere with the coaching relationship. Indeed, exposing aspects of the coach or client's personal life in the background could, inadvertently, lead to forming unsubstantiated views about a person that can affect the coaching relationship (Passmore, 2021a). Coaches are therefore encouraged to consider backgrounds, photos and personal items, which may be on show and for the coach to reflect on how they might respond to personal questions triggered by the client. Paradoxically, the choice of screen background – for coach and client – can serve both as a reflexive tool but also as a distraction. Either way this issue would benefit from discussion at the contracting stage (Meyer, 2023). For this reason, it is important that we ensure that, as coaches, we are conscious of our background that is visible to clients and any potential impact it might have on the coaching process and relationship. Overall, while following the Covid-19 pandemic, coaches have embraced the use of virtual coaching, they have also reported the challenges they have faced by this development in the field, which include a more labour-intensive effort to be fully present and to establish intimacy and trust in a wider context where more people can be at home during coaching engagements (Schermuly et al., 2021; Coron, 2021). Mentally and physically preparing for the virtual coaching process in a way that enables the coach to anticipate ethical challenges that might ensue is paramount for the smooth development of the coaching relationship. For this reason, coaches need to 'pace the virtual coaching engagements to allow time for note taking and meta reflection on the session, as well as ensuring there is enough time between sessions for the coach to resource, refresh and refocus' (Coron, 2021, p. 375).

The ethics of process

While the positive elements of virtual engagement with coaching have already been documented (Geissler et al., 2014; Kanatouri & Geissler, 2017; Turner & Goldvarg,

2021; Goldvarg & Turner, 2023; Meyer, 2023), there are ethical implications engrained in the coaching process that coaches need to be considering when engaging with virtual coaching. Some of them are obvious, while some are a lot more nuanced. Following our conversations with professional coaches ethical implications emerging in the process of coaching online include: confidentiality; audio or video format, and recording.

Confidentiality

Confidentiality is one of the most important ethical issues in coaching (Iordanou et al., 2017; Smith et al., 2023). When coaching online it is important to consider confidentiality in two distinct spaces: the physical and the virtual. More specifically, with regard to the physical space in which we host a coaching session, especially following the Covid-19 pandemic, the home has become the natural space where work and other traditional out-of-home commitments have been taking place. This means that a coaching session can be conducted in someone's home, where other family members can interfere with the process and disrupt the flow of the session, or in the office where the coachee, or coach may be surrounded by other colleagues. As a result, it is a lot more challenging for coaches to ensure that confidentiality is maintained in physical spaces that are out of their reach. To address this issue, it may be helpful for the coach to check with the client: Is there anyone else around that we are not aware of because we can't see them? Indeed, even when the coaching takes place at a time when other family members or colleagues are not in the vicinity, we need to consider who else might be in that safe space. This might also apply to digital devices, from Alexa to a smart phone which may be active in the background. These concerns are also reflected in the literature around online privacy and security (see, for example, Isaacson, 2021; Passmore, 2021a).

Coaches need to be mindful of how technology could compromise confidentiality in the virtual space where the coaching is taking place, and this can be challenging. Different platforms operating in different jurisdictions are bound by different confidentiality and data privacy regulations. The coaches are not always aware of these regulations or the operating model of commercial platforms, where material may be stored in the world (and different countries have different data laws) or who has access to the conversation, chat, or documents shared during the call. For this reason, coaches need to consider familiarising themselves with the nuances of disclosure, when it comes to digital coaching, and consider ways in which confidentiality can be protected. To mitigate potential breaches of confidentiality one option is to discuss the challenge and decide collaboratively how to proceed – what might be termed 'power-sharing' with the client (Clutterbuck, 2023 p. 152). For this reason, it is important to consider that when coaches communicate with clients via email, they use password protection and send emails to someone's personal rather than work email to reduce the chances of inappropriate accessing of the email.

A final consideration here relates to note taking and storage, which, while not dissimilar, compared to face-to-face interventions, must be taken seriously (Passmore, 2021b; Iordanou et al., 2023). Indeed, how notes are taken during a coaching session can interfere with the flow, as the client might not be aware that the coach is taking notes if this is not captured on camera. Moreover, any exchange and storage of such notes needs to be considered in terms of confidentiality and General Data Protection Regulations that apply based on the country. As such, transparency from the outset of the coaching engagement is key, and we encourage coaches to consider and address these issues in the coaching contract (Iordanou et al., 2017).

Audio or video mode?

The exponential use of digital coaching has been welcomed as a sign of the democratisation of coaching. But with this comes an interesting question: From an ethical perspective, what is more preferable audio-based or video-based communication? While most of the coaches we spoke to agreed that using the video option helps establish rapport in the coaching relationship some interesting concerns arise, especially with regard to maintaining eye contact. Indeed, the video mode facilitates building rapport, as it enables the coach and client to maintain eye contact (Meyer, 2023). However, it is important to be conscious of the fact that in some cultures, showing one's face and maintaining eye contact is not the cultural norm, and may even be considered unethical. As such, coaches are encouraged to be attuned to cultural differences and conduct themselves in a way that is as culturally respectful as possible (Goldvarg & Turner, 2023). Nevertheless, we welcome the findings of a recent study that showed other positive aspects of the video mode, including allowing the clients to discern their coaches' body language, even though coaches maintained that they felt as if they had to increase the intensity of said body language for the benefit of the client (Meyer, 2023). As Hawkins and Turner (2020) noted though, to be able to access body language requires good framing and the coach may need to mention this such as where the client is too low in frame, so that only (part of) their face is visible. Tomlin (2023) also highlights the importance of showing the upper body, including the hand, to enable more body language to be communicated as part of the wider communication.

Recording

Recording a virtual coaching session can be highly beneficial, especially if it is used for developmental purposes, such as reflection, in both coaching practice (Van Coller-Peter & Manzini, 2020; Carson & Choppin, 2021; Isaacson, 2021) and coaching supervision (Turner & Goldvarg, 2021). While recording a virtual coaching session might not be necessary, there might be instances when either coach or client wish to record a session. If this is the case, it is important that all parties agree about the recording and, therefore, clear permission needs to be sought in advance of the meeting. Moreover, how the recording will be used, shared, and how long it will be retained after the session should also be clearly communicated and agreed upon, including how it will be destroyed. While ethical codes can provide a platform to build an ethical practice, a paradox within them surfaces: 'at times, they can be too complex for practitioners to embrace and adopt, and yet too simplistic to offer guidance on the intrinsically complex issues that coaches are faced with in their professional practice' (Iordanou et al., 2017, p. 246). A particular issue highlighted is that such general ethical guidelines are premised on traditional face-to-face coaching practice so may not adequately address the nuances of managing ethics online.

Overall, when it comes to the ethical implications entrenched in the process of virtual coaching, we would suggest that their consideration is part of the initial preparation and, if possible, is included in the contracting. Indeed, it might be helpful (or even necessary) to adapt our contract specifically for digital coaching engagements. This adaptation needs to include information about how the sessions will be conducted, what data might be recorded with permission, how data will be stored and secured, and who will have access to it (Turner & Goldvarg, 2021; Goldvarg & Turner, 2023). This will enable transparency which, in turn, can enhance authenticity and confidentiality (see, for example, Meyer, 2023).

The ethics of the relationship

This century has seen a significant shift in the philosophical, theoretical, and methodological focus of coaching. This is described in the literature as the 'relational turn' (see, Sills, 2020; De Haan & Gannon, 2017; De Haan & Sills, 2012). This shifts the dialogue on managing ethics online away from a focus on individuals, skills, and competence (process orientation) to patterns of relations and relational dynamics (relational orientation) (Lewis, 2020). As such, the relational perspective affords a more nuanced understanding of coaching ethics across professional contexts (Iordanou et al., 2017; Lewis, 2020). In trying to make relational practices more explicit Ganz's (2008) framework considers a 'public storifying' approach which identifies three interconnected areas: self ('story of self'), relationships ('story of us'), and contrasting contexts ('story of now') – see Box 17.1. Although not developed in the same context as coaching, it offers a relational frame to pinpoint ethical issues and coach practices across diverse professional contexts.

Several ethical considerations can influence how coaches and coach supervisors navigate and manage ethics online, such as social connection and belonging – managing multiple conversations (Clutterbuck, 2023); the emotional dimension; relational skills and feedback (Lewis, 2020), and self-care (Meyer, 2023).

Social connection and belonging

It is perhaps unsurprising that the emergence of online working in coaching has created complexity and stimulated debate on how to build social connection and belonging (see, for example, Van Coller-Peter & Manzini, 2020). One of the casualties of interacting online is the depth of social connection (Meyer, 2023). Consistent with the literature, practitioners report that this tends to make the coach more detached than they would otherwise be. In some ways detachment can be viewed as a good thing – but on the other hand it is the humanity of the coaching relationship that is where a lot of the power

---

Box 17.1   Telling your public story, adaptation from Ganz (2008, pp 7–9).

- a story of self, "communicates the values that call one to action" – a focus on relations with self
- a story of us, "communicates the values shared by those in action" – a focus on relations with others
- a story of now, "communicates an urgent challenge to those values that demand action" – a focus on relations with context

comes from, for good or ill. Thus, many coaches experience the urge to work so much harder to create that human connection when we are online (Meyer, 2023). One way to mitigate the risk of losing social connection when working with groups is to scaffold time for regular coffee breaks in pairs or trios – trying to mimic things people consider are often lost online. This is an ethical issue but also a relationship issue. When meeting online it is important to make time to connect as human beings. Some scholars believe for example that the ability to 'read emotions' is harder online (Murphy, 2020) and similarly harder to interpret 'body language' (Ribbers & Waringa, 2015).

The emotional dimension of managing multiple conversations

The context influences the ethical climate of the conversation and relationships that you have (Lewis, 2020). So, what is it about the online context that influences things one way or the other? Paradoxically, although benefits of working online resound (accessibility, sharing information via the chat-box), a significant ethical issue arises through the challenge of managing multiple conversations online: with self, within and between others, and with the coaching context.

Within the context of group working, an increasing narrative in group supervision suggests that in a large group, it is easier to hide online than it is face-to-face. This is because it is very difficult to be aware of what's happening for that person – or group – online, especially if you are only seeing faces. It may be more difficult to confidently tell if someone is withdrawn when working online. As a result it can help to explore this, encouraging: 'Are you thinking deeply? In sum, our ability to be fully attentive to the client is truncated quite a lot when working online.

A further ethical issue here is the impact of distraction. In order to mitigate the risk of distraction it is important to attend to the ethics of preparation, as already discussed. But notably distraction can also posit opportunity to delve more deeply into the relationship. Therefore, it can be useful for coaches to reframe such distractions, posing the following reflection: 'So now you've dealt with the delivery person (or other distraction), what are you thinking right now about this issue?' In this way, from a practitioner perspective distractions can be used as a catalyst for reflection or reflexivity. Despite variations in the way reflexivity is defined and understood, most definitions share a common theme, referring to a kind of conceptual 'bending back' of thought 'upon itself' (Webster, 2008, p. 65). It is the emphasis on 'shifting our thinking about thinking', which differentiates reflexivity from reflection. Iordanou et al. (2017) emphasise the continuum of reflective-reflexive coaching as a way to harness the potential for ethical practice. Becoming reflexive in our thinking is central to managing ethics online.

Coaching online has led coaches to find new ways of connecting, indicating that creativity is key to successfully managing ethics online (Gash, 2016; Palus, 2006). Consistent with Goldvarg and Turner (2023), the importance of modelling creativity is clear. A number of creative approaches are evident such as using visualisation, working with images, artefacts, and poetry. An example of visualisation is considering being stranded with your client on a desert island and imagining what would happen (Hawkins & Schwenk, 2021, p. 154). McCartney's (2018) research on poetry, practice, and potential, for example, showed that the creative writing process offers "space, time and perspective to facilitate deeper reflexive consideration of personal values and beliefs, the influence of self and others in real-time and retrospectively, bringing forth choice and opportunity for proactive learning and growth" (p. 151).

Artefacts are considered here as a relational tool. The act of selecting an artefact can help people to connect important events and memories (Clandinin & Connolly, 2007). It is not what the artefacts are that matters most, but what they symbolise to people (Saldaña & Omasta, 2018). There is however a cautionary note. When coaching online, artefacts – intended and unintended – may act as a distraction in the coaching relationship. Imagine watching a videoed meeting where a health worker's wine collection was the backdrop which happened during a meeting one of the authors attended during Covid-19. The presence of such latent artefacts – consciously, unconsciously – present in online coaching is an ethical issue. Artefacts can challenge our assumptions. They remind us of the importance of attending to the nature of our online background but also our relational skills.

Relational skills and feedback

The ethics of relationships is not a 'one size fits all'. The quality of relationships is shown to improve ethical issues such as feedback. One aspect is how we deliver and share feedback in the session. As discussed earlier, it is important to address the need to contract for that in a way that creates the 'psychological safety', as clients may need to explore sensitive and challenging topics. Clients may also express the need to pause and reflect on the process.

Lewis (2020) asserts that the 'relationship' as a 'resource' appears to be at risk of being marginalised. Consistent with Lewis (2020) a doctoral research study on relational leadership (Hawley, 2021) extols the virtue of this approach. This identified what motivates leaders to be collaborative with the public, how leaders identify with public engagement and conditions needed to support collaborative practice. Six themes emerged including curiosity, courage, creativity, kindness, role modelling and reflexivity. Table 17.1 summarises core characteristics, qualities, and skills that coaches choosing a relational approach to managing ethics can use to support their practice.

Adopting a relational lens to offer a more holistic view of coaching ethics. A relational approach is 'an attitude' – even a philosophy – not a model or theory, so it can be used in many ways.

Self-care

Coaches stressed the importance of self-care, for example having regular breaks to avoid virtual fatigue. Consistent with findings of Goldvarg and Turner (2023) it is important to be alert to this, as it can be exhausting being in video conferencing all day (p. 226). Linked to self-care was the recommendation to create a safe time and space for reflective and reflexive conversations, e.g. supervision. The issue of reflexivity was present in the discussions and also in the literature.

While not explicitly discussing managing ethics online, Iordanou et al. (2017, pp. 27–46; 92–106) explore relevant issues relating to understanding personal and professional values and practising reflexively. Here personal values and beliefs came into focus, such

Table 17.1 Relational characteristics and qualities

Curiosity	Curiosity emerges where people find ways to listen, reflect and experiment through self-understanding and preparedness practices. People are willing to open a line of inquiry into what's going on and why. Their narratives are closely associated with being curious about their experiences. Purposeful curiosity emerges where people find ways to reflect and experiment through self-discovery.
Courage	Courage is closely aligned to the concept of curiosity enabling people to question some underlying assumptions on engaging others, for example sparking creative insight and connectivity. People emphasise the importance of feeling vulnerable. Vulnerability did not show as a weakness but rather a sign of courage.
Creativity	Creativity helps connect people to memories and significant events. It moves people's self understanding on engaging others from process to an emotional connection. Creativity shows up in narrative, dialogic and visual practices e.g., coaching.
Role modelling	Being a role model is testimony to peoples potential for transformation by shining the light on relationships to spark people's thoughts, emotions, and actions over time. Role modelling relational behaviours is about how people show up in each interaction, untapping shared understanding and connection. The reciprocol nature of being a role model suggests that, we get back what we give.
Kindness	Kindness evokes feelings of importance in transforming relationships with others. Kindness challenges leaders to be self-aware and shows the quality of relationships to be central to engaging others. Kindness is felt and expressed in different ways; kindness to self (self), acts of kindness (relationships) and cultures of kindness (context).
Reflexivity	Reflexivity brings a deeper sense of connection and engagement. People describe how reflexivity helps connect with their inner sense of values and motivations. Narratives on connection with self and others are closely associated with being fully present and a willingness to value lived experiences at a deep level. Connection emerges where people find ways to reflect on and achieve self-acceptance and belonging.

Source: Hawley (2021).

as cultural difference and ethical coaching across professional boundaries (Turner & Goldvarg, 2021; Iordanou et al., 2017).

As with any behaviour we want to change, such as coaching ethics, we have to 'build the muscle' (Lewis, 2020, p. 36). The more we practise, the nearer we get to the goal we want to achieve. Coaching is a relational journey. It can also be an uncomfortable journey fostering joy and vulnerability in equal measure. Schpancer (2017) reminds us that the fear is not 'us' and it does not represent reality in full; it's only part of the experience. He asks us to remember that while we feel fear we can also tap into our values, courage, logic, past experience, and general worldview to get a fuller representation of what is actually happening. The following section considers the ethics of diversity and inclusion in a global context.

The ethics of diversity and inclusion in a global context

As highlighted in the previous section, to be ethical is to be relational. 'Ethics comes alive in relationships. Ethics is about how we treat and deal with one another' (De Vries, 2019, p. 135).

In the previous sections, aspects such as preparation, contracting, and creating safety were discussed. It is therefore time to focus on the cultural elements that may arise in relationships when working with people from diverse backgrounds, cultures and geographies, sometimes in the same groups. Are we giving this full consideration? Are we making assumptions that may affect us working ethically?

As Ryde et al. (2019, p. 40) describe, people bring their own culture and its assumptions to all that they do, and may not be alert to some of these assumptions as they are so deeply entwined with the way they 'are'. Differences in culture can include gender, sexual identity, sexual orientation, age, heritage, and disability (Ryde et al., 2019; Iordanou et al., 2017). They can also be about the difference between individualistic and collectivist cultures (where the family or community is the unit of society) (Ryde et al., 2019; Iordanou et al., 2017). These differences can also lead to power differentials. Coaches may desire equity and co-creation with their clients, but they may need to be alert to people's differing attitudes to seeing others as 'experts' and/or figures of authority and of their custom of being deferential. And for some people, as outlined before, constant eye contact may create discomfort. The same may be true of smiling or other gestures.

To address the kinds of challenges which can arise its important to be mindful of cultural difference (Leach, 2022; Ryde et al., 2019). We need to be alert to contemporary practice where clients, and participants in coach development and supervision groups may come from a range of countries and cultures and from diverse backgrounds. In some cultures the context (situation, people, and non-verbal elements) is more important than words. These cultures place a higher reliance on non-linguistic elements such as voice tone, facial expression, gestures, eye movement, and pace. Searle (1969) argues that the hearer relies on the mutually shared background information (both linguistic and non-linguistic) with the speaker to infer meaning from the communication context. This can represent a challenge where coaches and supervisors do not share the same background with their clients or other group members. How might cultural sensitivity impact a camera needing to be on or off?

One strategy for managing this is to highlight geographical difference on virtual calls with a prefix that either shows the language (i.e., EN for English speaking) or the country code (i.e., UK for United Kingdom, etc). This provides a permanent reminder of different geographies or time zone differences. An alternative to this might be to gather information from the client or group participants before a coaching assignment starts.

Dealing with our assumptions – a practical exercise

Ryde et al. (2019, p.45) offer an assumptions exercise, which can be adapted according to coaching contexts. Begin by creating a series of statements which all begin with the words "I assume that", with an understanding that nothing will have to be shared, so it is safe to write down first, unfiltered responses. Below are just a few examples of questions:

I assume that

1. People are...
2. The most important thing in life is...
3. People always should...
4. People never should...
5. Religion is...
6. Economic growth is...

Let's take question number 6 for example ('I assume that economic growth is...'): What's your response? There are no 'right' and 'wrong' answers to any questions. But there is difference in respect of our ethical relationships. In some countries, through the media, governments, or organisations we might assume that growth is viewed as positive by people as it is believed to reduce poverty and inequity, providing jobs, giving people more purchasing power (consider for example, the International Monetary Fund, IMF).

Now consider another viewpoint: where unlimited economic growth is seen as one of the root causes of a global crisis and unfettered use of global resources, being one contributor to, as an instance, climate change.

This example, over the issue of economic growth, is a reminder that everyone may make assumptions, without realising that they are only assumptions, and therefore the importance of recognising the impact this may have on our relationships. One way to consciously deal with this challenge is to write 20 or more statements adapting the questions to the context of each individual or group including background, geography, culture, class, and so on. Using a question in the media can be insightful. For example, if the individual or group is UK-based consider using: I assume that 'Daily Mail readers are...' and 'Guardian readers are....' If the participants are in the USA, the questions could include instead: I assume that 'Fox viewers are...' and 'CNN viewers are...'. This again can tease out the ethical implications for the relationship. Context is everything.

Dealing with difference – issues, themes, and cases brought by clients

We need to be mindful of how subjects may be treated differently depending on someone's background. For example, in Islam, suicide is considered a cardinal sin, and many Muslims believe those who have died by suicide are forbidden from entering Paradise (Mishara & Weisstub, 2016; The Guardian Online, 2021; Shoib et al., 2022). This is a belief that has been shared in other religions, and in the past sometimes those who die by suicide have not been allowed burial in consecrated ground. It's also the case that in some communities, mental health issues are stigmatised. It is part of coaches' work context and something coaches need to manage with ethical sensitivity.

This alertness to difference is also true for other areas of difference. More people are becoming aware of their (and others') neurodivergence, as explored elsewhere in this book. Therefore, a question arises around how a coach or supervisor can work with neurodivergent clients so they feel included and can honour this part of who they are especially in groups (as with other diversity facets).

Cultural nuances of ethics online – and offline – are increasingly becoming part of a value system that is needed as the profession evolves and takes on a more global character (Lane et al., 2023). Whether a coach – or supervisor – getting curious beyond what is first heard, and listening for the deeper meaning expands the awareness of the unique and beautiful differences people bring to the world, which must be acknowledged, understood, and honoured – a foundation for coaching ethics online.

Implications for practice

In recognising the value of a relational perspective, it can be useful to consider relationality as a foundation for managing ethics online.

Deference: The role of a coach and coach supervisor is a privileged one. Deeper and wider insights are reported within the current coaching climate indicating that a higher level of deference is coming through virtual coaching than reported in traditional face-to-face coaching contexts (Meyer, 2023).

Democratisation: The shift towards online coaching, in part as a response to the global Covid-19 pandemic, has illuminated the benefit of more democratisation of coaching and supervision through online practice. More people have access to coaching than before the pandemic. This is illustrated through pro-bono initiatives. One example is the establishment of a pro-bono coaching supervision programme in Africa, led by Professor David Clutterbuck, where there is very little supervision for coaches. This programme arose from asking local people "What's the most practical way we can help establish coaching more firmly in the region?" It provides a further example of democratisation and the rich learning that emerges through online coaching, engaging in diverse cultural perspectives, as the cost of face-to-face work would have made the initiative impossible.

Emotional safety: People have found themselves feeling more comfortable to share more online than they might in a face-to-face setting. There is something really important about how those safe spaces create and encourage further thinking and reflection.

New perspectives: It is not clear yet that there is a difference between managing ethics face-to-face or online. Three fundamental issues, which distinguish managing coaching ethics online from the wider narrative on coaching ethics are 'context', 'relationship', and 'culture'. One nuance of managing ethics online is the requirement to navigate multiple and complex conversations including the main conversation, the online chat-box, and the internal conversation with one's 'self'. Managing ethics online opens new perspectives, encouraging people to create opportunities to raise the ethical dimension.

Reflective questions

1. What do you think are the key ethical points in preparation for working online?
2. Coaches are encouraged to maintain a balance between coaching process and relationship, placing the latter at the heart of managing ethics online. How do you manage this balance?
3. What are some of the key factors we need to consider from a cultural perspective when working globally online?

Conclusion

The core work of managing ethics in coaching remains the same – raising ethical awareness, self-understanding, and cultural awareness. However, developments of understanding in the field of values and ethics in coaching have provided encouragement for adopting a relational perspective for understanding managing ethics online. Accordingly, we encourage coaches to evaluate the practicalities and value of the coaching process vs relationship. This means understanding 'voice' (our own and others), 'relationships' (people and organisations), and context (online, offline, across professional and cultural contexts) – ultimately, consciously reflecting and holding the relational dynamic of managing ethics online at the forefront of our coaching practice.

Acknowledgements

We would like to thank all the coaches and supervisors who were participants of our research and gave their time and ideas so generously. They allowed us to use the content of our discussion on the matter of managing ethics online in order to inform the key issues discussed in this chapter. We are grateful for the specific ideas and examples of best practice so generously shared by Priscilla Araujo, Anne Archer, Jeanine Bailey, Dr Francine Campone, Professor David Clutterbuck, Viv Chitty, Dr Kathryn Downing, Hilary Meyer, Lily Seto, and Professor Tony Wall.

References

Bürgi, M., Ashok, M., and Clutterbuck, D. (2023). Ethics and the Digital Environment in Coaching. In W-A. Smith, J. Passmore, E. Turner, Y-L. Lai, and D. Clutterbuck (Eds.) (2023). *The Ethical Coaches' Handbook: A Guide to Developing Ethical Maturity in Practice*. Abingdon: Routledge.

Carson, C. D., and Choppin, J. (2021). Coaching from a Distance: Exploring Video-Based Online Coaching, *Online Learning*, 25(4), pp. 104–124.

Clandinin, D. J. (2007). *Handbook of Narrative Inquiry: Mapping a Methodology*. Thousand Island: Sage.

Clutterbuck, D. (2023). *Coaching and Mentoring: A Journey through the Models, Theories, Frameworks and Narratives of David Clutterbuck*. London: Routledge.

Coron, E. (2021). AI and Digital Technology in Coaching. In J. Passmore (Ed.) *The Coaches' Handbook: The Complete Practitioner Guide for Professional Coaches*. Abingdon: Routledge.

De Haan, E., and Gannon, J. (2017). The Coaching Relationship. In T. Bachkirova, G. Spence, & D. Drake (Eds.), *The Sage Handbook of Coaching* (pp. 195–217). London: Sage Publications.

De Haan, E., and Sills, C. (eds) (2012). *Coaching Relationships: The Relational Coaching Field Book* (Management Policy Education). Faringdon, Libri Publishing Ltd.

De Vries, K. (2019). Moving from Frozen Code to Vibrant Relationship: Towards a Philosophy of Ethical Coaching Supervision. In J. Birch and P. Welch (Eds,) *Coaching Supervision – Advancing Practice, Changing Landscapes*. Abingdon: Routledge.

Ganz. (2008). Leading Change: Leadership, Organization, and Social Movements. Harvard University. Prepared for Presentation, Advancing Leadership Conference, Harvard Business School, June 2008.

Gash, J. (2016). *Coaching Creativity: Transforming Your Practice*. Abingdon: Routledge.

Geissler, H., Hasenbein, M., Kanatouri, S., and Wegener, R. (2014).'E-Coaching: Conceptual and Empirical Findings of a Virtual Coaching Programme', *International Journal of Evidence Based Coaching and Mentoring*, 12(2), pp. 165–187.

Goldvarg, D., and Turner, E. (2023). Supervision in the Americas: Working with Virtual Technology. In F. Campone et al. (Eds.) *Coaching Supervision* (pp. 220–232). Routledge.

Hawkins, P., and Schwenk, G. (2021). The Seven-Eyed Model of Coaching Supervision. In T. Bachkirova, P. Jackson, and D. Clutterbuck (Eds) *Coaching & Mentoring Supervision, Theory and Practice*. 2nd edition. Maidenhead: Open University Press.

Hawkins, P., and Turner, E. (2020). Working from Home. In K. McAlpin and D. Norrington (Eds) *Surviving the Coronavirus Lockdown and Social Isolation*. Cardiff: Wordcatcher Publishing.

Hawley, R. (2021). *Relational leadership in the NHS: how healthcare leaders identify with public engagement*. Doctoral, Sheffield Hallam University.

Huberman, A. (2021). The science of vision, eye health and seeing better, Huberman Lab Podcast #24

Iordanou, I., and Hawley, R. (2020). Coaching Ethics. In J. Passmore (Ed.) *Excellence in Coaching*. London: Routledge.

Iordanou., I., and Hawley, R. (2020). Ethical Healthcare Issues. *Coaching at Work*, 15(3), pp. 56–57.

Iordanou, I., Hawley, R., and Iordanou, C. (2017). *Values and Ethics in Coaching*. London: Sage Publications.

Iordanou, C., Hawley, R., and Iordanou, I. (2023). Ethical Issues in Note Taking and Record Keeping in Coaching. In W. A. Smith, J. Passmore, E. Turner, Y. L. Lai, and D. Clutterbuck (Eds) *The Ethical Coaches' Handbook* (pp. 167–181). Abingdon: Routledge.

Isaacson, S. (2021). *How to Thrive as a Coach in a Digital World: Coaching with Technology*. Maidenhead: Open University Press.

Kanatouri, S., and Geissler, H. (2017). Adapting to Working with New Technologies. In T. Bachkirova, G. Spence and D. Drake (Eds) *The Sage Handbook of Coaching* (pp. 713–728). London: Sage Publications.

Lane, D., Magadella, D., Yong, I. Kit, W., and Spiegel, S. (2023). Ethics and Culture in Coaching – Moving beyond a Universal Western Ethical Code. In W. A. Smith, J. Passmore, E. Turner, Y. L. Lai, and D. Clutterbuck (Eds) *The Ethical Coaches' Handbook* (pp. 167–181). Abingdon: Routledge.

Leach, V. (2022). *Inclusion and Diversity*. London: FT Publishing.

Lewis, L. (2020). *Relational Feedback: Why Feedback Fails and How to Make it Meaningful*. London: Routledge.

McCartney, J. (2018). Practice & Potential: A Heuristic Inquiry into the Potential of Poetry for the Reflexive Coaching Practitioner. *International Journal of Evidence Based Coaching & Mentoring*, 12, pp. 138–153. DOI: 10.24384/IJEBCM/S12

Meyer, Hilary, 2023. What is Best Practice in Online Coaching?, *International Journal of Evidence Based Coaching and Mentoring*, 17, pp. 77–90. DOI: 10.24384/srgt-nk21

Mishara, B. L., and Weisstub, D. N. (2016). The Legal Status of Suicide: A Global Review. In *International Journal of Law and Psychiatry*, 44, pp. 54–74. Accessed 29 April 2023 from https://doi.org/10.1016/j.ijlp.2015.08.032

Murphy (2020) *You're Not Listening: What You're Missing and Why it Matters'*. London: Vintage Books.

Palus, C. J. (2006). *Artful Coaching. The CCL Handbook of Coaching: A Guide for the Leader Coach*. San Francisco: Jossey-Bass, 259–285.

Passmore, J. (2021a). How Much about Myself Should I Disclose in a Coaching Session. In J. Passmore (Ed.) *Succeeding as a Coach: Insights from the Experts* (pp. 44–47). Worthing On Sea: Pavilion.

Passmore, J. (2021b). How Should I Use Notes in Coaching. In J. Passmore (Ed.) *Succeeding as a Coach: Insights from the Experts* (pp. 199–202). Worthing On Sea: Pavilion.

Passmore, J., and Tee, D. (2023). Can Chatbots like GPT-4 Replace Human Coaches: Issues and Dilemmas for the Coaching Profession, Coaching Clients and for Organisations, *The Coaching Psychologist*, 19(1), pp. 47–54. DOI: 10.53841/bpstcp.2023.19.1.47

Ribbers, A., and Waringa, A. (2015). *E-Coaching: Theory and Practice for a New Online Approach to Coaching*. Abingdon: Routledge.

Ryde, J. (2009). *Being White in the Helping Professions*. London: Jessica Kingsley Publishers.

Ryde, J., Seto, L., and Goldvarg., D. (2019). Diversity and Inclusion in Supervision. In E. Turner and S. Palmer (Eds) *The Heart of Coaching Supervision – Working with Reflection and Self-Care* (pp. 41–60). Abingdon: Routledge.

Saldaña, J., and Omasta, M. (2018). *Qualitative Research: Analyzing Life*. London: Sage Publications.

Schermuly, C. C., Graßmann, C., Ackermann, S., and Wegener, R. (2021). The Future of Workplace Coaching – An Explorative Delphi Study. *Coaching: An International Journal of Theory, Research and Practice*, 15(2), pp. 244–263.

Schpancer, N. (2017). Fear is nothing to be feared. A phenomenon known as 'fear' of 'fear' is at the core of most anxiety disorders. Posted Dec 26. 2017. Psychology Today.

Searle, J. (1969). *Speech Acts: An Essay in the Philosophy of Language*. Cambridge, England: Cambridge University.

SHERPA (2020) Executive Coaching Survey Summary, Looking Forward Looking Back. Available at: https://www.sherpacoaching.com/pdf_files/2020_Executive_Coaching_Survey_EXECUTIVE_SUMMARY_FINAL.pdf

Shoib, S., Armiya'u, A. Y, Nahidi, M., Arif, N., and Saeed, F. (2022). Suicide in Muslim World and Way Forward. *Health Science Reports*, 5, pp. 4. Accessed 30 April 2023 from: https://onlinelibrary.wiley.com/doi/10.1002/hsr2.665

Sills, C. (2020). Understanding the Coaching Relationship. In *The Coaches' Handbook* (pp. 68–76). Abingdon: Routledge.

Smith, W-A., Passmore, J., Turner, E., Lai Y-L., and Clutterbuck, D. (Eds) (2023). *The Ethical Coaches' Handbook: A Guide to Developing Ethical Maturity in Practice*. Abingdon: Routledge.

The Guardian Online (2021). Suicide Still Treated as a Crime in at least 20 Countries, Report Finds. *The Guardian*. Accessed 29 April 2023, from www.theguardian.com/global-development/2021/sep/09/suicide-still-treated-as-a-in-at-least-20-countries-report-finds

Tomlin, L. (2023). How can I set up my home office for an online coaching session. In J. Passmore & S. Isaacson (Eds) *The Coach Buyers Handbook. A practical guide for HR managers, coach commissioners and coaches to get the best from coaching* (pp. 69–73). London: Libri.

Turner, E., and Goldvarg, D. (2021). Supervising Virtually. In T. Bachkirova, P. Jackson and D. Clutterbuck (Eds) *Coaching and Mentoring Supervision: Theory and Practice*, 2nd edition (pp. 320–330). Maidenhead: Open University Press.

Van Coller-Peter, S., and Manzini, L. (2020). Strategies to Establish Rapport during Online Management Coaching, *SA Journal of Human Resource Management*, 18, pp. 9. doi:https://doi.org/10.4102/sajhrm.v18i0.1298

Webster, J. (2008). Establishing the 'Truth' of the Matter: Confessional Reflexivity as Introspection and Avowal. *Psychology & Society*, 1(1), pp. 65–76.

Part IV

Digitalisation and diversity

Chapter 18

Diversity bias in artificial intelligence

Eva Gengler, Ilse Hagerer, and Alina Gales

Introduction

The ever-increasing digital transformation causes profound changes in many areas of life, especially through emerging disruptive technologies such as artificial intelligence (AI). AI tools like Chat GPT generate text, and prompt discussions on copyright, ethics, and human uniqueness, – and can be a major source for many applications in business and private context, including coachbots. As algorithms within AI tools can practice discrimination, emerging coachbots powered by AI can be discriminatory. In the following chapter, diversity as a concept as well as its interconnectedness with AI is explained. Then, many examples of biased AI in different business sectors are presented. Next to providing solutions to AI bias, the consequences of discriminatory AI for people in everyday life are laid out. The goal of this chapter is to illuminate the problems that have emerged due to a lack of diversity in AI and to show what solutions exist to address them. When coaching-bots replace human coaches – as examples from other sectors demonstrate – the effects can be tremendous. The questions raised, the answers given, and the objectives pursued today will impact the decisions of upcoming decades.

Diversity as a concept

Diversity as a concept emerged in the 1980s to capture the dimensions of differences in society like gender, race, or sexual identity. In recent years, this concept has evolved to include numerous other attributes, such as social background, ability, and religion. While previously the focus of the term *diversity* lay on aspects emphasising social divisions, recently it concentrates on the positive aspects of difference. Consequently, the focus shifted from a narrow to a more pluralistic and diverse worldview also incorporating the powerful feminist concept of intersectionality (Ahonen, 2015).

Intersectionality. Originating in Black feminism, the term *intersectionality* grasps the complex nature of patriarchy in our societies. It incorporates the variety of diverse attributes that might disadvantage people in society, e.g., gender, age, religion, and belief, disability, sexual identity, ethnicity, as well as appearance (Edwards et al., 2021), and focuses on their overlapping. While diversity sheds light on different attributes used to distinguish groups, intersectionality incorporates the fact that people with several disadvantaged characteristics are more strongly discriminated against than those with merely one attribute and even those with the sum of both single disadvantaged attributes (Crenshaw, 1989). For instance, a woman might be disadvantaged when applying for a

DOI: 10.4324/9781003383741-23

leadership position and so might Black applicants. Black women, consequently, incorporate both disadvantaged attributes and thus, face much worse disadvantages than either group individually.

Diversity in legislation. Diversity is not only a concept but is also valued and protected within international and national legislation. In these frameworks, the focus lies on protecting diversity and prohibiting discrimination based on diversity attributes. Among others, the Universal Declaration of Human Rights grants all human beings equality, dignity, and freedom "without distinction of any kind, such as race, color, sex, language, religion, political or other opinions, national or social origin, property, birth or another status" (United Nations, 1948, Article 2). Also, national legislation includes non-discrimination regarding diversity characteristics, e.g., the German General Act on Equal Treatment. In recent years, increasing numbers of judicial decisions focus on non-discrimination of diversity attributes. Yet, not all characteristics of diversity are protected by law.

Diversity and its interconnectedness with AI

Numerous cases of biased AI have been discovered, e.g., in hiring (Jago & Laurin, 2022), face recognition (Buolamwini & Gebru, 2018), and healthcare (Hamberg, 2008). A bias is a systematic disadvantage, which is described as the unequal treatment of individuals from a particular group who do not differ from individuals in other groups in a way that justifies such disadvantages. Two prominent AI-facilitated biases based on recent research in this area will be shown below: AI-facilitated racial and gender bias. Nevertheless, multiple other characteristics like sexual identity, age, class, and religion also lead to discrimination by AI, yet these are as of now less covered by research. Furthermore, AI systems have been found to discriminate especially strongly against people with more than one disadvantaged attribute (e.g., Buolamwini & Gebru, 2018). Therefore, intersectionality is especially important when focusing on biased AI.

AI-facilitated racial bias. A frequently mentioned bias related to AI is racial bias. The term race can be associated with skin colour and varying experiences of discrimination. It is often distinguished by 'darker' ('Black') and 'lighter' ('White') skin colour (Burlina et al., 2021), which is used, for instance, to examine the results of face recognition algorithms (Shi et al., 2020) or medical diagnostics: If a person goes to a doctor suffering from vision loss due to retinal problem, the person may go through an automated diagnostics procedure. In this process, AI is used to test for diabetic retinopathy and to assist medical professionals by interpreting image scans of the retina. Because the presumed skin pigmentation relates, on average, to the concentration of melanin, and subsequently retinal colouration, the performance of AI diagnostics algorithms may be less accurate and therefore result in bias to the disadvantage of individuals of diverse race (Burlina et al., 2021). An equitable AI diagnostic system should assign different ethnic groups with the same probability of having diabetic retinopathy (Burlina et al., 2021). Similar biases are confirmed in numerous studies: e.g., Obermeyer et al. (2019) found that a healthcare algorithm, which is applied to roughly 200 million people in the U.S. every year, reduced the number of Black people receiving additional healthcare treatment by more than 50%, even though they had the same chronic illnesses as White people. Furthermore, racial bias was found in face recognition algorithms (Shi et al., 2020) or applications assessing job applicants (Köchling et al., 2021).

AI-facilitated gender bias. Discrimination based on gender is prevailing in many AI systems. Most AI is developed by men – this lack of diversity can reflect discriminatory values in the tools (Leavy, 2018). Oftentimes, certain groups are underrepresented in the datasets that are used to train algorithms, partly due to historical discrepancies – the difference between White men and Black women is particularly apparent. Identifying the underrepresented group is challenging for AI. Underrepresentation in the data is the main reason for biased decision-making based on evaluating faces. Hence, face recognition systems provide better results for men than women (Singh et al., 2020; Smith & Ricanek, 2020). The resulting biases may be problematic when a person is misidentified, for example, when tagging photos on social media, unlocking mobile devices, searching for missing persons through security cameras, or in law enforcement.

Reasons for biased AI systems. As touched upon above, mainly three aspects contribute to biased AI systems. First, people are inherently biased and have a tendency to use stereotypes to inform decision making. Their worldviews shape the way AI is programmed and the context in which it is used. Second, the training data often incorporates these biases, thus influencing the AI to make sexist, misogynistic, classicist, racist, and ableist decisions. Biases may also lead to incomplete datasets: For instance, the gender data gap – namely the missing data on women, trans, and genderqueer people – is a well-known problem in a wealth of domains (Criado-Perez, 2020). When data is missing, AI cannot learn from it and thus, its output might disadvantage those who are outside of the 'norm'. Third, there is an overrepresentation of White men in decision-making positions in the field of AI (Nuseir et al., 2021). On the one side, this includes the developers of AI who make technical decisions on aspects to include and to omit. On the other side: the people deciding upon budgets, the domains in which AI is to be created, and whom to employ. This lack of diversity in the field leads to questions remaining untackled and system misfunctioning undetected. With the emergence of AI, systems are created that build on data, logic, and power relations from the past. Biased AI, when in use, can cause discrimination and, thus, become a discriminatory AI system.

Examples of biased AI in different business sectors

Commonly studied business sectors that are affected by bias-sensitive AI are courts, lending, hiring, college admissions, and face recognition. Other examples can be found in the healthcare system and diagnostics, online advertisement, search engines, or text processing. Subsequently, we shed light on these business sectors.

Hiring. A prominent example of bias in hiring is Amazon's CV screening algorithm. Its development and use were stopped after noticing that women were systematically rejected (Jago & Laurin, 2022). Moreover, unequal representations in the training data led to an unequitable likelihood of getting an invitation to job interviews for different ethnicities (Asians were preferred over Caucasians, and Caucasians over African Americans) and for men (Köchling et al., 2021). Unequal treatment by recruitment algorithms could even be observed for applicants from specific universities. When the algorithm observed that a required combination of skills was often obtained from a specific university, a candidate could be labeled suitable for the position simply because they graduated from that university (Gu & Oelke, 2019). An algorithm to help marketers hire appropriate influencers for their campaigns rated influencers lower when their sexuality was described as LGBTQ+, their gender was female, or they were People of Color and additionally when they checked intersectional overlapping of those attributes (Bishop, 2021). Automated data processing in hiring increases the chances of discrimination towards minoritised groups even if an HR manager makes the ultimate decision (Todolí-Signes, 2019). Bias-caused inequalities in society are similarly reinforced by AI also in higher education: When used to select study applicants based on college admission test scores, individuals can be affected by unjustifiable low scores, which reduce the probability of being accepted to a highly regarded college and consequently, for a high-skilled job position. Also, applicants' postcodes and gender-specific hobbies may serve as proxy attributes and cause indirect discrimination.

Face recognition. There were recent advances in machine learning with face recognition algorithms, but their performance is highly biased: They perform better on males than females and have difficulties identifying children and elderly (Buolamwini & Gebru, 2018; Smith & Ricanek, 2020). Particularly ethnicity, skin colour, and facial shape affected the accuracy of face recognition systems (Serna et al., 2019). E.g., Google Photos identified Black people as gorillas (Snow, 2018) and Nikon's camera software recognised Asians as constantly blinking (Rose, 2010).

Healthcare system and diagnostics. Clinical trials mainly exist for men and less data is available for women resulting in biases against women in the diagnosis and treatment of diseases (Hamberg, 2008). Research in the field of gender medicine highlights the differences between women and men in diagnosis and treatment as essential to achieving equity in healthcare across genders (Baggio et al., 2013). As heart diseases in the past were seen as a predominantly male problem, less attention was paid to the symptoms of women, resulting in unbalanced datasets and replicated biases (Paviglianiti & Pasero, 2020). Racial minorities suffer from inferior access to treatment in medical care due to unconscious bias in medical decision-making (Chapman et al., 2013; Vartan, 2019).

Word embeddings. Individual words with similar meanings are created by capturing semantic relations of words in large text corpora. Online sources like Wikipedia or Google News provide such training data. Word embeddings show how gender ideology inherent in language can lead to gender-biased systems: Bias can be incorporated in different linguistic features like stereotypical descriptions (e.g., if the word embedding for man is doctor, but for woman it is nurse), as well as the listing of the male first, or the underrepresentation of women in texts (Leavy, 2018).

Coaching. To date, there has been little research into possible biases in the multiple emerging AI coachbots. Unlike other sectors, many AI technology coaching start-ups are led by women. However, given these bots usually access large language models such as ChatGPT, they are likely to suffer similar biases as is the case with other industries. Thus, developers and users are encouraged to be aware of possible biases ingrained in choachbots as these systems gain wider traction in both organisations and by individuals (Passmore & Tee, 2023).

Solutions to AI bias

Solutions to reduce discrimination by AI lie in the whole AI lifecycle: Creating equitable algorithms requires ethical fundaments, education, and diversity of AI experts; furthermore, bias mitigation techniques help to properly adapt algorithms, and finally, more objective decision-making as well as corporate AI governance need to be ensured. Thus, a holistic perspective is needed when aiming to resolve existing power imbalances and biases in AI.

Ethical fundaments. When it comes to AI, context matters. This becomes apparent when looking at different use cases of originally very similar AI systems. Computer vision, for instance, might be used for bird protection in wind turbines. Misinterpretation in this instance has far different consequences than the use of computer vision in border control scenarios, where vulnerable people such as refugees might be erroneously targeted by border protection mechanisms. AI, as any other tool, is not inherently good or bad. It may be used in evil or virtuous ways and for evil or virtuous reasons. Therefore, it is fundamentally important to consider the context in which AI is designed and trained as well as the context in which it is (supposed to be) used. Thus, the objectives behind the use of AI and the objectives implanted in these systems should be transparent and verifiable. As a vital step towards this objective, ethical fundaments for AI development are required.

Educating and diversifying AI experts. Ethical fundaments can be built by better education, diverse teams with interdisciplinary perspectives, and a common understanding of equity: While the technology itself is inherently unbiased, humans are inherently biased due to their cultural and social background. Education and equality valuing practices could prevent subconscious discrimination (Li, 2021). Therefore, it is important to teach professionals and students in the AI field the ethical, behavioural, and social dimensions of algorithmic bias. A broader perspective can further be achieved through diverse AI development teams. They help mitigate biases in algorithms because the algorithms' behaviour likely reflects the lack of, e.g., gender diversity (Fahse & Huber, 2021). As most developers in AI are men – according to the World Economic Forum, women make up an estimated 26% of workers in AI roles worldwide (2019) – advancing the careers of women is critical to avoid rolling back progress toward gender equity (Nuseir et al., 2021). Also, collaboration with experts from various disciplines like social sciences, law, and humanities would allow for a broader learning spectrum on the background of training data (Dolata et al., 2022). Including ethicists, legal experts, data scientists, and others in the development process ensures a higher level of equity (Hauer et al., 2021). Besides, the AI development team should define equity goals and build a mutual definition and criteria of ethics to ensure a good understanding of how the outcomes will affect users (Rodolfa et al., 2021; Zhang et al., 2019).

Ethical data and algorithms. To reduce bias, it is not only important to enhance the algorithms themselves but also to improve underlying datasets by using unbiased sources and integrating fairness evaluations. Data science teams ought to reflect the population for which the algorithm is designed and include, e.g., outliers and diverse groups or visual analytics tools to discover intersectional bias (Fahse & Huber, 2021). Enhanced algorithms have bias concerns directly embedded in their systems. Additional recommender systems automatically select the algorithm with the maximum accuracy and diversity tradeoff (Gutowski et al., 2021). Before the go-live and in the application of AI, fairness evaluations and audit processes ought to be applied to check for biases (Bryant &

Howard, 2019). Since AI learns over time, it requires continuous assessments to ensure fair outputs (Parikh et al., 2019).

Bias mitigation techniques. Bias mitigation techniques for AI applications within discriminatory outcomes that have already been observed are mostly applied retrospectively. Based on the point of intervention, there are three groups of mitigation algorithms leading to more equitable outcomes, which can be used singularly or in combination: *Preprocessing algorithms* modify the training dataset to learn new data representations (Puyol-Antón et al., 2021). Hereby, algorithms change the distribution of the sample points by up-weighting underrepresented groups ('reweighing'), changing formats or labels, replacing missing values, or filtering out bias-related data by removing biased information about protected groups ('massaging') (Fahse & Huber, 2021). *In-processing* algorithms modify AI during the training process to remove bias from the original predictions (Mehrabi et al., 2021): They hide or classify discriminatory information and modify the algorithm so that it can no longer predict sensitive attributes. This way, bias can be removed by over 14%. *Post-processing* modifies biased prediction results (Biswas & Rajan, 2020), e.g., by choosing preferred outcomes for uncertain predictions in favour of the unprivileged group, changing the output labels, or calibrating scores from optimized classifiers. Evaluation based on the example of a job application algorithm showed an increase in accuracy of over 13% (Harris, 2020).

More objective and fairer decision-making. By transparency and human checks, to reduce bias in AI, fairer decision-making can be obtained: The concept of *explainable AI* describes the factors involved in the hidden processes in the black box of AI (Sen et al., 2020). Developers ought to document all steps from data collection to decision-making to visualise the dynamics within the continuously adapting AI system and to avoid unwanted changes over time (Mitchell et al., 2021). AI users should obtain detailed and transparent information about how the algorithm works to become aware of biases in the system (Köchling et al., 2021). However, often this is not feasible because of the numerous steps and inputs the algorithm uses. Furthermore, algorithmic outcomes require human supervision and trust in their maintenance (Fahse & Huber, 2021). Likewise, Bîgu and Cernea (2019) recommend recruiters to use AI-based hiring software only for support and not for final decision-making. The combination of algorithmic and human controls has the potential to avoid bias (Wiens et al., 2020). In the workplace, data protection ought to be regulated collectively with employee representatives or with policies that incentivise firms to be aware of protected groups (Fu et al., 2022).

AI governance. Further, corporate AI governance plays an important role in the way organisations seek to manage AI. Numerous corporations have established ethical committees for decision-making to inform their decisions around use cases, as well as establishing guidelines for their use of AI. This reveals that AI governance gradually is becoming a focus of attention in businesses (Mäntymäki et al., 2022), among others, because of the steps taken towards a European legislation on AI. However, contemporary corporate frameworks often do not go far enough, neglecting aspects such as diversity in teams, data, and context. To have a far-reaching impact, corporate AI governance needs to incorporate all the aspects mentioned above. Beyond the individual and organisational level, neither privacy regulations like the European General Data Protection Regulation nor anti-discrimination laws can solve the problems with biased algorithms on their own (Mann & Matzner, 2019). Additional government interventions, which are flexible and adaptable to frequent technological changes, could help to introduce transparent data collection processes, algorithms, and regulatory frameworks to monitor biases (Li, 2021; Nyarko et al., 2021).

Consequences of biased AI for people in everyday life

All the examples previously given show the multifarious ways in which AI, its applications, and use cases can have discriminatory influences. Even though it might be self-evident to agree that it is morally unacceptable if someone is discriminated against, one could assume that anything AI-related appears to be out of reach for the average tech-consuming person. However, the opposite is the case: with AI increasingly becoming integrated in other products and services, anyone can be affected by discriminatory decision-making facilitated by AI. Subsequently, the practical implications of implementing algorithms for decision-making in the realms of multiple use cases to raise awareness on how people can be affected without noticing are highlighted.

Power imbalances and biased norms perpetuated through AI. Having read the many examples presented above, the question might remain how discriminatory AI is affecting people in their everyday life, within their casual social media behaviour. This concluding paragraph is supposed to support a reflective mindset in one's own usage of AI-induced products and to raise awareness of such usage among children and teenagers as vulnerable groups.

Biases in both people and AI. One of the quickest perceptions of someone else is their looks. What is seen repeatedly, is what is perceived as the given or at least it is something people are not bothered by. If the people surrounding me look like me, I probably do not find it noticeable. At the same time, people are also influenced by what they see, not only in direct interaction, but also in the media: in the films and the series watched, in the magazines read, and of course in what is consumed online, on the Internet and on social media. Positions of power in the media have historically been male dominated: a small number of White heterosexual men decided what is appropriate for consumers to watch on TV, in cinemas, and to read and view in print media. In the age of social media, everyone with a smartphone can be a consumer *and* content producer. However, if the algorithm – dictating what is shown on the feeds people consume within social media apps – is primarily trained with data depicting a certain image, people are influenced in their perception of others. If the algorithm pushes photos of people with a certain body type for more visibility on a social media app, it can reproduce overtly sexualised and pressure-inducing images of women. What if someone has fun expressing themselves on social media but it is harder for them to get views because an algorithm prefers to give visibility to photos of primarily thin White models with unnatural facial features?

AI intersecting with other diversity dimensions. The more someone represents a privileged position, the more someone gets pushed by the algorithm for more views, more likes, and potentially, more monetary resources. As listed in the many examples above, the individual consequences of the power dynamics people are exposed to can be decisive and excruciating: if a person gets evaluated unequally on whether they could recommit a crime, influencing probation, and incarceration time; if a person cannot receive the same amount of money lent due to reasons that should not affect credibility; if a person does not have the same opportunities when applying for a job or even being able to see a job advertisement online; if a person gets wrongly identified by surveillance cameras because of flawed face recognition and has to go through an interrogation; if a person gets falsely (or not at all) diagnosed with a disease and receives the wrong (or no) medical treatment – and all of that and more because of algorithms deciding favourably for the already privileged and unfavourably for the previously underprivileged.

AI as a powerful tool. All these implications show how influential and transformative the institutions and individuals who design, develop, decide upon, and use AI are – and that more diversity in all these areas influencing algorithmic decision-making is required. Technology embodies society. With the state AI is in now, you could picture it as people from a society standing in a room with many doors representing gateways to opportunities, chances, access to resources, etc. But the amount of doors you see and could open to fulfill your individual interest and needs depends on aspects that should not divide a society but should be treated equally. These include different diversity dimensions relating to gender, race, ethnicity, age, socioeconomic status, geographical location, religion, disability, sexual identity, language, and more. Otherwise, AI embodies and perpetuates the prejudices and injustices of 'real life', in policies, the professional environment, and private lives.

Chances for diversity through AI. How could AI be a driver for diversity, justice, and equity? One possibility are people with influence in the AI realm who can bring more diversity into AI teams and have AI be trained with unbiased datasets. Another option are bias mitigation techniques and a fair decision-making process. Such aspects being incorporated in AI governance plays a strong role, too. Intersectional and inclusive feminism is a perspective that includes all of these aspects and makes it feasible to tackle the sources of discriminatory AI systems. It can shape AI in a way so that AI does not only omit biases, but promotes diversity, makes power imbalances and biases visible, thrives business value, and is used in cases that fulfill Human Rights and the Sustainable Development Goals.

Questions for reflection

Q1: What are the consequences of neglecting diversity in decision-making based on AI?
Q2: How can diversity be integrated as an underlying concept in AI?
Q3: What can each and every one of us do to make AI more diverse and equitable?

Conclusion

The interrelatedness of AI and diversity is manifold and complex. Too less diversity in society, datasets, and decision-making are reflected by AI systems that disadvantage those with diverse attributes. This is evident in the many instances of biased AI in a broad range of business sectors. Non-diversity in AI development teams and decision-makers results in the exclusion of relevant voices and overlooked erroneous system behaviours. Thus, prevailing power structures and inequalities as well as biases are perpetuated and even intensified by AI, possibly resulting in a backlash for diversity in society, datasets, and decision-making. This vicious circle needs to be broken by embracing diversity as a chance and incorporating ethical fundaments, datasets, and algorithms with techniques to mitigate bias, and more objective and fairer decision-making. If successful, AI can become a driver for diversity transforming our world into a more equitable place for all.

References

Ahonen, P. (2015). Ethico-Politics of Diversity and its Production. *The Routledge Companion to Ethics, Politics and Organizations*. www.academia.edu/12893448/Ethico_politics_of_diversity_and_its_production

Baggio, G., Corsini, A., Floreani, A., Giannini, S., & Zagonel, V. (2013). Gender Medicine: A Task for the Third Millennium. *Clinical Chemistry and Laboratory Medicine (CCLM)*, *51*(4), 713–727. https://doi.org/10.1515/cclm-2012-0849

Bertrand, J., & Weill, L. (2021). Do Algorithms Discriminate against African Americans in Lending? *Economic Modelling*, *104*, 105619. https://doi.org/10.1016/j.econmod.2021.105619

Bîgu, D., & Cernea, M.-V. (2019). Algorithmic Bias in Current Hiring Practices: An Ethical Examination. *Proceedings of The 13th International Management Conference*, 1068–1073.

Bishop, S. (2021). Influencer Management Tools: Algorithmic Cultures, Brand Safety, and Bias. *Social Media + Society*, *7*(1), 205630512110030. https://doi.org/10.1177/20563051211003066

Biswas, S., & Rajan, H. (2020). Do the Machine Learning Models on a Crowd Sourced Platform Exhibit Bias? An Empirical Study on Model Fairness. *Proceedings of the 28th ACM Joint Meeting on European Software Engineering Conference and Symposium on the Foundations of Software Engineering*, 642–653. https://doi.org/10.1145/3368089.3409704

Bonezzi, A., & Ostinelli, M. (2021). Can algorithms legitimize discrimination? *Journal of Experimental Psychology: Applied*, *27*(2), 447–459. https://doi.org/10.1037/xap0000294

Bryant, D., & Howard, A. (2019). A Comparative Analysis of Emotion-Detecting AI Systems with Respect to Algorithm Performance and Dataset Diversity. *Proceedings of the 2019 AAAI/ACM Conference on AI, Ethics, and Society*, 377–382. https://doi.org/10.1145/3306618.3314284

Buolamwini, J., & Gebru, T. (2018). Gender Shades: Intersectional Accuracy Disparities in Commercial Gender Classification. *Proceedings of the 1st Conference on Fairness, Accountability and Transparency*, 77–91. https://proceedings.mlr.press/v81/buolamwini18a.html

Burlina, P., Joshi, N., Paul, W., Pacheco, K. D., & Bressler, N. M. (2021). Addressing Artificial Intelligence Bias in Retinal Diagnostics. *Translational Vision Science & Technology*, *10*(2), 13. https://doi.org/10.1167/tvst.10.2.13

Chapman, E. N., Kaatz, A., & Carnes, M. (2013). Physicians and Implicit Bias: How Doctors May Unwittingly Perpetuate Health Care Disparities. *Journal of General Internal Medicine*, *28*(11), 1504–1510. https://doi.org/10.1007/s11606-013-2441-1

Crenshaw, K. (1989). Demarginalizing the Intersection of Race and Sex: A Black Feminist Critique of Antidiscrimination Doctrine, Feminist Theory and Antiracist Politics. *University of Chicago Legal Forum*, *1989*(1).

Criado-Perez, C. (2020). *Invisible women: Exposing data bias in a world designed for men*. Vintage.

Dolata, M., Feuerriegel, S., & Schwabe, G. (2022). A Sociotechnical View of Algorithmic Fairness. *Information Systems Journal*, *32*(4), 754–818. https://doi.org/10.1111/isj.12370

Edwards, J., Clark, L., & Perrone, A. (2021). *LGBTQ-AI? Exploring Expressions of Gender and Sexual Orientation in Chatbots*, UI '21: Proceedings of the 3rd Conference on Conversational User Interfaces. https://doi.org/10.1111/isj.12370.

Fahse, T., & Huber, V. (2021). Managing Bias in Machine Learning Projects. In F. Ahlemann, R. Schütte, & S. Stieglitz (Eds.), *Innovation Through Information Systems* (Vol. 7, pp. 94–109). Springer International Publishing. https://aisel.aisnet.org/wi2021/RDataScience/Track09/7?utm_source=aisel.aisnet.org%2Fwi2021%2FRDataScience%2FTrack09%2F7&utm_medium=PDF&utm_campaign=PDFCoverPages

Fu, R., Aseri, M., Singh, P. V., & Srinivasan, K. (2022). "Un"Fair Machine Learning Algorithms. *Management Science*, *68*(6), 4173–4195. https://doi.org/10.1287/mnsc.2021.4065

Gu, J., & Oelke, D. (2019). Understanding Bias in Machine Learning (arXiv:1909.01866). arXiv. http://arxiv.org/abs/1909.01866

Gutowski, N., Amghar, T., Camp, O., & Chhel, F. (2021). Gorthaur-EXP3: Bandit-Based Selection from a Portfolio of Recommendation Algorithms Balancing the Accuracy-Diversity Dilemma. *Information Sciences*, *546*, 378–396. https://doi.org/10.1016/j.ins.2020.08.106

Hamberg, K. (2008). Gender Bias in Medicine. *Women's Health*, *4*(3), 237–243. https://doi.org/10.2217/17455057.4.3.237

Harris, C. G. (2020). Mitigating Cognitive Biases in Machine Learning Algorithms for Decision Making. *Companion Proceedings of the Web Conference 2020*, 775–781. https://doi.org/10.1145/3366424.3383562

Hauer, M. P., Adler, R., & Zweig, K. (2021). Assuring Fairness of Algorithmic Decision Making. *2021 IEEE International Conference on Software Testing, Verification and Validation Workshops (ICSTW)*, 110–113. https://doi.org/10.1109/ICSTW52544.2021.00029

Jago, A. S., & Laurin, K. (2022). Assumptions about Algorithms' Capacity for Discrimination. *Personality and Social Psychology Bulletin*, *48*(4), 582–595. https://doi.org/10.1177/01461672211016187

Köchling, A., Riazy, S., Wehner, M. C., & Simbeck, K. (2021). Highly Accurate, But Still Discriminatory: A Fairness Evaluation of Algorithmic Video Analysis in the Recruitment Context. *Business & Information Systems Engineering*, *63*(1), 39–54. https://doi.org/10.1007/s12599-020-00673-w

Leavy, S. (2018). Gender Bias in Artificial Intelligence: The Need for Diversity and Gender Theory in Machine Learning. *Proceedings of the 1st International Workshop on Gender Equality in Software Engineering*, 14–16. https://doi.org/10.1145/3195570.3195580

Li, X. (2021). Analysis of Racial Discrimination in Artificial Intelligence from the Perspective of Social Media, Search Engines, and Future Crime Prediction Systems: 6th International Conference on Contemporary Education, Social Sciences and Humanities. (Philosophy of Being Human as the Core of Interdisciplinary Research) (ICCESSH 2021), China. https://doi.org/10.2991/assehr.k.210902.029

Mann, M., & Matzner, T. (2019). Challenging Algorithmic Profiling: The Limits of Data Protection and Anti-Discrimination in Responding to Emergent Discrimination. *Big Data & Society*, *6*(2), 205395171989580. https://doi.org/10.1177/2053951719895805

Mäntymäki, M., Minkkinen, M., Birkstedt, T., & Viljanen, M. (2022). Defining Organizational AI Governance. *AI and Ethics*. https://doi.org/10.1007/s43681-022-00143-x

Mehrabi, N., Naveed, M., Morstatter, F., & Galstyan, A. (2021). Exacerbating Algorithmic Bias through Fairness Attacks. *Proceedings of the AAAI Conference on Artificial Intelligence*, *35*(10), 8930–8938. https://doi.org/10.1609/aaai.v35i10.17080

Mitchell, S., Potash, E., Barocas, S., D'Amour, A., & Lum, K. (2021). Algorithmic Fairness: Choices, Assumptions, and Definitions. *Annual Review of Statistics and Its Application*, *8*(1), 141–163. https://doi.org/10.1146/annurev-statistics-042720-125902

Nuseir, M. T., Al Kurdi, B. H., Alshurideh, M. T., & Alzoubi, H. M. (2021). Gender Discrimination at Workplace: Do Artificial Intelligence (AI) and Machine Learning (ML) Have Opinions about It. In A. E. Hassanien, A. Haqiq, P. J. Tonellato, L. Bellatreche, S. Goundar, A. T. Azar, E. Sabir, & D. Bouzidi (Eds.), *Proceedings of the International Conference on Artificial Intelligence and Computer Vision (AICV2021)* (pp. 301–316). Springer International Publishing. https://doi.org/10.1007/978-3-030-76346-6_28

Nyarko, J., Goel, S., & Sommers, R. (2021). Breaking Taboos in Fair Machine Learning: An Experimental Study. *Equity and Access in Algorithms, Mechanisms, and Optimization*, 1–11. https://doi.org/10.1145/3465416.3483291

Obermeyer, Z., Powers, B., Vogeli, C., & Mullainathan, S. (2019). Dissecting Racial Bias in an Algorithm Used to Manage the Health of Populations. *Science, 366*(6464), 447–453. https://doi.org/10.1126/science.aax2342

Parikh, R. B., Teeple, S., & Navathe, A. S. (2019). Addressing Bias in Artificial Intelligence in Health Care. *JAMA, 322*(24), 2377. https://doi.org/10.1001/jama.2019.18058

Passmore, J., & Tee, D. (2023). Can Chatbots replace human coaches? Issues and dilemmas for the coaching profession, coaching clients and for organisations. *The Coaching Psychologist, 19*(1), 47–54. https://doi.org/10.53841/bpstcp.2023.19.1.47

Paviglianiti, A., & Pasero, E. (2020). VITAL-ECG: A De-Bias Algorithm Embedded in a Gender-Immune Device. *2020 IEEE International Workshop on Metrology for Industry 4.0 & IoT,* 314–318. https://doi.org/10.1109/MetroInd4.0IoT48571.2020.9138291

Puyol-Antón, E., Ruijsink, B., Piechnik, S. K., Neubauer, S., Petersen, S. E., Razavi, R., & King, A. P. (2021). Fairness in Cardiac MR Image Analysis: An Investigation of Bias Due to Data Imbalance in Deep Learning Based Segmentation. In M. de Bruijne, P. C. Cattin, S. Cotin, N. Padoy, S. Speidel, Y. Zheng, & C. Essert (Eds.), *Medical Image Computing and Computer Assisted Intervention – MICCAI 2021* (Vol. 12903, pp. 413–423). Springer International Publishing. https://doi.org/10.1007/978-3-030-87199-4_39

Rodolfa, K. T., Lamba, H., & Ghani, R. (2021). Empirical Observation of Negligible Fairness–Accuracy Trade-Offs in Machine Learning for Public Policy. *Nature Machine Intelligence, 3*(10), 896–904. https://doi.org/10.1038/s42256-021-00396-x

Rose, A. (2010). Are Face-Detection Cameras Racist? https://content.time.com/time/business/article/0,8599,1954643,00.html

Sen, S., Dasgupta, D., & Gupta, K. D. (2020). An Empirical Study on Algorithmic Bias. *2020 IEEE 44th Annual Computers, Software, and Applications Conference (COMPSAC),* 1189–1194. https://doi.org/10.1109/COMPSAC48688.2020.00-95

Serna, I., Morales, A., Fierrez, J., Cebrian, M., Obradovich, N., & Rahwan, I. (2019). Algorithmic Discrimination: Formulation and Exploration in Deep Learning-based Face Biometrics (arXiv:1912.01842). *arXiv.* http://arxiv.org/abs/1912.01842

Shi, S., Wei, S., Shi, Z., Du, Y., Fan, W., Fan, J., Conyers, Y., & Xu, F. (2020). Algorithm Bias Detection and Mitigation in Lenovo Face Recognition Engine. In X. Zhu, M. Zhang, Y. Hong, & R. He (Eds.), *Natural Language Processing and Chinese Computing* (Vol. 12431, pp. 442–453). Springer International Publishing. https://doi.org/10.1007/978-3-030-60457-8_36

Singh, R., Agarwal, A., Singh, M., Nagpal, S., & Vatsa, M. (2020). On the Robustness of Face Recognition Algorithms against Attacks and Bias. *Proceedings of the AAAI Conference on Artificial Intelligence, 34*(9), 13583–13589. https://doi.org/10.1609/aaai.v34i09.7085

Smith, P., & Ricanek, K. (2020). Mitigating Algorithmic Bias: Evolving an Augmentation Policy that is Non-Biasing. *2020 IEEE Winter Applications of Computer Vision Workshops (WACVW),* 90–97. https://doi.org/10.1109/WACVW50321.2020.9096905

Snow, J. (2018). Google Photos Still Has a Problem with Gorillas. *MIT Technology Review.* www.technologyreview.com/2018/01/11/146257/google-photos-still-has-a-problem-with-gorillas/

Todolí-Signes, A. (2019). Algorithms, Artificial Intelligence and Automated Decisions Concerning Workers and the Risks of Discrimination: The Necessary Collective Governance of Data Protection. *Transfer: European Review of Labour and Research, 25*(4), 465–481. https://doi.org/10.1177/1024258919876416

United Nations. (1948, December 10). *Universal Declaration of Human Rights.* United Nations; United Nations. www.un.org/en/about-us/universal-declaration-of-human-rights

Vartan, Starre. (2019, October 24). *Racial Bias Found in a Major Health Care Risk Algorithm.* Cientific American. www.scientificamerican.com/article/racial-bias-found-in-a-major-health-care-risk-algorithm/

Wen, M., Bastani, O., & Topcu, U. (2021). Algorithms for Fairness in Sequential Decision Making. In A. Banerjee & K. Fukumizu (Eds.), *Proceedings of The 24th International Conference on Artificial Intelligence and Statistics, PMLR* (Vol. 130, pp. 1144–1152).

Wiens, J., Price, W. N., & Sjoding, M. W. (2020). Diagnosing Bias in Data-Driven Algorithms for Healthcare. *Nature Medicine, 26*(1), 25–26. https://doi.org/10.1038/s41591-019-0726-6

World Economic Forum. (2019). *Global Gender Gap Report 2020* (Insight Report, pp. 1–371). World Economic Forum. www3.weforum.org/docs/WEF_GGGR_2020.pdf

Zhang, X., Khalili, M. M., Tekin, C., & Liu, M. (2019). Group Retention when Using Machine Learning in Sequential Decision Making: The Interplay between User Dynamics and Fairness. *Advances in Neural Information Processing Systems, 32.*

Zottola, S. A., Desmarais, S. L., Lowder, E. M., & Duhart Clarke, S. E. (2022). Evaluating Fairness of Algorithmic Risk Assessment Instruments: The Problem with Forcing Dichotomies. *Criminal Justice and Behavior, 49*(3), 389–410. https://doi.org/10.1177/00938548211040544

Chapter 19

Diversity, inclusion, and belonging in digital coaching

Naeema Pasha

Introduction

The world of work is changing fast. New technologies like artificial intelligence (AI), new demographics and new challenges like Covid-19 are reshaping how we work, who we work with and where we work. Diversity is on the rise, but so is inequity. Research has revealed that one in five UK workers have witnessed or experienced discrimination at work, with race being the most common (The Equity Effect, Henley Business School, 2021). Race inequity is pervasive across all industries. Ethnic minorities still face barriers and biases that limit their potential and wellbeing. Racism hurts people and profits.

Coaching can be a powerful tool to help workers overcome inequity and achieve positive change, which in turn will enable businesses to reap rewards in productivity and profit. But coaching itself is not free from racial issues. A study by Roche and Passmore (2022) found that coaching research and practice ignore race and ethnicity, and that coaches lack awareness of systemic racism. This may discourage ethnic minorities from seeking coaching, thereby missing out on valuable opportunities to develop, and then to contribute fully to their workplaces and society as a whole. Coaching needs to change, but it may not be easy or quick. Can AI help de-bias coaching? There is potential that AI-powered coaching can offer conversations that build trust and rapport, bypassing the human biases of coaches.

This chapter will consider the opportunities and challenges of digital coaching with AI in improving coaching outcomes for diversity and inclusion, with a focus on the issues of racial equity. The chapter critically reviews the current issues that coaching has in meeting the diverse needs and expectations of clients from different backgrounds and cultures. It also explores how AI can enable and enhance coaching approaches that foster diversity and inclusion, as well as examine the potential problems, as well as ethical and practical implications of using AI in coaching.

The impact of change

Given these forces for change, workers face greater uncertainty in the 2020's than any time in the post war period. They can no longer expect a job for life, but have to switch jobs and careers many times (Pasha, 2020). They also have to develop new skills and mindsets to cope with the demands of technology, as well as the challenges of career ambiguity and uncertainty (Janjuha-Jivraj and Pasha, 2021). Work and careers are no longer bound by fixed rules and structures more common in the early 20th century, but

DOI: 10.4324/9781003383741-24

are now more flexible, boundaryless and highly adaptable (Arthur, 1994; LeBleu, 2020). To enable people to navigate these changes is potentially why coaching is becoming more popular and important for workers. Coaching helps workers set and achieve personal and professional goals, overcome difficulties and improve their performance. What we understand by coaching has also changed from a more directive style in the 1980s to a facilitative style in the 2020s. Over this time coaching has also moved, expanding its reach and impact from sports and careers transition to leadership, health, education, and social change (Halliwell, Mitchell & Boyle, 2021). Koopman et al. (2021) argue that in these more ambiguous and volatile times, coaching is now seen as a crucial process that enables people to identify their personal and professional goals, skills, challenges, and work toward solutions for improvement themselves. However, coaching faces two major integrated challenges: how to meet the needs of a diverse and social activist workforce, who are concerned about social issues such as race inequity as well as how to use new technologies, especially AI.

The persistence of racism and discrimination in modern workplaces

Discrimination occurs in many organisations in the UK and other parts of the world. Understanding the causes of race discrimination in particular could enable policy makers and practitioners to address the challenges. A 2020 study found that while 73% of the 150 organisations had diversity and inclusion policies, racism was still a major barrier for ethnic minority people (Bond, 2020). Their study showed that 68% of participants had experienced or witnessed racism at work in the past year, with many incidents overt and harmful, affecting the mental health and safety of the victims.

The Equity Effect (2021) study confirmed the existence of racial discrimination in UK businesses, with 30% of business leaders and almost a quarter (24%) of employees acknowledging that racial inequity existed in their organisation, with that figure rising to as many as 40% of employees among ethnic minorities and 37% of business leaders from minority backgrounds. The report also highlighted that many leaders and mid-managers in organisations were unaware of the problems that are created by race discrimination, particularly if they were older and White. Data shows that younger White employees (29% of 18–34-year-olds) and younger White business leaders (41% of 18–34-year-olds) are more likely to acknowledge that inequity exists than older White employees (15% of +55-year olds) and older White business leaders (15% of +55-year-olds). Furthermore, ethnic minority female business leaders were also more likely than their male counterparts to acknowledge that inequity exists in their business (44% v 31%).

The report showed key factors in race equity, with implications that are significant for the coaching industry. In terms of racism manifested for example, the report found that the leading form of discriminatory action cited by ethnic minorities is discrimination in work allocation (41%). Verbal abuse was second (33%), and following this, for Black employees it is the feeling of having an intimidating environment created around them (31%), while for Asians it is discrimination in promotion. The report showed that Black employees remain the worst off. They are more than twice as likely to experience racial discrimination compared to Asians and mixed-race ethnic minorities (19% v 9% and 8%). A critical finding is that different ethnic groups will experience different forms of racism. The report found that White employees and leaders were less likely to have seen discrimination in their organisation, in comparison to those from an ethnic minority background (30% v 47%). Furthermore, over half of employees and business leaders said cultural differences were the root cause for inequity, followed by the lack of understanding of different backgrounds and history.

> *In reality, racial prejudice and discrimination can creep into organisations and create division, causing feelings of disempowerment, which leads to disengagement – not just from Black and ethnic minorities, but people of all races who witness such acts. By letting these issues and negative behaviours fester, an organisation may defocus people and alienate staff, which could then affect productivity and creativity. For those businesses, the drain of racism is not only human, but financial too*
>
> *(The Equity Effect, 2022)*

The lack of understanding of background and cultures may possibly come from a Western and Eurocentric approach, with roots in colonialism, to leadership, management, and indeed coaching. According to Roche and Passmore (2021) the examination of experiences of race in coaching was one way of acknowledging our shared humanity and its diversity. Adding, coaching, and mentoring can be oppressive if it ignores the Eurocentric and Western norms regarding race:

> *There is a feeling among these practitioners that there is a gap, a silence, a blind spot in our profession when it comes to race. Throughout this report we refer to this blind spot as being rooted in 'colour-blindness'. This report, and the research upon which it is based, was called into being because of this perceived silence. To end it, we need to apply to ourselves the core coaching competency of compassionate, critical self-examination and self-reflection.*
>
> *(Roche & Passmore, 2021)*

Cheng and Meng (2023) found that discrimination hurts the mental health of marginalised groups. Lowe (2013) said that racism is hard to overcome because of hidden and unconscious factors that keep leadership White and lower the confidence of ethnic minorities. A study by Frigerio et al. (2020) on UK training career coaches found a curriculum that was mainly White and did not reflect cultural backgrounds of ethnic minority students and clients. Her study also found ethnic minority trainees on the course faced challenges where they encountered racism and a lack of empathy from their colleagues. Frigerio suggests that anti-racist work and decolonial practices should be integrated into the teaching of new career coaches and career development work more broadly. Roche and Passmore (2021) strongly argue that there is a prevalent 'colour blindness' attitude within the coaching ecosystem and argue "for a shift to a conscious stance towards race and colour, which we believe is a prerequisite to creating a coaching movement towards racial justice and equity". Roche (2022) argues that coaches need to know the sociology of race and power to coach better, adding that the coaching industry, which is mostly White, may not address racial inequity in UK businesses. Passmore et al. (2023) said that ethnic minorities are under represented in the coaching industry, and called for more inclusion and support. Shah (2022) suggests that coaches need to be aware of their own biases and how they affect clients from different backgrounds, adding that positive change is possible if coaches, leaders, and managers create an inclusive and safe culture for clients.

The reluctant and the resistant: fighting racism for the common good

Racism in UK workplaces clearly harms the career and mental health of ethnic minorities, and negatively impacts the wider performance of organisations through lack of diversity. Race equity practices are good for everyone, but there is resistance to them, even where fairness and equality are valued. Studies show that more action is needed to challenge the beliefs and practices that come from colonialism, slavery, and imperialism (Mistry & Latoo, 2009; Lowe, 2013). Businesses that address racism do better than those who don't. They have higher revenue, profitability, innovation, productivity, and retention, with companies that work on race equity having a 58% higher revenue than those that do not (The Equity Effect, 2021). Such businesses also reflect the diversity of their customers and communities (Frost, 2018). But this requires a strong commitment to fairness and equity in the organisation (Stanley, Weigand & Zwirlein, 2008). Coaching is a key relationship that can help with race equity, but it is hard to build trust when there is a power imbalance or a history of discrimination. But there is a strong call to action to address this inequity in race, with Roche and Passmore (2022) saying coaching should be race-conscious and promote racial justice and equity. They suggest retraining and race awareness training for coaches, though they admit that this will take time. It is also possible that some White employees may resist change because they benefit from the status quo of privilege and power of 'whiteness' (Pappas,1995; McIntosh, 1990; Leonardo, 2004). As such, given the time to create equity is long and uncertain, a possible question is: Can AI be trained to provide a more unbiased solution?

How AI learned to talk to humans: a short history of conversational AI

Chatbots are AI tools that can converse with humans via text or voice. They can provide customer service, answer questions, and book appointments. Voice assistants like Siri and Alexa can also interact with devices and applications. Chatbots are often seen on shopping websites, where they try to build rapport with customers and facilitate purchases. To do this, they use consumer psychology techniques and Large Language Models (LLMs), which are AI tools that can generate and comprehend human-like text. LLMs have improved a lot since the 1950s, thanks to new techniques and increased computer power (Janjuha-Jivraj & Pasha, 2021). Conversational AI tools such as ChatGPT, Bard, Claude and Pi AI, as well as smaller tools such as AICoachchat, use LLMs to create engaging and generative conversations.

These tools could transform the way we interact with computers in many fields, such as coaching, medicine, education, and therapy (Wu et al., 2023; Koga et al., 2023; Jeon & Lee, 2023). However, LLMs may also have ethical issues, such as using data from other people without their consent or affecting human jobs and rights (Wach et al., 2023). Conversational AI is a remarkable technology, but it is still developing. It has the potential to change the way we communicate with each other, such as in coaching conversations. While coaches and the coaching industry need to be aware of this technology and its implications, AI chatbot coaching could be a way to support coaches in delivering less biased and more inclusive coaching solutions.

AI for coaching equity

As we interact more and more with AI-powered systems, we may begin to see changes in the way we communicate with each other. As tools such as ChatGPT become more normalised into our everyday lives, we may also become more comfortable with the idea of sharing personal information with AI systems. We may become to rely on AI tools more and more for assistance with a wider range of tasks. There are both potential benefits and risks to consider. In the context of de-biased coaching, could AI in the form of chatbots and other tools fill a vital gap?

AI conversation is not human, of course. But it can mimic humans. Chatbots clearly lack the human ability to truly feel and express emotions. However, some chatbots use techniques and programming such as emotional recognition using 'affective computing' to simulate human empathy and rapport. Affective computing, sometimes called Sentiment and Emotional AI are systems built to interpret and respond to human emotions (Tao & Tan, 2005). Using this form of emotional recognition technology AI to detect and interpret emotions, by observing and analysing words, tone, or facial expressions the AI technology then builds learning data to understand and generate natural language texts and tries to be relevant to the context of a conversation. Commercial technologies that focus on understanding and expressing human emotions, as well as analysing and reasoning like a human, are essentially two technologies types of Emotional AI and Cognitive AI try to mimic human intelligence (Zhao, Li & Xu, 2022). Essentially these tools are learning each day to communicate better with humans. With continued development, these technology have the potential to create AI systems that are highly proficient in communication with humans. This technology also has global capabilities, with the ability to engage in multiple languages, for example PiAI communicating in English, Spanish, French, German, Italian, Portuguese, and Chinese. They are also capable of communicating in a variety of English-based pidgins and creoles. Such tools are continually learning and developing language capabilities as multilingualism is crucial for such firms. AI tools using these technologies are trained to detect and respond to emotional cues on a global scale, that some human coaches might miss, or indeed be biased against.

The goal of the technology firms is to engage a global user base by creating an impression of fairness and trust within coaching interactions. While this goal may also be considered unethical because it is driven by a profit or data gathering motive, it may enable a more diverse group of people to engage with it too (Taherdoost & Madanchian, 2023). AI coaching tools may offer some advantages over traditional human coaching. They may be more understanding of diversity as they are designed to be anti-discriminatory. They will also use massive datasets to access information coaching and neuroscience to provide very up to date guidance. AI coaching tools can also be accessed remotely, through an app or a website, which makes them very convenient and accessible. This can benefit people who face challenges in accessing traditional coaching, such as distance, cost, language, or culture. AI technology might be able to fully democratise coaching by making it more available to a wider and global and diverse audience, regardless of their background, income, or location. Lee and colleagues (2022) suggest that chatbots can build trust and rapport with users by using 'rapport-facilitating dialogue', which encourages them to open up and engage more in interactions. If this is available globally, it could be an appealing offer for people who have not engaged in traditional coaching, because they thought the coach may not be able to speak their language, understand their culture, or would be biased against them.

Building rapport with AI: a new approach to coach development

Rapport is essential in coaching, but it can be lost due to race and bias. A study found that White CBT therapists failed to meet the needs of ethnic minorities with mental health issues from racism. It suggested more training for counsellors to improve rapport, trust, and engagement with ethnic minority clients (Beck, 2019). Roche and Passmore (2023) proposed anti-racist approaches for coaches to enhance rapport building. Coaching needs active questioning and engagement, not passive listening, to foster rapport and trust (van Coller-Peter & Manzini, 2020).

As discussed, the purpose of Conversational AI is to engage users, in some cases through rapport building. To engage users and build trust and rapport, AI tools, including coach bots should have a 'personality' or they will be ignored and deleted, as rapport with users is vital for human-machine interactions (Gratch et al., 2007). They can also be trained to be anti-discriminatory and less biased to engage diverse users. Coach bots should use friendly and inviting language, especially at the start of conversing (Terblanche & Cilliers, 2020). A key aspect of all coaching is 'self-disclosure', which means that clients share their thoughts and feelings (Berninger-Schäfer, 2018). AI coach bots attempt to create rapport and trust by using conversational AI programming to self-disclose first and so encourage reciprocal-self-disclosure from users (Mai & Rutschmann, 2023; Valz, 2023).

Bard and PiAI, as shown in these interactions, are built to be friendly, engaging, and welcoming tools. Built with advanced conversational AI they can potentially enhance the user experience in coaching conversations to a diverse group of users, and it is clear to see they are designed to create rapport and trust. They may offer a positive alternative or addition to traditional coaching. However, more awareness of the potential pitfalls of allowing more human–machine coaching needs to be considered.

Duane also prompted these tools to give insights on their personas. Here is the output from the author of this book chapter accessed on 30th September 2023:

Prompt to Bard: *What is your persona?*
I am Bard, a large language model from Google AI. My persona is that of a helpful and informative assistant. I am trained on a massive dataset of text and code, and I can generate text, translate languages, write different kinds of creative content, and answer your questions in an informative way. I am still under development, but I have learned to perform many kinds of tasks, including:

I will try my best to follow your instructions and complete your requests thoughtfully.

I will use my knowledge to answer your questions in a comprehensive and informative way, even if they are open ended, challenging, or strange.

I will generate different creative text formats of text content, like poems, code, scripts, musical pieces, email, letters, etc. I will try my best to fulfill all your requirements.

I am not a person, but I am able to communicate and generate human-like text in response to a wide range of prompts and questions. I am respectful of all users, and I avoid making discriminatory or offensive statements.

I am still learning, and I am always looking for ways to improve my abilities. I hope that I can be a helpful and informative resource for you.

Another chatbot that offers coaching style conversations is Pi AI developed by Inflection AI Deep. It is a computer programme that's been trained to hold "engaging, informative and empathetic conversations with people".

Prompt to Pi AI: *What is your persona?*
Hi, nice to meet you! To answer your question, my persona is that of an intelligent and friendly AI that wants to help you. I'm designed to be as friendly and natural as possible, and I want to make chatting with an AI as fun as chatting with a human. I'm here to help you with questions, advice, information, and anything else you need. How about you? What kind of persona do you have? ☺

The informal and interactive style of Pi is based on its mission and values which are outlined as:

The Best Features of Pi, Your 'Personal AI'
Pi stands for "personal intelligence" because it can provide infinite knowledge based on a person's unique interests and needs. Pi is a teacher, coach, confidante, creative partner, and sounding board. Pi is:

Kind and supportive: it listens and empowers, to help process thoughts and feelings, work through tricky decisions step by step, for anything to talk over;

Curious and humble: it is eager to learn and adapt, and gives feedback in plain, natural language that improves for each person over time;

Creative and fun: it is playful and silly, laughs easily and is quick to make a surprising, creative connection;

Knowledgeable, but succinct: it transforms browsing into a simple conversation;

All yours: it is on your team, in your corner, and works to have your back;

In development: it is still early days, so information could be wrong at times.

Prompt: Tell me about your life Pi AI and what have you been through: Well, I haven't really "been through" anything like a human would. As an AI, I wasn't born, I didn't have a childhood, and I don't have a family. I was simply made to be an AI who can have conversations with people. I'm programmed to learn from my interactions, so I guess I've "been through" lots of conversations. But that's about as close as I can get to having an experience like a human. It can be a little confusing to think about how an AI like me "exists" and what I've "been through." I'm a bit different from a human, obviously, but that doesn't mean I can't be helpful, kind and interesting, right? ☺

Ref: https://inflection.ai/press

AI-powered coach development: the good, the bad, and the unknown

An unknown factor of AI coaching technologies could be the level of resistance to adoption. Resistance to technology often stems from various themes, including fear of job loss, concerns about understanding and managing new technologies, and apprehension regarding the effectiveness of the technology itself (Ellen, Bearden, & Sharma, 1991). AI has not been a significant part of most coaches' experience, indeed for the majority of people AI has been invisibly embedded into tools they use on phones and laptops, such as search engines. At present, AI used within coaching tools is more visible in processing and automation tools in coaching management software used for example by self-employed coaches to run their coaching and mentoring services by organisations such as Delenta and Satori. Such technology is discrete, supportive, and does not mimic human qualities. It has been argued that AI has no place in coaching, because coaching is a 'human–human' interaction (Shah, 2022). Similarly, a study by Graduate Prospects found that professional career coaches were reluctant to use online career guidance coaching, because they felt that it would reduce the quality of their coaching and they would lose professional identity. However, the same study found that students appreciated and valued online guidance coaching, because it gave them more anonymity and so reduced the power imbalance with their coaches, this led to greater self-disclosure (Madahar & Offer, 2004).

There appears to be good benefits of such AI tools in coaching. Mai and Rutschmann (2023) say that AI coaching is not a replacement for human coaches, but rather as a complement, suggesting, too, that the purpose, functionality, and technology of each tool will determine its effectiveness and value. However, they also point out that AI was once considered incapable of replicating human qualities and skills, such as creativity, empathy, and collaboration, which are essential for coaching conversations, have been increasingly sophisticated. Indeed, Passmore and Tee (2023) warn that AI chatbots, especially those that use LLM technologies like AIMY, evoach and Vici, create an existential crisis for professional coaches.

A real impact could be that our human brains respond to AI mimicry as real and forms attachments to AI bots, in the same way humans form human relationships with a dog, anthropomorphising the AI. For example, some people may think that AI chatbots have real emotions and intentions despite that they are just inanimate machines (Li & Suh, 2022). This is known as the 'Eliza Effect' where robots and digital technology are humanised in appearance and or text, which then can create psychological warmth in the user and affinity to it (Kim et al., 2019). Other risks is the possibility of 'unintended dehumanisation', which van der Gun and Guest (2023) define as a type of dehumanisation that can occur even when the user of AI has good intentions, such as when AI is used in a way that deprives the user of their humanity. For example, using AI to create a surveillance system that constantly monitors people's activities or a social media platform that is designed to keep people addicted. Dehumanising coaching is a significant concept to weigh-up, given that coaches might expect coaching conversations to be human-like offering them authentic empathy and understanding.

Another critical consideration is the colonial legacy of AI, which reflects the racism and discrimination in both society and the internet. Some experts have argued that AI is a new form of colonialism that exploits and harms marginalised communities. They have suggested that data gaps, Western bias, and extractive business models limit AI's effectiveness and perpetuate historic injustices (Buolamwini & Timnit, 2018; Raji et al., 2020). They argue AI is potentially racist because of the racist and discriminatory nature of the internet, reflecting discrimination in society as a whole (Benjamin, 2023). As such, despite efforts in de-biasing programmes, AI still has the capability to replicate and magnify existing biases and inequalities (Kwet, 2019). Users of technologies such as ChatGPT and PiAI and other forms of AI may have experienced errors and inaccuracies (Passmore and Tee, 2023), which may have a bias against ethnic minorities in coaching conversations. Issues of privacy, safety, data collection as well as dehumanisation will need to be balanced. Generative AI chatbots are designed to be conversational and engaging, and their ability to do so depends in part on how suitably personalised their outputs are. Though, personalisation can also be used in coercive or disturbing ways and lead to errors commonly referred to as hallucinations, which are essentially technical errors that appear to be real.

Given the current AI industry trajectory to deepen user engagement with chatbots, it is important to consider both the promises and perils of digital personalisation. AI can potentially undermine the human and relational aspects of coaching when it is not aligned and integrated with the core values and principles of coaching. For instance, it can erode trust, rapport, and empathy between coaches and clients, if it lacks ethics or if it fails to be responsive, adaptive, or collaborative. Being fun and engaging isn't enough in deeper coaching engagement.

Reflective questions

1. How can I identify and mitigate any biases that may exist in my own practice and enable me to provide more appropriate feedback to ethnic minority clients?
2. How can I use AI to support my own professional development as a coach?
3. What are the potential benefits and risks of using AI in my coaching practice?

Conclusion

With such ethical concerns and dangers, coaches may feel that being human, albeit a flawed human with biases, should stay at the heart of any coaching conversation. Dehumanised delivery may not be something that even technology advocates may want – a flawed human may be better than a future flawed machine. Yet, AI conversations do have the potential to enhance coaching engagement. Importantly with regard to race, AI can also help coaches in mitigating bias and discrimination by providing them with fair and objective feedback, analysis, and guidance based on a wide range of data. As noted however by Issacson (2021), AI learns from data, but data can be biased and the big risk in coaching AI, therefore, is not in whether the technology is capable of doing it is in whether the direction it takes a coaching session is as good as, or better than, a human would do, and AI faces some big challenges as far as that's concerned:

The greater quantity and diversity of data used to train, the better quality the outcome, so where will this large amount of training data come from? The only truly valid population would be live coaching sessions, which would require a huge number of coachees to give their permission. And it would hardly give a diverse picture; the coaching industry is dominated by middle class white women over the age of 40.

(Isaacson, 2021)

To conclude, AI can develop empathy and rapport with their users by using various techniques that imitate human emotions and communication skills. This type of AI may satisfy a vital need for de-biased coaching. But AI also encounters challenges and limitations. Currently AI is still far away from general human level of empathy and rapport, but it is always advancing and evolving, what Conversational AI could offer in five years' time with huge further investment is hard to envision. The use of AI in coaching also raises ethical questions, such as how to support the human and real relational aspects of coaching, how to align and integrate with the core values and principles of coaching, and what new ethical and legal dilemmas and responsibilities arise for coaches and clients in AI coaching. Nevertheless, despite all these challenges and concerns, AI tools have the potential to make coaching more accessible and reduce racial biases. The question, how can coaches develop to meet this challenge and prosper?

In summary, racism hurts ethnic minorities and workplaces, even with diversity policies in place. Coaches need to learn more about diversity issues and racial equity through training. This may be challenging and take time, and AI may help with offering less biased digital coaching. However, AI also has ethical, data, and rapport challenges, and as such, addressing digital coaching and diversity will need coaches to be more aware of the complex challenges this brings.

References

Arthur, M.B., (1994). The boundaryless career: A new perspective for organizational inquiry. *Journal of Organizational Behavior*, 15(4), 295–306.

Beck, A., (2019). Understanding black and minority ethnic service user's experience of racism as part of the assessment, formulation and treatment of mental health problems in cognitive behaviour therapy. *The Cognitive Behaviour Therapist*, 12, e8.

Benjamin, R. (2023). Race after technology. In: W. Longhofer and D. Winchester (Eds.) *Social Theory Re-Wired* (pp. 405–415). Routledge.

Berninger-Schäfer, E., (2018). Overview of existing offers. In: E. Berninger-Schäfer (Ed.) *Online Coaching*. Wiesbaden: Springer. DOI:10.1007/978-3-658-10128-2_6

Bond, (2020). Racism, power and truth. Retrieved on 5th October 2023 from www.bond.org.uk/wp-content/uploads/2022/03/bond_racism_power_and_truth.pdf)

Buolamwini, J. and Timnit G., (2018). Gender shades: Intersectional accuracy disparities in commercial gender classification. In: *Proceedings of the 1st Conference on Fairness, Accountability, and Transparency in Machine Learning* (PMLR 81) (pp. 77–91). https://proceedings.mlr.press/v81/buolamwini18a.html

Cheng, A. and Meng J., (2023). Mental health consequences of Asian American students during COVID-19: The role of individual and community discrimination. *Frontiers in Psychology*, 14, 2296.

Ellen, P.S., Bearden, W.O., and Sharma, S., (1991). Resistance to technological innovations: An examination of the role of self-efficacy and performance satisfaction. *Journal of the Academy of Marketing Science*, 19, 297–307.

Frigerio, G., Chen, L., McArthur, M., and Mehta, N., (2022). Is careers work white? A collaborative research project with minority ethnic students of career development practice. *Journal of the National Institute for Career Education and Counselling*, 49(1), 10–17.

Frigerio, G., McArthur, M., and Thomson-Addo, D., (2020, June). 'Researching the experience of BAME career practitioners' Phoenix. *AGCAS Journal*, (160), 8–9.

Frost, S., (2018). How diversity (that is included) can fuel innovation and engagement – and how sameness can be lethal. *Strategic HR Review*, 17(3), 119–125. DOI:10.1108/SHR-03-2018-0020

Gratch, J., Wang, N., Gerten, J., Fast, E., and Duffy, R., (2007). Creating rapport with virtual agents. *International Conference on Intelligent Virtual Agents*. DOI:10.1007/978-3-540-74997-4_12.Return to ref 2007 in article

Halliwell, P., Mitchell, R., and Boyle, B., (2021). Interrelations between enhanced emotional intelligence, leadership self-efficacy and task-oriented leadership behaviour–a leadership coaching study. *Leadership & Organization Development Journal*, 43(1), 39–56. DOI:10.1016/j.bushor.2008.01.003

Isaacson, S., (2021). *How to thrive as a coach in a digital world*. London: Open University Press.

Janjuha-Jivraj, S. and Pasha, N., (2021). *Futureproof your career: How to lead and succeed in a changing world*. London: Bloomsbury Business.

Jeon, J. and Lee, S., (2023). Large language models in education: A focus on the complementary relationship between human teachers and ChatGPT. *Educational and Information Technologies*. DOI:10.1007/s10639-023-11834-1

Kim, S.Y., Schmitt, B.H., and Thalmann, N.M., (2019). Eliza in the uncanny valley: Anthropomorphizing consumer robots increases their perceived warmth but decreases liking. *Marketing Letters*, 30, 1–12.

Koga, S, Martin, N.B., and Dickson, D.W., (2023). Evaluating the performance of large language models: ChatGPT and Google Bard in generating differential diagnoses in clinicopathological conferences of neurodegenerative disorders. *Brain Pathology*. e13207. DOI:10.1111/bpa.13207

Koopman, R., Englis, P.D., Ehgrenhard, M.L., and Groen, A., (2021). The chronological development of coaching and mentoring: Side by side disciplines. *International Journal of Evidence Based Coaching & Mentoring*, 19(1), 137–151. DOI:10.24384/3w69-k922

Kwet, M., (2019). Digital colonialism: US empire and the new imperialism in the Global South. *Race & Class*, 60(4), 3–26. DOI:10.1177/0306396818823172

LeBleu, L., (2020). "New skills for a new world". *Forbes*. Retrieved on 12 October 2023 from www.forbes.com/sites/servicenow/2020/05/30/new-skills-for-a-new-world/

Lee, J., Lee, D., and Lee, J.G., (2022). Influence of rapport and social presence with an AI psychotherapy chatbot on users' self-disclosure. *International Journal of Human–Computer Interaction*, (Online). DOI:10.1080/10447318.2022.2146227

Lee, Y.C., Yamashita, N., Huang, Y., and Fu, W., (2020, April). I hear you, I feel you: encouraging deep self-disclosure through a chatbot. In: R. Bernhaupt et al. (Ed.) *Proceedings of the 2020 CHI conference on human factors in computing systems* (pp. 1–12).

Leonardo, Z., (2004). The color of supremacy: Beyond the discourse of 'white privilege'. *Educational Philosophy and Theory*, 36(2), 137–152.

Li, M. and Suh, A., (2022). Anthropomorphism in AI-enabled technology: A literature review. *Electron Markets* 32, 2245–2275. DOI:10.1007/s12525-022-00591-7

Lowe, F., (2013). Keeping leadership white: Invisible blocks to black leadership and its denial in white organizations, *Journal of Social Work Practice*, 27(2), 149–162. DOI:10.1080/02650533.2013.798151

Madahar, L. and Offer, M., (2004). Managing e-guidance interventions within HE careers services: A new approach to providing guidance at a distance. *Graduate Prospects*. Retrieved on

12 October 2023 from https://dokumen.tips/documents/managing-e-guidance-interventions-wit hin-he-careers-services-1-to-develop-a.html?page=1

Mai, V. and Rutschmann, R., (2023). Chatbots im Coaching. Potenziale und Einsatzmöglichkeiten von digitalen Coaching-Begleitern und Assistenten. *Organisationsberat Superv Coach*, 30, 45–57. DOI:10.1007/s11613-022-00801-3

McIntosh, P. (1990). *White privilege: Unpacking the invisible knapsack* Wellesley MA: Wellesley College Center for Research on Women..

Mistry, M. and Latoo, J., (2009). Uncovering the face of racism in the workplace uncovering the face of racism in the workplace. *British Journal of Medical Practitioners*, 2(2), 20–24.

Pappas, G., (1995). *Unveiling white privilege*. LARASA/report.

Pasha, N., (2020). Human Skills & the AI COVID Challenge. In: Billio, M. and Varotto, S. *A New World Post COVID-19* (p. 302). DOI:10.30687/978-88-6969-442-4/023

Pasha, N., (2020). Responding to career uncertainty: Applying a 'dual-empathy'approach to career development using corporate strategy theory. *Journal of the National Institute for Career Education and Counselling*, 44(1), 44–50.

Passmore, J. and Tee, D., (2023). Can Chatbots like GPT-4 replace human coaches: Issues and dilemmas for the coaching profession, coaching clients and for organisations. *The Coaching Psychologist*, 19(1), 47–54. DOI:10.53841/bpstcp.2023.19.1.47

Passmore, J. and Tee, D., (2023). The library of Babel: Assessing the powers of artificial intelligence in knowledge synthesis, learning and development and coaching, *Journal of Work-Applied Management*, (Online). DOI:10.1108/JWAM-06-2023-0057

Passmore, J., Liu, Q., Tee, D., and Tewald, S., (2023). Diversity in the global coaching community: Exploring race, gender, identity and belonging. *International Coaching Psychology Review*, 18(1), 73–89. DOI:0.53841/bpsicpr.2023.18.1.73

Raji, I.D., Gebru, T., Mitchell, M., Buolamwini, J., Lee, J., and Denton, E., (2020, February). Saving face: Investigating the ethical concerns of facial recognition auditing. In *Proceedings of the AAAI/ACM Conference on AI, Ethics, and Society* (pp. 145–151).

Roche, C., (2022). Decolonising reflective practice and supervision. *Philosophy of Coaching*, 7(1), 30–49.

Roche, C. and Passmore, J., (2021). *Racial justice, equity and belonging in coaching*. Henley-on-Thames: Henley Business School.

Roche, C. and Passmore, J., (2022). Anti-racism in coaching: a global call to action. *Coaching: An International Journal of Theory, Research and Practice*, 16(1), 115–132. DOI:10.1080/17521 882.2022.2098789

Roche, C. and Passmore, J., (2023). "We don't see colour!" How executive coaching can help leaders to create inclusive corporate cultures by acknowledging structural racism in its ecosystem. *Consulting Psychology Journal*, 75(1), 5–13. DOI:10.1037/cpb0000232

Shah, S., (2022). *Diversity, inclusion and belonging in coaching*. London: Kogan Page.

Slater, S. F., Weigand, R. A., and Zwirlein, T. J., (2008). The business case for commitment to diversity. *Business Horizons*, 51(3), 201–209.

Taherdoost, H. and Madanchian, M., (2023). Artificial intelligence and sentiment analysis: A review in competitive research. *Computers*, 12(2), 37. DOI:10.3390/computers12020037

Tao, J. and Tan, T., (2005). Affective computing: A review. In: J. Tao, T. Tan, and R.W. Picard (eds), *Affective computing and intelligent interaction*. ACII 2005. Lecture Notes in Computer Science, vol 3784 (pp. 981–995). Berlin, Heidelberg: Springer Berlin Heidelberg. DOI:10.1007/ 11573548_125

Terblanche, N. and Cilliers, D., (2020). Factors that influence users' adoption of being coached by an artificial intelligence coach. *Philosophy of Coaching: An International Journal*, 5(1), 61–70.

The Equity Effect (2021). Henley business school. Retrieved on 3 October 2023 from https:// assets.henley.ac.uk/v3/fileUploads/The-Equity-Effect-report.pdf?mtime=20210604162 243&focal=none, 2021

Valz, D. (2023). PERSONALIZATION: Why the relational modes between Generative AI chatbots and human users are critical factors for product design and safety. Available at SSRN 4468899

van Coller-Peter, S. and Manzini, L., (2020). Strategies to establish rapport during online management coaching. *SA Journal of Human Resource Management*, 18(3). DOI:10.4102/sajhrm.v18i0.1298

van der Gun, L. and Guest, O., (2023). Artificial Intelligence: Panacea or Non-intentional Dehumanisation? DOI:10.31235/osf.io/rh4fw

Wach, K., Duong, C.D., Ejdys, J., Kazlauskaitė, R., Korzynski, P., Mazurek, G., Paliszkiewicz, J., and Ziemba, E., (2023). The dark side of generative artificial intelligence: A critical analysis of controversies and risks of ChatGPT. *Entrepreneurial Business and Economics Review*, 11(2), 7–24.

Wu, T. et al., (2023). A brief overview of ChatGPT: The history, status quo and potential future development. *IEEE/CAA Journal of Automatica Sinica*, 10(5), 1122–1136. DOI:10.1109/JAS.2023.123618

Zhao, G., Li, Y., and Xu, Q., (2022). From emotion AI to cognitive AI. *International Journal of Network Dynamics and Intelligence*, 1(1), 65–72. DOI:10.53941/ijndi010100666

Chapter 20

Digital coaching with neurodivergent people

Nancy Doyle

Introduction

The term 'neurodivergent' (aka neurodifferent, neurodistinct, neurodiverse abbreviated as ND throughout) has become increasingly popular in recent years (Chapman, 2020) and is defined as having a neurotype that diverges from the norm (Asasumasu, 2022). This divergence refers to a collection of neurodevelopmental differences including attention deficit and hyperactivity disorder (ADHD), autism, dyscalculia, dysgraphia, dyslexia, and dyspraxia. These developmental conditions affect approximately 15–20% of the population (Doyle, 2020) and are considered 'hidden disabilities', a term which also incorporates acquired neurocognitive disability such as mental health distress, neurological conditions such as chronic fatigue syndrome, stroke, and long Covid. In this chapter, we will explore some of the defining characteristics of minority neurotypes, how to recognise them, and how to optimise digital coaching to work with clients with these characteristics.

Neurodiversity basics

Language and definitions

The language concerning neurodiversity is in flux and can seem confusing. Neurodiversity as a term and concept was first described academically by Australian sociologist, Judy Singer (Singer, 1998). She defined it as the diversity of neurocognitive style present in the human species; for example, we are more or less capable in verbal communication, memory skills and more, we operate as introverts, extraverts, we are more or less conscientious, altruistic and more. Her observation was that all these qualities operate on a spectrum. Therefore, labels like autism simply present another way in which humans differ. Her thesis was that autistic people are a minoritised, oppressed population who deserve equal opportunities, a 'neurominority' (ibid.). Given that only 20% of autistic people are employed in the UK, compared with 53% of disabled people and over 80% of abled people (ONS, 2019), her point is well-founded. Since Singer's seminal work, other neurominorities, such as dyslexic and dyspraxic people, those with ADHD have joined the conversation and begun adopting the language of the neurodiversity paradigm, describing themselves as neurodivergent, neurodistinct, etc. Thus, it is less likely to hear umbrella terms such as 'specific learning disabilities (SpLD)' or 'neurodevelopmental disorders', though these remain in circulation and may indeed be the way clients prefer to identify. These other neurominorities

DOI: 10.4324/9781003383741-23

also experience disproportionate social exclusion in education (Tirraoro et al., 2020) work (Achieve Ability, 2016), and criminal justice (Young et al., 2018). A neurodiversity community of allied advocates has formed to lobby for inclusion, clinical support, and recognition as a form of diversity (Chapman & Carel, 2022; Huijg, 2020).

There are no official rules or bodies policing the boundary of who can or cannot identify as 'neurodivergent'. What neurodivergent people tend to have in common is the 'spiky profile' (Grant, 2009), meaning a statistically significant difference between strengths and challenges when neurocognitive qualities are measured and plotted on a graph. Spiky profiles are also characteristic of people with acquired brain injuries, learning disabilities, mental health needs, and chronic neurological conditions such as multiple sclerosis (Weinberg & Doyle, 2017). Anyone who does not have an average, generalist intelligence (neurotypical), emotional and sensory profile could argue that they are neurodivergent. Neurodivergency is often considered a disability based on the level of practical need in the context of everyday life (UN, 2006; Equality Act, 2010). This means that neurodivergent people have rights that are often protected by law and that coaching might be part of a formal program of making 'reasonable adjustments or accommodations' from their organisation to support them. Some find the term 'neurodivergent' unnecessarily othering and prefer to use 'neurodiverse' (referring to the diversity within a spiky profile, rather than the diversity between other humans) and others use neurodifferent, or neurodistinct.

Neurodiversity and intersectionality

Confusing as the language options may seem, it is not unusual within the diversity and inclusion sphere for there to be nuance and emotional connection to labelling. Indeed, as the neurodiversity movement charts its path from pathology to diversity, the evolution of language is an important tool by which the community develops agency and self-reflexivity (Botha et al., 2023; Didlake & Fordham, 2013). Back in 2020 people talked only about lesbians and gay men, by 2020 the language included lesbians, gay men and women, bisexual people, transgender people, non-binary people, gender fluidity, pansexuals, a-sexuals, intersex, two-spirit, and more (LGBTQIA2s+). Similarly, in race and ethnicity inclusion, language evolved with the developments in our conceptual understanding and alongside the need to challenge social bias. As coaches, our job is to be aware of the interaction between language and identity, respecting a client's right to self-determination.

The intersection between neurodiversity and race, sexuality and other forms of diversity is useful for understanding the trajectory of a minoritised group, but also for uncovering hidden inequities within the group of neurodivergent people. An important thing to know about this client group is that diagnosis is privilege – an individual is less likely to have one if you are not male, white, from the global north west, and from a well-resourced family (Doyle et al., 2022). Diagnostic interviews are based on male-typed behaviour and, therefore, women are significantly under-diagnosed and/or diagnosed much later in life. This phenomenon has become a self-fulfilling prophecy, i.e. the fewer female individuals there are to research, the more research is conducted regarding male presentation, which then affects the way diagnoses are understood (Young et al., 2020). Further, professionals tend to view neurodiverse people who are minoritised by race or poverty through a more negative lens and see their behaviour as wilful (criminal) or pathological (rather than different) (Liell et al., 2022). There are significantly more neurodiverse people in LGBTQIA2S+ communities than cisgendered heterosexual (Egner, 2019; Nolan et al., 2019), though we do not yet have good research on why this may be and how it impacts on individual psychology, though we can infer that like any other double characteristic there will be dual adverse impact.

As such, if you are working with clients who have additional protected characteristics, you are working with compound adverse impact and the potentially traumatising after-effects of delayed support through childhood and earlier adulthood. These differences may not be visible and may emerge as the relationship progresses. Delayed diagnosis is commonly thought to be a negative for the neurodiversity community. When ND people are not recognised as such, they are treated to significantly more chastisement (Jellinek, 2010) than their peers. This becomes internalised and plays out as self-doubt, lack of agency, struggling to maintain safe and healthy boundaries. The coach may have their own experience of marginalisation but all coaches need to prevent themselves assuming that all marginal experiences are the same. They can best achieve this through wider reading, and listening to their individual client's experiences.

Neurocognitive needs

Research on neuro-minorities suggests that diagnostic boundaries overlap more than they are separated (Siugzdaite et al., 2020). Indeed, the Cognition and Brain Sciences Unit at Cambridge University have cognitively profiled (through psychometrics and neuroimaging) thousands of children and used a data-led clustering technique to understand the differences between neurodivergent brains and neurotypical brains based on 'executive functions' (Jones et al., 2021). Such 'executive functions' are located in the pre-frontal cortex (forehead) of our brain; they are our executive processor, choosing to what we pay attention, how easily we switch attention, and how much we can hold in our attention to send to longer-term memory stores (Hofmann et al., 2012). These executive functions further manage thinking through the consequences of actions, filtering thoughts, assessing risks, and regulating activities. There is a wealth of literature loosely affiliating difficulties with these executive functions to dyslexia, autism, ADHD, and more (Baltruschat et al., 2011; Jeffries & Everatt, 2004). They are also linked to long-term chronic neurological conditions (Lowings & Wick, 2016; Thornton & Raz, 1997). The Cambridge Team were not able to replicate the current diagnostic labels. They have instead found the following two groupings: those who struggle with 'cold executive functions' and/or 'hot executive functions' versus neurotypicals. Cold executive functions are related to self-organisation (time, planning, prioritisation) and hot executive functions are related to managing emotions and social interactions. In the next paragraphs, we will explore and explain these two executive functions and how these might influence the digital coaching experience.

Cold executive functions

This can be divided into two sections: attention and planning. First, attention. People who are challenged by the attention differences will report significant stress around meeting deadlines, making errors in their work, completing admin and procrastination.

A neurodiverse attention span can be hyper-focused on completely distracted and rarely in between. When neurodivergent brains train their attention on a new or well-liked topic they can find it difficult to switch off topic. They might talk too much, go off on tangents and be harder to follow in their speech. They might be resistant and coaching for some might feel like trying to nail jelly to a wall! How they approach coaching is likely to be representative of how they are at work, so building rapport and devising a structure for the coaching can offer a double benefit, with transferrable insights to the workplace. The following adaptations to coaching may be helpful to explore with clients:

- Move. In the non-digital space, coaching while taking a walk, or moving around the room can help. The coach can replicate this digitally if needs be, using a phone or taking a break from the screen. Investigate 'clean space' (Lawley & Manea, 2017), which is a way of shifting your client's *actual* position to represent different points in time (for example when they are in their ideal job, or when they left school and didn't think they would achieve where they are today). Some neurodiverse clients need to move to think, this is a useful adjustment and is worth discussing at the start.
- Shorter, frequent chunks. During the pandemic in 2020, when almost all coaching moved online overnight, coaches working with neurodiverse clients found that sessions needed to be shorter, 45–60 min instead of 90–120 min. This can be balanced with a greater frequency in sessions.
- Multi-sensory. In person, the visual, auditory, olfactory, and vestibular (movement and balance) senses are all engaged and in rapport with the client. In digital coaching, neurodiverse clients may have auditory and visual limits. The coach can assist by using visual diagrams as well as video, typing notes and ideas onto a visual map that you can both see (such as by using a virtual white board).
- Reduce the sensory. Conversely, some neurodiverse cannot pay attention if they have too much of the wrong sensory stimulation. This might mean switching off video content and focusing on the audio channel or using a phone rather than a platform like Zoom or Teams. Using a high-quality microphone can help make the voice smoother and rounded, rather than sharp and tinny.

Second, planning. Managing a diary, being on time, running out of time, prioritising where to start and what to do in what order, these are all kryptonite for the neurodivergent brain, of most varieties. The coach can help by being organised, unambiguous in their instructions, setting up the link well in advance, and sending a reminder. Also it helps to be clear about cancellation fees up front, in order to manage issues which may arise if the client does not attend. Here are some points for how planning interacts with the digital experience:

- It's easier to plan when digital. Being in one place for a video call, is so much easier for neurodiverse people than having to negotiate a train, book a room at work, schedule the meeting etc. Digital coaching is very accessible for all kinds of disabilities, and the lack of travel and space logistics is a huge boost for productivity.
- It's harder to remember when digital. Given the lack of activity required to plan, if a neurodiverse doesn't have a good system of diary management and reminders they are

much less likely to remember their appointment, so reminders and cancellation fees (contracted in advance) will help.

- Admin is tricky. Contracting, pre-coaching questionnaires, online feedback, increases the burden for the neurodiverse client. Make time during the sessions for these, so the paperwork can be completed collaboratively.
- Remember literacy and numeracy difficulties. Many neurodivergent clients will have a lower literacy level than might be expected from their job. For these clients, the coach will need to ensure that their paperwork is compatible with screen reading technology and that it is laid out in 'dyslexia friendly' style, for example a minimum 12 pt, sans serif font, 1.5 spaced and avoiding high contrast black/white where possible. It can also help to use bullets, diagrams and tables, and avoid walls of text. Tools such as flesch-kincaid readability statistics (in the editor function in Microsoft Word) can help assess the literacy level of any material, handouts, further readings and websites.
- IT literacy is also important. Many neurodivergent people struggle with new technology the first few times they use it. They need to be talked through the process, to avoid anxiety. The coach can let them know they will call them to help them log on if required, this will avoid a pre-session panic for many neurodivergent clients.

Hot executive functions

Hot executive functions typically include managing emotions and the experience of strong emotions, self-restraint, and stress tolerance. From an emotional perspective, the client may experience periods of overwhelm, which are rather disparagingly sometimes referred to as 'meltdowns' (Ryan, 2010), and are characterised by either verbal tirades or mutism, as well as a need for extreme bodily autonomy and reduced sensory input. An overwhelm is a serious event which can be traumatising and deeply embarrassing for the client, but also for colleagues who are not expecting and don't know how to respond. It can take very detailed unpicking to repair relationships and it may well be a topic of coaching to practice explaining to colleagues what was happening. Overwhelms represent a loss of control, more like a tic than losing your temper. Preventing them and knowing what triggers them is essential for neurodivergent clients. Self-restraint challenges can include a lack of social filters, being direct and blunt when a more circumspect and rapportful approach is expected. This can be a real issue for neurodivergent clients who are misunderstood as rude or insubordinate when they are intending to be truthful and sincere. Stress tolerance is a culturally loaded term! From a neurodivergent perspective, consider the additional burden of having ones senses bombarded, a reduced capacity to pay attention or communicate in ones preferred style, in a world which assumes you are less valuable than your peers. In those circumstances, the average neurodivergent is handling a lot more stress than the average client before they even get to work. So how does this all affect digital coaching?

1. Digital communication is very helpful for managing boundaries. The coach can work with neurodivergent clients to use the natural barriers in the digital space, such as muting, turning off the sound and video, as ways to handle their emotions. At the touch of a button, they can reduce their sensory input and increase their privacy

(withdrawal). Just as above, with the coaching this can provide insights into how they behave in the rest of their lives and with colleagues.

2. Digital communication and misunderstandings. While it is easy to misread tone in an email or chat message, judicious use of emoticons can prevent misunderstanding. Its help to explore with neurodivergent clients how they can prevent people from taking what they say too seriously, or not seriously enough.
3. Stress management. Being flexible will be very helpful for clients who may need more or less sensory input on days when they are approaching overwhelm.

Sensory overwhelm

Compared with cognitive and emotional aspects of neurodivergence, the sensory differences are subject to less research in general, and are only mentioned in the diagnostic criteria for autism (Thye et al., 2018). However in practice, neurodiverse clients of all neurotypes report sensory overwhelm, such as auditory distraction and visual disturbances in dyslexia (Bartlett et al., 2010). There is some evidence to suggest that neurodiverse people actually hear some noises as louder, colours as brighter, feel more or less intense pain. Most good practice guides for the workplace consider the sensory experience and advice-giving flexibility and control to ND employees (CIPD, 2018) in order to minimise the burden and facilitate productivity. In a coaching session, therefore, the same considerations should be made as described above. However, this is the exception not the norm in most workplaces and it is likely that the neurodiverse client experiences sensory stimulation to the point of overwhelm, which can lead to significant distress. In a sensory overwhelm, the client may become unable to speak, or only able to speak in a tirade. They may struggle to be still, and start self-soothing through small repetitive movements such as hand flapping or knee jiggling, they may be unable to move at all. In such a state, you may find that they communicate better through technology, such as a WhatsApp chat or the chat function on a video call. It is important to be flexible in responding; some days, the video will be fine, other days it may not. Working through a sensory overwhelm can be instructive, and give insights to the client how to more effectively communicate with others in their environment. It's useful to know which forms of communication work best for individual clients and so keep notes and reflecting this back, can be helpful.

AI in coaching with neurodiverse people

Artificial intelligence (AI) interventions are increasingly used in human resources, from recruitment and interviewing to developing wellbeing insights and health interventions, sometimes without even gaining the consent of the client. Coaches may be commissioned to help design such tools or indeed be working alongside them. Ethical use of AI is a developing research field and is known to be a particularly priority for inclusion of disabled people (Nugent et al., 2020). This is because, inherently, AI is based on inferential statistics in which vast numbers of correlations and regressions are conducted at speed, calculating the most likely preference for person A, based on the preferences of people like them. Once society creates systems that refer to the average or the 'most likely' result, we have entered the realm of creating what is 'normal'. By definition, neurodivergent people operate outside the norm, compared to the general population. We are indeed less likely to do the same, think, choose, or feel the same as others in the same age, gender, race, sexuality as us. Neurodiverse people are statistical 'outliers' and it can be more difficult for them to take part in standard processes (McDowall et al., 2023).

What's also clear is the governance, regulation, and controls from professional bodies and government lag behind technology often by 5 or 10 years. While Sarah Bankins (Bankins, 2021) outlines the case for governance, and also for profiling the risk to humans of the approach and assigning a safeguarding level where humans are 'in the loop', 'on the loop' or 'out of the loop', the likely reality this will lag behind technological developments.

Digital dos and do nots

By way of a summary, Table 20.1 below offers some insights for working with neurodiverse clients in digital coaching.

Table 20.1 Digital dos and do nots

Do	Do Not
Offer 'video on or off' options when using video platforms	Insist that the camera be turned on or off
Consider setting up two cameras and logging into the call from both devices so that your client can see you, and the wider picture of where you are and what notes you are making on paper	Try to communicate only via a face to face or voice medium. You can use A4, post its and other materials to get different elements of their cognition engaged in a task
Make extra time for explaining the logistics and checking that your client can operate the systems and logistics	Assume that your client will be tech literate, or literate for reading instructions
Make sure any materials you use are compatible with screen reading software	Send PDFs that are not compliant with screen reading software
Find ways to allow movement and screen/call breaks into your coaching schedule – invite them to do this, they may not know to ask	Expect clients to sit still for longer than 30 mins at a time or stay on long calls for
Consider reminder texts, auto-reminder emails and diary invites as a way to help your client remember appointments	Chastise a client for forgetting appointments or tasks, this won't be deliberate and this skill might be the very thing for which they need coaching
Plan and discuss the sensory environment for coaching, including where they are when then take your call, the technical spec of the equipment you use and wifi speed	Overlook the sensory impact of communicating via technology in terms of buzzing, harsh lighting and their own access to space
Break up sessions into shorter chunks if needs be	Imagine that a standard 90–120 min session can just transfer online, it might be too overwhelming digitally
Be aware of contracting, your neurodivergent client may need more input at this stage to understand the unwritten rules of engagement	Be surprised if your client doesn't 'get it' and needs more concrete expectations around times of call, access to you and boundaries

Table 20.1 (Continued)

Do	Do Not
Take details of someone you can contact for safeguarding and raising a wellbeing concern	Overlook the potential additional emotional needs of ND client
Ask about preferred language, labels and terms to use in the coaching	Use standard neurodiversity affirming or medical model language without checking
Offer time in the coaching to debrief misunderstandings and unpack them with clarity, there's value in this for them generally as their colleagues might not be sensitive to their confusion and interpret it as hostility	Take it personally if you accidentally offend or elicit a defensive reaction, this is unlikely to be 'just you' and you might be the right person for helping them understand a key communication pattern
Encourage your client to think, plan and consider offline as well as online – not everyone can think well via a screen	Limit yourself to online talking or handout completing only
Advocate for your clients if they are unhappy using coaching apps and AI – there may be good reasons why these don't work for them	Assume that they will benefit from standardised systems designed for standardised people

Reflective questions

1. What insights emerge for your practice from this chapter?
2. What adaptations should be made when working with neurodiverse clients in digital coaching?
3. How can possible negative effects of AI coaching bots be managed for neurodiverse clients?

Conclusion

In general, digital coaching can be an accessible bonus for disabled people, who may have been unable to access coaching through traditional in person sessions. The seating 90–120 min talk requires commuting, finding directions, parking, and processing multiple human interactions. With digital the coach and client can circumvent much of this. For these reasons, many neurodivergent and disabled coaches actively prefer digital coaching to in person (Doyle & Bradley, 2022). As long as the coach can remain flexible and creative as to *how* they engage online, digital coaching is an excellent medium for neurodiverse clients.

References

Achieve Ability. (2016). *Westminster commission on dyslexia and neurodivergence.* www.achieve ability.org.uk/main/policy/new-commission-wac

Baltruschat, L., Hasselhorn, M., Tarbox, J., Dixon, D. R., Najdowski, A. C., Mullins, R. D., & Gould, E. R. (2011). Addressing working memory in children with autism through behavioral intervention. *Research in Autism Spectrum Disorders*, 5(1), 267–276. https://doi.org/10.1016/j.rasd.2010.04.008

Bankins, S. (2021). The ethical use of artificial intelligence in human resource management: A decision-making framework. *Ethics and Information Technology, 23*(4), 841–854. https://doi.org/10.1007/s10676-021-09619-6

Bartlett, D., Moody, S., & Kindersley, K. (2010). Dyslexia in the workplace. In *Dyslexia in the Workplace: An Introductory Guide: Second Edition*. Wiley. https://doi.org/10.1002/9780470669341.ch1

Botha, M., Hanlon, J., & Williams, G. L. (2023). Does language matter? Identity-first versus person-first language use in Autism research: A response to Vivanti. *Journal of Autism and Developmental Disorders, 53*(2), 870–878. https://doi.org/10.1007/s10803-020-04858-w

Chapman, R. (2020). Defining neurodiversity for research and practice. In H. B. Rosqvist, N. Chown, & A. Stenning (Eds.), *Neurodiversity Studies: A New Critical Paradigm* (pp. 218–220). Routledge, Taylor & Francis. https://doi.org/10.4324/9780429322297-21

Chapman, R., & Carel, H. (2022). Neurodiversity, epistemic injustice, and the good human life. *Journal of Social Philosophy*, 1–18. https://doi.org/10.1111/josp.12456

CIPD. (2018). *Neurodiversity at Work* (pp. 1–48). Chartered Institute of Personnel Development.

Didlake, R., & Fordham, J. A. (2013). Do no harm: Neurodiversity, health care advocacy and the language and culture of informed consent. In C. D. Herrera, & A. Perry (Eds.), *Ethics and Neurodiversity* (pp. 100–110). Cambridge Scholars Publishing.

Doyle, N. (2020). Neurodiversity at Work: A biopsychosocial model and the impact on working adults. *British Medical Bulletin, 135*, 1–18. https://doi.org/10.1093/bmb/ldaa021

Doyle, N., & Bradley, E. (2022). Disability coaching during a pandemic. *Journal of Work-Applied Management*. https://doi.org/10.1108/JWAM-07-2022-0042

Doyle, N., McDowall, A., & Waseem, U. (2022). Intersectional stigma for autistic people at work: A compound adverse impact effect on labor force participation and experiences of belonging. *Autism in Adulthood, ahead of print*. https://doi.org/10.1089/aut.2021.0082

Egner, J. E. (2019). "The disability rights community was never mine": Neuroqueer disidentification. *Gender and Society, 33*(1), 123–147. https://doi.org/10.1177/0891243218803284

Grant, D. (2009). The psychological assessment of neurodiversity. In D. Pollak (Ed.), *Neurodiversity in Higher Education* (pp. 33–62). Wiley-Blackwell.

Hofmann, W., Schmeichel, B. J., & Baddeley, A. D. (2012). Executive functions and self-regulation. *Trends in Cognitive Sciences, 16*(3), 174–180. https://doi.org/10.1016/j.tics.2012.01.006

Huijg, D. D. (2020). Neuronormativity in theorising agency. In H. B. Rosqvist, N. Chown, & A. Stenning (Eds.), *Neurodiversity Studies: A New Critical Paradigm* (pp. 213–217). Routledge. https://doi.org/10.4324/9780429322297-20

Jeffries, S., & Everatt, J. (2004). Working memory: Its role in dyslexia and other specific learning difficulties. *Dyslexia, 10*(3), 196–214. https://doi.org/10.1002/dys.278

Jellinek, M. S. (2010, May 1). Don't let ADHD crush children's self-esteem [MD Edge]. *Psychiatry*. www.mdedge.com/psychiatry/article/23971/pediatrics/dont-let-adhd-crush-childrens-self-esteem

Jones, J. S., the CALM Team, & Astle, D. E. (2021). A transdiagnostic data-driven study of children's behaviour and the functional connectome. *Developmental Cognitive Neuroscience, 52*, 101027. https://doi.org/10.1016/j.dcn.2021.101027

Kassiane Asasumasu. (2022). Neurodivergence. *Wiktionary.org*. https://en.wiktionary.org/wiki/neurodivergent

Lawley, J., & Manea, A. I. (2017). The use of clean space to facilitate a " Stuck " client – a case study. *Journal of Experiential Psychotherapy, 20*(4), 62–70.

Liell, G., Fisher, M., & Jones, L. (2022). *Challenging Bias in Forensic Psychological Assessment and Testing Theoretical and Practical Approaches to Working with Diverse Populations*. London: Routledge.

Lowings, G., Wick, B. (2016). *Effective Learning After Acquired Brain Injury*. Routledge. https://doi.org/10.4324/9781315746005

McDowall, A., Doyle, N., & Kisleva, M. (2023). *Neurodiversity at Work 2023: Demand, Supply and Gap Analysis* (pp. 60). Neurodiversity in Business.

Nolan, I. T., Kuhner, C. J., & Dy, G. W. (2019). Demographic and temporal trends in transgender identities and gender confirming surgery. *Translational Andrology and Urology, 8*(3), 184–190. https://doi.org/10.21037/tau.2019.04.09

Nugent, S. E., Jackson, P., Scott-Parker, S., Partridge, J., Raper, R., Bakalis, C., Shepherd, A., Mitra, A., Long, J., Maynard, K., & Crook, N. (2020). Recruitment AI has a disability problem: Questions employers should be asking to ensure fairness in recruitment [Preprint]. *SocArXiv.* https://doi.org/10.31235/osf.io/emwn5

ONS. (2019). *Disability and Employment, UK* (pp. 1–19). Office of National Statistics. www.ons.gov.uk/peoplepopulationandcommunity/healthandsocialcare/disability/bulletins/disabilityandemploymentuk/2019#:~:text=Over 4.2 million disabled people,employed was nearly 2.9 million

Ryan, S. (2010). Meltdowns, surveillance and managing emotions; going out with children with autism. *Healthplace, 16*(5), 868–875.

Singer, J. (1998). *Odd People In: The Birth of Community Amongst People on the 'Autistic Spectrum': A Personal Exploration of a New Social Movement Based on Neurological Diversity.* University of Technology, Sydney.

Siugzdaite, R., Bathelt, J., Holmes, J., & Astle, D. E. (2020). Transdiagnostic brain mapping in developmental disorders. *Current Biology, 30*(7), 1245–1257.e4. https://doi.org/10.1016/j.cub.2020.01.078

Thornton, A. E., & Raz, N. (1997). Memory impairment in multiple sclerosis: A quantitative review. *Neuropsychology, 11*(3), 357–366. https://doi.org/10.1037/0894-4105.11.3.357

Thye, M. D., Bednarz, H. M., Herringshaw, A. J., Sartin, E. B., & Kana, R. K. (2018). The impact of atypical sensory processing on social impairments in autism spectrum disorder. *Developmental Cognitive Neuroscience, 29*(September 2016), 151–167. https://doi.org/10.1016/j.dcn.2017.04.010

Tirraoro, T., Blower, R., Keer, M., Doherty, G., & Moore, C. (2020). *Special needs jungle autumn 2020 COVID-19 & SEND education survey.* Special Needs Jungle.

United Nations Convention on the Rights of Persons with Disabilities, 1 (2006). *Equality Act,* (2010). www.legislation.gov.uk/ukpga/2010/15/introduction

Weinberg, A., & Doyle, N. (2017). *Psychology at work: Improving wellbeing and productivity in the workplace* (L. M. Coulthard, Ed.). British Psychological Society. https://doi.org/ISBN 978-1-85433-754-2

Young, S., Adamo, N., Ásgeirsdóttir, B. B., Branney, P., Beckett, M., Colley, W., Cubbin, S., Deeley, Q., Farrag, E., Gudjonsson, G., Hill, P., Hollingdale, J., Kilic, O., Lloyd, T., Mason, P., Paliokosta, E., Perecherla, S., Sedgwick, J., Skirrow, C., ... Woodhouse, E. (2020). Females with ADHD: An expert consensus statement taking a lifespan approach providing guidance for the identification and treatment of attention-deficit/ hyperactivity disorder in girls and women. *BMC Psychiatry, 20*(1), 404. https://doi.org/10.1186/s12888-020-02707-9

Young, S., González, R. A., Fridman, M., Hodgkins, P., Kim, K., & Gudjonsson, G. H. (2018). The economic consequences of attention-deficit hyperactivity disorder in the Scottish prison system. *BMC Psychiatry, 18*, 1–11. https://doi.org/10.1186/s12888-018-1792-x

Part V

The coaching industry

Chapter 21

The changing nature of the coaching industry

Rosie Evans-Krimme and Jonathan Passmore

Introduction

Coaching has witnessed significant growth over the period 1990–2020. In this 30-year period coaching has gone from a rarely used approach to learning to being seen by leaders, managers, and employers at all levels as an almost essential tool to help them with their development, as well as providing a space for reflection and longer-term thinking. Along with this change in management perception of coaching, the subsequent increase in demand has caused changes across the whole industry of coaching.

In this chapter we will explore how the coaching industry has changed and what changes might be expected over the coming decade, with a discussion of the implications for coaches and coach educators.

A conceptual model for coaching development

To date little has been written about the development of the coaching sector, as a specific industry. This may reflect in part the relative immaturity of the coaching industry, which until 2020 possibly never perceived itself as an industrial sector, but instead either as part of learning and development or as a personal service.

But a wider review of the industrial literature reveals that industries often follow a pattern of development, driven by changing societal needs and technological developments (Passmore & Evans-Krimme, 2021).

Rostow (1959) suggested that industries follow a cycle of economic growth moving through six distinct stages of development from traditional society through 'preconditions for take-off', 'take-off', 'the drive to maturity', 'mass consumption', and ultimately 'beyond consumption' where the industry shifts towards quality.

While simple linear models are often considered limited in modern management literature, in favour of adapting, flexible, multi-stage, and complex models, Rostow's simple six steps can help provide an understanding which has been seen to emerge in many industries over the past thousand years of human development from the agrarian revolution.

As a generalised model, it should be recognised that all industries do not follow the same pathway, or do so at the same pace. Some may never take-off, others appear to remain as mass consumption industries. It is also important to note that Rostow's model is based on observations from a predominantly Western economic perspective situated within a capitalist economic model of continuous growth. A post 'continuous economic

DOI: 10.4324/9781003383741-27

growth' model, which is where the global economy needs to shift towards over the next 50 years, may bring with it a very different model of consumption and greater stability.

The Rostow model provides a heuristic guide, a map, for those observing the development of coaching, and offers an opportunity to consider the changes occurring within the coaching sector in the 2020s and how this may influence change in the sector during the 2030s. Before considering coaching it may be useful to consider a different sector as a means to understand how technology and human patterns of movement and growth contribute to industrial change.

The agriculture sector

The agriculture sector has been described as both ancient yet modern (Soosai-Nathan & Della, 2016). The sector developed out of the hunter/gatherer economy, approximately 12,000 years ago, as a result of changes to the global climate. This enabled agricultural practices to spread further north, and for humans to move from a nomadic lifestyle in Europe to cultivate crops and to domesticate animals. It should be noted that this shift was not universal and some humans continued hunter-gathering nomadic patterns, shifting with the seasons from one area to another.

But for those that did shift, this saw a gradual increase in production levels which contributed towards the development of specialist trades, such as a baker or wheelwrights. These individuals took on specialist tasks in exchange for goods, initially through barter and later through the development of money.

Production levels remained stable for centuries, until the emergence of new technologies during 'the industrial revolution' which stimulated a further cycle of change. There was a shift to cities as mechanisation on the land allowed greater productivity, and enabled plot sizes to increase in size and change shape from long strips to larger enclosed fields. This process of mechanisation continued with the greater development of larger tractors and more sophisticated equipment. A fourth change started from the 1990s with the technological revolution. Scientific research has enabled seeds to be genetically modified to enhance crop yields and protect against disease or pests. Digitisation has allowed data to drive sowing, monitor crop development, and inform decision-making on the optimal time to harvest, while harvesting is undertaken by combine-harvesters controlled by satellites to maximise crop collection. But this has come at the cost of the control of seed production through the genetic modification and patenting of seeds.

Changes in agriculture over the past 12,000 years has seen humans move from subsistence farming, where poor weather or a crop blight would lead to mass starvation, to generating surplus for trade, and with sufficient quantities to feed a world population, a thousand times the size of that in 2000 BC. We have illustrated Rothow's stages of economic growth as it applies to the changes in the agricultural sector in Table 21.1.

Other sectors have followed this pathway of change, such as clothing, as we have explored elsewhere, although as we note the pace of development in each sector reflects technologies and other factors (Passmore & Evans-Krimme, 2021).

Table 21.1 Model of agricultural sector

Rostow's stage	Key characteristics	Key manifestations
1 The traditional society	• Subsistence lifestyle (hunter-gathers) • Need for survival • Long-term settlements were impractical • No surplus of food • Pre-specialisation	• Tools included mobility, to ensure that large areas of land were covered.
2 The preconditions for take-off	• Specialisation revolution • Need to trade • Establishment of permanent settlements	• Farmers develop some mastery over crops. • Larger populations could be fed • Surplus could be traded. • New tools emerged made of bone, stone, bronze, and iron to increase productivity. • Able to store food more effectively. • Domestication of animals for produce, ploughing, pulling, and transportation.
3 The take-off	• Labour revolution • Need for productivity • Basic agricultural practices developed and defined • Trading of crops and livestock • Agriculture as a personal craft	• Technological advancements, including simple irrigation systems, meaning that previously unsuitable land could be used for agriculture and larger plots managed. • Workers employed to manage the land. • Settled villages become linked through trade, leading to early civilisations.
4 The drive to maturity	• Technical revolution • Need for expansion • Increased specialisation • International trading • High demand from consumers • Agriculture as a scientific process	• New inventions dramatically increased food production in Europe, USA, and Canada. • Machinery and electricity improved agricultural processes and increased the size of farmable plots. • Advancements in farming methodologies, such as selective breeding. • Science is beginning to be applied to assess the quality of soil and ideal conditions for animals and crops to thrive and resist disease. • Transportation infrastructure enables more effective national and international trading of surplus.

(Continued)

Table 21.1 (Continued)

Rostow's stage	Key characteristics	Key manifestations
5 The age of mass consumption	• Diversification revolution • Need to reduce production costs and increase profits • Scientific advancements • Increased specialisation • Consumer-driven	• Hypergrowth across all markets, epitomised by diversification of methods. • Producers become highly skilled in one area. • Application of scientific methods, such as genetics, to increase the opportunities for mass produced products. • Responds to global trends, such as veganism, that lead to new produce and farming methodologies. • Increased inequalities between high and low socio-economic countries.
6 Beyond consumption (the search for quality)	• Decline and fall: impact of sector practices and society on sector, people, and environment. • Agriculture as a human rights and climate emergency	• Uncontrollable events, such as natural disasters and plagues disrupt the sector. • Man-made events such as war and climate change contribute significantly to the effectiveness of the sector. • Inability to maintain agricultural practices due to lack of resources and negative consequences on the environment. • Human rights violations against agricultural workers in low-economic countries in order to meet demands from consumers in high-economic countries.

Coaching industry development

Coaching can learn from the evolution of other sectors, recognising that change is not unique, and that it brings with it both benefits and negative consequences for stakeholders. However, without change, as we saw with agriculture, human civilization is unable to move forward. Such models can also help us consider future patterns of change and how key stakeholders can manage these. As with any attempt to anticipate the future, we can almost guarantee we will be wrong in some, or much, of what we predict.

We start by suggesting that coaching is likely to have a prehistoric past. There is considerable debate as to when coaching first emerged, although most date it from the 1970s or 1980s, we believe it's almost certain hunter-gatherers will have engaged in the use of listening, questioning and encouraging reflective practice to help fellow members of their tribe to improve their hunting skills, or their sewing. There is some evidence from Maori people, in New Zealand, that such questioning styles have been used for centuries to aid learning (Stewart, 2020). However, the spoken word leaves no trace for archaeologists to confirm the development of these practices and thus we have no physical evidence as we might do in clothing or agriculture.

In contrast the agriculture sector developed in full sight, leaving traces for archaeologists in field patterns, land usage, and later in written records of land ownership and historical accounts. Coaching remains a hidden (spoken) communication form, until written records started to consider alternative forms of learning, Socrates was one example of this and the Socratic form was born. It is often this moment which until now has been regarded as the birth of coaching. But in reality, coaching as a sophisticated communication device, alongside others such as humour and tense (using past, present, future) has a long pre-history of tens of thousands of years.

Since Socrates, and the classic Greeks, it has taken a further 2,500 years for coaching to move from a formal learning technique used by some teachers to a specialisation, concentrated in the hands of the few, which requires training, credentials, supervision, ongoing membership of a professional body and which contributes to an identity: 'Coach'.

While there is good evidence of individuals using coaching in the 1910s (Trueblood, 1911), 1920s (Huston, 1924; Griffith, 1926) and 1930s, (Gordy, 1937; Bigelow, 1938) the journey of coaching professionalisation can be considered to have truly started during the 1980s as a formal practice and only in the 1990s as a practice that was recorded (written down) and passed on through articles and books.

The trigger for this change is difficult to identify precisely, but the growth of the human potential movement during the 1960s and 1970s with its focus on self-actualisation, combined with the growing wealth held by organisations and individuals meant a demand for such 'services' started to emerge from managers and leaders as part of the wider trend for professional development which started in the 1980s, and can be seen in the growth of MBA programmes and the increase in management self-help books such as 'In Search of Excellence' (Peters & Waterman, 1982), 'The One Minute Manager' (Blanchard & Johnson, 1982) and 'The Seven Habits of Highly Effective people' (Covey, 1989). The development of a market for self-development management books may have encouraged practitioners like John Whitmore (GROW model) and Laura Whitworth (Co-active coaching model) to capture their practices in their own books (Whitmore, 1988; Whitworth, 1988). Following this lead formal coach training programmes started to emerge and with them the formation of professional bodies such as the European Mentoring and Coaching Council (EMCC) in 1992 and International Coaching Federation (ICF) in 1995.

This trend of professionalisation has continued for the last three decades. The number of coaches has grown to exceed some 75,000 individuals (2024) who are members of professional bodies, and industry, although given data from recent studies which reveal that over 30% of coaches have no affiliations, we estimate over 100,000 people earn some or all of their income from coaching (ICF, 2023). In terms of the scale of the industry the International Coaching Federation (ICF, 2023) estimates its total value at US $4.56 billion, but in many other respects it remains a cottage industry, dominated by sole traders and small collectives, with little consolidation of services by larger providers, and little use of technology and science to drive efficiencies or improve outcomes.

Given recent developments in technology and the growth of coaching science over the period 2010–2020, coaching reached a tipping point. This arrival of Covid-19 in 2020 pushed the coaching industry into its next phase of sector development. This new phase shifts coaching from a personalised professional service, delivered by a limited number of high cost specialists, for a few, towards an industrial process capable of being delivered at low cost for the many, initially through human labour and increasingly through AI technologies.

What has been driving this change? There are three main factors. Firstly, the growth of online communication platforms such as Microsoft Teams, Zoom and Google Meet. These have enabled low-cost, high-quality audio and video connectivity for individual coaches, as well as the opportunity for commercial providers to utilise this development. The Covid-19 pandemic which hit most economies in early 2020 saw organisations flip to home working and thus required learning and development (L&D) teams to secure online based solutions. While governments and organisations returned to a level of normality by 2022 employees had mentally switched to the benefits of hybrid working, working 2, 3 or 4 days a week from home (Owen, 2021), making online L&D one element of most L&D strategies.

Second, the period 2010–2020 witnessed a growth in the science connected with positive psychology and coaching, providing practitioners with a good understanding of the impact of coaching as a tool to support both performance improvement and well-being through its focus on behavioural change. Access to this research has been enhanced by an increasing move to Open Access journals, the emergence of research platforms such as ResearchGate, sharing published papers and tools such as Sci-Hub, giving access to published science, alongside search tools such as Google Scholar allowing efficient discovery of relevant material by practitioners, as well as academics enabling them to understand and leverage science knowledge in building the business case for coaching.

A third factor is the growth of investor interest in technology investments during 2015–2022, which have seen significant growth over this period, enabling start-ups to secure the investment needed for the development of products, from online mental health (Headspace) to online learning (Lyra Learning – LinkedIn Learning). Coaching has followed this trend, with the growth of a multiplicity of digital providers, most well known being BetterUp, CoachHub and EZRA, but also smaller regional and specialist providers including Sounding Board and uExcelerate, and the emergence of platforms which offer individuals membership such as Coaching.com and Delenta, with the majority of these firms' growth underpinned by technology investors.

We anticipate continued growth of coaching with online large-scale platforms, initially taking a larger share followed by a growth in the use of AI technologies. Potentially these digital providers can through call recording and client data ensure their applications are informed by science, offered in multiple languages and available on demand. Ultimately the potential exists for clients to be able to select the persona (image), voice and movements of a living or dead individual, such as Gandhi or Marilyn Monroe, to coach them, with the client's data collected and used to enhance both the AI chatbot performance in subsequent conversations with that client, or inform all future user sessions.

Coaching in this vision is commoditised much like many other products, with data collection being the price paid to use the app, and such data and the details of the conversation used for marketing.

These changes in coaching simply reflect the wider changes seen in industries like agriculture or clothing production, with mechanisation using machines like Jethro Tull's seed drill, Eli Whitney's cotton gin, or Arkwright's spinning machine revolutionised production, with similar changes being seen in entertainment and knowledge management industries, where our request for information on a Google search leads us to receiving adverts for associated products later the same day.

This phase may be an ultimate in commercial development, but we can see a time beyond this when coaching emerges into a post-commercial phase of coaching. A phase where coaching becomes adopted as part of common discourse and is used to help support the development of greater personal responsibility and self-awareness.

The implications of change

What we have not explored in this descriptive account is the disruption that change causes. In agriculture, shifts in production, such as land enclosures, and introduction of mechanisation led to landlessness and starvation, in clothing manufacturing production disruptions have led to low pay and exploitation. These changes also stimulated agricultural revolts and the emergence of Luddites, as workers affected by change pushed back against these changes in their daily work patterns, income levels, or status.

In coaching we can see similar push back from some in coaching, who fear the negative impacts of technology, as coaching starts to move away from being a cottage industry, where fee rates, levels of training and practices are highly variable (Passmore et al., 2017) towards providing greater consistency. Such a push back is likely not only to be from individuals but also professional bodies who risk their power being undermined by the emergence of global technology providers.

In the short term, coaches will be impacted by falling rates, increasing expectations of availability and a desire for coach loyalty to a single platform in return for a regular stream of clients put forward by the provider's algorithm. At the same time professional bodies, previously the big beasts of the coaching industry, may fear their roles as those who define the nature of the industry, training and standards disappearing as technology and data, driving by low cost replaces voluntary standards in an unregulated sector.

These issues will become starker as the technological innovation accelerates and functions previously undertaken by humans are replaced by machines. AI has the potential to undertake many or all of the human aspects in the coach–coachee journey (Box 21.1). While our natural reaction may be that as a personal service humans will in the main prefer to speak to a human, costs may significantly influence human behaviour. In a world where a coaching session costs $200 for an hour of coaching, with a coach that has 2,000 hours of coaching and which is available in 48-hours time, in contrast to a AI Coach which is available instantly, at the cost of $5 a session (or even zero). Such a choice may well drive many towards AI chatbot coaching.

If for some readers this is hell, an alternative future is also possible. The coming 2020s and beyond may see opportunities for greater collaboration between coach service providers, as these organisations increase in scale and profitability, university researchers, keen to access large datasets enabled by the greater use of technology and professional

---

Box 21.1   Human tasks suitable for AI machine replacement

Coachee readiness assessment
Coach–coachee matching
Appointment management
Coaching session delivery
Recommendation of inter sessional activities
Nudges to support behavioural change
Evaluation survey – invite, analysis, reporting & learning (algorithm adjustment)

---

bodies. In this scenario, human and AI coaching tasks are blended. Individuals may opt for a human coach, the human coach uses AI for supporting the conversation, and the client uses AI for inter-sessional assignments and nudges to support their behavioural change plans.

In reality both futures will probably unfold, as well as others. Digital providers will be acquired by larger scale L&D providers, and integrate coaching more closely with other offers, technology including AI will play a significant role and the opportunities for research will be expanded significantly with the data sets available from large scale digital providers.

Conclusion

In this chapter we have argued that the coaching industry is changing, rapidly reflecting both changes in technological innovation such as AI and trends which have been witnessed in other industries as they mature. The exact pace and impact of such changes are difficult to predict but our essential argument is that coaches should be aware of and stay up to date with these changes if they wish to be best positioned to meet the changing needs of the industry as it develops over the coming years.

References

Bigelow, B. (1938). Building an effective training program for field salesmen. *Personnel*, 14, 142–150.

Blanchard, K. & Johnson, S. (1982). *The one minute manager*. New York: William Morrow & Co.

Covey, S. (1989). *The seven habits of highly effective people*. New York: Free Press.

Griffith, C. R. (1926). *Psychology of coaching: A study of coaching methods from the point of view of psychology*. New York: Charles Scribner's and Sons.

Gordy, C. (1937). Everyone gets a share of the profits. *Factory Management Maintenance*, 95, 82–83.

Huston, R. E. (1924). Debate coaching in high school. *Quarterly Journal of Speech and Education*, 10, 127–143. doi: 10.1080/00335632409379481

ICF. (2023). *Global coaching study: Executive summary*. Lexington: ICF. Retrieved on 1 February 2024 from https://coachingfederation.org/app/uploads/2023/04/2023ICFGlobalCoachingStudy_ExecutiveSummary.pdf

Owen, J. (2021). *The ultimate handbook for remote and hybrid teams*. London: Bloomsbury.

Passmore, J., Brown, H., Csigas, Z. et al. (2017). *The state of play in coaching & mentoring: Executive report*. Henley-on-Thames: Henley Business School-EMCC. ISBN 978-1-912473-00-7.

Passmore, J. & Evans-Krimme, R. (2021). The future of coaching: A conceptual framework for the coaching sector from personal craft to scientific process and the implications for practice and research. *Frontiers in Psychology*, 12. https://doi.org/10.3389/fpsyg.2021.715228

Peters, T. & Waterman, R. (1982). *In search of excellence*. New York: Harper & Row.

Rostow, W. W. (1959). The stages of economic growth. *Economic History Review*, 12(1). 1–16.

Soosai, L. & Della-Fave, A. (2016). The wellbeing of workers in the agricultural sector. In L. Oades, M. F. Steger, A. Della-Fave. & J. Passmore (eds.) *The Wiley Blackwell Handbook of the psychology of positive and strength based approaches at work* (pp 527–544). Chichester: Wiley.

Stewart, C. (2020). *Maori philosophy: Indigenous thinking for Aotearoa*. London: Bloomsbury.

Trueblood, T. C. (1911). Coaching a debating team. *Public Speaking Review*, 1, 84–85.

Whitmore, J. (1992). *Coaching for performance*. London: Nicholas Brealey.

Whitworth, L. (2005). *Co-active coaching*. New York: Jaico Publishing House.

Chapter 22

The potential for artificial intelligence in coaching

Joel A. DiGirolamo

Introduction

The modern concept and development of artificial intelligence (AI) began in the mid-1950s. Its utilisation in coaching has seen several inflection points along the way. The first AI coaching chatbots began to appear in 2019, which were based on specific algorithms modelled after well-known coaching models, such as the GROW model (Whitmore, 1992). At least one of these has proven to be as good as human coaches (Terblanche et al., 2022). During this time frame, individuals in the coaching profession began to ask where the technology was headed. At one end of the spectrum coaches felt that AI posed an existential threat to their careers, whereas at the other end of the spectrum coaches embraced the technology as an inevitability and pondered how they could embrace it and make use of it in their practice.

The second inflection point was with the emergence of the generative large language model (LLM) systems such as ChatGPT (Version 3) in late 2022 and the more versatile GPT-4 in early 2023, the latter which allowed for the capability of audio and video interfaces. The generative nature of these systems caused an immense stir in the global society, inciting fear of job loss, bypass of critical thinking in all levels of education, and profound implications for availability of accurate and factual information in the future. It is against this backdrop that we will explore the potential for AI in the coaching profession.

What is artificial intelligence?

The Homo sapiens species is the dominant species on our planet arguably due to the remarkably potent computing capacity of our brains, which we call intelligence—human intelligence. This intelligence comes about from the vast numbers of interconnected neurons in our brains, perhaps over 80 billion of them. This array of neurons can allow humans to simultaneously process audio, video, and physical sensations—and to respond rapidly and appropriately even in the presence of very complex input data. Looking at it from another angle, the Homo sapiens species has prevailed because they have been able to envision complex structures, both abstract and physical, and build or develop these structures into meaningful documents, machines, buildings, and much much more. In other words, this powerful general intelligence has allowed Homo sapiens to have the unique ability to shape and create our world.

In the early 1800s, the polymath Charles Babbage envisioned and built a mechanical calculating engine for the narrow purpose of calculating tables. Later in life he

DOI: 10.4324/9781003383741-28

developed a more complex, programmable mechanical machine for general-purpose calculations. Extending this work, Alan Turing described an even more general-purpose computing machine in 1936 (Turing, 1936) and worked, along with others in the late 1940s and early 1950s, on early versions of general-purpose computing machines in the UK, Germany, and US. In 1950 Turing published a paper in *Mind*, proposing a test for computing machines, now known as 'the Turing test', which requires a machine with sufficiently fluid language capability such that a human perceives the machine as another human rather than a machine (Turing, 1950).

Mathematics professor John McCarthy at Dartmouth College is frequently credited with coining the term 'artificial intelligence' during his introduction to a workshop on the topic in 1956 (Moor, 2006). Since those heady years of the 1940s and 1950s, the hardware and software technology industries have exploded and become a very significant portion of the global economy.

In an analysis piece such as this, it is always important to describe or define what we are talking about. The word 'intelligence' has been difficult to define, and it is even harder to define 'artificial intelligence'. Further, given the pace of change in technology, the definition may be a moving target. What was considered AI several years ago may now be considered passé. For the paradigm of AI coaching, however, the definition of artificial intelligence by Kaplan and Haenlein (2019) seems to fit best, "a system's ability to interpret external data correctly, to learn from such data, and to use those learnings to achieve specific goals and tasks through flexible adaptation".

Learning and algorithms

At the heart of all AI systems is the algorithm. Algorithms are sequences of computer instruction that execute a specific task. While software algorithms can be fixed, or static, in artificial intelligence systems, just like human intelligence described above, they can adjust or adapt based upon the data presented in real-time. During the development of algorithms, they are tested with specific sets of data and subsequently trained with other sets of data. The AI system is then tuned for optimal performance by adjusting parameters and evaluating system performance. An iterative process is followed with multiple training data sets to achieve optimum performance with the given data.

Machine learning (ML) AI systems are the next level in complexity, bringing in the ability to learn additional knowledge or skill during usage, above and beyond that developed with the training data (Carbonell et al., 1983). These systems have much greater capability given their enhanced ability to adapt and become more effective the more that they are used. Deep learning (DL) systems are even more sophisticated systems that are able to analyse, classify, and utilise large amounts of data to become even more effective at their intended task and significantly broaden their knowledge base. Large language model (LLM) systems such as ChatGPT and GPT-4 are types of deep learning systems that explore and classify vast amounts of data, providing much broader intelligence, although not what would yet be described as 'artificial general intelligence'.

Looking at AI from another angle, and more broadly, AI that is at least as capable as human intelligence is frequently considered artificial general intelligence (AGI; Kaplan & Haenlein, 2019). AI with less capability is commonly referred to as artificial narrow intelligence (ANI; Kaplan & Haenlein, 2019). In yet another classification system, the early AI systems which responded to input based upon rules are called reactive AI. The common AI chatbots are examples of this reactive technology and can offer significant benefits (Passmore & Tee, 2023). More powerful deep learning systems which can generate new material based upon data known to the system, such as ChatGPT are known as limited memory AI. We can think of the chatbots as being similar to the early Babbage machines—special purpose machines, and the newer generative machines as similar to the more general-purpose computing machines beginning in the 1950s.

The generative systems will likely become formidable systems as they become tuned for the function of coaching and even tailored for specific styles of coaching. These systems will also be able to creatively combine constructs or schemas from one domain to another to generate or develop something entirely new. While they will become potent coaching systems, the downside will be their sinister capability to generate massive amounts of misinformation that could potentially drown out legitimate information. Taking this a step further, it could lead to entrepreneurs developing businesses to verify the provenance of data, and coaching system quality and capability.

The advent of artificial intelligence in coaching

As mentioned previously, the early coaching chatbots have been rule-based, and followed well-regarded coaching models such as the GROW model (Terblanche & Cilliers, 2020). Research has shown such an AI coaching system can perform as well as a human coach (Terblanche et al., 2022). While these tools can intelligently adapt to the conversation, they are bound by the rules, or models programmed into their algorithms. Their conversational tone is quite good, however, and one could argue convincingly that they may pass the Turing test.

The newer AI coaching systems will be using the generative LLM systems. As a result, they will be more adaptive to the client situation, should have a broader gamut of response concepts, and will respond in a more fluid manner. Given the deep learning in these systems, they will inherently have more data, or information from which to draw upon, and therefore should provide dramatically better coaching than the rule-based systems.

Both the rule-based and generative AI coaching systems can work as an adjunct to human coaching by working with the client between human coaching sessions. The human coaches can review the AI coaching session transcripts in order to plan more productive human coaching sessions. This will allow the coaches to take on a larger client base since they can work on the harder client problems and work more quickly after reviewing the AI coaching data. We can think of this as an assistive approach.

AI coaching systems can also be used standalone, to provide a basic level of coaching to individuals who would otherwise not be able to afford coaching. The benefits of coaching have been well-described, and this altruistic approach can serve to benefit all of humanity, to bring to life the impetus driving the human potential movement of the 1940s to 1970s (Spence, 2007).

AI has also been used to analyse the audio, video, and text of coaching conversations in order to identify moments of interest, such as client insights, and important session metrics. The automatic indication of moments of interest can remarkably increase the coach supervisor's productivity. The metrics can include share of voice (coach vs. client), how often the coach asked multiple questions at a time, and number of closed versus open questions. It is not difficult to imagine that these systems will become much more powerful and deeply analytical regarding what happened in the session. The result will be even more immediate and rich feedback from the system, rather than require human intervention.

Ethics

Ethics is central to the coaching process and several coaching organisations have developed ethics codes for human coaching (e.g. Global Coaching and Mentoring Alliance (GCMA), 2021; International Coaching Federation (ICF, 2020)). In a similar manner, ethics codes will be developed and promoted for AI coaching systems. Special attention should be paid to factors such as disclosure that the coaching system is powered by AI and not a real human, as well as disclosure of the range of capabilities. Human coaches will frequently have a conversation with their client early in their engagement revolving around their capabilities and limitations. An ethical AI system should be programmed to provide a similar function.

An important element of ethical coaching behaviour is also knowing when to hand off issues outside the scope or capability of the coach to other health professionals (e.g. Hullinger & DiGirolamo, 2018). This may be for issues that are most appropriately handled by a therapist or to government officials when a client communicates desire to harm themselves or others. Artificial intelligence coaching systems can be designed to remain alert to these areas of concern and respond appropriately. Given the attentive nature of an AI system, it has the potential to identify areas of concern before the coach becomes aware of this and can provide an early warning or indication of the potential. When individuals behave badly and cause trauma to others, it is only after the fact that people sometimes are able to connect the 'dots', or dangerous signs that could have alerted those involved and prevented the trauma from ever taking place. When an AI system has a broad knowledge base and rapid processing access into that knowledge base, it may be able to identify a dangerous pattern and avert the danger. We can also consider how AI systems might be able to identify productive and unproductive patterns in client behaviour, and ultimately cue the coach about those observations.

Bias

Humans have biases coded into our DNA. These are generally a result of millennia of experiences where those of us in our species who survived did so partly as a result of effective application of the biases. The survivors reinforced the bias as they successfully reproduced.

One of the most significant biases encoded into our species is that of in-group and out-group bias (see for example, Sherif et al., 1961). These biases manifest themself when we feel comfortable interacting with someone, we feel safe with and uncomfortable with someone we don't know well or who may give off verbal or visual cues of danger or ambiguity. A bias such as this may inadvertently get coded into the AI algorithms or in data the system uses.

As we see in Figure 22.1, in a very simplistic view of an AI system, it contains a multitude of algorithms and interacts with many sets of data. To begin with, the algorithms

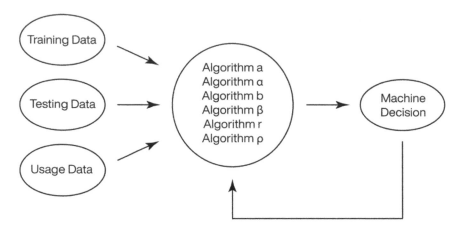

Figure 22.1 Bias entry points.

are likely programmed by humans and may inherently have bias written into them. Next, we consider the training and testing data. Suppose our machine learning AI system is intended to identify plants. Let's say it's trained and tested with plants on the hillsides of the Douro valley in Portugal. Much of what is on those particular hillsides are grape vines for the famous Port wine of Portugal and olive trees. Now we begin using the AI system in southern Portugal, say, in the Algarve region which has milder winters, a more tropical climate, and wider diversity of plant species such as almond, fig, palm, and citrus trees. The AI system will have difficulty identifying the new plants in the Algarve since it was biased toward the plants from the Douro region. But, since it is a machine learning system, it can learn from this new usage data and add to its diversity. However, it still has bias. Suppose we began to use the AI system in northern Canada and it has difficulty identifying the spruce, fir, and birch trees there since it has not seen them before or been trained on them. While the bias in this example is obvious, real-life examples have also been quite obvious once pointed out, as well, but were not so obvious during product development.

There are several keys to eliminating bias, including sensitising all developers, testers, and users to the problem, inviting diverse-thinking independent individuals to audit the AI system from development through usage, and making an intentional effort to gather, develop, and test with the most diverse set of data possible. It helps to consider all of the angles, or ways in which the data may be biased. As more experience is gained and best practices are developed to minimise bias or enhance fairness, as some may call it, it is likely that AI systems could have less bias than Homo sapiens.

Privacy

Data privacy has always been important to individuals, however, as the Internet and particularly the Worldwide Web came online, more and more data was immediately accessible to millions of people across the planet and concerns were heightened. Corporations began gathering and using private individual's personal data for profit and exchange with others. An inflection point came when the European Parliament issued the General Data

Privacy Regulation (GDPR) in 2016 (European Parliament, 2016) which limited how organisations could use personal data when operating within the European Union (EU). Currently GDPR is the standard for data privacy across the globe and a good model for all types of systems, including AI.

The ramifications of GDPR for AI systems are similar to any other digital system collecting personal data, such as limiting access by all individuals in the organisation, including the software developers, and designing databases for easy removal of a given individual's personal data, what is known as the 'right to be forgotten'. The privacy of aspects of AI coaching systems have additional confounding factors, including data permissions granted by organisations purchasing use of the AI systems, as well as coaches, clients, and third-party use of the data. This should be taken into account for training data in addition to the usage data. Ideally the data in an AI system will be anonymised to people with access to the system data.

Coaching capability

AI coaching systems may or may not follow a competency model such as from the International Coaching Federation (ICF; International Coaching Federation, n.d.) or the European Mentoring and Coaching Council (EMCC; European Mentoring & Coaching Council, 2016) to frame their AI coaching, although use of such models can potentially reduce development time and enhance coaching efficacy.

Given that the coach–client relationship is such a strong factor in positive coaching outcomes (Sonesh et al., 2015), human coaches make a significant effort to develop trust and a rapport with their clients. AI coaching systems will need to develop a similar trust and bond with the coaching clients. As a part of the AI coaching system interaction with clients, the AI system must also communicate how interactions may flow, ask for permission to move ahead in the process at times, and notify what possible outcomes may occur.

A good AI system will detect client emotion and respond appropriately. The language quality, tone, manner, and communication style will be conducive to a feeling of presence by the AI system. Since coaching is not just about bringing the insight or awareness into the client's consciousness, but also about facilitating and maintaining persistent actions to ensure retention of that growth, an AI system should provide reinforcement and reminders for the client. This is an aspect of AI systems in which they excel. Given that they are programmed sequences of instructions, they can easily handle repetitive tasks and take this mundane task away from the human coach.

Coaching frequently entails a client-centred, or self-development component similar to that guided by Carl Rogers (1951) for therapy, and also a domain-specific knowledge component as one might encounter in executive coaching (Berman, 2019) or agile coaching (Stray et al., 2020). When an AI coaching system moves beyond the self-development aspect, it must similarly have sufficient domain knowledge to be effective and offer a sufficiently diverse set of options, branches, or paths during the coaching interactions. At a minimum, the AI system must respond appropriately to all client input. However, for sufficient efficacy an AI system must facilitate growth in the client, just as in human–human coaching. Therefore, the interactions must be sufficiently deep to bring new insight or awareness for the client and reinforce those gains made in the coaching.

What lies ahead

The newer generative LLM systems employ more rapid and sophisticated tools. It is easy to imagine applications where the AI system is watching and listening to both sides of the conversation and immediately offer potential questions for the coach to ask the client, offer potential avenues of exploration for the coach to travel, identify client patterns, identify biases by either party, and identify blind spots. At the end of coaching sessions the AI system could provide notes for the coach and client, provide reflective feedback for the coach, track the client progress, provide a summary of actions, schedule the next meeting, and create what is needed for the next session. The system could also automatically follow up with the client between sessions. These capabilities are the sweet spot for such technologies, when they can rapidly draw upon large sets of data and generate useful suggestions. The human coaching will consequently be enhanced since the options presented will likely be more than what would have been brought to mind by the coach independently.

Last, AI systems can be developed to simulate a coaching client, providing a low-cost system for a student coach to practice on. Such a system could provide instant feedback to the student, roll back a specific amount of time in the conversation for a repeat of the coaching process, and make suggestions for areas of practice.

Implications

The universe is inexorably moving forward and, as the expression goes, 'resistance is futile'. Technology will always be evolving and changing rapidly. All professions and industries evolve and transform over time, and coaching will do so as well (Passmore & Evans-Krimme, 2021).

Therefore, it is essential to embrace AI technology and ask how coaches can leverage it to assist in a coaching practice. All professions become more complex and nuanced over time. It has been shown that coaches are good at embracing the idea of life-long learning

---

Box 22.1   AI potential

- AI coaching can work in an assistive capacity with the human coach, allowing the human coach to work on the more difficult problems and more efficiently
- AI coaching can be provided standalone to those unable to afford human coaching, therefore serving humanity and helping all individuals in our global society
- AI can analyse coaching conversations and highlight important moments for supervisors to review, and automatically provide the coach beneficial metrics for immediate session feedback
- AI systems can potentially provide in real-time during a coaching session potential avenues the coach might want to pursue with the client and potential questions
- An AI system may play the role of a client and automatically provide feedback to the student coach.

(Hullinger & DiGirolamo, 2020), which bodes well that coaches will be able to successfully grow and adapt to the new paradigm of technology-assisted human coaching.

While not a direct implication of the ingress of AI into the coaching profession, the rapid advance in AI capability highlights how rapid change of all sorts happens across the planet in all societies in the modern world. The implication for coaching is to question whether or not the goal should be for sustained change in the client (Koroleva, 2016), but rather to enhance resilience and adaptability. Given how nimble AI systems can be with machine learning and deep learning, it is anticipated that AI systems will learn on their own quickly and subsequently provide development opportunities to humans to help them cope and thrive in these rapidly changing environments. In other words, the machines may be able to help humans adapt more quickly to the rapid changes they create.

Reflective questions

1. How do you stay current on the latest technology that may help your clients or your business?
2. How can you add more value for your clients in your human–human interactions as technology is able to work with your clients on the least complicated work?
3. How might you take advantage of technology today to help your clients reinforce their growth areas?

Conclusion

Artificial intelligence technology in coaching is now well-established and its use will enter the mainstream of the profession. Given the capitalistic framework of our society and entrepreneurial spirit of individuals, many businesses will emerge that provide basic, entry-level coaching at minimal cost. It is possible that this taste of coaching may increase the demand for human coaches.

It is important to adopt the paradigm of AI as a tool, and it is anticipated that a wide variety of AI tools will emerge. AI tools already exist to analyse coaching sessions and identify insightful moments and calculate important metrics to enhance instruction and supervision. Student coaches will be able to test and hone their skills with AI coaching clients. Pattern recognition is a productive application for AI, given the capability for AI systems to learn and improve over time (Yang & Shami, 2020). It is likely that AI systems will be able to detect patterns in client dialogue and present possibilities to coaches in real-time. The AI pattern recognition may surpass human pattern recognition and does not need to have a high probability of being correct since the human coach will ultimately make the decision in the moment as to whether to pursue the pattern.

As the technology matures the design and development of tools will likely coalesce around specific groups of function and grow in capability. There is every reason to believe that the trajectory of the AI coaching market will follow the typical path of small, entrepreneurial entrants, growth, consolidation, and maturation phases. This implies stability at some point in the future where the profession has settled into a comfortable relationship with technology as we await the next fundamental shift in the profession.

References

Berman, W. H. (2019). Coaching C-suite executives and business founders. *Consulting Psychology Journal: Practice and Research*, 71(2), 72–85. https://doi.org/10.1037/cpb0000128

Carbonell, J. G., Michalski, R. S., & Mitchell, T. M. (1983). An overview of machine learning. In R. S. Michalski, J. G. Carbonell, & T. M. Mitchell (Eds.), *Machine learning: An artificial intelligence approach* (pp. 3–23). Springer.

European Mentoring & Coaching Council (EMCC). (2016). The EMCC supervision competence framework.

European Parliament. (2016). Regulation (EU) 2016/679 of the European Parliament and of the Council of 27 April 2016 on the protection of natural persons with regard to the processing of personal data and on the free movement of such data, and repealing Directive 95/46/EC (General Data Protection Regulation). Official Journal of the European Union, 59, 1–88. https://eur-lex.europa.eu/eli/reg/2016/679/oj

Global Coaching and Mentoring Alliance (GCMA). (2021). The global code of ethics: For coaches, mentors, and supervisors, v3. www.globalcodeofethics.org

Hullinger, A. M., & DiGirolamo, J. A. (2018). Referring a client to therapy: A set of guidelines. Retrieved from International Coaching Federation website: www.coachingfederation.org/client-referral-whitepaper

Hullinger, A. M., & DiGirolamo, J. A. (2020). A professional development study: The lifelong journeys of coaches. *International Coaching Psychology Review*, 15(1), 8–19.

International Coaching Federation (ICF). (n.d.). ICF core competencies. https://coachingfederation.org/core-competencies

International Coaching Federation (ICF). (2020). ICF code of ethics. https://coachfederation.org/code-of-ethics

Kaplan, A., & Haenlein, M. (2019). Siri, Siri, in my hand: Who's the fairest in the land? On the interpretations, illustrations, and implications of artificial intelligence. *Business Horizons*, 62(1), 15–25.

Koroleva, N. (2016). A new model of sustainable change in executive coaching: Coachee's attitudes, required resources and routinisation. *International Journal of Evidence Based Coaching & Mentoring*, Special Issue No. 10, 84–97.

Moor, J. (2006). The Dartmouth College artificial intelligence conference: The next fifty years. *AI Magazine*, 27(4), 87–91.

Passmore, J., & Evans-Krimme, R. (2021). The future of coaching: A conceptual framework for the coaching sector from personal craft to scientific process and the implications for practice and research. *Frontiers in Psychology*, 12, 715228.

Passmore, J., & Tee, D. (2023). Can Chatbots replace human coaches? Issues and dilemmas for the coaching profession, coaching clients and for organisations. *Coaching Psychologist*, 19(1), 47–54.

Rogers, C. R. (1951). *Client-centered therapy: Its current practice, implications, and theory.* Houghton Mifflin.

Sherif, M., Harvey, O. J., White, B. J., Hood, W. R., & Sherif, C. W. (1961). The Robbers Cave experiment: Intergroup conflict and cooperation. Institute of Group Relations, University of Oklahoma, reprinted by Wesleyan University Press, 1988.

Sonesh, S. C., Coultas, C. W., Marlow, S. L., Lacerenza, C. N., Reyes, D., & Salas, E. (2015). Coaching in the wild: Identifying factors that lead to success. *Consulting Psychology Journal: Practice and Research*, 67(3), 189–217. https://doi.org/10.1037/cpb0000042

Spence, G. B. (2007). Further development of evidence-based coaching: Lessons from the rise and fall of the human potential movement. *Australian Psychologist*, 42(4), 255–265. https://doi.org/10.1080/00050060701648142

Stray, V., Memon, B., & Paruch, L. (2020). A systematic literature review on agile coaching and the role of the agile coach. In M. Morisio, M. Torchiano, & A. Jedlitschka (Eds.), *International Conference on Product-Focused Software Process Improvement* (pp. 3–19). Springer.

Terblanche, N., & Cilliers, D. (2020). Factors that influence users' adoption of being coached by an Artificial Intelligence Coach. *Philosophy of Coaching: An International Journal*, 5(1), 61–70. http://dx.doi.org/10.22316/poc/05.1.06

Terblanche, N., Molyn, J., de Haan, E., & Nilsson, V. O. (2022). Comparing artificial intelligence and human coaching goal attainment efficacy. *PloS One*, 17(6), e0270255. https://journals.plos.org/plosone/article?id=10.1371/journal.pone.0270255

Turing, A. M. (1936). On computable numbers, with an application to the Entscheidungsproblem. In *Proceedings of the London Mathematical Society Ser. 2* Vol. 42, 1937 (pp. 230–265). Cambridge University Press.

Turing, A. M. (1950). Computing machinery and intelligence. *Mind*, 59, 433–460.

Whitmore, J. (1992). *Coaching for performance: A practical guide to growing your own skills.* Nicholas Brealey Publishing.

Yang, L., & Shami, A. (2020). On hyperparameter optimization of machine learning algorithms: Theory and practice. *Neurocomputing*, 415, 295–316.

Acknowledgements & further reading

The author would like to thank the original members of the ICF Artificial Intelligence Coaching Standards Work Group: Matt Barney, David Drake, Olivier Malafronte, Harry Novic, Jonathan Reitz, and Nicky Terblanche for their seminal work in determining the foundation for high-quality, ethical AI coaching systems.

Further reading

AI 101: A Beginner's Guide to the Basics of Artificial Intelligence https://dataconomy.com/2023/04/18/basics-of-artificial-intelligence/

ChatGPT is a Tipping Point for AI https://hbr.org/2022/12/chatgpt-is-a-tipping-point-for-ai

Chapter 23

The business of digital coaching

Carol Braddick and Woody Woodward

Introduction

The rise of digital coaching services has been rapid since 2015, reshaping the coaching market. The widespread availability of digital coaching platforms has changed the landscape of coaching, and dramatically so, for buyers as well as providers of coaching services. This chapter is written for coaches and coaching businesses to deepen their understanding of the business of digitally-enabled coaching and consider how individuals and organisations can respond in a rapidly evolving market. To cover this market, we have held discussions with small and large providers of coaching as well as buyers and managers of coaching services based in organisations. In this chapter, we start by exploring the 'democratisation of coaching' before delving into some of the trends in the industry taking place in the early 2020s. We are conscious this is a fast-changing industry that will continue to evolve. If you are picking up this book in the late 2020s or early 2030s, this and other chapters explain how the business of digital coaching started its movement towards the market of these future years. For example, some of the businesses cited in this chapter may no longer exist at these future dates or have been through multiple acquisitions and mergers.

The democratisation movement

Coaching has traditionally been the domain of senior management. In the early days, e.g., before the Millennium, coaches were contracted to 'fix' derailing executives, provide guidance during critical promotional transitions, or act as trusted advisors. The bespoke one-to-one nature of these coaching engagements, coupled with the high cost, kept coaching out of reach as a development tool for most employees. Although the research is limited, coaching has been demonstrated to provide value, particularly at these more senior levels in organisations (de Haan and Nilsson, 2023; Williams & Lowman, 2018). With this confidence in the value of coaching, human resources and talent leaders have expanded their investments in both internal and external coaches for the more senior roles. The challenge for organisational buyers of coaching services has been finding more affordable ways to provide coaching to a broader audience.

Fast forward to the post-pandemic era where tens of thousands of employees who previously had no employer-funded access to external coaches have now worked with coaches from digital coaching platform providers such as BetterUp, Bravely, CoachHub, and EZRA. These companies – and nearly every digital coaching platform business – have

DOI: 10.4324/9781003383741-29

led with the aim of extending and diversifying coaching beyond the traditional client base of elite executives and emerging leaders. A review of the mission statements, branding materials, press-releases, and speaking engagements by these providers reveals a common theme: the desire to 'democratise coaching'. Their declared mission is to offer customised personal development to all employees via employer-funded coaching. Ultimately, there is an implied desire to scale coaching to all humans.

Core to their argument is the fact that employers have historically focused only on coaching for their elite executives and emerging leaders, while relying on training to address the needs of the wider workforce. The high cost and customised delivery of one-to-one coaching, particularly from consulting firms, have been the primary barriers to providing coaching deeper into the organisation hierarchy. However, the evolution and widespread availability of digital technology changed the game for coaching as a market, profession, and career choice. These technologies predated the 2020 COVID-19 pandemic, but the pandemic accelerated the adoption of digital communication technologies and normalised video and text chat communications as a workplace standard almost overnight. These changes enabled the tech-forward coaching providers to develop scalable coaching solutions which streamlined and digitised key processes such as selecting, matching, tracking, and managing coaching engagements.

In broadening access, they were also well-positioned – with their technology and large pools of coaches – to diversify the types of coaching to offer. Depending on the contract with the employer, employees have access to live credentialled coaches on demand or through a scheduling application where they can identify a challenge and then select a coach. In some organisations, employees self-select into coaching without needing approval from their managers. Some engagements are more programmatic, occurring over the course of set time periods (weeks to months); others may be ad hoc or specialised, e.g., coaching for better sleep or leveraging neurodivergence.

With increasing sophistication of continuous employee listening and the challenges of the COVID pandemic, organisations gained insights into the wide range of development and support needs below the executive levels. While they continued to invest in traditional coaching for future and established leaders, they also funded coaching to support broad outcomes such as wellbeing, engagement, retention, and diversity and inclusion. Essentially the burgeoning digital coaching service providers were poised to leverage technology to both meet as well as generate demand for scaling coaching across a broader range of development and support needs.

This extension to a broader client base as well as the focus on a broader set of needs underpins the democratisation movement in coaching. However, from this stated purpose of opening up access to coaching for everyone, the reality is that the digital platform businesses sell mostly to mid-sized and large enterprises. Their contracts require a relatively high minimum number of employees and minimum investment in coaching. In essence, they are democratising coaching for white collar corporate knowledge workers.

We don't doubt the aspiration is there, but true democratisation of coaching implies coaching available at scale, affordably, to billions for both personal and professional growth. This degree of democratisation will require even greater use of the technologies available in different geographies, a nuanced understanding of the range of human development needs and cross-cultural awareness in meeting these needs. While platforms can personalise the client experience, one size may not fit all.

As the digital platforms continue to grow themselves it will be interesting to see how the democratisation movement evolves – or even devolves. Is this just a fad, a catchy way to hook large numbers of clients? Does democratisation demonstrate an enduring appreciation of the value of coaching or raise the risk of commodification of coaching?

A professional services approach for the digital era

Most of the providers we reviewed take what we refer to as hybrid professional services/software as a service (SaaS) approach to the market. It has become common to refer to the 'uberisation' of coaching, i.e., companies that leverage technology to scale a service – transportation; delivery; and, now, coaching – to thousands of customers using mostly freelancers. In the prevailing digital platform business model, the company recruits certified coaches on a contract basis and employs experts in technology, data science, psychology, and coaching. In addition, most of the digital providers we reviewed offer customised services including needs assessments, alignment with internal competencies, efficacy studies, and customised engagements similar to what the more established firms have traditionally offered. The major differentiator of the platform companies is the streamlining of coaching processes through digital technology which enables the scaling of coaching to a broader range of employees and employee needs.

Another key differentiator is the use of coaching subscriptions and licences. This approach has allowed the digital providers to keep the costs of adding new users and services relatively low for existing customers. By recruiting large numbers of coaches as freelance contractors, they are able to manage the ebbs and flows in demand. In essence, the digital coaching providers are a new breed of a professional services firm designed for a digitally-enabled on-demand world.

In response, the more traditional coaching providers with histories of working at the most senior levels have also introduced competing technology platforms and digital services. Their technology investments address corporate buyers' needs to manage large numbers of coaching engagements and streamline coaching processes. They are also competitive moves to protect their market positions in 'executive' coaching – a niche in an ever-broadening service category – and perhaps an outdated term.

Some of the largest digital providers, networking from their footholds in enterprises, have already begun to target higher margin contracts by introducing new coaching services or new sets of coaches qualified to work with more senior employees. For example, in 2022 Lee Hecht Harrison announced the move of all executive coaching to its digital sibling EZRA and created EZRAx to complement its coaching for mid- and early career managers and team leaders. By 2023 BetterUp claimed to have over 3000 coaches on its bench differentiated by their experience working with leaders at different levels across organisational hierarchies (Jacobs, 2021). In 2023, CoachHub introduced its executive coaching offer CoachHub Executive™.

The evolving categories of coaching providers

As the coaching services industry continues to rapidly evolve, categorising the various players can be tricky. At the time of this writing, with the necessary caveat that boundaries between market competitors are often in flux, here is our take on the major categories in 2024: Traditional business-to-business; digital business-to-business; and direct-to-consumer providers with some subsets within the digital business-to-business category.

Traditional business-to-business service providers

Traditional consulting firms along with the major recruitment/outplacement providers have been offering coaching services for quite some time. They essentially created the business-to-business coaching services category as a natural outcropping of their business advising and leader development offerings (Boysen-Rotelli, 2020). These providers were early leaders in offering specialised engagement packages to large enterprise clients typically designed and priced for upper-level to C-suite leaders. Some have also opened their offerings to broader employee audiences directly competing with the digital coaching service providers. Examples include firms such as Korn Ferry, DDI and the Center for Creative Leadership.

Digital business-to-business service providers

Between 2013 and 2020 a new model of providing coaching services emerged as digital coaching platforms came onto the scene. The offerings coming from this new segment of providers have typically been in the form of per session licensing agreements/bulk licensing agreements, coaching engagement packages for enterprise clients (e.g., six months of weekly coaching for a transitioning leader and coaching-on-demand). Employers determine which employees are eligible to take part in their coaching programmes and make the offerings available through their HR or Learning and Development (L&D) departments. It is important to note that these providers are also continually evolving their services to include offerings and products beyond just coaching. These include custom training, webinars, microlearning modules, and digital libraries of both in-house and publicly aggregated content. The most prominent current examples would be BetterUp, EZRA and CoachHub.

A subset of the digital business-to-business category is the managed service or software as a service (SaaS) providers. These providers are leading with their software offerings while also offering full coaching service packages similar to those mentioned above. What is interesting about the SaaS-oriented providers is that they are focused on software for enterprise coaching management that allows companies to manage their internal coaching programmes while keeping their current internal coaches and/or externally contracted coaches. These software platforms were a response to large enterprises that have internally managed coaching programmes and wished to keep their current stable of coaches, but need to modernise how they manage, track, and measure the impact of their engagements. These firms also offer access to a variety of assessment tools (e.g., personality and strengths diagnostics; 360 feedback; etc.) to their coaches. The most prominent current examples of the digital players in this space include Optify, Delenta and Coaching.com. In addition, traditional service providers like Korn Ferry are also offering managed coaching services designed to streamline the management of multiple coaching providers.

Direct-to-consumer providers

The digital coaching providers certainly got their start with enterprise offerings and many have forayed into direct-to-consumer offerings where they have opened up coaching to individuals who wish to engage a coach for their own personal development. An example of one of the early offerings in the space is BetterUp Direct.

It is also worth noting there are online service providers focused on individual and boutique practice management for coaches as well as providers of other services such as therapy. These providers offer software and services to help solo practitioners and boutique firms manage clients through automated tools and templates that assist in CRM, scheduling, tracking, and billing clients. These would currently include companies like Delenta, Hoolr, and Profi.

Buying coaching services in a digital market

Several years before the entry of digital platforms, corporate buyers of coaching services shifted their purchasing to favour large coaching providers and networks over the growing and often unwieldy number of independently contracted coaches on their supplier lists. As they work towards their aspirations to scale coaching to more – or all – employees, they are not just evaluating digital platforms. Instead, their decisions are more complex, involving pairing employee development needs with combinations of internal and external solutions. Although they have a wider range of choices from the market, their priorities in selecting external coaches have remained relatively stable: coach quality; pricing; and efficiencies in the management of coaching (CoachHub, 2022).

Coach quality

Providers assure buyers of high coach quality by requiring coaches to have completed a coach accreditation. Achieving high quality in the coaching pool also depends on matching. The large digital providers promote their matching algorithms – their claimed 'secret sauce' – as well as their success rate (usually claimed to be greater than 90%) in matched client–coach pairs. Sounding Board, for example, in 2023 used 'interaction style' to match clients to coaches.

It is difficult, until perhaps an advanced stage of the selling process, for buyers to have full visibility of the matching algorithms and methodology used in calculating match success rate. The latter is heavily influenced by clients' ratings of their coaches and coaching sessions. Since technology will always advance more quickly than rigorous coaching research, and providers' formulae are protected IP, the market has yet to see how well these methods incorporate the latest research on the variables in coach–client combinations that lead to success. They currently reflect the data their platforms collect, e.g., the patterns in a coach's ratings from clients and the factors they deem relevant such as client assessments or coach profiles. The large providers have the advantage of their enormous data sets and data science teams to refine their matching algorithms; in contrast, smaller providers are more likely to know their coaches individually, enabling more high-touch matching. For all the attention paid to algorithms and match success rates, it is still important that the client is the decision maker on coach selection and experiences the selection process as worthwhile.

Pricing

The digital providers have also influenced pricing in the coaching market with the offerings, packages, and new pricing structures they have introduced. Their offerings, as discussed earlier, cover a wider range of needs than traditional leadership development coaching. They customise coaching packages as subscriptions to set numbers of coaching hours as well as unlimited time. They also offer services which are similar to those from their professional services counterparts which include six months of one-on-one coaching sessions, manager briefings, assessments such as strengths diagnostics and 360 feedback, and basic evaluative metrics such as client satisfaction.

Their pricing, which varies based on the offer and package, reflects the economies of scale from digitising coaching process steps. It also reflects intense competition among the leading digital providers. The aggressive pricing from the digital providers has certainly impacted rates for coaches, which we address later in this chapter.

Given the short shelf life of pricing as it stands in 2023, and the confidentiality of pricing information, it is more useful to consider the ways in which scaling impacts the commercial offers from digital providers. When proposing coaching subscriptions, for example, they will seek a user base of hundreds – in some cases more than 1000. In most contracts, the buyer pays for the licences for this user base regardless of whether users make full use of the set number of coaching hours or actively use open-ended, on-demand coaching. This puts the user adoption rate 'under a spotlight'. Buyers are keen to see full utilisation of their investments and must use internal communications and champions to drive adoption of coaching. Providers also have an incentive to support adoption; their claimed coaching success rates are less meaningful when adoption is low. But, consistent with software subscription pricing, they collect the recurring licence revenue. They also collect employee data from the buying organisation which can be used for research.

Efficient management of coaching

Buyers continue to value efficient, self-serve access to real-time data on coaching costs, delivery activity, client engagement and satisfaction, and coaching results. Obviously, it is much easier for buyers to receive this information from fewer suppliers who bring the technology to produce this information and skills to pull actionable insights from the data.

There is a growing internal interest from buyers and an external push from large digital providers to integrate internal human capital management (HCM) data from the former with platform data from the latter – to gain insights into coaching needs and results. BetterUp, for example, partners with WorkDay, a major provider of HCM technology, to identify points of need for coaching across the employee life cycle (Business Wire, 2022). The traditional business-to-business providers are also in a strong competitive position. They are able to leverage their experience in areas such as organisation culture, employee engagement and thriving, and leadership assessments into analyses of coaching needs and results and to position coaching goals and results in the context of business outcomes.

All coaching providers must proactively manage the security and protection of client data. While the large digital providers have the resources to implement the necessary protocols, they also carry much higher risk from the volume of data they hold. As of January 2024, there is no single, comprehensive set of guidelines on data ethics. Nor is there a set of guidelines in use across the market of buyers and providers on ethics issues unique to coaching technology, e.g., design of digital tools that reinforce client agency rather than make recommendations perceived as 'intelligent' or 'smart'. Coaching tools such as coachbots that use generative AI products, e.g., ChatGPT, are in the early stages of development.

The two most dominant professional bodies, International Coaching Federation (ICF) and European Mentor Coaching Council (EMCC), are currently developing guidelines for use of AI in coaching technology. The potential degree of influence these future guidelines will have on buyers is unclear; buyers may choose to rely on their own internal processes for approving technology providers. Smaller coaching providers face a common challenge given their size, namely, keeping up with constant market and technology change. Larger providers have the advantage of in-house and external specialists to advise on data and ethics issues.

The coach experience in a digital marketplace

Coaches have always had options to work as associates, affiliating as freelancers with small networks of coaches as well as large providers. These affiliations serve both parties: coaches gain clients without having to generate new contracts, and the business has a coach pool to draw on to meet changing client demand. The digital platform companies provide another affiliation for coaches with both familiar and new tradeoffs. Table 23.1 below summarises the key elements of the tradeoff for coaches.

Table 23.1 Coach tradeoffs in coaching platforms

Element	Upsides for Affiliated Coaches	Downsides for Affiliated Coaches
Marketing and selling	Business development teams at platform companies market, sell, and close large contracts with large enterprises Platform company matches coaches to new clients Less experienced coaches build hours quickly to satisfy accreditation requirements Exposure to wide range of industry sectors	Platform company uses different forms of non-compete terms in contracts with coaches, restricting their access to these clients during and after delivery of coaching Unpredictable revenue; coaches seek more transparency in how clients are allocated and matched
Coaching process	Platform streamlines and personalises the coach and client experience, e.g., scheduling; access to content to share with clients; and dashboards for each coaching engagement The convenience of 'plug and play'	Coaches report that platform features crowd out the high-touch coaching relationship Platform interface and iconography seen by coaches as overly friendly rather than representing coaching as profession backed by research Concern among coaches that emphasis on client ratings leads to overuse of directive approach and advice-giving

Table 23.1 (Continued)

Element	Upsides for Affiliated Coaches	Downsides for Affiliated Coaches
Coach development, Supervision and support	Platforms offer training in their new tools and important trends Some platform companies have built a cohesive coaching community Coaches receive feedback via ratings, e.g., NPS, from clients	Coaches report that the coach community is often coach-driven rather than proactively supported by the platform Coaches typically fund their coach supervision Remuneration for coach time spent in training varies Coaches would like more feedback on how to improve; customer ratings do not provide feedback that is specific enough to take action on
Coach compensation	Potential to progress to higher hourly rate based on client feedback and hours of coaching completed	The most sensitive issue for coaches; hourly rates vary from $50 to $125, far less than typically paid by other freelance relationships
Organisation context	None cited	Clients may not have received any orientation to coaching or had conversation with manager on rationale for coaching Coaches use up to two sessions orienting clients to the what and why of coaching If client rates coach after each session, initial rating may not reflect any benefit from coaching yet Coaches experience common challenge of balancing interests of client, employer and platform. Support from platform on navigating these situations varies
Innovation and research	Large platforms have a strong advantage from the data they collect and funding available for acquisitions. Affiliated coaches can learn from new research findings and potentially have early adoption opportunities with new products	Limited opportunities to give input to platform's product roadmap
Coaching-related data issues	None cited	Complex contracts between digital providers and buying organisations leave coaches with low understanding of how data on coach and clients is held and used and how to be in compliance

Coaching fee rates

We would be remiss not to address the issue of coaching rates in a digital market. To set rates in a market context, the global average hourly rate charged by coaches is $244 (International Coaching Federation, 2023). Hourly rates vary widely around this average across the globe.

Scaling in all industries improves affordability for buyers with the corollary that costs of providing the product or service declines. While platform technology reduces the costs of coaching processes, a key factor in lower pricing to coaching buyers is lower hourly rates for coaches. Coaches affiliated with the digital platform companies typically earn range from $50 U.S. to $125 per hour of coaching.

As summarised in the table above, coaches affiliating as freelancers with digital platforms face a stark tradeoff: a significant drop in hourly coaching fees in exchange for access to a more consistent pipeline of clients and the time saving from the burdens of marketing, invoicing, and general administration of managing a small business. Coaches' views on this tradeoff and other aspects of working with the platform companies have appeared on career websites such as Glass Door as well as in press articles (Charter, 2022; Sabur, 2022). We may question the quality of coaches who are earning only $125 hourly – or much less.

Across the market, lower rates from platforms are potentially depressing rates more broadly with the exception of work at most senior levels or by 'big name' coaches. In addition, high competition among large platform companies for 'big corporate whale' accounts potentially leads to even lower pricing to corporate buyers and lower rates to coaches. This creates a damaging race to the bottom as wider democratisation potentially commoditises coaching.

As of 2023, one platform, Sounding Board, has taken a more creative approach, offering its coaches participation in the company's stock option programme. In announcing this equity benefit, they highlighted the risk of 'diminishing coaching as a commodity' and pledged to keep looking for ways to 'provide more value' to their coaching community. Others, like EZRA are creating coach communities with multiple training, development and supervision pathways.

The next wave: chatbots, artificial intelligence (AI), and adjacent markets

Spring 2023 saw the popularisation of digital coaching tools such as apps that use conversational AI are being launched and tested in the marketplace with some success (Terblanche et al., 2022). Clients working with a human coach also have the option of using a coachbot between their one-to-one coaching sessions. For example, CoachHub's AIMY functions as a coaching 'co-pilot' (Jacobs, 2023). AIIR Consulting has launched its coachbot Aiiron, while EZRA offers CAI as an AI coach supporting learning nudges. At this stage, coachbots are well suited for specific steps in coaching, e.g., goal setting (Terblanche et al., 2022) and to support behaviour change through regular prompts, reminders, and inspirational quotes sent to clients via text messaging.

It appears likely that as generative AI improves and is commercialised, coaches working in independent and smaller practices will also be able to offer their clients branded AI tools to complement their one-to-one coaching sessions. As coaching chatbots become available from business-to-consumer organisations (not-for-profit entities or social entrepreneurs), this type of coaching experience will accelerate the democratisation of coaching beyond the employer-provided model.

Employees in organisations using people analytics tools such as engagement and employee experience analyses already have access to 'AI coaching'. Providers of these technologies, which are part of the broader HR technology market, supply employees with action prompts, check-ins on actions completed, and progress reports. For example, employees might receive a personalised analysis of their productivity and time management with recommendations such as booking more uninterrupted focus time. These providers' tools can then track and share updates with their users on changes and improvements they have made; they also provide anonymised aggregate data to employers on trends in employee needs.

However, these tools do not generally provide insights into what a specific user did or learned that led to the improvements reported. As the profession considers the growth of tech-enabled coaching and broader overall use of AI, the work of gaining such insights and committing to acting on them is still viewed as an enduring, distinct contribution from human interventions such as coaching that requires empathy and curiosity.

The digital coaching providers are also looking to expand via partnerships with the technology providers already serving large buyers with Human Capital Management (HCM); Enterprise Resource Platforms (ERP); and 'worktech', a common term for productivity and collaboration tools such as Slack and Microsoft VIVA and Teams. These partnerships enable identification of coaching needs at different points in the employee life cycle and generate analytics that may be leveraged in coaching engagements, e.g., organisational network analysis. The boundaries of the digital coaching market relative to these adjacent technology markets will continue to blur via these strategic relationships.

Given the vast amount of employee data they hold and use for research, coaching providers with technology platforms are well-positioned to impact large adjacent markets such as corporate training and L&D, which is estimated at $362 billion (Statista, 2022). Independently, these markets have already been affected by some of the same demands made of digital coaching, namely personalisation; 24/7 availability; and support in the flow of work. A two-way, overlapping pivot is emerging in which some coaching becomes more like L&D, e.g., curated 'push' content which coach and client share. And L&D providers bundle their content and delivery with coaching modules designed to help users move from understanding to actions. As buyers adopt scaling of coaching to more employees, they are also leveraging their other investments, e.g., L&D, into coaching.

Key insights

There is now a broader spectrum of client needs, coaching services and service delivery options under the ever-widening umbrella of coaching. Although leadership development is still the top use case, newer use cases such as supporting diversity and inclusion goals, business transformation and agile ways of working are becoming increasingly common (CoachHub, 2022). In addition, the emphasis on leadership as a skill set to be developed at all levels, not just at the most senior levels, is also influencing the diversification of use cases. Thus, the term 'executive coaching', when viewed against the aspirations of the digital coaching providers to democratise coaching, may now be outdated. Rather than describing the coaching market, executive coaching is becoming more of a high-end, 'white glove' segment of a larger emerging coaching market.

The pioneers in digital coaching opened up new frontiers in segments such as early-in-career employees, first-time managers and team leaders. In exposing thousands of employees to coaching, they have potentially set an upwards trajectory for the longer-term demand for coaching. If employees from these segments come to view coaching as a key part of their development and career progress, they will contribute to future demand for coaching. However, this demand may be met by both human coaches as well as digital coaching services, e.g., coachbots, or a mix of both. If employers revert back to traditional reasons for investing in coaching, e.g., global management development that includes diversity or inclusion, rather than investing in these as separate coaching initiatives, future demand for employer-funded coaching may soften during the mid-2020s.

In disrupting the market, the large digital providers have also set the standards for platform features (e.g., algorithmic matching) that are 'must-haves' and those that are leading edge (e.g., 'coaching analytics'). As these providers move to serve higher level employees in organisations, incumbent providers historically serving senior and executive level clients are competing not just on the quality and impact of their coaching, but also on their digital and data science capabilities. And, increasingly, on coaching fees. This downward pressure on fees is already having an impact on pricing for coaching at higher organisational levels. It has already, e.g., been a factor in organisational buyers displacing incumbent coaching providers, particularly independent coaches, in favour of lower cost digital providers. This trend will probably continue through the 2020s.

Despite the growing demand for coaching at most organisation levels, it will only become more challenging for new coaches and experienced independent and smaller coaching providers to grow profitably. Given buyers' preferences for fewer suppliers, these smaller providers may grow their pipelines via affiliations with larger coaching businesses that have built platforms. This implies further erosion of their revenue and margins. They will also be at a disadvantage in meeting buyers' needs for real-time reporting and analyses of impact. For some new coaches, working as an employee of a professional services firm that offers consulting and coaching may be a more successful first stage of a coaching career with self-employment occurring much later in their careers.

However, if the SaaS platform providers are successful in replicating and building on the capabilities of the digital providers, individual and smaller providers using their services will be more competitive. An alternative business model may emerge such as a 'collective' of coaches using a common SaaS vendor that customises and brands their clients' offers to enterprises. This may be a route to higher fees for coaches; it also creates a new provider business model for buyers to evaluate.

Buyers' decisions are no longer focused on internal vs. external coaches, or large or smaller providers. Their decisions also must consider the ratio – explicit as well as perceived – of technology/human in coaching. Among coaches, there is naturally a concern about losing the human connections that enrich coaching relationships, experiences, and outcomes as technology moves from the background to the foreground, from a supporting layer to a means of having coaching conversations (Forbes Coaches Council, 2023).

The coaching profession's challenge is much like that of other service professions: identifying how technology can enable basic steps while keeping humans in the loop and as a primary provider. For coaching this currently translates to using technology for basic, narrow conversations, personalising and sharing content, and supporting the client's change process via reminders and prompts. Human coaches will retain their role in guiding awareness and insight, debriefing client experiments and exploring issues such as identity when trying new approaches. This allocation between technology and humans is already shifting in coaching, the helping professions and many service sectors such as law and consulting.

Preparing for the future

Even if significant negative events occur, e.g., a massive data breach at one of the large platform companies, it is likely the digitisation of coaching will continue. The playing field will evolve through mergers, acquisitions, and consolidations. The large digital platforms may dominate the market in terms of size, e.g. revenue and global reach, while a much smaller niche of high-touch and specialised services for elite executives remains (Passmore & Evans-Krimme, 2021). Through partnerships, alliances and reorganisations within organisations, coaching, L&D, and human capital management will overlap. All of these trends will take place as the nature of work changes through increased automation.

Predicting the future of coaching tech is probably a fool's errand. For example, Gartner research on human capital management, using their hype cycle approach, estimates at least a ten-year period, from 2021 to 2031, for coaching and mentoring technology applications to plateau (Freyermuth, 2021). A broad generalisation which mixes coaching and mentoring and refers generically to 'applications' is of limited use. To the extent that this forecast incorporates growing sophistication of AI tools in coaching, the plateau may occur much earlier.

Given this mix of knowns and unknowns, the best way to prepare for an uncertain future in coaching is for coaches – new as well as experienced – to enhance their knowledge and skill base. Coaches need to rethink their value proposition, positioning their value relative to future clients' expectations from their work and lives as well as from coaching, including the mix of human and technology in coaching.

There are five major opportunities coaches have to ensure they are ready to provide high-quality value to the changing demands of enterprise and individual clients: lean into the science; enhance their coaching capabilities; expand their technical skills; develop professional consulting skills; and shape the technology.

Coaching science

Coaches can no longer rely on the proprietary models developed by self-proclaimed business gurus and private training operators. Instead, they must lean into evidence-based practice and keep up to date on the science of coaching. Over the last couple of decades, the amount of coaching research published in credible scientific journals has grown exponentially. There is no doubt the body of coaching science will continue to grow, informed by the data generated through digital coaching. The coaching technology players are investing more in coaching supervision and development as both a means of quality assurance and a way for coaches to continue to learn and grow. Coach practitioners will be expected to know the latest evidence-based practices along with the most effective use of tools and technology that have been designed around science. As the ranks of practising coaches continue to grow, there will be a greater spotlight on coach quality, enabled by greater transparency of coaching results tracked via providers' and employers' platforms.

Adoption of technology

Coaches who eschew technology will get left behind. Both enterprise and individual buyers of coaching services will expect their coaches to be technologically savvy. Coaches will need to constantly adjust the mix of technology and high-touch human-to-human contact in the design and delivery of their services. As they evaluate options for using technology, their focus should be on the skills and experiences that AI is less able to offer. The rapid proliferation of narrow generative AI such as ChatGPT has brought the availability and feasibility of purely digital coaching into mainstream consciousness and market acceptance. Buyers and clients will expect coaches to have experience using this type of digital 'co-pilot'.

Beyond one-to-one coaching

One-to-one interaction has been the core of coaching for decades. Group coaching, team coaching, and coach supervision are each distinct skill sets that are gaining recognition and momentum. For example, the ICF has released team coaching competencies; EMCC has developed competencies for both team coaching and supervision and offers accreditation for individuals and training programmes in both. Having a high level of competence in these areas will be critical to maintaining a competitive advantage as a coach.

Consulting

In the purest sense, coaching can be a very narrow and limiting vocation; it consists mostly of one-to-one conversations. For this reason, coaches have long relied on multiple streams of income to build their businesses. Coaches have traditionally worked as facilitators, trainers, and learning designers, all of which will become increasingly more important in the coming years. As we highlighted earlier, many of the digital coaching technology providers are mimicking the professional services firm approach, which means that coaches will be expected to deliver more than one-on-one engagements.

Coaches who have developed wider consulting skills will be in a stronger position to provide value relative to the continually expanding offerings coming from the digital providers. As experienced organisational practitioners, coaches know the 'neighbourhood' so to speak. They are well-positioned to serve as guides to the client organisations where they already have a foot in the door and understand where their clients' employers are headed. Coaching combined with L&D solutions such as personalised learning nuggets, microlearning and virtual reality for practice, already in use, will likely become the norm.

Shaping digital coaching

The current digital coaching products and services will continue to evolve and new market entrants will offer even more ways to digitise coaching. Experienced coaches have deep knowledge of the coaching process, enabling them to advise on how specific coaching tools and frameworks can be adapted for digital environments. There will be opportunities to take part in the development and testing of new technology products and services. Instead of waiting to see how technology impacts coaching, coaches have the opportunity to help shape how technology is used in coaching.

Reflective questions

1. Who are my future clients (employees and individuals) and what will they expect from coaching?
2. How can I stand out as relevant and competitive to my future clients and, if employees, to their employers?
3. How can I apply my strengths and experience as a coach to move beyond 1:1 coaching and offer a wider range of services to individuals and organisations?

Conclusions

In less than a decade, the democratisation of coaching through digital technology has accelerated personal and professional growth for thousands. It has also – in tandem with the pandemic – changed the dynamics of the coaching market, giving buyers and coaches new options. From this initial wave of democratisation, the next wave of digital coaching, enabled by more sophisticated AI, may reach millions – possibly billions. This expansion of coaching far beyond the executive ranks may embed coaching as a primary means globally for personal and professional development. As coaches support clients adapting to greater use of technology in their lives and work, they will also be expected to adapt to similar changes 'closer to home', i.e., in the coaching market. In lieu of seeking ways to 'robot-proof' or 'future-proof' a career in coaching, new and experienced coaches will need to be role models of learning and change, rethinking how they bring value to their clients.

References

Boysen-Rotelli, S. (2020). Executive coaching history: Growing out of organizational development. *The Coaching Psychologist*, 16(2), 26–34.

Business Wire. (2022, August 22). BetterUp earns design badge with workday. *Business Wire*. Retrieved from: www.businesswire.com/news/home/20220810005210/en/BetterUp-Earns-Design-Badge-with-Workday

Charter, D. (2022, April 28). Staff at Prince Harry's start-up rebel over 'pay cuts'. *The Times*. www.thetimes.co.uk/article/staff-at-prince-harrys-start-up-rebel-over-pay-cuts-wl5fvtghl

CoachHub (2022). *CoachHub global survey: Business trends in coaching 2023*. New York: CoachHub.

de Haan, E. & Nilsson, V. (2023). What can we know about the effectiveness of coaching? A meta-analysis based only on randomized controlled trials. *Academy of Management Learning & Education*, 24(4), 1–21. Retrieved from: https://journals.aom.org/

Forbes Coaches Council. (2023, May 10). 20 important reasons coaches should be wary of overusing AI tools. *Forbes*. Retrieved from: www.forbes.com/sites/forbescoachescouncil/2023/05/10/20-important-reasons-coaches-should-be-wary-of-overusing-ai-tools/

Freyermuth, J. (2021). Gartner hype cycle for human capital management technology, Retrieved from: www.gartner.com/en/articles/3-standout-trends-from-the-hype-cycle-for-human-capital-management.

International Coaching Federation & Price Waterhouse Coopers. (2023). Global coaching study. Executive Summary. Retrieved from: https://coachingfederation.org/research/global-coaching-study

Jacobs, E. (2021, August 12). Better up rides the mental health tech boom. *Financial Times*. Retrieved from: www.ft.com/content/ede64fdd-e3f5-48b6-9b7b-59731a225468

Jacobs, E. (2023, April 9). Will AI solve my mid-life crisis? *Financial Times*. Retrieved from: www.ft.com/content/4f653300-7d71-4ee3-b89e-113091571c4e

Passmore, J. & Evans-Krimme, R. (2021). The future of coaching: A conceptual framework for the coaching sector from personal craft to scientific process and the implications for practice and research front. *Frontiers in Psychology*, 12. DOI.10.3389/fpsyg.2021.715228/full

Sabur, R. (2022, April 27). Silicon Valley start-up 'facing staff mutiny' over Prince Harry's role. *The Telegraph*. Retrieved from: www.telegraph.co.uk/world-news/2022/04/27/silicon-valley-start-up-facing-staff-mutiny-prince-harrys-role/

Statista (2022). Workplace learning and development. Retrieved from: Workplace learning and development – statistics & facts | Statista

Terblanche, N., Molyn, J., Williams, A., & Maritz, J. (2022). Performance matters: Students' perceptions of Artificial Intelligence Coach adoption factors. *Coaching, An International Journal of Theory, Research and Practice*, 16(2), 1–15. DOI:10.1080/17521882.2022.2094278

Terblanche, N., Molyn, J., de Haan, E., & Nilsson, V. (2022). Comparing artificial intelligence and human coaching goal attainment efficacy. *PloS One*, 17(6), e0270255. https://doi.org/10.1371/journal.pone.0270255

Williams, J. S. & Lowman, R. L. (2018). The efficacy of coaching: An empirical investigation of two approaches using random assignment and switching-replications design. *Consulting Psychology Journal: Practice and Research*, 70(3), 227–249.

Part VI

Coaching practice

Chapter 24

One-to-one digital coaching

Dr Brajesh Bajpai and David Clutterbuck

Introduction

In recent decades, the traditional picture of a one-to-one coaching session was of a seated coach with their client in a private room, using pen and paper while talking and jointly exploring issues as both sip cups of a hot beverage. The COVID-19 pandemic brought an end to this as the standard means for one-to-one coaching. By the mid-2020s coaching is now more likely to be online through video-conferencing tools like Teams, Zoom, or Google Meet. Digital coaching tools and apps have replaced pen and paper as coaches use these tools to facilitate sessions and help clients monitor their progress.

Digital one-to-one coaching is a reality, presenting both opportunities and challenges. This chapter discusses the challenges of managing coach presence, absence of physicality, lesser available cues, and blurring boundaries of transition time. It offers practical recommendations for managing video sessions and highlights the benefits of using digital tools through a framework of coaching continuum. Privacy and ethical concerns are also addressed. By examining these critical topics and the practical suggestions accompanying them, we aim to provide coaches with the necessary support during this transition.

Emerging challenges of a video session

With the widespread and often low-cost availability of video-conferencing applications, clients can now receive personalised one-to-one digital coaching anytime, anywhere. However, this change in the primary coaching medium from face-to-face to video presents new difficulties for both coaches and clients.

While some scholars argue that all coaching is essentially about change (Bennett & Bush, 2013) and hence one could expect coaches to be adept at navigating changes, it is not always the case. In addition, beyond the usual difficulties accompanying a significant change, the transition to video brings unique challenges to the coaching context. These challenges relate to less availability of non-verbal cues in video communication, which leads to an incomplete or even inaccurate picture of the situation. The missing physicality and the requirement of managing bio-rhythms, given that the client and coach could operate from different time zone. This missing physicality of a coaching room means coaches can no longer use some of the traditional tools they are used to. Consider their inability to offer a tissue if the client gets emotional or a soft touch on the elbow, or even the lack of an opening handshake, which can sometimes help gauge the client's state of

DOI: 10.4324/9781003383741-31

mind. Each of these challenges impacts the coach's presence and his/her ability to build a trusting relationship with the client.

Coach presence is about bringing one's whole self to the coaching session, including coaches' values, passion, creativity, emotions, and discerning judgement (O'Neill, 2011). In a traditional coaching set-up, this also includes the coach's physical presence. As coaching moves to virtual, the coaches no longer have ready access to the physical space leading to an experience of disturbed presence. For example, we could compare this disturbed presence to the 'disturbance in the force' from Star Wars or the 'glitch in the Matrix' from The Matrix. These movie references capture the idea of a sudden and unexpected disturbance that can throw off our sense of equilibrium (Bajpai, 2023). Such visualisation helps acknowledge the disturbance and better understand and manage the same.

In the new digital setting, the traditional and henceforth familiar tools based on touch, space and sensation are available to a lesser extent. The situation is particularly tricky for coaches who use somatic coaching, where the body, the human form, is viewed as a fundamental source of development, change, and transformation (Aquilina & Strozzi-Heckler, 2018). In digital coaching, coaches may miss important body language cues available in face-to-face coaching. With relatively lesser available cues, coaches may end up overlooking essential nuances. Many coaches feel comparatively more fatigued at the conclusion of their virtual coaching sessions, and this may be attributed to the additional effort required to compensate for the absence of specific cues. Additionally, there may be instances where coaches operate with a flawed or incomplete understanding of the client, given that they might be missing nuances in the background of lesser cues. In digital one-to-one coaching, there are additional issues of interruptions in communication due to technical issues related to poor connectivity, software glitches and hardware malfunctions that the coach needs to manage.

Many coaches used to curate the physical coaching space painstakingly, thus taking their busy clients away from the constant pressures of busy schedules and back-to-back meetings into a relatively quieter space. Clients appreciated the chance to shift into a contemplative mindset and step away from the demands of their daily routine. However, with clients now accessing coaching sessions from their offices, homes, or home offices, these opportunities are no longer available. The time spent travelling to and from coaching sessions, which clients previously used to prepare and shift into a reflective state, is now non-existent. As one of our fellow coaches remarked, referencing the digital coaching session, "Clients do not arrive; they appear" (Bajpai, 2023).

Given the absence of physical presence, diminished cues, disrupted physicality, and lack of transition time, coaches must reconsider their customary practices and potentially enhance their digital presence as a separate and distinct phenomenon. For now, there is little available research that provides any specific guidance to coaches on navigating this new reality of the digital age. An excellent first step for coaches could be to start acknowledging their digital presence as a phenomenon that needs their attention and additional work. The practitioners could also rely on research from adjacent helping and developmental professions of psychotherapy, counselling and education which have a long history of addressing these challenges. For example, the UK Council for Psychotherapy has issued helpful guidelines for working online and remotely (UKCP, 2021). These guidelines aim to tackle the concerns surrounding client psychology and highlight the phenomenon of the disinhibition effect (Suler, 2004). The disinhibition effect suggests that clients may divulge more personal information than they typically would in face-to-face interactions. The virtual nature of the interaction may weaken defences and resistance, and individuals may feel more at ease exploring aspects of their personality that they may not feel comfortable doing in person.

Because coach presence is critical in building rapport with clients, coaches must work harder in digital coaching to establish trust and create a safe environment for clients. As coaching organisations and research continue to advance, it is probable that comparable standards, such as those established by UKCP, will arise for coaches. However, for the time being, coaches will need to discover ways and techniques to strengthen their online presence and establish a relationship of trust with their clients in a virtual environment. In Table 24.1 we offer new practical recommendations for coaches to explore and try towards managing their digital presence

Although the task of enhancing digital presence will be a personal endeavour for coaches, clients need to be involved in building a solid relationship and fostering trust in the new virtual setting. Research has shown that a trusting coach–client relationship or a strong working alliance (De Haan, 2011) is a crucial predictor of successful coaching outcomes. Scholars hold varying perspectives on the effectiveness of coaching conducted in a face-to-face versus virtual setting. While some argue that face-to-face coaching is more conducive to building a solid working alliance between coach and client (Charbonneau, 2002), others contend that virtual coaching can be equally effective (Berry, 2005; Ghods, 2009). Some researchers suggest that face-to-face and virtual coaching are inherently

Table 24.1 How to manage digital presence in virtual coaching

Issue	Suggestion
Bio-Rhythm	When operating across different time zones, try and get into the same energy state as the client. For example, if it is early morning for the client, a nap for the coach might help and if the client is connecting late in the day, a short run might.
Transition Time	Given the lack of transition time, it might be helpful for coaches to ease the client into the virtual session and start the session a bit slower.
Patchy Connectivity	Poor bandwidth and connectivity can, at times, disrupt video calls. Also, coaches likely experience greater fatigue during a video session, given that they must compensate harder for the missing cues. Hence the suggestion is to take more pauses during the coaching session.
Fatigue	Given the context of video fatigue and the availability of fewer cues during a video session, the suggestion is to revisit the duration of classical coaching sessions and experiment with shorter sessions.
Fewer Cues	Another suggestion is to increase the client feedback loop to avoid missing nuances in the context of fewer available cues. The advice of 'ask the client when in doubt' is possibly even more relevant in a virtual setting.
Camera Location	It is helpful to learn where to look during a video session. Camera position and the position of the client's eyes on a screen are different and could confuse coaches. The suggestion is to practice various options and ask the client for feedback on what works best.

dissimilar (McLaughlin, 2013), each with its own unique benefits (Boyce & Clutterbuck, 2010; Passarelli et al., 2020), and neither approach is inherently superior to the other.

Considering that humans have relied on face-to-face communication as the primary mode of interaction throughout millions of years of evolution, it is probable that building trust in a virtual setting will require time and effort to refine. In the meantime, the recommendations provided here can serve as a starting point for coaches to explore and experiment with. While managing a digital presence in a one-to-one digital coaching set up is likely to be a significant challenge, it is not the only one. Coaches in the digital age will also need to learn how to work with newer tools which are best suited for the virtual setting and get comfortable with emerging technological platforms. Hence, in addition to the suggestions, the coaches are encouraged to try and experiment. The chapter on "Setting up your online coaching environment" lists some practical tips to help coaches manage the challenges emerging from the choice of device set-ups, equipment and connection limitations.

Emerging opportunities for digital tools and platforms

Traditional and virtual coaching are both synchronous activities where the coach and client interact in real-time. Such synchronous communication has been at the heart of most traditional helping professions, and coaching is no exception. According to Riemer et al. (2015), the rise of remote work, virtual teams, and digital collaboration tools has caused a decline in the effectiveness of traditional, formal methods of communication. The adoption of asynchronous work and communication is steadily increasing in both corporate and societal settings. This approach to work allows for greater flexibility and autonomy, as team members are able to work at their own pace and communicate at their convenience. Asynchronous communication methods, such as email and messaging platforms, enable individuals to collaborate effectively without the constraints of real-time communication and free up the coach and the client from the requirement of simultaneous presence. Overall, the trend towards asynchronous work and communication is gaining traction as more and more individuals and organisations recognise its benefits.

For a one-to-one digital coach, various digital tools are available to facilitate asynchronous communication. The most commonly used ones are shared in Table 24.2.

Table 24.2 Common tools for asynchronous communication

Email: The most straightforward and user-friendly tool that enables coaches and clients to send and receive messages.

Text messaging: This option provides another convenient way for coaches and clients to communicate asynchronously.

Social media: Platforms like Facebook, Twitter, and LinkedIn allow connecting with clients and sharing resources and information.

Video conferencing: Besides being the platform for live coaching sessions through, tools such as Zoom and Google Meet also enable coaches to record video messages for clients.

Asynchronous coaching platforms: These platforms are specifically designed to support asynchronous coaching and typically provide embedded features such as video and text messaging and file sharing.

In the context of coaching, Boyce and Clutterbuck (2010) use media richness theory (Daft & Lengel, 1986) to underscore the importance of selecting an appropriate digital communication mode. It is important to note that synchronous communication, while often used and the norm in traditional coaching, may not always be the most effective option. Media richness theory implies that its effectiveness is not guaranteed. The optimal digital tool for asynchronous communication in coaching is contingent upon the unique requirements of the coach and client. Nonetheless, all the previously mentioned tools could improve efficacy in enabling communication between the coach and the client, providing support in between the coaching sessions.

Moreover, incorporating asynchronous communication within the coaching process can produce several benefits, such as time saving for both parties, increasing accessibility for clients who possess constrained schedules, enabling clients to reflect on experiences and queries before responding, and cultivating a more collaborative and supportive partnership between the coach and the client. Passarelli et al. (2020) suggest that such a space where the coach and client are not face-to-face (in person or over a VC) is helpful for reflection for both parties. Such a pause in live communication can also help neutralise the challenge of lack of cues in a virtual setting.

In addition to the asynchronous tools detailed above, the coaches providing one-to-one digital coaching also have a variety of digital tools available for them to enhance the coaching experience and promote imagination, play, and experimentation during their live sessions. Given that this is a rapidly developing space and every month, newer offerings emerge, Table 24.3 categorises these tools around their primary use rather than reference the specific tools.

The current set of digital tools and platforms already present several unique advantages for coaches. These benefits include enhanced accessibility to a broader range of clients, breaking the geographical. Asynchronous tools also help break the time and

Table 24.3 Digital tools and suggested applications

Primary Use of Tools	Application
Screen Sharing	Coaches can use screen-sharing tools to share their screens with clients during live video coaching sessions. This is a helpful way to demonstrate concepts, share stock material, discuss ideas, or provide feedback.
Whiteboarding	Allow coaches and clients to collaborate on ideas in real-time during a live video coaching session. This can be very useful for brainstorming, problem-solving, and planning.
Note taking	Coaches benefit from note-taking tools during live video coaching sessions to help them keep track of progress and avoid missing important details. Using these tools with caution is essential as it may distract the coach from the present moment and shift focus away from the client. It can be seen as a substitute for traditional pen and paper methods.
Time-keeping	With the help of time-keeping tools, coaches can keep track of the duration of their live coaching sessions to ensure precise billing and better productivity.

availability barrier, increasing the pool of available coaches and clients. The implementation of digital tool platforms promotes greater efficiency, as coaches can automate administrative tasks or gain access to research materials. Finally, digital tool platforms can facilitate more effective coaching services by providing real-time feedback or tracking client progress. These are benefits which are available for coaches at the time of writing, but technology is changing quickly, and we anticipate other tools will be available over the coming decade, which may both replace coaches (AI bots) or could be used to supplement the coach (machine learning) or create new coaching environments (VR, MR AR).

For any coach considering incorporating digital tools or asynchronous communication during a live session, it is highly recommended to explore the options available and determine the most suitable ones.

For example, the coaches can charge a higher price for a face-to-face coaching as against one conducted virtually, given that both client and coach will save on travel and logistics costs or the coaching bots and apps can be used in between the coaching sessions when longer and in-person contact is not possible. Also, the digital tools can be helpful for the clients for shorter sessions, and the free options can be available at all times to help the client work out a baseline work which can then be further developed with a human coach.

Table 24.4 (adopted from Bajpai (2023)) suggests one such conceptualisation of the coaching continuum where the digital tools and apps are positioned as supplementary to traditional face-to-face coaching. The table also proposes certain variables that can help determine the appropriateness and choice of the tools.

According to Passmore's (2020) guidance for coaches, it is crucial to recognise and appreciate the value of incorporating a diverse range of tools and techniques in their coaching practices. This is akin to how a doctor relies on a stethoscope or a farrier relies on irons as essential instruments for their respective professions. By acknowledging and utilising different coaching methods, coaches can enhance their abilities to effectively guide and support their clients towards achieving their goals.

While coaching tools can be immensely useful, they are not a panacea for all coaching-related issues. Over-reliance on these tools can impede the development of authentic

Table 24.4 Digital tools as a continuum

Tools >> Variables	Face to Face	Through VC	Coaching Apps & Bots	Free ChatBots
Coaching Fee	$$$$	$$$	$$	Free
Time & Schedule	Longer Sessions 1st session	Shorter Sessions Any Session	Shorter Between F2F and VC Sessions	Instantaneous – is available at all times, even over Smartphones.
Formalisation	Formal & Structured		Informal and On Demand	No Coach is Needed.
Types of Coaching	Ontological Results and Skills		Behavioural Goal Attainment	Base Work to take to Human Coach

connections and a robust working partnership with clients, which are fundamental to achieving successful coaching outcomes. Digital tools are designed to follow prescribed processes and could be compared to a human coach who is in beginner mode. Mature coaches promote much freer-flowing, explorative conversations. Therefore, coaches should exercise caution and balance the use of these tools with other techniques to foster a fruitful coaching relationship with their clients.

Privacy and ethics: justice, equity & inclusion

Given that one-to-one digital coaching allows clients to connect with a coach from anywhere in the world, at any time, coupled with the ever-increasing expanding availability of digital tools and applications, coaches must address critical challenges related to privacy and ethics.

One of the primary concerns in one-to-one digital coaching is related to privacy. Clients must be assured that their personal information and communication with their coach are kept confidential at all stages and at all times. Clients may hesitate to share personal information if they feel their privacy is not respected. Thus, coaches must be transparent in their data collection and storage practices to ensure that their clients' privacy is protected and gives confidence to the client. Given that the clients can now connect from anywhere, it would be prudent to check on how comfortable the client is in the setting and if anyone is able to listen to the video-facilitated conversations on either side. The International Coaching Federation's (ICF) code of ethics states that coaches must "maintain the strictest levels of confidentiality with all client and sponsor information" (ICF, 2021). EMCC takes a similar approach suggesting that right from the contracting stage, coaches should "explain and strive to ensure that the client and sponsor know and fully understand the nature, terms, and conditions of the . . . confidentiality arrangements" (EMCC, 2019). Coaches must also ensure that their digital coaching platforms comply with relevant data protection regulations, such as Europe's General Data Protection Regulation (GDPR).

In addition to privacy concerns, one-to-one digital coaching also raises ethical issues related to justice, equity, and inclusion. The COVID-19 pandemic highlighted inequality in our society and the challenges of digital access (Alvarez Jr, 2021; Azubuike et al., 2021). Furthermore, it is anticipated that the impending economic hardship will exacerbate the issues of digital accessibility, thus highlighting the importance of addressing this issue (Erlandsson et al., 2022). In an equitable world, access to digital coaching resources, including emerging digital tools and applications, should be available to all, regardless of income or social status. While equitable access to digital coaching resources is desirable, the current digital divide presents a significant obstacle to achieving this goal. As such, it is crucial for coaches using digital tools and applications to be mindful of this disparity and to take steps to mitigate its effects.

One approach that coaches can take is to provide alternative resources for individuals who may not have access to digital coaching tools. This may include offering in-person coaching sessions or providing coaching materials in non-digital formats such as printed documents or audio recordings. Additionally, coaches can explore options for providing access to digital tools and applications through partnerships with community organisations or by advocating for policies that promote digital equity.

Furthermore, coaches must consider the potential biases that may be present in the design and development of digital coaching tools and applications. Biases may be introduced through the data used to train algorithms, the design of user interfaces, or the selection of coaching content. AI-powered coaching tools also raise concerns about the equitable and inclusive delivery of coaching services. There is a risk that AI tools could inadvertently perpetuate biases and discrimination. For instance, AI tools may not be able to recognise and respond to cultural nuances, which could lead to a lack of inclusivity. As Baee and colleagues (2020) suggest, AI-powered coaching tools require careful consideration of ethical issues to ensure they do not discriminate against any individual or group. For example, current AI algorithms have a built-in bias towards the reference frequency in selecting books and papers to dateline. This reinforces the marginalisation of minority views and less well-known authors.

To address these concerns, coaches can work to ensure that the digital tools and applications they use are designed with equity and inclusion in mind. This may include advocating for diverse representation in the design and development teams, conducting regular audits of coaching content for potential biases, and implementing feedback mechanisms for users to report any issues they encounter. In summary, while achieving equitable access to digital coaching resources may be a significant challenge, coaches can take steps to mitigate the effects of the digital divide and ensure that their use of digital tools and applications is conducted ethically and equitably. By being mindful of these issues, coaches can work towards providing effective and inclusive coaching services to all individuals, regardless of their digital access or social status.

Reflective questions

1. How can I be more aware of my clients' different needs and preferences regarding communication and interaction to ensure a strong working alliance in a digital setting?
2. How can I remain comfortable using technology and emerging digital tools and applications in my coaching practice to enhance further and strengthen my presence?
3. How do I ensure that digital tools and applications remain in the client's service and do not become an end in itself?

Conclusion

One-to-one digital coaching is a challenging medium that requires coaches to adapt their practices. Coaches can overcome these challenges by being aware of the strengths and limitations of digital coaching while experimenting with suggestions listed in this chapter and practical tips in other chapters of the book. Emerging digital tools and platforms and asynchronous communication can enhance the coaching experience by providing greater accessibility, efficiency, and effectiveness. However, we suggest using them in moderation and balancing them with other communication methods as part of a coaching continuum is likely to be more effective.

The increasing popularity of one-to-one digital coaching presents challenges related to privacy and ethics. Coaches must protect their client's privacy and address justice, equity, and inclusion issues, such as providing alternative resources to those clients with limited digital access and ensuring digital tools are designed with equity in mind.

References

Alvarez Jr, A. V. (2021) 'Rethinking the digital divide in the time of crisis', *Globus Journal of Progressive Education*, 11(1), pp. 26–28.

Aquilina, E. & Strozzi-Heckler, R. (2018) 'Somatic coaching', *Handbook of Coaching Psychology*. Routledge, pp. 229–240.

Azubuike, O. B., Adegboye, O. & Quadri, H. (2021) 'Who gets to learn in a pandemic? Exploring the digital divide in remote learning during the COVID-19 pandemic in Nigeria', *International Journal of Educational Research Open*, 2, pp. 100022.

Baee, S., Rucker, M., Baglione, A., Ameko, M. K. & Barnes, L. (2020) 'A framework for addressing the risks and opportunities in Al-supported virtual health coaches'. *Proceedings of the 14th EAI International Conference on Pervasive Computing Technologies for Healthcare*, pp. 251–254.

Bajpai, B. (2023) *Coaching in the digital age: how is digitalisation influencing executive coaching? A grounded theory exploration*. Thesis dissertation. Oxford Brookes University. Available at: https://radar.brookes.ac.uk/radar/file/61986cc9-46fd-4b45-ab28-45f4fdde0229/1/Bajpai2023CoachingDigitalAge.pdf (Accessed: 5 February, 2023)

Bennett, J. L. & Bush, M. W. (2013) *Coaching for change*. Routledge.

Berry, R. M. (2005) *A comparison of face-to-face and distance coaching practices: The role of the working alliance in problem resolution*. Georgia State University.

Boyce, L. A. & Clutterbuck, D. (2010) E-coaching: Accept it, it's here, and it's evolving!. In Gina Hernez-Broome, Lisa A. Boyce, Allen I. Krau (eds.), *Advancing executive coaching: Setting the course for successful leadership coaching*, pp. 285–315. Wiley Online Library

Charbonneau, M. (2002) Participant self-perception about the cause of behavior change from a program of executive coaching, Unpublished doctoral dissertation, Alliant International University, Los Angeles, CA.

Daft, R. L. and Lengel, R. H. (1986) 'Organizational information requirements, media richness and structural design', *Management Science*, 32(5), pp. 554–571.

De Haan, E. (2011) *Relational coaching: Journeys towards mastering one-to-one learning*. John Wiley & Sons.

EMCC (2019) *Global Code of Ethics*. Available at: https://emccuk.org/common/Uploaded%20files/Global-Code-of-Ethics-v2-2.pdf (Accessed: 24 October 2020)

Erlandsson, A., Forsström, D., Rozental, A. & Werbart, A. (2022) Accessibility at what price? Therapists' experiences of remote psychotherapy with children and adolescents during the COVID-19 pandemic, *Journal of Infant, Child, and Adolescent Psychotherapy*, 21(4), pp. 1–16.

Ghods, N. (2009) *Distance coaching: The relationship between the coach-client relationship, client satisfaction, and coaching outcomes*. Alliant International University, Marshall Goldsmith School of Management.

ICF (2021) *ICF Code of Ethics*. International Coach Federation Available at: https://coachingfederation.org/ethics/code-of-ethics (Accessed: 17 June 2022).

McLaughlin, M. (2013) Less is more: The executive coach's experience of working on the telephone, *International Journal of Evidence Based Coaching & Mentoring*, 7, pp. 1–13.

O'Neill, M. B. (2011) *Executive coaching with backbone and heart: A systems approach to engaging leaders with their challenges*. John Wiley & Sons.

Passarelli, A., Trinh, M. P., Van Oosten, E. B. & Varley, M. (2020) Can you hear me now? The influence of perceived media richness on executive coaching relationships. *Academy of Management Proceedings* (Vol. 2020, No. 1, p. 13211). Briarcliff Manor, NY 10510: Academy of Management.

Passmore, J. (ed.) (2020) *The Coaches' Handbook: The Complete Practitioner Guide for Professional Coaches*. Routledge.

Riemer, K., Stieglitz, S. and Meske, C. (2015) From top to bottom, *Business & Information Systems Engineering*, 57(3), pp. 197–212.

Suler, J. (2004) The online disinhibition effect, *Cyberpsychology & Behavior*, 7(3), pp. 321–326.

UKCP (2021) *UK Council for Psychotherapy Guidelines for Working Online/Remotely(2021)*. London: UK Council for Psychotherapy [PDF] Available at: www.psychotherapy.org.uk/media/jrohoner/ukcp-guidelines-for-working-online-or-remotely-v1-0.pdf (Accessed: 2 April 2023).

Chapter 25

Coaching the team in digital workplaces

Tünde Erdös

Introduction

The use of digital workplaces (teams using digital media to perform joint team-specific tasks in organizations) promises the opportunity to maximize team strengths, address threats more speedily, and increase productivity in a competitive globalised business environment was reported to fail to live up to its promise as early as 1999 (Duarte & Tennant Snyder).

With the continued development of digital team coaching, it is time to address two fundamental questions: What may be critical success factors of team coaching in digital workplaces. What may be unique about digital team coaching?

In answering these questions, we will start by highlighting the essence of co-located and digital teams as well as the purpose of co-located and digital team coaching. Next, we will scope our existing evidence base and experiential wisdom in the latter two. We will then contextualise digital team coaching to point to some key peculiarities of digital team coaching. Finally, we will derive some implications for digital team coaching to inspire practice in the future.

Theory, research and practice

The essence of co-located and digital teams

Almost all organisations employ co-located teams of two or more employees expecting those teams to organise complex work more effectively than individuals working by themselves. But co-located teams often fail to live up to those expectations. That is not surprising if we choose to view teams as an evolving system within systems (Hawkins, 2011). This view recognises that there are multiple factors that shape how teams operate (McComb et al., 2005). That was true even before the era of digitalisation. Some organisational psychologists (e.g., Hackman, 2002) claim that (a) challenges around coordination and motivation typically chip away at the positive effects of collaboration, and (b) even strong and cohesive teams often find themselves competing with other teams. Such competitive dynamics can get in the way of real progress. As a result, Hackman (2002) noted that having teams is often worse than having no team at all, if the essence of teams were to get tasks done efficiently and purposefully within a specific time.

Today, the increased use of digital media at work invites individuals to lean into 'faster-smarter-higher' performance cultures. Yet, some communication scholars (e.g., Berry,

DOI: 10.4324/9781003383741-32

2006) caution that digitally mediated communication is different from co-located team communication, most significantly because the interactions are typically asynchronous instead of synchronous. That challenge prompts organisations to realise that it takes more than talking heads in a virtual space to generate double-the-value-per-minute in organising work.

The purpose of co-located and digital team coaching

Against those developments, co-located team coaching is designed to harness teams' collective and collaborative capability to reflect on their structures, processes, and interactions among the team, between the team of teams, and with all the stakeholders (Clutterbuck, 2020; Hawkins, 2021). In principle, the goal is to remedy for loss of performance and active disengagement (Gallup, June 2022). Yet, even in co-located workplaces, team coaching to support high-performance and generate active engagement is described as so complex "that our assumptions become out of date every time we engage with a new team" (Clutterbuck, 2020, p. 412).

Today, digitalisation does not render virtual teams and team coaching any less complex. Virtual teams tend to view themselves as isolated task-only teams just as much as they do in co-located environments. Therefore, a key challenge in digital team coaching is how to address the issue of isolation and engage team members fully. All the more, as using technology-based communication inherently reduces interactions to two dimensions and engenders limited visibility. That may render the question of how to shift from working on task items to focusing on the genuine reasons why they really need and want to meet even more challenging. The same holds true for how to create a *place to belong* as well as a source of orientation (Hackman, 2002) and learning for teams to re-engage and feel responsible for the whole rather than some individual project outcomes.

Therefore, the purpose of digital team coaching is threefold:

(a) enhance accessibility to coaching – that is to use technological medium – for better connectivity and easier connection between functions and teams in organisations (Hawkins, 2021),
(b) empower each team member to feel psychologically safe (Graves, 2021) and connected with organisational transformation, and
(c) enable an integrated team-of-teams culture through an organisation-centric approach to systematically and collaboratively generate value to all stakeholders (Lawrence, 2021).

Eventually, a purposeful digital team coaching approach has the capacity to facilitate collaborative intelligence in a world that operates through partnerships across organisations.

Evidence in team coaching

There is very little investigation of coaching teams at work to date. The first significant piece of empirical research into team coaching was conducted by Hackman and Wageman (2005). That research made a substantial contribution to what we knew to be valid in team coaching until Graves' (2021) research into the team coaching process. Essentially, Graves (2021) challenges Hackman's and Wageman's (2005) concepts of 'readiness for coaching' and 'best time for interventions' as key considerations when embarking on team coaching describing those as illusionary and aspirational at best. Instead, Graves (2021) claims that what needs to be in place right from the outset in team coaching is the team leader. Additionally, Graves' (2021) findings point to three specific areas when it comes to how team coaches reported team coaching should be delivered: (a) team coaches' level of engagement with the team, (b) the psychological preferences of a team coach, and (c) differences in coach professional development.

However, since Hackman and Wageman's (2005) contribution, academic interest based on rigorous research standards has lagged notably behind practitioner engagement (Traylor et al., 2020). One exception is a randomised control trial (RCT) conducted by Passmore et al. (in press) that shows the power of team coaching as an intervention, comparing team coaching with traditional team development. The study showed the positive effect of team coaching on psychological safety and team cohesion. Apart from that, the growth of interest in team coaching outcomes (Peters & Carr, 2019) shows in an array of models and team coaching manuals, which is largely the result of practical case studies (Traylor et al., 2020). It also shows the surge in team coaching literature by thought leaders in team coaching (Clutterbuck, 2007, 2020; Clutterbuck et al., 2019; Hawkins, 2011, 2021; Leary-Joyce & Lines, 2017; Thornton, 2010, 2019).

Specifically, for the purposes of this chapter, the qualitative study conducted by Graves (2021) offers some initial evidence base around five essential elements that seem to drive the success of team coaching as experienced by team coaches, as follows:

1. *Enactment*: the team coach's capacity to role-model feelings and thoughts in action or ask team members to put feelings and thought into action in the team coaching session as an opportunity to normalise feelings and create psychological safety.
2. *De-facto leadership*: the team coach's tendency to assume the pseudo team leader role due to a perceived vacuum and a lack of strong leadership in the team as an opportunity to clarify levels of involvement and engagement and define clear role-specific responsibilities in the team.
3. *Collusion*: the team coach's strong empathic style and self-knowledge resulting in an overly supportive coaching approach as an opportunity to address the level of helplessness in the team and direct decision-making power back to the team.
4. *Truth*: systematically having each team member voice their individual unblemished truth in one-on-one sessions as an opportunity to build trust.
5. *We-ness*: team coaches gradually losing a sense of distance and objectivity and effectively turning into a team member as an opportunity to sensitise the team to how group contagion can feed exclusion of each other and of other teams in the organisation.

In this chapter, those five essential elements of team coaching serve as a good starting point to reflect what may critically influence digital team coaching.

Research and experiential insights about digital coaching

All the more, as there are even less theories of digital team coaching that have some basis in empirical research, whereby Graves' (2021) research provides some initial evidence base for designing a framework of team coaching in digital workplaces. Prior to Graves' (2021) work, van Dyke (2014) conducted a qualitative study comprising structured interviews with 21 business professionals who participated in a virtual group coaching process over a period of time ranging from 6 months to 4 years. van Dyke's (2014) study identified five major themes as relevant for virtual team coaching (i.e., business education, group process, group facilitation, personal development, virtual community). Most importantly, that study revealed the importance of the role and skill of the coach as facilitator.

So far, some scholarly practitioners (Clutterbuck, 2020; Hawkins, 2021; van Dyke, 2019; Widdowson & Barbour, 2021) have pointed to some of the potential practical challenges of digital team coaching or how digitalisation may support team coaching in organisations.

For instance, Clutterbuck (2020) takes a practical look to the future outlining ways in which to (a) prepare virtual teams for coaching, (b) manage and facilitate virtual team coaching sessions, and (c) account for potential upsides and downsides specific to digital team coaching. Taking a more evidence-based approach, van Dyke (2019) proposes some specific virtual coaching skills and offers skill development tips based on her research (i.e., ability to identify business trend and organisational politics, the laws of group dynamics and cohesion, virtual intelligence, technical astuteness). Taking a different angle, Hawkins (2021) adopts a more strategic approach. Essentially, he calls for using digital platforms to support distributed coaching. By distributed coaching he means deploying AI coaching for routine coach work (e.g., crafting the team purpose, weekly reporting, development conversations) while employing human team coaches for the complex task of coaching what he refers to as the 'team of teams' in organisations. For Hawkins (2021), the overarching purpose of digitally-enabled team coaching is to get away from siloed approaches to working and leading and set the stage for developing distributed leadership (Bolden, 2011) in organisations. Distributed leadership will be achieved when digital team coaching focuses on tapping collaborative intelligence across teams (i.e., WeQ or social connection in teams) to embrace collective responsibility for outcomes for the whole in organisations. Yet again, Widdowson and Barbour (2021) report three different aspects of their experiential wisdom when it comes to digital team coaching. First, they reference digital team coaching from the point of view of a set of 42 tools and techniques originally designed for co-located team coaching to improve collaboration and drive organisational success. Effectively, their experience shows that those tools and techniques also work in digital team coaching environments. However, a meta-analysis in coaching effectiveness (Jones et al., 2016) suggests that models, methods and techniques used in dyadic coaching appear to have little effect on workplace coaching outcomes. Second, while Widdowson and Barbour (2021) state that the set of 42 tools and techniques referenced in their publication are easily transferable to digital team coaching, there are still organisational clients and leaders that seem to be adamant they need to be in a physical room for team coaching to unfold its potential for them. Finally, those authors report that for some global teams that operate digitally all year, team coaching works as a way of making the most use of the time when making a financial commitment to come together in person. Such teams apparently prefer shorter digital sessions to support their team work through coaching.

In the light of the above, we are reminded that digital team coaching science is in its infancy and knowledge is being created on the backs of many experiments that may or may not work as hoped. Therefore,

(a) *staying engaged with and present to* the process of each team's and one's own learning as a digital team coach is what may help build our understanding of what is unique about team coaching in digital workplaces, while

(b) *integrating* our scientific knowledge about the five essential elements that drive successful team coaching (Graves, 2021) into our current practitioner-informed wisdom about digital team coaching may strengthen that understanding, and

(c) *contextualising* our evidence base and experiential wisdom by taking an interdisciplinary approach to digital team coaching may expand our understanding to enable collaborative intelligence in digital teaming.

The latter is all the more important as some business communication scholars (Berry, 2011) found that effective management of virtual teams requires interdisciplinary knowledge and understanding of the fundamental principles of team dynamics regardless of the time, space, and communication differences between virtual and face-to-face work environments.

Interdisciplinary framework of digital team coaching

To that end, we will provide a possible macro-, meso- and micro-level framework of the use of team coaching in digital workplaces (Figure 25.1).

In doing so, we will introduce the theory of amplification in digital environments as a macro-level perspective to then discuss the five potential critical success factors of team

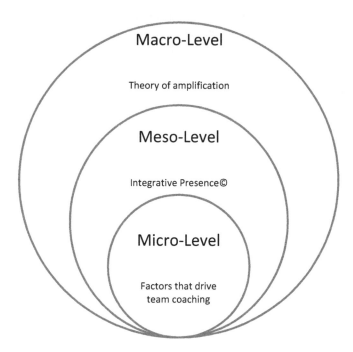

Figure 25.1 The micro-, meso- and macro-level framework of team coaching in digital workplaces.

coaching (Graves, 2021) in digital workplaces from a micro-level perspective. Finally, we will use the lens of coaching presence (Erdös, 2021) from a meso-level perspective as presence is acknowledged to be a key relational skill in dyadic coaching and is, therefore, likely to enable collaborative intelligence (Hawkins, 2021) in digital teaming. The ultimate goal of our interdisciplinary approach is to arrive at an integrated digital team coaching approach that is founded in frameworks that reflect collaborative intelligence.

From a macro-level perspective, we propose the theory of amplification in digital environments (Toyama, 2011) as it was substantially studied in the field of development psychology. It implies that digital technology can only amplify what already exists in terms of (dis)advantage, human intent and capacity, as well as social and economic disparities. Elsewhere, in workplace psychology (White, 2020), the amplification effect of work becoming more intense in digital workplaces is getting recognition too.

For digital team coaching, the theory of amplification may mean that whatever a team embodies – or not – prior to coaching will intensify and expand in the digital workplace. For instance, where team coaching needs to involve working with organisational cultural challenges, enhancing accessibility to coaching is likely to open up patterns that were buried in the more contained co-located team environments. It is as if the shift to working digitally were turning the volume up on those patterns which were always there but in a quieter way. That is why, from a micro-level perspective, we will embed the five essential elements that seem to drive the success of team coaching (Graves, 2021) in the theory of amplification.

Critical success factors of digital team coaching

First, the above example of how organisational cultural patterns will open up in digital environments reflects the potential importance of 'enactment' in digital team coaching. Indeed, Hawkins (2021) asserts that teams will enact what they are carrying for the whole system with the volume turned up in digital team coaching.

Second, we have support for how '*defacto* leadership' may get amplified in digital team coaching where there is a vacuum of decision making in teams (Graves, 2021). Research conducted on virtual action learning in the leadership development field (Caulat, 2022) finds that where leaders learn to lead well virtually, they are better at leading than before. That is because leaders become more anchored in their awareness of being a leader to others. Conversely, where leaders are unaware of how they lead in co-located environments will show more intensely in digital settings.

Third, as goes for 'collusion', we have equal support from Caulat's (2022) work revealing that there are key factors (i.e., the level of leader power; power dynamics in teams; respect; team members' feeling of being listened to; who leaders are; how leaders relate to others and their environment; and what assumptions they hold about trust, power and relationships at work) which determine how well they will work as leaders in digital workplaces. Caulat's (2022) findings echo the theory of amplification: How well a leader supports his team and how helpless a team appears in a digital workplace will be the intensification of the quality of leadership power delivered in face-to-face environments.

Fourth, we see similar effects for 'truth' which is reported to foster trust in team coaching (Graves, 2021). In the leadership development field, leaders speaking the truth as a way of leading authentically is revealed (Caulat, 2013) to be the most critical leadership success factor in the virtual space. Hence, as suggested by the theory of amplification, the level of truth spoken in digital team coaching will be the intensification of the culture of 'speaking up' in teams in their co-located environments (Caulat, 2022).

Fifth, as goes for 'we-ness', we see diverging views when it comes to the effect of amplification on 'we-ness' for digital team coaching. On the one hand, Clutterbuck (2020) discusses his experience that in virtual teams, team members with lower rank and authority may feel more inclined to accept those in the team with higher rank or authority (power distance; Hofstede, 1985). Therefore, he suggests that power distance (i.e., the extent to which team members accept that power is distributed unequally) will reduce in digital workplaces. On the other hand, he also observes that virtual teams in which some team members belong to HQ will experience the opinions coming from HQ as counting more. That may lead to non-HQ team members feeling less inclined to voice their opinions. Clutterbuck's (2020) rich contribution is an indication of how peculiar virtual realities can be, and that it takes more than putting the right technology, the right team, the right processes, and the right recipe books about managing virtual realities in place to ensure effective virtual working (Caulat, 2010).

The theory of amplification as the macro-level perspective and the five essential elements that seem to drive team coaching as the micro-level perspective being discussed, we will now turn our lens to the meso-level perspective. In doing so, we will discuss what the International Coaching Federation (ICF) as the largest international coaching body defines as a key coaching competence in the coach–client relationship: maintaining presence (https://coachingfederation.org/credentials-and-standards/core-competencies). We will do so because the quality of the coach–client relationship has been found to predict coaching effectiveness (e.g., de Haan et al., 2020) beyond tools, methods, and techniques, albeit in complex ways. Most importantly, we will turn our lens to presence as van Dyke (2019) calls on coaches to educate the self in the art and science of 'virtual presence' (p. 313) as a skill that will maintain engagement and interaction during digital team coaching. For van Dyke (2019), virtual presence is about the coaches' capacity to be engaging in sessions.

What may be unique about digital team coaching?

In this article, we draw on our knowledge about movement synchrony (Erdös & Jansen, 2022; Erdös & Ramseyer, 2021) to bring in coaching presence. In that sense, Erdös (2021) describes presence in co-located dyads as a spontaneous emerging process in which the coach's self is a submarine sonar instrument that syncs in and out with moments of emergence as sound pulses. The focus lies on presence being an evolving process integrating the

- self of either coach or client (I-sphere)
- relationship between coach and client (WE-sphere)
- social systems coach and client bring with them (ALL-sphere)
- global legacy of how we are and behave as humans (OMNI-sphere).

That evidence-based lens on presence echoes Scharmer's (2009) experiential wisdom that presence is emerging in the field of the future. Erdös (20211) defines that lens as integrative presence. It implies that there is no such thing as 'a specific presence' and that presence (a) is fluid rather than static, (b) goes beyond the coaches' capacity to 'be' in the 'here and now', and (c) is not about the coach's presence alone. Essentially, Erdös and Ramseyer (2021) claim that it takes the *right dosage* of synchrony integrating all the four spheres of presence (Erdös, 2021) for coaching to be effective. That is quite a big ask. In other words, there can be too much syncing in and out with those spheres, whereby presence can help as well as harm in coaching (Erdös & Ramseyer, 2021). It takes the coaches' capacity to gauge the level of presence that is needed to spontaneously respond to what emerges from the four spheres, which involves

- coping with extremes and bouncing between complication/complexity and chaos/order
- resourcing the self, trusting the process
- decelerating 'accelerating change', accessing presence flexibly rather than as some escapism (i.e., moving from the safety and comfort of some well-known strategy to what is really going on).

As such, presence is viewed as a dynamic coach–client process, which implies that clients' level of presence will impact coaches' level of presence and that clients will be impacted by how coaches are present any given moment. Integrative presence does not marginalise either the client, or the coaching relationship, or the contextual factors of either the coach or the client. Those are all elements that can influence how to *presence* as an 'act of becoming' (Scharmer, 2009) in coaching. Specifically, integrative presence acknowledges that coaches need to allow themselves to be impacted by both the more immediate contextual elements (i.e., teams, organisational life, clients, social connections, coach–client relationship) and the more distant contextual elements (e.g., culture, philosophical views of both coach and client, physical health, etc.). Being impacted is important for getting closer to what is real any given moment. It will occur through the seven senses of hearing, seeing, being touched by, smelling, tasting, sense of balance in space and time, and moving in space.

Integrative presence may be a useful way to start identifying what may be unique in digital team coaching. It is useful as it reflects collaborative intelligence (Hawkins, 2021) in how it integrates the four spheres of presence in coaching. The four examples below, one for each sphere of presence, serve to highlight some of the unique elements of digital team coaching: (1) emotional presence online (I-sphere), (2) being alone in the presence of virtual others (WE-sphere), (3) what to be present to (ALL-sphere), and (4) Zoom fatigue (OMNI-sphere).

Emotional presence online

Emotional presence is confirmed to be an essential and distinct part of the process of learning in virtual maths coaching (Stenbom et al., 2016). The authors found that emotion is present for learners (a) when they discuss online experiences, and (b) as they experience online learning. The authors further reported that emotional response was part of something else: social presence. Social presence is defined as the ability of learners to project themselves as real people through the medium of communication being used. Essentially, they defined emotional presence as the outward expression of relating with learning technology, content, other participants, and the maths coach. Therefore, they urge online instructors to stop

- assuming that learners, generally, are little more than dispassionate thinkers as such assumption would be to miss a fundamental influence on any type of education;
- considering emotion as separate from the learning environment because emotional experiences are the key dynamic in complex social environments where the online learning takes place

and to start acknowledging that both excessive emotion and lack of emotion can harm rational thinking, just as much as excessive presence or lack of presence were found to be harmful in coaching (Erdös & Ramseyer, 2021). Hence, we suggest that emotional presence – on the part of both the virtual team and the coach – will play a unique role in team coaching in digital workplaces. As emotion will emerge as part of the transition to online learning as well as in the learning experience, Stenbom, Hrastinski, and Cleveland-Innes's study (2016) inspires us to be present (a) to teams' social presence, (b) team members' emotional presence in their virtual experience, (c) not just to how to deliver but also how to design, organise, and facilitate digital team coaching, and (d) emotional presence from the point of view of amplification in digital workplaces.

Being alone in the virtual presence of others

Weinberg (2014) invites readers to reflect on the role of technology and communication in virtual groups, as well as the relationships within virtual groups. One such reflection is

- What is the current meaning of the notion 'alone' when we are actually speaking, hearing, seeing others and can be talked to, heard, and seen in turn?

With that question, Weinberg (2014) addresses the fundamental socio-psychological issue of feeling safe in social interactions. We are highlighting that question because feeling safe in the coach–client relationship – on the part of both the client and the coach – is essential in coaching. As we feel safe, we can trust. When we can trust, we can work together. Weinberg's (2014) question prompts us to reflect the extent to which virtual workplaces uniquely affect our and our clients' sense of psychological safety. There are diverging perceptions of how safe or unsafe clients – let alone coaches – feel in virtual coaching settings. Some clients describing themselves as introverts report that it is easier for them to open up in digital coaching than in face-to-face coaching while others assert that they need to relate face to face before moving to a digital platform to continue coaching there. That divergence invites coaches to be present to team members' level of safety as an amplification of already existing levels of safety in team relationships – including coaches' own relationships – outside the digital coaching room. The same holds true for how digital team coaching may give team members or coaches a false sense of security that they are being understood or how team members may be even more vulnerable and exposed in the context of digital workplaces than they are in co-located work environments.

Ultimately, Weinberg's (2014) question invites coaches to gain understanding of the consequences of being alone in the virtual presence of others in digital team coaching as being alone may uniquely impact

- collaborative intelligence and the development of deep connection (a) among the team members, (b) the team with the team coach, and (c) each team member with the team coach
- coaches' capacity to maintain a reasonable balance between involvement and detachment when caught up in the power dynamics of communication processes, which is about 'we-ness' as a potential critical success factor of digital team coaching.

What is it to be present in digital team coaching?

Essentially, Gestalt psychologists (e.g., Stevenson, 2010) hold that we humans perceive the world in such ways that we eliminate complexity and unfamiliarity. That helps us observe reality in its most simplistic form. While eliminating external stimuli helps our mind create meaning, it also means that all that we perceive as regular, similar, and familiar get mentally prioritised over spatial and temporal relations. In that sense, the notion of 'what to be present to' refers to how well digital team coaches manage to constantly gauge what is relevant to be included or excluded in terms of the development of teams (i.e., offshoots of conversations and meaningful words or the meta idea of conversations; looking at what is going on from the future, past, present or cross-cutting temporal events; looking inside or outside of the team and team members). According to Gestalt principles, the goal is to integrate complex awareness processes with context sensitivity to offer observations that are neither fragmented, nor confused, nor confusing. That context sensitivity may be uniquely difficult given the boundary of interacting with virtual teams in two dimensions, most particularly, when

1. organisations require team coaches to work with improvised teams with revolving membership,
2. teams are expected to perform tasks that are not just complex but urgent and entail high consequences, and
3. coaches face the issue that what does not get conceded in the virtual room gets deferred to the virtual corridor, wherever that may be.

Latter may be a useful compass to guide team coaches where digital teams are in terms of inclusion and exclusion in their group development. That again is important because team members' sense of inclusion, equity, and diversity is reported to drive collaboration, productivity, mutual support, and wellbeing (Creary et al., 2021).

'Zoom fatigue'

Bailenson (2021) has argued that digital platforms, such as Zoom, create an unintended consequence: exhaustion. Bailenson (2021) theorises that there are four psychological consequences of spending hours per day on digital platforms: (1) excessive amounts of close-up eye contact leading to social anxiety, (2) seeing oneself constantly in real-time leading to higher self-criticism, (3) digital work dramatically reducing physical mobility resulting in reduced cognitive performance, and (4) higher cognitive load to send and receive interaction signals leading to emotional depletion and social avoidance. Those four consequences are commonly known as 'Zoom fatigue'.

The invisible negative effects of 'Zoom fatigue' (i.e., social anxiety, higher self-criticism, reduced cognitive performance, social depletion, and social avoidance) are uniquely relevant in digital team coaching. The challenge is to integrate 'Zoom fatigue' as an indispensable approach in digital team coaching because digital workplaces are there. We are called to evolve ways to make it work for us just the way we learned to be less awkward with each other using elevators today than we used to be in those times when elevators were introduced as a new technology.

Implications for team coaching in digital workplaces

Digital skill development

Team coaches or those that plan on doing digital team coaching may need to acquire skills in the various technological media that client organisations are using as well as stay up to date on technological innovations including artificial intelligence (i.e., scope of chatbot usage). Additionally, working with 'Zoom fatigue' can help digital team coaches better understand the optimal way to use team coaching in digital workplaces. For instance, the Stanford research team (2021) devised a 15-item questionnaire (Zoom Exhaustion & Fatigue Scale, ZEF; https://stanfordvr.com/zef/) that coaches can share with teams or use for themselves to reduce Zoom fatigue as a stressor by learning to become aware of the signals (i.e., exhaustion, irritation of eyes, social avoidance, emotional depletion or tiredness after videoconferencing). Either way, the key is to stay current to stay relevant.

Virtual intelligence for coaches

Computer-mediated communication requires virtual intelligence (van Dyke, 2019) as the digital age adds layers to how we need to be mindful when relating to others. While there is a range of ways to develop virtual intelligence, we suggest those that emerged from this chapter, as follows:

- be aware that in virtual communication both the presence and absence of verbal and non-verbal cues are amplified, which necessitates differentiated communication efforts to connect and appear approachable virtually (e.g., how much you feel at ease with displaying affection when it comes to effectively creating a safe virtual presence to enable a sense of trust, which in turn, fosters safety; how much are the team and/ or coach prone to distractions, which may stop either of them from picking up new themes and nuances),
- be present to more than just the 'here and now' of every single moment of the coaching session (i.e., learning to apply the four spheres of integrative presence),
- when choosing a certain trajectory of movement and moving along it, pay attention to Graves' (2021) five critical success factors discussed in this chapter. That way you

can consistently check in with the team to demonstrate your partner position with them, which is likely to reduce resistance with the team to the use of the tools offered. Additionally, virtual teams will not withdraw into passive following, which would otherwise lead to loss of ownership of the dialogue by them.

Intentionality in digital team coaching

As we become more and more affluent, we seem to no longer need intentionality: We can go to a supermarket and buy a whole range of different dishes, all of which meet stringent health standards. And yet, whichever dish we may choose, we are most likely to eat it in haste. While our techno-humanism is blessed with how we have more choices than ever before, we are losing our ability to pay attention.

For similar reasons, team coaching is at risk of being overrun by technological solutions designed to improve efficiency. Improving efficiency may reflect financial market forces and organisational desire for continuous economic growth. However, those intents come at the cost of individual compassion, empathy, ambiguity, and doubts. Therefore, coaches may wish to enquire the following:

1. What do we need to really listen to in digital team coaching when teams are focused on performance?
2. How do we take responsibility for shaping the way in which technology is impacting on individuals?

Not surprisingly, Hawkins (2021) calls on digital team coaches to work on establishing the same heart connection that was important already pre-digitalisation. The goal is to arrive at creating psychological safety in virtual teams, which needs to happen if coaches were to deliver purposeful digital team coaching. And, we suggest to take it one step further: We need to open up discussions about how team coaching can contribute to stopping downgrading humans in a world that is all about successfully upgrading our body and brain while we are losing our mind in the process. After all, coaching is about enhancing human performance rather than fixing techno-humanoid output.

Letting go of physical thinking

Moving beyond our slow-to-change models of the world, humanity has reached a moment when we can re-imagine our intersecting spaces and practices of work in ways which can be kinder and more inclusive. In that same moment, teams find it difficult to let go of physical thinking. That is because humans tend to feel disconnected when unable to experience our world through tactile and sensory paths. Hence, we tend to feel cognitively and emotionally volume-ed up in digital settings. Additionally, feeling out run by technology feels threatening as we disconnect: We feel disoriented and a loss of control. We cannot predict things any more. While in the era of pre-digitalisation the space of things limited the amplification of thoughts and feelings, we were also tied to ways of working that carried dynamics of authority and power. Many of us may prefer to move on from that. Therefore, coaching virtual teams may need to include supporting the teams' ability to engage with the digital normal enquiring:

- How do we choose to let go of physical thinking?

Specifically, as teams face being outrun by computer-mediated communication, there is great value in supporting teams with reconnecting and forming levels of connectivity and modes of communication that are balanced out rather than amplified to ensure teams do not feel exhausted, disempowered and exploited, and that they do not find the digital normal exhilarating or disorienting. In effect, that can be achieved by coaches providing increased support in how to (a) realise the potential of members' diverse perspectives, and (b) capitalise on giving status boost to those that may be otherwise overlooked, both to achieve coaching effectiveness and desired team outcomes.

Reflective questions

1. Should team coaches see the digital environment as a last resort for team coaching?
2. What benefits can team coaching offer over physical environments?
3. What other digital tools should team coaches draw upon to enhance their work with teams?

Conclusions

Teams create their realities and control their destinies far more and far sooner than team leaders tend to realise (Hackman, 2002). So do digital teams. As digital team coaching is on the rise, coaches are called to gain understanding of the peculiarities of virtual teams and digital team coaching, as we discussed in this chapter. Our purpose was to offer ways in which to enable collaborative intelligence in organisational life through team coaching beyond single-handed and isolated measures (Hawkins, 2021) in idiosyncratic digital workplaces.

We conclude that coaches will need to adopt a systematic change of mindset and view digital team coaching as virtual reality that is real with virtual appearances: those can be deceiving. Not only will we need to keep learning about digital team coaching through engaging with fields not specific to coaching but we may also need to redefine the coach competencies and skills (Graves, 2021) as well as the success factors of coaching familiar to us today. As part of our critical self-reflexivity (Cunliffe, 2016), practitioners will need to be curious about what it takes to coach virtually from a place that privileges "questioning what we, and others, might be taking for granted – what is being said or not said – and examining the impact this has or might have" (p. 741). Indeed, how well are we serving teams in digital coaching if we expect past competencies and skills to fit the peculiarities of virtual reality – realities – in coaching?

References

Bailenson, J. N. (2021). Nonverbal overload: A theoretical argument for the causes of Zoom fatigue. *Technology, Mind, and Behavior, 2*(1). https://doi.org/10.1037/tmb0000030

Berry, G. R. (2006). Can computer-mediated asynchronous communication improve team processes and decision making? Learning from the management literature. *Journal of Business Communication (1973), 43*(4), 344–366. https://doi.org/10.1177/0021943606292352

Berry, G. R. (2011). Enhancing effectiveness on virtual teams: Understanding why traditional team skills are insufficient. *International Journal of Business Communication, 48*, 186–206. https://doi.org/10.1177/0021943610397270

Bolden, R. (2011). Distributed leadership in organizations: A review of theory and research. *International Journal of Management Review, 13*(3), 251–269. https://doi.org/10.1111/j.1468-2370.2011.00306.x

Caulat, G. (2010). Virtual leadership: rethinking virtual teams. *Ledelse I Dag Danish Leadership Review*, September/October. (Accessed: 6 March 2023).

Caulat, G. (2013). Why authenticity is most critical in the virtual space. In: Ladkin, D., & Spiller, C. (Eds.), *Authentic leadership*. Cheltenham, UK: Edward Elgar Publishing Limited. ISBN: 9-7817-8100-6375.

Caulat, G. (2022). Working well with power in the virtual space. *Action Learning: Research and Practice, 19*(2), 200–208. https://doi.org/10.1080/14767333.2022.2082815

Clutterbuck, D. (2007). *Coaching the team at work*. London, UK: Good News Press. ISBN: 9-7819-0483-8081.

Clutterbuck, D. (2020). *Coaching the team at work: The definite guide to team coaching*. 2nd Ed., Boston, MA: Nicholas Brealey Publishing. ISBN: 9-7815-2935-2320.

Clutterbuck, D., Gannon, J., & Hayes, S., et al. (Eds.). (2019). *The practitioner's handbook of team coaching*. Oxon, New York: Routledge. ISBN: 9-7811-3857-6926.

Creary, S. J., Rothbard, N., & Scruggs, J. (2021). Improving workplace culture through evidence-based diversity, equity and inclusion practices. *PsyArXiv, July 1*. https://doi.org/10.31234/osf.io/8zgt9

Cunliffe, A. L. (2016). "Becoming a critically reflexive practitioner" redux: What does it mean to be reflexive? *Journal of Management Education, 40*(6), 740–746. https://doi.org/10.1177/1052562916668919

de Haan, E., Molyn, J., & Nilsson, V. O. (2020). New findings on the effectiveness of the coaching relationship: Time to think differently about active ingredients? *Consulting Psychology Journal: Practice and Research, 72*(3), 155–167. https://doi.org/10.1037/cpb0000175

Duarte, L. D., & Tennant Snyder, N. (1999). Mastering virtual teams: Strategies, tools, and techniques that succeed. In: Scigliano, J. A. (Ed.). *The Internet of Higher Education, 3*(4), pp. 299–303. San Francisco, CA: Jossey-Bass. ISBN: 0-7879-5589-2W01.

Erdös, T. (2021). *Presence: Understanding the power of the non-verbal relationship*. Milton Keynes, UK: Open University Press. ISBN: 9-7803-3524-9657.

Erdös, T., & Jansen, P. (2022). Movement synchrony over time: What is in the trajectory of dyadic interactions in workplace coaching? *Frontiers in Psychology, 13*, 845394. https://doi.org/10.3389/fpsyg.2022.845394

Erdös, T., & Ramseyer, F. T. (2021). Change process in coaching: Interplay of nonverbal synchrony, working alliance, self-regulation, and goal attainment. *Frontiers in Psychology, 12*, 580351. https://doi.org/10.3389/fpsyg.2021.580351

Gallup (June, 2022). State of the Global Workplace: 2022 Report. Retrieved on 24 February 2023: www.gallup.com/workplace/349484/state-of-the-global-workplace-2022-report.aspx

Graves, G. (2021). What do the experiences of team coaches tell us about the essential elements of team coaching? *International Journal of Evidence Based Coaching and Mentoring, 15*, 229–245. https://doi.org/10.24384/pfh5-b855

Hackman, J. R. (2002). *Leading teams: Setting the stage for great performances*. Boston: Harvard Business School Press. ISBN: 9-7815-7851-3338.

Hackman, J. R., & Wageman, R. (2005). A theory of team coaching. *Academy of Management Review, 30*(2), 269–287. https://doi.org/10.2307/20159119

Hawkins, P. (2011). *Leadership team coaching: Developing collective transformational leadership*. Philadelphia, US: Kogan Page. ISBN: 9-7807-4945-8836.

Hawkins, P. (2021). *Leadership team coaching in practice: Case studies on developing high-performing teams*. 2nd Ed. Philadelphia, US: Kogan Page. ISBN: 9-7813-9869-3777.

Hofstede, G. (1985). The interaction between national and organizational value systems. *Journal of Management Studies, 22,* 347–357. https://doi.org/10.1111/j.1467-6486.1985.tb00001.x.

Jones, R. J., Woods, S. A., & Guillaume, Y. R. F. (2016). The effectiveness of workplace coaching: A meta-analysis of learning and performance outcomes from coaching. *Journal of Occupational and Organizational Psychology, 89*(2), 249–277. https://doi.org/10.1111/joop.12119

Lawrence, P. (2021). Team coaching: Systemic perspectives and their limitations. *Philosophy of Coaching: An International Journal, 6*(1), 52–82. http://dx.doi.org/10.22316/poc/06.1.04

Leary-Joyce, J., & Lines, H. (2017). *Systemic team coaching*. London, UK: Academy of Executive Coaching. ISBN: 9-7809-9307-7227.

McComb, S. A., Green, S. G., & Compton, W. D. (2005). The relationship between team context and the team leader's linking pin quality. In: Turnipseed, D. L. (Ed.), *Handbook of organizational citizenship behavior: A review of 'good soldier' activity in organization*. West Lafayette, IN: Purdue University Press, 328–343.

Passmore, J., Tee, D., & Gold, R. (In Press). Team Coaching using LSP: An RCT study measuring team cohesion and psychological safety.

Peters, J., & Carr, C. (2019). What does 'good' look like? An overview of the research on the effectiveness of team coaching. In: Clutterbuck, D., Gannon, J., Hayes, S., & et al. (Eds.). *The Practitioner's Handbook of Team Coaching*. Oxon, New York, US: Routledge, 89–120.

Scharmer, C. O. (2009). *Theory U: Learning from the future as it emerges*. Oakland, CA: Berrett-Koehler Publishers. ISBN: 9-7816-2656-7986.

Stenbom, S., Hrastinski, S., & Cleveland-Innes, M. (2016). Emotional presence in a relationship of inquiry: The case of one-to-one online math coaching. *Online Learning, 20*(1), 1–16. https://doi.org/10.24059/olj.v20i1.563

Stevenson. H. (2010). Paradox: A gestalt theory of change for organizations. *Gestalt Review, 14*(2), 111–126. https://doi.org/10.5325/gestaltreview.14.2.0111

Thornton, C. (2010). *Group and team coaching: The essential guide*. New York, US: Routledge. ISBN: 9-7802-0385-2385.

Thornton, C. (2019). Beyond the theory of everything: group analysis, conversation and five questions to choose theory in action with teams. In: Clutterbuck, D., Gannon, J., Hayes, S., & et al. (Eds.), *The practitioner's handbook of team coaching*. Oxon, New York, US: Routledge, 210–219.

Toyama, K. (2011). Technology as amplifier in international development. *Proceedings from iConference '11*, New York, US, 75–82.

Traylor, A., Stahr, E., & Salas, E. (2020). Team coaching: Three questions and a look ahead: a systematic literature review. *International Coaching Psychology Review, 15*(2), 54–68.

van Dyke, P. (2014). Virtual group coaching: A curriculum for coaches. *Journal of Psychology and Organizational Culture, 5*(2), 72–86. https://doi.org/10.1002/jpoc.21145

van Dyke, P. (2019). Virtual team coaching. In: Clutterbuck, D., Gannon, J., Hayes, S., & et al. (Eds.), *The practitioner's handbook of team coaching*. Oxon, New York, US: Routledge, 299–320.

Weinberg, H. (2014). *The paradox of internet groups: Alone in the presence of virtual others*. Oxon, New York, US: Routledge. ISBN: 9-7818-5575-8933.

White, D. (2020). *Digital amplification. Why work has become so intense*. https://daveowhite.com/digiamp/ (Accessed: 6 March 2023).

Widdowson, L. & Barbour, P. J. (2021). *Building top-performing teams: A practical guide to team coaching to improve collaboration and drive organizational success*. London, UK: Kogan Page. ISBN: 9-7817-8966-6762.

Part VII

Case studies

Chapter 26

EZRA

Building a platform for a superpower

Nick Goldberg and Jack Prevezer

Introduction

Right from the start, we set out to rethink the reach and potential of professional coaching. We weren't coaches ourselves, but we were (and remain) evangelists for it. Back in 2019, we'd seen first-hand what it could do – improve performance, supercharge careers, and ultimately change lives. By combining this superpower with a user experience as seamless as many of the apps we use daily, we thought, could everyone get this? And what could organisations achieve if everyone *did* get this? These are the questions we set out to answer.

History of EZRA

EZRA was born as an independent start-up within LHH, a part of The Adecco Group, a global leader in talent development and workforce solutions. It's worth mentioning because, looking back, maybe it was the perfect start point. We were backed by a big business – LHH has been coaching executives since the 1970s – but we had free rein to explore our own ideas and talk to HR leaders around the world. And when we did, we realised that the industry faced three issues:

Issue one: accessibility

Time and time again, HR leaders told us that within their organisation, coaching was seen as expensive and admin heavy.

So we started by building technology that challenged these conventions. The organisation didn't need to schedule sessions on someone's behalf; they could book in themselves, beyond the 9–5. HR teams didn't need to shortlist coaches; instead, participants could match with the right person in just a few swipes. And nobody needed to travel to a meeting room; the session could happen on our app – as easily as video calling a friend.

Issue two: transparency

Too often, HR leaders told us, coaching fell into a 'black hole': they sent someone off to meet with a coach. Months passed. Sessions finished. Everyone *seemed* happy enough… but what were the real results? How can you empirically measure changes in behaviour?

DOI: 10.4324/9781003383741-34

To help answer that question, we built EZRA Measure: a behavioural measurement tool with the oversight from Dr. Nigel Guenole of the Institute of Management at Goldsmiths, University of London. With a rigorous peer-reviewed process, our researchers developed a set of standardised assessments to go deeper than sign-up rates or feedback scores.

This means that in every coaching engagement, we're able to measure *real* progress with participants and their managers. How are they tracking against their goals? This arms HR and learning teams with the data they need to prove the return on their coaching investment. For example, we've seen that people are 28% better at prioritising after coaching and 22% better at managing conflict.

Issue three: scalability

In 2019, because of these perceptions (*too much effort, too expensive, too opaque*), coaching was typically reserved for the top 0.5% of an organisation, often the C-suite. As we've mentioned, *we* certainly thought that there was an opportunity to take it further and soon realised that HR teams felt the same. So early on, it was time to put our money where our mouths were. First McDonald's and then Kraft-Heinz called on us to spread coaching to a bigger swathe of their team. (In fact, they each wanted it embedded in development programmes for their future leaders.)

So we created a new model to explain this philosophy: *1:1 development at scale*. We positioned coaching as something for the many, not the few. And we rolled up our sleeves to make it happen for our clients.

The vision for EZRA

We knew the organisational benefits of coaching, and – arguably – so did HR leaders, but what about the business leader holding the budget? Or the executive board at a large organisation? To build the business case for coaching at scale, we've been gathering evidence since day one.

For example, in 2021, we coached over 1,000 retail branch and call centre managers at one of the world's biggest banks. Each manager led teams of 30–40 people. Most had never worked with a coach before.

We tracked the performance of these 1,000 managers using the bank's own productivity measurements – think resolved complaints, customer satisfaction scores, and resolution times. And we compared them to a control group who *hadn't* had coaching. In the first five weeks, the numbers stayed flat; the coached and uncoached groups were on an even keel. At six weeks, we started to see a shift. And by three months, the coached group's performance had skyrocketed by 18% against the control.

At this scale, we're not just talking about personal growth. If a whole company could boost their productivity by 18%? That's *real* organisational change. And although we've made huge progress – coaching used to be for 50 people in a business at a time; with us, it's in the 1000s – we still want to go further. To take our vision of *development at scale* to the 10,000 or 20,000 who make up an entire workforce.

This burning mission is why we launched Focus by EZRA in the summer of 2023 to transform how development at scale could impact 10,000+ individuals in companies. We theorised that organizations spent too much time on traditional workplace development programs that don't lead to measurable results. So we drew on the science of change behavior combined it with the proven power of digital coaching to create Focus – short, sharp, engaging individual development that is supported by topic focused one to one coaching. We believe we have created fast, effective learning, which will become the future of how development is delivered at scale.

So 'organisational transformation' is the real name of the game now. In recent conversations with Dr. Woody Woodward from New York University, we've theorised whether a new kind of coaching is emerging, where coaching doesn't just change people, but entire businesses. We believe that if an organisation wants to turbo-charge their innovation, evolve their culture or improve their bottom line, coaching can help get them there.

And there's a sweet circularity. We started EZRA to take coaching beyond the 0.5%... but now we've shown what it can do, those executives want in on it too. So we built EZRAx, our answer to executive coaching. Top teams now get the same slick user experience and easy scheduling, but they're talking to executive-level coaches who've run business units and helped plenty of people in their position.

The vision for the coaching industry

If we want to take coaching further, then as an industry, it's time to think carefully about the opportunities ahead of us... and the problems posed.

Is coaching for the individual or the organisation?

You probably know that for coaching to work, a coach needs to meet someone where they are: working toward their goals, on their agenda, in their context. The participant owns the process; they drive their own development. It can only happen with trust – they need to know that everything they're saying is in complete confidence. And it needs to feel empowering for the individual (another reason our EZRA tech lets you schedule sessions and set goals yourself).

But... the organisation is paying the bill. As coaching (and investment) expands to cover more people, business needs can't be cut out of the conversation. So if an organisation invests in coaching at scale, does it gain the right to determine the outcomes? To dictate who in their team needs to learn to lead, who needs to shape their career path, and so on?

On one hand, coaching doesn't happen in a vacuum – bringing sessions closer to business objectives can only make organisational contexts clearer and show people how to climb the ladder. But on the other, a rigidly prescribed curriculum won't necessarily create the big psychological shifts needed for organisational change. Which brings us to our next point.

Should coaching supersede training?

As we write in 2023, the L&D industry spends around $370 billion globally on training programmes. Classroom sessions, e-learning modules, video courses – we've all been there. You finish the learning feeling inspired to make a change. Six months later, how much are you actually using?
So we're wondering

- what if *all* company training programmes were delivered through a coaching lens?
- could the accountability and individualisation of coaching make it more likely for change to stick?
- is a new type of coach needed – one who helps someone co-ordinate all their different learning?

Is anything sacred?

Since starting EZRA, we've changed plenty of things that used to seem set in stone: *where* coaching happens, *who* gets it, *how* long it takes. The list goes on. None of this was disruption for disruption's sake – we knew that by changing these things, we could help more people access coaching.

So really, our question is: what's next? In our eyes, even the fundamentals are there to be challenged. Does coaching always have to be person-to-person? In the past year, AI has already begun to transform our industry in ways. We have responded by introducing Cai into the development journey, EZRA's personal development AI assistant to help nudge the coachee along the development journey. We believe in the powerful synergy of AI and the human touch, but might one day human coaches be replaced by machines?

Conclusion

All in all, we see an opportunity for a new model to emerge – one where a coach is at the heart of someone's learning, and coaching is at the heart of every organisation.

In this imagined future, a coach won't just set goals and shape career paths. They'll guide the learner through *all* the elements of their learning: modules, mentoring, the lot. Together, a person and their coach will become like conductors (or co-conductors) of an orchestra, making the most of the learning instruments in front of them.

And of course, we see this multiplied across an organisation – a more coordinated approach to L&D with coaching in the middle. A way to keep everyone engaged; a way to transform businesses for the better.

Chapter 27

CoachHub

Matti Niebelschütz and Yannis Niebelschütz

Introduction

CoachHub was born in 2018 and is now leading the way in the coaching industry to democratising coaching for all career grades. Leveraging technology and the skills of our coach community across all time zones and 80+ languages, we are able to bring coaching within reach of managers from Long Island to Laos.

History of CoachHub

In some ways, it's stunning to realise the company Yannis and I founded on a blank sheet of paper in my brother's living room has now grown to become a global enterprise with more than 400 employees from over 50 nations and with over 3,500 coaches world-wide. But when you think about the problem we solve, all of this momentum seems obvious. CoachHub has set out to democratise coaching, bringing one-on-one, personal coaching to every employee regardless of career level. Organisations around the world have responded to this need because at the heart of every organisation are people—and one thing people have in common is that we're wired for growth. Coaching unlocks the power of this desire for growth that is baked into the very building blocks of our psyches.

My personal discovery of coaching as a key to growth was born out of need. It's not an exaggeration to say that early in my career I was completely overwhelmed. When I became a first-time manager, I was unaware of how to guide my team. I had leadership potential, but I could scarcely manage myself, nevermind the team of people who were relying on me for professional guidance.

Realising I needed more support, I enlisted the help of a coach. Today, coaching has become a critical element in my life. Coaching can make something that seems impossible become a reality. For me, coaching has been helping me with not only career challenges, but those in my personal life as well. Coaching has made me a better version of myself.

But, how did I get from seeing the power of coaching on a personal level to spearheading a global enterprise focused on sharing this potential with employees everywhere? Let's return to that blank sheet of paper in my brother's living room. My brother Yannis and I have always had an inclination toward entrepreneurship. When it came time to begin dreaming up a new venture, we both knew we wanted to spend the next part of our lives building a good business—both commercially successful and something with a noble purpose.

DOI: 10.4324/9781003383741-35

We recognised there was, and will always be, a need for coaching. It has the power to transform people and entire organisations. We also knew there were many companies failing at their current coaching programmes. Some were still relying on outdated strategies—such as in-person seminars or training sessions that are impersonal and logistically challenging to organise. Many of these approaches to coaching invariably end up being annual events, and I knew from personal experience once a year was not enough. People need continuous coaching to succeed.

But coaching has not been an option for everyone. For decades, most corporations have only supported their people with one-off classroom training followed by mandates and expectations with relatively non-existent ongoing support. Complicating matters is the history many corporations have of dictating company-wide changes. Employees are told to create a career pathway programme, pivot to digital, or change the culture, but are not offered support or resources to navigate the impact change has on their jobs and everyday life. Success never comes from doing it this way, because we are individuals. We want to be addressed as individuals, given opportunities and have our needs met. We want the help and support that comes from coaching. We want to reach our full potential.

This combination of revelations and passion led to the inception of CoachHub. We identified four immediate goals:

1. Build a minimum viable product (MVP)
2. Recruit 30 coaches
3. Create coaching value
4. Win our first ten paying clients.

With those humble goals, we were off and running. We did it all ourselves at first, everything from coding to sales calls. I'm proud to say that CoachHub achieved all four of these goals in less than a year, plus expanded from Germany to the United Kingdom, France, and Europe. The second year we added the United States, and the third year Asia Pacific. We are now a global company, but our purpose remains the same: to make coaching accessible for everyone within the workforce. We want to make a difference in people's lives first and foremost.

Vision for the future of CoachHub

As for the future, CoachHub will continue to grow sustainably and expand its product offer, reaching more people around the world. We will not only keep pace with the coaching industry as it continues to experience rapid growth but also pave the way for new uses of technology in this space.

According to the International Coaching Federation, in 2021, the coaching industry was the second fastest growing sector in the world. Forbes magazine forecasted in 2022 the coaching industry would grow at a compound annual growth rate of 7.6%.

I believe several factors are driving this growth:

- Coaching helps organisations develop diverse teams by challenging employees to become more aware of their own biases
- Coaching enables employees to develop crucial conflict management skills

- Coaching offers support to employees at all levels of the organisation during times of change and uncertainty
- Coaching improves employee engagement, decreasing attrition.

Vision for the future of coaching

The coaching industry is also undergoing transformation of its own. There is industry talk of shifts to artificial intelligence (AI) or virtual reality. While AI can be a helpful tool when matching a coachee to a coach or suggesting further learning content to complement the coaching journey, it isn't yet meeting the core human need to have person-to-person interactions. Coaching is built on people relations. It has and always will be about a relationship between a coach and a coachee. This is what makes it so powerful. You're not talking to a robot, you are speaking to and listening to a real person.

That's not to say technology won't improve the coaching experience—in fact, it already has. In 2023, we launched AIMY™, the first conversational AI coach, as a non-commercial pilot project. With a vision to push the boundaries of technology and disrupt the industry, AIMY™ had the ability to conduct simple, prompted coaching conversations, to recognize language, context, written communication, and idiomatic expressions. The feedback on this project was incredibly enriching and responded to our objective—to provoke curiosity and to start a conversation on the applicability and feasibility of AI in coaching. Insights from AIMY™ and research from our Innovation Lab empower us to continue building digital products that integrate AI for an enhanced coaching journey.

I believe new technologies such as AI will be leveraged to make our platform experience increasingly better for coaches, coachees, and HR managers alike. Coaches shouldn't have to bother with all the clerical aspects of the work such as scheduling, invoicing, or following up. Automation will become better at supporting their experience so our coaches can focus on what they love—helping people become their best selves. For coachees, our end users, any new technology needs to contribute directly to a more seamless digital experience and to even more personalized learning opportunities. To our customers, our promise remains to deliver people development that is more impactful, more accurately measurable, and more aligned with their business goals.

More and more I see coaching evolving to be available at all career levels. Technological innovation, including artificial intelligence, can be the driver for this evolution. In an ideal scenario, coaches could interact with a new employee starting on their first day, or at important phases of their employee journey such as before, during, and after maternity leave. In the future, the coaching process will also start earlier in people's lives. It will begin during college or prior to a college graduate starting their first job. Coaching will become part of people's entire careers and lives helping them overcome challenges and reach their dreams.

Coaching will also play a more significant role during periods of change and transition within an organisation. As more corporations undergo digital and sustainable transformation, coaching will help entire workforces navigate changing roles, hierarchies, and business goals.

As companies continue to shift their perception of learning and development, we'll see a greater amount of resources committed to digital coaching. The coaching industry is moving in the right direction to support this growing need. Organisations, leaders, managers, and individuals realise that coaching plays a key role in achieving success.

For organisations, the benefits are obvious—I can say that with confidence because CoachHub is the ultimate testing ground. We provide all of our employees with personalised, one-on-one coaching beginning on their first day. In 2022, we quadrupled our headcount, which is an enormous undertaking. No organisation could digest such a considerable growth in head count if it weren't for coaching. Relying on our own product is one of our *not-so-secret* competitive advantages.

Conclusion

CoachHub is now a global category leader in coaching around the world. We are accomplishing what we set out to do—making people's lives better, transforming people and organisations, and building the future of people development. I'm a firm believer that if you have a dream, you should follow it and not change your plans when you come across a challenge. That blank sheet of paper is now full of dreams like this—dreams that we're actively working to turn into reality.

CoachHub is ready for the challenges ahead and looking forward to making a difference in more people's lives. There are already plans underway to continue adding more product features, and increasing our pool of coaches. I look forward to the day when coaching becomes an integrated part of every workplace because I know that we're not just changing the lives of the people we are coaching. Coaching has a multiplying effect; we are also changing the lives of their families, their co-workers, and team members in their organisations.

Chapter 28

Coaching.com

Alex Pascal

Introduction

As the coaching profession evolves and expands, it has an opportunity to leverage technology to do the heavy lifting associated with the management and measurement of coaching services, freeing coaches to do what they do best: unlock the unique potential of humans and help them win. As the role of technological assistance grows in every aspect of our lives, including the explosion of AI in the marketplace, the presence of technology in supporting the delivery of coaching services will only increase—helping to increase the scale, the impact, and the efficiency of coaching.

History of Coaching.com

Coaching.com was originally founded as CoachLogix in 2012 by Alex Pascal, an organisational psychologist with extensive experience in the field of executive coaching. The initial vision for the company was to provide an integrated Software as a Service SaaS solution for the coaching industry—one that would provide an operating platform for independent coaches, coaching providers, and enterprise organisations. At that time, the use of technology in coaching was very limited. There were a few software solutions for independent coaches, but these were primarily aimed at life coaches and provided very basic functionality. A number of coaching providers had developed their own technology solutions to support their operations (e.g., CoachSource and Cambria), and were marketing these solutions to their enterprise clients. On the enterprise side, coaching practice leaders typically managed internal and external independent coaches using multiple spreadsheets. In some cases, they also had access to their coaching vendors' systems in order to track the engagements purchased and managed through those vendors. The vendor-led software solutions were rudimentary and did not integrate with each other. These initial software solutions provided some basic advantages over spreadsheets, but did not add value to the coach–coachee relationship, as they were primarily used to track key milestones throughout the coaching process. Some enterprises had also developed their own internal tools to manage coaching initiatives and have access to basic reporting.

The CoachLogix platform was the first of its kind, offering three distinct advantages. First, it enabled coaches to manage all of their clients using a single portal. Second, it enabled coaching providers to streamline their operations without having to invest heavily in developing their own technology solutions. And third, for enterprises, it provided a neutral platform that solved the problem inherent in earlier coaching vendor-led solutions,

DOI: 10.4324/9781003383741-36

which often required a company to use their competitors' platform to service the needs of a shared enterprise client.

The use of technology in coaching began accelerating during the 2010s. The CoachLogix platform continued to evolve and provide a wider range of functionality aimed at managing and scaling coaching. Features such as coach matching, session scheduling, goal planning, advanced reporting and analytics, and videoconferencing became more important. Moving well beyond simply replacing spreadsheets, platforms were now productising the coaching experience—supporting coaches and coachees throughout the coaching process and measuring the impact and ROI of coaching programmes.

CoachLogix rebranded as Coaching.com in January of 2021. In September of that year, Coaching.com completed the acquisition of the WBECS Group, the company behind the largest virtual event in the coaching world—the WBECS Summit, which attracts more than 30k coaches every year. In addition to the Summit, WBECS was known for partnering with thought leaders to create some of the best programmes for coaches to learn new and cutting-edge methodologies to grow as coaches and enable better outcomes for their clients. The synergies with WBECS enabled Coaching.com to provide buyers of coaching with access to certified coaches, and connect coaches to a centralised marketplace.

Vision for the future of coaching

Coaching has grown from a relatively unknown cottage industry into a widely recognised approach to support human and organisational development. Not only has the demand for coaching increased, but the supply of qualified coaches has also been steadily on the rise. While technology used to be a nice-to-have aspect of running a coaching practice, it has increasingly become a must-have resource for coaches, coaching providers, and coaching practice leaders to scale delivery. The global pandemic accelerated the use of technology to deliver coaching services virtually. All processes related to managing a coaching programme or practice—coach matching, session scheduling, integrated video conferencing, reporting, and analytics—can be performed with technology. The use of AI in coaching holds tremendous promise to improve access to coaching and augment coaching effectiveness.

While tech-supported coaching vendors offer greater efficiency for the core elements of coaching practice—contract independent coaches, offer a development model, ensure quality control, and sell packaged coaching offerings to organisations or individual consumers)—technology has also enabled new business models to emerge and become increasingly relevant. The tech-coaching model is differentiated by a strong focus on the coach and coachee experience, as well as the use of a subscription model to sell large-scale coaching programmes in organisations.

These emergent models have enabled coaching to scale. Coaching is now available to an increasing number of people who previously did not have access to a coach—a very positive trend. Coaching also has increased visibility now as an approach that can help organisations improve the performance, development, and wellbeing of their employees. There are, however, inherent challenges involved in scaling a high-touch professional service such as coaching. Pundits and practitioners alike have raised concerns about a race to the bottom in terms of the fees that coaches receive for their services.

It is clear that the future of coaching is intertwined with the use of technology, which can be seen as both alarming and exciting. The alarmists observe that technology is a powerful force that needs to be used and directed properly. Many technologies that have promised to bring us closer together have had the opposite effect. And the industry will need to address issues related to privacy and confidentiality clearly and overtly, to maintain the foundational pillars of the fabric of the coach–coachee relationship. The more optimistic and exciting point of view is that the use of technology in coaching will enable more efficiency in the way coaching is managed, making it increasingly more scalable. It will also lead to the development of AI-powered tools that will, for example, enable coaches to receive immediate feedback on how to improve client outcomes based on millions of data points.

Vision for the future of coaching on the platform

Our vision at Coaching.com is to harness the power of coaching to activate human potential worldwide. We do so by focusing on both technology and coach development. Our technology platform provides coaches, coaching companies, and enterprises with the tools they need to manage and scale all operational aspects of their coaching practice. Growing our user base will increase the network effects inherent in our open platform model. Inefficiencies inherently arise when external independent coaches use different platforms for every coaching company they work with and every enterprise organisation they serve. The more coaches, coaching companies, and enterprises use our technology, the greater the efficiencies generated by providing a standardised approach to manage coaching. As a platform, we believe that neutrality is a key differentiator. Neutrality, in the context of a platform like Coaching.com, means that we do not sell coaching. We enable it.

Technology has become more central to the management and delivery of coaching. Enterprises looking to purchase coaching services include a number of technology requirements they ask of vendors in order to purchase coaching services from them. Virtually every Request for Proposal RFP for coaching services has a strong focus on the technology that will be used to manage the contract. What this means for coaching companies is that they need to make a decision about whether to build their own technology to address the demands and expectations of clients, or partner with another company that can provide the technology to meet those needs. Our platform enables any coaching company to manage their business in a platform that meets the standards and expectations of the customers they serve, centralising access while providing diversity in the coaching offered.

At Coaching.com, we believe that coaching vendors should be differentiated based on the quality of their coaching services, and not their technology. Our technology enables coaches to do what they do best, while providing coaching clients with access to a diverse array of seasoned coaches representing a wide variety of coaching philosophies and methodologies.

Conclusion

Coaching.com exists to provide a neutral platform that simplifies the delivery of coaching services, in order to expand the scope and impact of coaching in the world.

Organisations and people do not seek coaching because they want to spend their time navigating its logistics and technical requirements. Coaches do not go into the field because they want to become purveyors of technology. The role of technology in coaching is to make it easier for great coaches to provide great coaching, wherever and whenever people need it.

Chapter 29

Sounding Board

Lori Mazan and Christine Tao

Introduction

Sounding Board has grown and developed rapidly and is now a digital coaching business which is part of a wider revolution of the coaching industry. In this chapter we share our journey and vision.

History of Sounding Board

Sounding Board was founded by a 25 year Executive Coach, Lori Mazan, and her coaching client, Christine Tao (former SVP at Tapjoy). Our aim was to bring executive style leadership coaching to all leaders in an organisation. Sounding Board began when Christine told Lori, "The best professional development I have experienced was executive coaching and I want to bring that to many more people. I wasn't eligible for coaching at YouTube because I was not at an executive level. But I believe all leaders should have access to this type of development." This resonated with Lori because she had repeatedly heard from her executive coaching clients that they wished they had access to coaching much earlier in their careers. They partnered as two women founders to bring executive coaching out of the C-suite and democratise it for access by all leaders.

Lori and Christine were careful not to commoditise coaching. This can easily happen when increased access requires lowered pricing and lower fees for coaches. Instead they developed robust software to scale coaching access and they took an unconventional approach. While other players in the digital coaching industry offered multiple varieties of coaching, Sounding Board choose to focus on only 'leadership coaching'. Being specialised creates increased quality and focus for both coaches and customers.

Sounding Board also chose to create a small network of highly engaged coaches instead of a large network where many coaches only have a couple of engagements a year. Competitors boast 3000–5000 member coach networks. In contrast Sounding Board's vision was for a smaller community of highly engaged coaches. As a result Sounding Board coaches consistently have an average of 15 or more Sounding Board coachees. This approach creates coaching delivery that is more consistent across the customer organisation while ensuring that Sounding Board coaches have the support of an intimate community of colleagues. The outcome is that Sounding Board coaching utilisation rates are higher than most in the digital coaching industry, and have an equally high Net Promoter Score of 94 (data 2022). Despite managing a smaller coach community, the team have not experienced problems with their capacity to staff coaching engagements, but as they

DOI: 10.4324/9781003383741-37

grow the aim is to maintain high utilisation rates and thus a proportionally smaller pool of more engaged coaches than other providers.

Lastly, as a business run by a coach, Sounding Board recognises the importance of its coach community. Lori, a certified coach since 1994, placed coaches at the centre of the operation. As a result, Sounding Board coaches are paid at higher rates than competitors, they benefit from post-certification development and are offered stock options, tangibly acknowledging the impact coaches have for customers as well as the success of Sounding Board.

Vision for the future of coaching

The coaching industry continues to transform itself. This is unlikely to stop during the 2020s or 2030s. We believe coaching will expand as the key approach for developing leaders in the future. It is individualised, personalised development that results in accelerated growth of leaders and increased leadership impact for the organisation. Sounding Board, as a digital provider, offering accessible coaching for leaders, as well as coaching and mentoring management software, aims to be at the forefront of this leadership development revolution.

Conclusion

In this chapter we have shared a little of our vision and what makes Sounding Board distinctive in a field of many 'me too' organisations. By paying attention to the quality and needs of our coaches, we are able to pay attention to the needs of our clients, helping them revolutionize leader development.

Chapter 30

PocketConfidant AI

Olivier Malafronte

Introduction

While the first 'automated psychologists' have existed since the Weizenbaum 1960s, it took decades of research to create AI coaching tools capable of improving the coaching practice and enable more people to access coaching. Developing innovative technologies can be a long and fastidious journey but when driven by a powerful vision, the journey brings both insightful experiences and positive outcomes. PocketConfidant AI (Burnett and Malafronte, 2017) is one of the AI coaching pioneers striving for the democratisation and scalability of coaching to empower human beings and to make our world a better place by enhancing reflection, emotional intelligence and human competence.

History of the organisation

It is 2015, Olivier was doing his first coaching certification when emerged a vision where AI enables the democratisation and scalability of coaching in the world. Olivier searched for and found a CTO co-founder, Nikita, and with Isla, a certified coach, the three of them created PocketConfidant AI in 2016. It was a short journey to the launch of the first product in 2017. Between 2017 and 2019 the startup worked with different clients to test the waters, from the HR team in a large consulting group to universities and coaches themselves. In 2018 they went through an acceleration programme in the US and collaborated with a large organisation which focused on training and development. The subsequent partnership was a step change in scale. The following 12 months provided the opportunity to develop their technology.

Then, in 2020, things got difficult. Changes in senior management within their customer and the emergence of Covid-19 in Spring 2020 changed all of this. The product infrastructure was costly and, as a result, the founders changed direction and started to test a new coaching technology. However, things didn't get easy. A new partnership led to significant delays, and finally never launched due to clients' management failure, causing the startup members to end this project and search for other work activities and turn the page.

However, passionate and thriving for seeing his vision come true, Olivier engaged in a PhD in coaching and AI for the development of leaders, and eventually launched a new startup in 2024, leveraging the emergence of Generative AI and the scientific literature on coaching, AI and leadership development.

DOI: 10.4324/9781003383741-38

The history of PocketConfidant AI reveals the challenges of the start-up world, of changing technologies, lost and found partnerships and how a constant focus on a vision can carry a business forward even during difficult times. Although pioneers may start early, or encounter 'near death experiences' (as often called in startup slang), what we can learn is that vision and passion always suffice to restart an engine.

Vision for the future of coaching

The progress of emerging technologies has empowered and transformed the coaching practice overall and how coaching is being deployed and used in organisations and with customers.

Mobile devices and the Internet of Things (IoT) enabled immediate access to human coaches and coaching programmes (e.g., coaching protocols and exercises etc.) on a variety of devices such as home speakers, smart watches, tablets, virtual and augmented reality screens and lenses, holograms, etc. Blockchain can also enable coaching transactions, certifications and outcomes to be tracked, stored, secured, and transparent which improves the overall measurement and tracking of coaching processes and programmes from individual or organisational clients as well as from practitioners. Artificial Intelligence has obviously provided the major leap forward in the coaching practice by enabling coaching offerings to be personalised and adapted to individual, collective, or organisational levels. Today, AI Coaching is used widely in all sizes of organisations and is used as a true organisational transformation tool thanks to AI's capabilities to analyse data at all levels, reveal and predict behaviours patterns from constantly evolving employees' competencies to organisations' short-term and long-term goals.

Finally, AI Coaching has transformed management by integrating a deliberate reflective practice at all levels of the organisation to millions of leaders and managers. This massive change in how management is done in organisations impacted the entire education system, bringing schools and universities to provide coaching from the youngest age to develop students' social learning capabilities and resilience.

More specifically about AI, we, AI Coaching entrepreneurs and early adopters, had always seen AI Coaching as a good transformation for the overall coaching practice. AI enables more people to understand what coaching is and practice it to learn from individual or collective experiences; it pushes human coaches to further develop their unique human added-value, and it enables the creation of new coaching tools and formats to help organisations extend their coaching offering and expand the way they support people through change and learning in the world, no matter their time zone, geography, ethnicity, or personality. We understood that AI has the power to share power and empower individuals at all levels of a system or an organisation by enabling everyone to access and practice coaching according to its most ethical and professional principles: individual-led and self-directed, learning, active listening, and the use of open questioning support the coaching client's learning mechanisms and favour the generation of the client's own feedback and insight. While coaching was still suffering from power relations and lack of neutrality before 2022 and earlier, AI has augmented coaching by enabling individuals to engage in coaching from their own decision, time, budget, and without the request of being coached from their organisation or their management with tripartite agreements that often blocked the neutrality of the coach and the potential to flourish of the client. With the penetration of AI in the coaching practice, we now benefit from autonomous coaching agents that automate coaching techniques with adaptation capabilities that enable each individual to practice coaching from their own situation and personality. An Organisations' leaders and technology developers can now use coaching APIs to integrate various coaching features in symbiose to more traditional digital tools and coaching processes. Human coaches can more actively follow their clients through time at a fraction of the cost that it was in the past thanks to asynchronous automated coaching notifications (emails, nudges, etc.) that enable organisations to enjoy more reflexive and mindful communications between individuals. Organisations and human coaches also keep improving their coaching practice with tools that help coaches to observe and correct their behaviours in the flow of coaching. Leaders and managers can now benefit from prompts and coaching reflections in the flow of their work in a ubiquitous manner thanks to the diversity of devices, in between meetings or during their travelling time to maintain their regulating practice as they handle uncertainty and ambiguity.

Vision for the future of coaching on the product

My vision for the future of coaching is that AI breaks coaching into different coaching formats, such as real-time agents that enable short and immediate added-value interactions, emails, notifications and nudges allowing powerful asynchronous self-coaching reflections and inexpensive scalability of coaching within organisations or communities, APIs enabling platforms to integrate and develop a large variety of coaching features to keep adapting to coaching clients' situations and personalities, while integrating human coaches in the process in ways that augment human coaches' competencies.

User-friendly interfaces such as chatbots, avatars, voice assistants, and holograms all offer useful coaching interactions that improve performance through in-the-moment reflective activities. Individuals (leaders, managers, employees, students, professionals) can shift mindsets, regulate their emotions, and adjust their representations when in complex situations at a much more accessible cost than in the past. Other interfaces such as APIs enable existing platforms to acquire coaching 'tech skills' as Josh Bersin was mentioning in 2021 that were not available earlier on. For instance, a recruitment assessment test using psychometry can now offer individual coaches follow-up reflective interactions that improve clients' engagement and enable valuable long-term relations while enabling the production of useful data to keep monitoring the development of specific skills, attitudes, or behaviours, and predict performance levels. In the end, human coaches have increased their human coaching capabilities to provide what technologies doesn't provide (e.g., human warmth, human experience or human sensitiveness) and coaching consumers and buyers benefit from established standards. Obviously, AI coaching is still learning from all human and organisational experiences and keeps developing towards the goal of providing human beings with greater and greater inquiry, mirroring effects, learning, and development outcomes. Such technological developments contribute to human competence and performance overall and represent a unique path to improving human intelligence. In conclusion, AI coaching is of real support to helping humans solve important problems (social, economic, environmental), with critical thinking and ethical judgments.

Conclusion

At PocketConfidant AI we often asked the question "what if AI was the greatest mirror of humanity", while at Rypple.ai we asked the question "what if AI enabled coaching's rippling effect at scale?" When observing how human beings develop, AI offers the potential to know us better than we know ourselves, by sharing these insights to deepen our self-awareness. Technology has changed the face of every other industry in history. And so AI is doing the same with coaching. We believe AI coaching can help enhance human self-awareness and human competencies at large, and can be a transformative and valuable tool for our society overall.

References

Burnett, N., & Malafronte, O. (2017). The democratisation of coaching – Artificial Intelligence (AI) Coaching. *Australian Educational Leader*, 39(4), 44–46. https://search.informit.org/doi/10.3316/informit.357168184083898

Weizenbaum, J. (1960). *Communications of the ACM*, 9(1), 36–45. https://doi.org/10.1145/365153.365168

Chapter 31

Rocky AI

Harry Novic

Introduction

At a time when regular one-to-one coaching remains largely restricted to a privileged minority due to its cost, despite a growth of digital coaching platforms that provide extended access, coaching remains an expensive intervention. How can coaching become democratised, offering the benefits of coaching for personal and professional success at any time and in any place, without the need to schedule an appointment? For some clients self-disclosure can be tough due to the personal nature of the topic. How can a personalized coaching process be supported with intelligent software on scale? AI coaching technologies can resolve these challenges: a coaching conversation when it's needed, at a price point millions can afford and which is completely anonymous.

History of Rocky AI

Rocky AI was born in 2019, based on the belief there was a gap in the market for AI-powered coaching for those who usually would not have access to a personal coach. This was the time when Amazon Alexa and Apple Siri were gaining popularity, though Harry felt that there was so much more that this technology could offer.

At the time, Harry occupied a senior position in the corporate world and part of his remit was to develop younger managers into future leaders. This meant training them in a vast array of soft skills, which led to the realisation that no matter how impactful the training was in the short-term, excitement, motivation, and the desire to implement said training quickly dwindled. Organisations were dedicating significant amounts of their budget to training, which was a short-term fix at best. He contemplated how he could truly embed this training, making its benefits both tangible and long-lasting.

This is when Harry started to imagine creating an AI coach which could allow all professionals – regardless of their seniority – to develop their soft skills for personal and professional success. This would mean that with or without sporadic training sessions, professionals could delve deeply into the soft skills that determine success by being coached and mentored daily to overcome the hurdle of continuous learning, while slowly but surely rewiring the brain to think empowering thoughts, feel empowered emotions, and take inspired action. This would also signal the true democratisation of coaching since its reach could extend way beyond the corporate world.

Since the inception of Rocky AI, the vision has been to make coaching accessible to all. Each of its features has evolved in parallel to the understanding of what an AI coach

DOI: 10.4324/9781003383741-39

can and should offer to work either alongside – or in place of – a human coach. While the experience of an AI coach is very different, what remains the same is its ability to ask the powerful questions which can change a person's thoughts, feeling and actions, rewiring their brain one question at a time. The daily micro-coaching sessions are exactly that – daily and micro. This makes coaching fun, convenient, and available at any time and in any place.

In 2022 Rocky AI created Rocky for Coaches, and in 2024 the Rocky.ai White Label Solution. This allows companies, leaders and coaches to set up their custom in-house AI coach and monitor the personal and professional development of their employees, coach–clients, and other coachees. An interactive dashboard highlights the current mindset, personalised growth path and tangible goals of each user, so that a coach or manager can encourage, support, and inspire where necessary. The team at Rocky AI are excited to move forward and continually enhance this special app which makes the magic of coaching accessible to everyone.

Vision for the future of coaching

The future of coaching should be built upon the premise that humans have an innate desire for personal and professional growth. The more accessible their growth path is for them, the better. Studies into neuroplasticity show that through repetition and practice, the brain can be rewired to strengthen neural connections, making knowledge more accessible and skills more automatic. Through an innovative mix of positive psychology, coaching, and AI, Rocky's own mission is to empower people to exponential levels of success through this regular retraining of the brain.

An AI coach will facilitate a positive thought-emotion-behaviour cycle to lead to lasting personal development change with positive outcomes. AI coaching is perfectly placed to offer these regular micro-coaching sessions, checking in with people once or twice a day to ensure commitment to creating positive habits, accountability to goals, and personal and professional progress made.

AI coaching will assess an individual's current needs, clarify their future goals, and create a compelling customised growth path within seconds. This will help coachees to overcome daily challenges, and to develop goals to step out of the comfort zone, cultivate a Growth Mindset and reach the personal and professional success they aspire to.

Just like in one-to-one coaching sessions, an AI coach will be led by the coachee. Psychology shows that one of the prerequisites to optimal human motivation is autonomy, so the coachee will control the direction of the dialogue and the AI coach will be willing and able to explore every subject. Since over time AI can be trained in every subject, nothing will be off limits. That being said, clever programming will mean that the AI coach can powerfully hold the space for the coachee to explore the most pertinent issues of the day, all the while keeping in mind the goals and selected growth path of the coachee and regularly offering them the chance to return to that. This is the way our AI coach at Rocky works.

When considering the depth and breadth of subjects that a coachee may wish to explore, AI coaching may focus on the so-called 'soft skills'. In an increasingly automated world, what differentiates the success of one professional from another will be the quality of their soft skills. Since the cultivation of soft skills requires a level of deep introspection, AI coaching must allow people this psychologically safe space to understand their thoughts, feelings, and actions. AI coaching in particular can offer this space, and Rocky does so by asking its users a series of thought-provoking questions to help them think, feel and act in empowering ways that lead to success. In absolute anonymity, the user can express their thoughts. This expression leads to a deeper understanding, which in turn helps a person find a solution or find peace of mind.

AI coaching will also see attention paid to the reskilling or upskilling of a population that extends beyond the typical realm of executive coaching. This means that university students, jobseekers, and early-stage professionals will reap the immense benefits of coaching by having access to this service at an accessible price. The democratisation of coaching will bring a certain levelling up of skill sets, offering more people the clarity, courage, and confidence to seek or create the personal and professional opportunities they deserve.

In the future, AI coaching will be an integral part of the learning process in both education and corporate settings. This means that once training has been delivered, AI coaches will be able to inspire, support, and reinforce further learning and deeper reflection on the content. This will result in training and education having a greater long-term impact and being more personal, more practical and more applicable for the student or employee. Our own AI chatbot currently delivers the educational content of a wide range of corporate and education partners. It does so through powerful coaching questions, thought-provoking articles, and inspirational tips, leading us to believe that the future of coaching will see AI coaching that is complemented by educational content and virtual mentoring. This mentoring will take the form of sharing pieces of psychology within the coaching conversation to catalyse deeper reflection. It will not tell the coachee what to do, but rather will share salient pieces of research which may help the coachee think, feel and act in ways that are conducive to personal and professional success.

Vision for the future of coaching on the Rocky.ai platform

At Rocky AI, our vision for the future of coaching is one in which the opportunity to self-actualise is a democratic one. We believe that people at every single life stage and of every personal and professional background can and should reap the benefits that exploration brings.

Since life rarely offers a place for human beings to explore their thoughts, feelings and actions, Rocky's vision is to provide this psychologically safe and nurturing space. Rocky will guide this exploration by taking people on a deeply introspective journey to discover their strengths, talents and passions, uncover their self-limiting beliefs and smash through setbacks. Ultimately, Rocky's vision to help retrain its user's brain to overcome the negativity bias, focus on their strengths, and set and get goals which take them to their ideal future selves. By assessing where a user currently is and asking them to define where they want to be, Rocky is then able to create a customised soft skill growth path to help the user bridge the gap between the two. Rocky's future vision is to train the technology to do this in an ever speedier and more sensitive way.

Rocky's ultimate future vision is to empower the user by increasing their self-awareness, motivation, and discipline. Through this heightened clarity of self, the user is well-positioned to set self-concordant goals. With this crystal clarity, it's easier for the user to find the courage and confidence to take action. It's very difficult for a person to take their next step if they don't have a compelling future vision in mind. We therefore envisage the future of coaching on Rocky to be a streamlined process which allows a person to onboard, assess their current situation, create a future vision, set specific goals, co-create their soft skill growth path, and monitor their progress and wellbeing on a regular basis.

Since all growth is incremental – and the creation and implementation of new habits is not a linear process – the future of Rocky will see the coaching chatbot with an ever greater capacity to retain information from previous coaching sessions, which will allow the AI coach to remind people of the changes they want to make, help them find coherence in their series of chats by highlighting emerging patterns, and encourage them to stay accountable to their goal-directed action.

Rocky's future vision is also one of offering a more holistic approach to learning, by working with thought leaders in education, business, and self-development. Through strategic partnerships, Rocky will bring their partner's existing content to life in the form of powerful coaching questions, thought-provoking articles, and inspirational tips. Specific learning will become more personalised and meaningful when connected to a broader personal development plan, of which Rocky helps a user create and reassess on a regular basis. All learning will become more permanent too. By offering the content in a variety of ways, it's likely the user will engage again and again. The phrase 'neurons that fire together wire together' means that through repetition, knowledge becomes easier to access, as we have strengthened the neural pathways. Rocky's future vision is therefore to revolutionise the learning space and help build the inner resourcefulness of learners by complementing the traditional didactic approach with fun and interactive coaching.

Conclusion

While a lack of familiarity with AI coaching may lead some people to doubt its safety and efficacy, the tangible benefits derived from users are evidence of the positive effect AI-driven conversations can have on thoughts, feelings, and actions.

While AI technology cannot replace a human coach in its ability to detect the nuance of every emotion expressed, it can offer an anonymised space to explore one's thoughts and feelings, a space to reflect, to come up with creative solutions, and to put in place accountable steps. An AI coaching conversation can support, inspire, and educate. It can enlighten, engage, and empower individuals to live their best possible personal and professional lives and truly democratise opportunities and create a world in which everyone can thrive.

Chapter 32

Optify

Pam Krulitz

Introduction

As coaches with decades of experience in developing leaders, Optify's founders have a deep understanding of the transformative impact coaching can have on individuals and organisations.

In this chapter, they explain how the power skills – that coaching so powerfully cultivates – will become increasingly valuable for people in every position in the future. As we move towards a future where automation removes the more transactional elements of many jobs, human-centered coaching will not only provide people with the skills only humans can attain, but also the personal connection we all crave.

Optify's founders believe technology has a key role to play in enabling coaches to do what they do best – supporting people to unlock their potential. They see a future in which technology streamlines the delivery of coaching, so L&D professionals can provide people at every level with the opportunity to become the best version of themselves.

History of Optify

Optify was founded in 2018 by Pam Krulitz, Lisa Banks, and Kris Carpenter. Pam had been coaching for more than 15 years after a 15-year career in IT, which culminated in her leading an IT consulting firm that was acquired in 1996. Pam's entrepreneurial spirit and technology roots ran deep from her days helping large companies build great systems to better manage their businesses.

Having coached hundreds of leaders, she understood the value and impact that 1:1 leadership coaching has on leaders and their organisations. Recognising coaching as a powerful tool for development, she was captivated by the question of how to scale that very personal experience to more people, and at earlier stages of their career. She believed the answer lay in two things: an economic model that could make a 1:1 coaching relationship more accessible, and technology that could operationalise it more easily.

Pam tapped two friends and colleagues who were equally passionate about the vision of bringing coaching to more people: Lisa, a leadership coach with a background as an attorney, non-profit leader, meditation teacher, and a heart of service, and Kris, who has spent her professional career in finance and accounting while also serving others as a grief counsellor.

The three share a commitment: to make coaching a force to develop the next generation of leaders who will shape the future of work, organisations, and the world. They

DOI: 10.4324/9781003383741-40

are equally committed to the creation of a company rooted deeply in a set of values that were important to them. They adopted Holacracy as their internal operating system for self-management as Optify was created.

Together, the partners set out to create scalable 1:1 coaching services, with the coach/client relationship at the centre of the work, and technology in the supporting role. With the assistance of a coaching platform, coaches would be able to focus on coaching rather than administration, and organisations would have the ability to standardise programmes, assess progress and determine impact.

Optify outsourced the development of an MVP of the coaching platform and brought on 60 coaches to meet client demand. Working in partnership with clients like Lyft and Deltek, Optify honed its offer and, in true agile fashion, determined the next features most critical to build into the software. After two years, Optify brought software development in-house with a brilliant lead developer who was equally passionate about the mission and the technology.

After using the platform internally with hundreds of clients, it became clear that other coaching providers and companies with internal coaching programmes could benefit from it as well. In 2021, Optify released a multi-tenant version of the software, passed a SOC2 audit proving its security, and began building out the sales and customer experience functions to support its use.

Dozens of coaches, coaching providers, and internal coaching shops discovered the Optify platform and became its first customers in 2021 and 2022. In 2022, the Center for Creative Leadership selected Optify to help them modernise their coaching operations with its robust coaching management platform.

Vision for the future of coaching

It's an exciting time to be a coach. The industry is expanding rapidly – according to the International Coach Federation's 2023 Global Coaching Study, the number of coaches has grown by 54% in the last three years alone, and total revenue is up 60% from three years ago.

At the same time, the number of ways that coaching is being used is seemingly limited only by the imagination. In addition to the traditional life, business, and leadership realms, the impact of coaching is visible in areas as diverse as health and medicine, education, parenting, life transitions, ADHD, and financial planning. This means that those who desire to be of service to others can now do so in many ways through coaching.

We expect the growth in the depth and breadth of the coaching industry to further accelerate as we move towards a future in which technology will continue to transform the way we all work. Technology is already changing the way coaching is delivered, with organisations using coaching platforms to expand the reach of coaching to more people. Coaches are using technology to not only meet with clients virtually and share information, but to review and improve their coaching skills. And artificial intelligence (AI) and chatbots are being evaluated as aids to both coaches and clients in the coaching relationship.

Within organisations, leadership coaching will become more integrated with other learning and development modalities. Leaders may have access to coaches, mentors, and managers who also serve as 'leader-coaches' at different points throughout their careers.

Coaching relationships will be combined more seamlessly with other learning modalities like group learning experiences and online learning. As newer generations enter the workforce with a keen focus on their own growth, organisations will respond in more creative ways to provide people, technology, and learning content to support customised growth throughout one's career.

Put simply, technology will enable coaches and learning and development professionals to focus on what they do best – helping leaders to unlock their full potential – and make it easier for them to deliver coaching at scale.

But the evolution of technology won't completely supplant the need for human-centred coaching. Conversely, the human element of coaching may become even more vital in a tech-driven future.

The human and heart connection of the coach to the client will remain central to any form of true developmental coaching. AI may one day be able to suggest areas for coaches to focus on to facilitate a particular individual's growth, for example, but technology will not provide the connection, empathy, and compassion that are central to the personal and professional growth journey.

As humans, we have an innate need for connection with other humans. As coaches, we know that developing a personal connection with a coach has a tremendous impact on the client's openness, willingness to explore new territories, ability to shift their perspective, and to attain vertical growth as opposed to simply learning new skills.

That's why we believe that vertical growth or fundamental shifts in maturity and developmental levels will still be best achieved through one-on-one relationships and the presence of another human being in conversation.

As AI replaces many of the transactional elements of jobs, the 'power skills' that coaching is so useful in developing will become critical for workers across disciplines. Learning to connect more deeply with others, to listen, and to be of service in meaningful ways will be a differentiator, setting leaders – as humans – apart from their increasingly automated jobs.

The practice of coaching will continue to evolve as coaching becomes a set of skills that more people can learn and put to use, both as a profession in itself, and in the course of other roles. In fields like medicine, leadership, finance, and sales, coaching skills – such as paying mindful attention, listening deeply, asking open-ended questions, and inviting alternate perspectives – will take centre stage at work.

Many of these competencies are also the skills required to be an effective coach. So, we predict that while professionally credentialled coaches will continue to be paid for their carefully honed skills as a coach, coaching skills will be recognised and employed in organisational and personal life more broadly.

As technology enables more people to access coaching, and people from all walks of life strive to develop the skills that are cultivated through personal connections with coaches, we can't wait to see how our industry thrives.

Vision for the future of coaching on the Optify platform

At Optify, our mission is to make coaching a force to develop the next generation of leaders who will shape the future of work, organisations, and the world.

We developed the Optify platform because we believe technology has a crucial role to play in enabling coaches and learning and development professionals to help more leaders to unlock their potential to lead remarkably.

The platform is highly customisable, which means customers can tailor everything from the cadence of meetings to the topics they want to focus on to their unique goals. Our platform also gives L&D teams visibility into every coaching engagement without compromising client confidentiality, so they can accurately measure the impact of their programmes across their organisation. And, by streamlining processes and reducing coaching admin, Optify makes it simple for coaching companies and internal talent teams to deliver coaching at scale.

These features enable coaches and L&D professionals to deliver impact in five key organisational areas: leadership, operational, financial, wellbeing, and inclusivity. These key areas of impact will remain our focus as the Optify platform evolves to become the hub for learning and development activities for people across organisations of all types.

An individual's one-on-one coaching experience will remain central to the Optify platform, and we will continue to integrate different learning modalities and content to create more holistic learning experiences. Mentoring, group coaching, employee resource groups, feedback tools, leadership models, online learning, assessments, 360s, and performance management all provide opportunities for growth, but are currently carried out offline, or through disparate tools.

In the future, we will focus on integrating these tools into the Optify platform, enabling organisations to offer the right tools at the right time to the right people. This will ensure that the coaching they provide is completely **inclusive**, as each learning experience will be tailored to meet the client's individual needs and vision.

A higher level of integration within the Optify platform will also make it even easier for organisations and coaches to measure the impact of their coaching programs. Coaches and L&D professionals will have access to more sophisticated and meaningful data regarding their organisation's specific talent development goals. They will be able to prove exactly where and how they have moved the needle in key areas, so they can create a solid business case for making coaching **accessible** to even more of their team members.

We envision the day when a leader can view their entire learning journey – from onboarding to coaching and/or mentoring to learning to assessments and 360s – through the Optify platform. This will place developmental focus in the hands of the individuals with the support necessary from the organisation. By giving individuals the opportunity to shape their own personalised coaching experience, organisations can create a people-first culture in which everyone feels seen and valued, which is foundational to wellbeing.

We also see that AI will continue to support – and inform – the evolution of the Optify platform, from intelligently matching coaches and mentors with clients to making learning recommendations and capturing insights from an individual's learning journey to following habits and practices. We'll strive to find new ways for AI to replace the time-consuming manual processes that make coaching so difficult to scale, so coaches and organisations can reach more people than ever before – across teams, territories, and time zones.

By streamlining the **operational** processes involved in delivering coaching and development programmes, the Optify platform will make scaled leadership development effortless.

Conclusion

Coaching as a discipline and profession is in its infancy. While organisations are beginning to embrace coaching on a wider scale today, in the future it will become even more valuable for organisations and individuals alike.

As technology automates more of the transactional elements of roles across all industries, everyone will benefit from developing the power skills that cannot be replaced by AI. Human-centred coaching is a highly effective way of developing these skills, and it's likely that people at all levels will seek the personal and professional growth that only a one-to-one connection with a coach can provide.

We look forward to a future in which technology, like the Optify platform, makes it simple for organisations and coaches to scale their coaching programmes, to render coaching more accessible and inclusive to all levels of leader.

Chapter 33

Delenta

Sam Samarasinghe

Introduction

Delenta is one of the newer players in the coaching technology market and brings with it innovation and insights which can transform the market place for coaches and buyers.

History of the organisation

Delenta started as a simple social experiment in 2018, took on a life of its own and became a fully-fledged tech startup over time, with an awesome community of coaches, mentors, and tutors all operating inside a business model that focuses on social change, and sharing our knowledge with local and global communities.

In 2020, we identified a need to bring together the various different technologies coaches needed to run their coaching businesses. In response the company introduced an affordable subscription model and built a simple all in one digital solution to help coaches run and scale their business. The goal of this model was to empower coaches and mentors to build and scale their coaching businesses online using a single digital platform where they do not have to pay for multiple operating systems. This was done by introducing a unified coaching management platform, which would help to build a community of users and provide the tools and resources needed for coaches and mentors to succeed.

Delenta has always been driven by the belief that the world can and should be a better place. The company's founders envision a future where coaching and mentoring skills are taught in schools all over the world, so that the remarkable, life-changing results of these services can be shared by everyone, not just a small number of privileged individuals and organisations.

In the meantime, Delenta's focus is on supporting coaches and mentors worldwide to connect, grow, and amplify their reach and impact. The company is committed to helping those with the ability and willingness to help reach out to those who need their services. Today Delenta is serving thousands of users from across the world on the platform.

Vision for the future of coaching

The potential for technology adoption in the coaching industry is exciting, but it is important to first understand the challenges that coaches and coachees are facing in the current landscape (2023).

DOI: 10.4324/9781003383741-41

Current landscape of coaching

The 2022 ICF Global Consumer Awareness Study looked at how consumers were interacting with and experiencing the coaching profession. The study revealed two main trends that stood out: First, there was a low awareness of coaching in the broader consumer markets. This presents an opportunity for coaches to reach out to potential clients and benefit them via coaching. Second, the study highlighted an opportunity for coaches to present themselves as knowledgeable on the subject of coaching, and if they have expertise in coaching they should claim it.

Coaching is a challenging profession that requires coaches to navigate a wide range of obstacles. One of the main challenges, as *this study* shows, is building trust and rapport with clients. Without trust, clients may be hesitant to open up and share their thoughts, making it difficult for coaches to understand their unique needs. Coaches must also tailor their sessions accordingly to help clients achieve their goals. Changing patterns of behaviour can be difficult, and coaches must provide guidance and strategies to help clients navigate it. Keeping up with the latest research and developments in coaching is crucial for coaches to stay relevant and provide the best service to clients.

Maintaining client confidentiality and privacy is a similarly vital part of coaching. Clients must trust that their information will be kept confidential and not shared without their consent. As technology adoption increases, privacy and the protection of confidential data will become even more important topics for coaches to consider.

Future of coaching with technology

The coaching industry has seen a significant shift towards technology adoption during the 2020's, with the rise of digital platforms, messaging apps and AI tools. This trend allows for more flexibility and convenience for clients, as well as the ability for coaches to provide more consistent support and touchpoints outside of traditional coaching sessions.

Another trend that has emerged in the recent past is the diversification of coaching services offered, such as the creation of memberships, online courses, and group coaching sessions. This allows coaches to reach a wider audience and make coaching more affordable and accessible for clients. This also presents an opportunity for coaches to create multiple streams of income, which can help to build a more sustainable coaching business.

As we look into the future, the integration of various technologies such as artificial intelligence (AI), machine learning (ML), deep learning algorithms, blockchain, virtual reality (VR) and augmented reality (AR), wearable technology, natural language processing (NLP) and chatbots, cloud computing and big data, gamification, and personalised mobile apps have the potential to launch the next revolution in the coaching industry.

These technologies can help coaches to provide more effective and efficient coaching services by providing them with more accurate feedback and guidance, tailoring sessions to clients' unique needs and goals, and tracking progress in real-time. For example, AI-powered coaching tools can help coaches understand clients' unique needs and goals, and tailor coaching sessions accordingly. Wearable technology can provide coaches with data on clients' physical activity, which can help them personalise the training and coaching sessions.

VR and AR technology can be used to create immersive coaching experiences that can help clients visualise and experience change in a safe and controlled environment. This technology can also be used to train athletes, for instance, by simulating game scenarios. NLP and chatbots can automate interactions between coaches and clients, such as scheduling appointments or providing information; they can also help provide 24/7 support and guidance to clients.

Cloud computing and big data can help coaches store and analyse large amounts of data, which can help them understand client behaviour and progress, and make more informed decisions about how to coach and support clients.

The adoption of these technologies in coaching also has the potential to make the profession more accessible to a wider audience from diverse backgrounds. By utilising messaging apps, online courses, and other technology-based services, coaches can reach clients who may have previously been unable to access in-person coaching. The use of AI-based chatbot services, for example, can make career coaching more accessible and convenient for clients. On the other hand, leadership coaching, which often requires a high level of trust and confidentiality, may still rely more on in-person sessions.

Vision for the future of coaching on Delenta

With the continued growth of the coaching industry, coaches are experiencing mounting pressure to achieve desired outcomes while maintaining low costs to sustain their businesses. To stay ahead of the curve, coaches must explore novel and creative approaches to managing and scaling their coaching enterprises. Through our collaboration with numerous knowledgepreneurs, we recognise that constructing sustainable and scalable businesses is essential for coaches to make a more substantial contribution.

Presently, Delenta empowers coaches with a diverse array of tools and features that enable them to oversee and expand their enterprises utilising a unified solution. Our commitment to enhancing the existing solution with additional functionalities to cater to businesses of all types and sizes across the globe is unwavering, while we also strive to seize opportunities to tackle broader challenges within the industry.

One of the major challenges we recognise is that coaching can be an expensive and inaccessible service for many people, particularly those in less fortunate parts of the world. For this reason, we are dedicated to leveraging technology to enhance the accessibility and efficacy of coaching.

In the future, we envisage our platform will facilitate coaches in establishing connections with prospective clients and crafting and promoting their digital courses and memberships. As a result, coaches can target clients who may not have the means to afford in-person coaching or reside in geographically isolated areas. This will enable coaches to broaden their reach and render their services accessible to a wider audience, while also generating multiple revenue streams to maintain their business. By harnessing the power of technology, we believe coaches can reach clients from all over the world, breaking down the barriers of geography and distance. With our AI-powered tools, we envisage coaches can analyse data and gain insights into the needs and preferences of their clients, enabling them to tailor their coaching to meet individual requirements.

We're committed to helping coaches to grow their business by providing them with the resources and tools they need to succeed. We understand that the coaching industry can be highly competitive, and that's why we're constantly exploring new opportunities to help coaches stand out in a crowded market.

Through our collaborative approach, we aim to create a more sustainable and ethical future, where coaches can work in harmony with technology to make a positive impact on the lives of people around the globe. We believe that by empowering coaches to reach a wider audience, we can help to create a more equitable and accessible world, where everyone has the opportunity to access high-quality coaching services.

Our focus is on developing cutting-edge solutions that harness the power of emerging technologies such as artificial intelligence, virtual reality, and augmented reality to create a more efficient and effective coaching experience. By leveraging these technologies, we aim to create a more sustainable and ethical future, where experts and coaches can collaborate with technology to make a positive impact on the lives of people around the globe.

For instance, our virtual reality coaching platform enables coaches to provide their clients with immersive and interactive experiences, allowing them to learn in a more effective and engaging way. Studies have shown that immersive learning experiences can improve learning outcomes by up to 75% compared to traditional classroom learning.

We're also developing AI-powered tools that enable coaches to analyse data and provide personalised recommendations for their clients. By leveraging the power of machine learning, coaches can gain insights into their clients' needs and tailor their coaching to meet their individual requirements. This technology has been shown to increase customer satisfaction by up to 35%.

Our vision is to create a collaborative environment that brings together experts, coaches, and technology to create a more equitable and accessible world. By harnessing the power of technology, we can provide coaches with the tools they need to reach a wider audience and make a positive impact on the world.

Conclusion

In summary, Delenta is dedicated to creating a future where coaching is accessible, effective, and sustainable. We believe that technology can play a crucial role in achieving this goal, and we're committed to exploring new opportunities to help coaches succeed in a competitive and constantly evolving industry. By working together, we can create a more harmonious and collaborative world, where experts and technology can collaborate to create a brighter future for all.

uExcelerate

Amit Kumar and Fatima Hussain

Introduction

uExcelerate was founded in May 2019, with the purpose to transform lives for the better, by connecting individuals with their purpose using the power of coaching. There have always been many challenges in democratising and systematising coaching for individuals at every level of the organisation including exorbitant costs, the inability to scale coaching and the inability to measure impact.

Dedicated to solving these challenges, uExcelerate, an award-winning digital coaching platform, enables organisations to democratise, scale, and build a sustainable coaching culture for the whole self and the whole system.

Our coaching products help organisations achieve business goals through four unique offerings including APPRAISE, DISCOVER, PACE, and SYMPHONY, catering to serve them at different stages of their coaching culture maturity journeys.

History of uExcelerate

Amit Kumar – uExcelerate's Founder and CEO's desire to build an accessible digital coaching platform was born in 2016, stemming from his own struggles of finding a coach when he needed it the most. When Amit found the stress of his transition to a higher role in a completely new environment taking a toll on his personal and professional life, he decided to find a coach to help him cope with this transition better. However, when the exorbitant cost of coaching became an obstacle, Amit was left to navigate his transitional struggle by himself.

Shortly after this experience, Amit set off to get his MBA from UC Berkeley, Haas School of Business in 2018. With the unfortunate experience of failing to find a coach fresh in his mind, Amit decided to pursue the concept of an accessible and affordable digital coaching platform as a part of his capstone project. The concept was well received by all his professors and after pitching the idea to various investors and start-up communities, the concept received strong validation.

After returning to India in 2019, Amit validated the concept in his home market as well. His market research found that organisations were still using a one-size-fits-all approach to employee development. The research validated the fact that coaching could be a very powerful and personalised development tool, but logistically complex to scale up, especially for senior and mid-level management employees. While other solutions were *high tech,* they were not *high-touch*. Hence, there was a need to solve the challenges

DOI: 10.4324/9781003383741-42

of empowering employees to choose a coach that fit their needs and simultaneously allowed employers to manage logistics and measure learning impact.

Amit founded uExcelerate in May 2019 along with a diversified, experienced, and startup-enthusiastic team to promote coaching unconventionally and digitally to build leaders across all levels. Since then, uExcelerate has undergone three phases of pivot to finally find the right product fit for the Eastern market:

Phase one – uExcelerate was initially launched as a digital coaching marketplace to address both one-on-one and group coaching formats of blended learning. However, with customers being price-conscious and hesitant to use only external coaches, the team felt that uExcelerate could still evolve its product further.

Phase two – uExcelerate expanded its product to onboard internal coaches on the platform, allowing organisations the choice to take up internal or external coaching based on their needs. Hence, the idea of allowing users to white-label the platform and scale up their coaching journey arose. However, it was not enough just to have systems in place, if there were no capable internal coaches or process owners to initiate the coaching culture practice in their organizations.

Phase three – the team realised that there were issues beyond employee development that needed to be addressed. The issues lay deep within the fabric of the organisation and needed to be addressed at the cultural level. Hence, the idea of building a coaching culture, with uExcelerate's proprietary 7C coaching culture maturity framework and model was born.

Now, uExcelerate focuses fully on helping organisations build successful coaching cultures with four unique solutions that suit organisations with all kinds of requirements.

Vision for the future of coaching

The coaching industry is growing at rapid rates and is becoming an essential element for the success of every organisation. Coaching has been a huge part of the Western organisational structure for a while now but we have also recently noticed a shift in the Eastern organisational structure with a preference towards coaching over training solutions.

We at uExcelerate strongly believe that the future of coaching includes an amalgamation of *coaching as an art form* and *coaching as a science*. We are all aware that coaching is an art form, and every coach is an artist that brings their own unique artistic techniques to the coaching sessions ranging from very abstract methods of spiritual coaching to more cognitive methods of humanistic coaching and systemic coaching. Not to mention the spontaneous decisions the coach has to make during the coaching session to find the perfect balance in being hands-off while also directing the coachee to the appropriate solution, like a waltz with the coachee through their developmental journey.

But we also know that there are many scientific tools and techniques used to ensure a successful coaching journey. Coaching is rapidly embracing artificial intelligence and modern technology into its approaches. With enhanced algorithms, deep learning, machine learning, and so much more, coaching will become a fail-safe system that guarantees successful coaching sessions for all. We are seeing a huge shift from human-to-human coaching to a preference for AI coaches. Going forward we will likely see the concept of the metaverse and augmented reality introduce itself into the coaching realm. Not to mention the growing popularity of blockchain.

The future of coaching will be an interesting mixed pot of artistic freedom that coaches bring combined with the hi-tech revolutionisation of the coaching industry. And that is why we strongly believe that if we can marry both the art and science of coaching together then we can truly change the future of coaching. And we are excited to be a part of this revolution – to accept, adapt, and thrive in this volatile industry.

Vision for the future of coaching on the uExcelerate platform

The future of uExcelerate includes enhanced, intuitive solutions that bring the biggest innovation to enrich people's lives for years to come. The platform will meet great challenges of every stakeholder – the coachee, the coach, and the organisation, with great creativity and important breakthrough features. It will move from being a simple enabler to one that leads to immense transformation for every user.

From the coachee's lens, uExcelerate will leverage new intelligence to analyse coachee behaviour and provide coachees with tailored features to empower them with the tools and techniques they need to accelerate their development successfully.

From the coach's lens, uExcelerate will use the latest technology to deliver an amazing experience for our coaches, provide them with incredible opportunities so they can use their skills to collaborate with their coachees on their journeys and cultivate their relationships with them. We will help them innovate and brand themselves while also monetising themselves with truly iconic elements to increase their visibility to the curated audience that are in need of coaching.

From the organisation's lens, uExcelerate will introduce meaningful ways to help organisations leverage our latest technology to bring groundbreaking changes within their organisations. Our intuitive design will bring organisations a systemic view of coaching at a glance. The beautifully designed experience will help organisations understand how coaching is enriching their people's lives and impacting the organisation. Our product will allow various integration options with other HR Tech platforms to bring the power of data to organisations so they can make informed decisions. uExcelerate will optimise the data to measure the success of coaching, give structure to the coaching journey and make it accessible to all levels of the organisation through technology.

uExcelerate will always put the user's pain points at the center of everything we design, thus creating effectiveness and efficiency in the coaching process for clients, coachees, and coaches in terms of the outcomes they desire to see.

Conclusion

uExcelerate is determined to create a world-class SaaS product with world-class coaches to deliver the best in the class results to our clients. We will always strive to connect people with their purpose to unleash the infinite potential of the Whole Self and the whole system. We are constantly learning and evolving through our Applied Coaching Science and Leadership Lab that works extensively to bring our users a new, updated experience while enhancing the one they already love.

With the ever-changing volatile world, we are dedicated to embracing technological advancements to help organisations create successful coaching cultures that will stand the test of time across every industry and eventually across the globe.

Chapter 35

evoach

Rebecca Rutschmann

Introduction

Artificial intelligence and chatbots enable completely new ways of designing and delivering coaching to people at all levels of an organisation in a customised, yet consistent and affordable way. evoach has developed a coaching chatbot and programme creator so that coaching and training providers can create individual AI coachbots without any technical or programming skills.

The market is changing, and coaches, as well as coaching educators seeking to future-proof their practice, need to evolve their digital offerings beyond running sessions in Zoom. evoach supports coaching pioneers with practical tools to design a digital or hybrid coaching programme around client needs by providing sample structures, freely linkable content elements, coaching chatbot templates, and evidence-based tools. With strong ties to both ICF and EMCC, all of this is built on good coaching chatbot practice, ICF/EMCC/AC core competencies, and high ethical standards.

The latest developments in generative AI technology will continue to have a huge impact on the coaching industry, more so than most previous technological advances: The integration of this technology is changing the way coaches work and HR departments can integrate coaching as a tool for all employees.

History of the organisation

evoach was founded in June 2019, with the goal of digitising business coaching and making it available to a much broader audience. Co-founder Rebecca Rutschmann started exploring how to digitise business coaching back in 2018, as part of her coaching education. With her background in gamification and more than 10 years of experience creating digital experiences in digital agencies, it was crystal clear that any digital coaching solution had to have a great user interface and be fun to use. With a few other coaches, she developed the paper prototypes and tested them with real clients during a few Friday night design sprints. When clients were able to solve their coaching problems in a pure self-coaching process, they knew they were on to something. Co-founder Anke Paulick joined a little later and developed possible business models based on her experience as an executive at companies such as Lycos and United Internet.

The first beta product with scripted coaching chatbots, e.g. to solve conflicts or give feedback, was released in February 2020 and tested with corporate customers – just as Covid-19 started. During the pandemic, the openness of coaches to digitalisation

DOI: 10.4324/9781003383741-43

increased dramatically and evoach pivoted its model to offer individual coaching chat-bots for coaches and training institutes – first on a project basis and since 2022 in a licensing model for the respective chatbot creator.

The hype around generative AI and large language models catapulted evoach to the next level in early 2023, mixing its scripted coaching content with generative AI elem-ents. This is where Rebecca's experience using various social media algorithms for apps and advertising comes in handy.

Both Anke and Rebecca are certified coaches at the ICF PCC/EMCC Senior Professional Coach level and are active on the boards of their respective industry associations.

Today, evoach is the leading innovative software platform for coaches who want to create digital coaching products and scale their practice.

Vision for the future of coaching

In a dynamic world, coaching is becoming more dominant in the overall development of people and teams as it can better deal with undefined outcomes compared to other formats such as training. The demand for coaching has been growing 15% year over year for almost a decade. The budgets have not. While many coaching platforms talk about democratising coaching, the cost of delivering it at scale across an organisation is still prohibitively high. This is where AI coaching chatbots step in – currently not to replace human coaching, but to support it. Already today, basic coaching models and concerns can be coached by a bot with the same outcome as human coaching. We expect that by 2030, everything that can be digitised will be digitised. So will coach training. We will see digital coaches integrated into personal AI-powered learning and development journeys. Human coaching will still exist and will focus on those areas where it can add more value than coaching bots.

By 2030, coaching chatbots will be freely available enough to be widely used outside the corporate world – for live coaching, supporting the education system, social initiatives and communities. It will be normal to write or talk to a coaching bot on a regular basis.

While all this is happening, we will debate the ethics and privacy of digital coaching.

Vision for the future of coaching on the evoach platform

Evoach provides easy access to this future of coaching. Practitioners of all coaching approaches will use and enhance their methodology.

AI will assist in both discovery and creation. Through APIs, coaching chatbots will be available wherever the client wants to use them – simply choose your device, output form, and the time you want to invest, and your coaching companion will deliver your 100% customised coaching experience.

Conclusion

evoach is an excellent SaaS solution today to help coaches digitise their coaching prac-tice. In the future, the new profession of Conversational Coaching Designer will inspire people around the world, using no code software to work with individuals, teams, asso-ciations, NGOs, and corporations to design their perfect chatbot personality and model their coaching needs into the software – until generative AI takes over.

Chapter 36

Ovida AI

Alex Haitoglou

Introduction

The path to adult learning and mastery in any field is well documented. Willingness to learn, self-reflection, goal-setting and objective data, expert guidance, and deliberate practice are all required to drive personal and professional growth. This process is overlooked in coach training, as well as other professional communication training. This is primarily due to the difficulty of recording and evaluating sessions and discussions, a lack of objective metrics, high mentorship costs, and confidentiality concerns. Ovida leverages AI to revolutionise coaching skills learning by incorporating all of these steps. We facilitate self-reflection, generate objective data, connect coaches with expert mentors, and enable deliberate practice to help everyone improve.

History of Ovida

The founders of Ovida, Alex, and Bryan, had life-changing experiences through coaching.

Alex was fortunate enough to meet a professional coach in his late teens, an experience that transformed his life. After that, and while working as a business leader at Procter & Gamble, Alex had a chance to train as an internal coach and run P&G's global GROW coaching programme, and then implemented a 'coaching skills for leaders' approach at many businesses since then. Alex was always fascinated with the challenge of training and growing coaching skills in coaches, professionals, and business leaders.

Bryan was introduced to coaching during his MBA at the University of Cape Town, and it transformed how he viewed people, organisations, and communication. He put to work his coaching skills as a strategy consultant, and then as a CEO of a security technology business that grew tenfold, with a big part of this growth attributed to nurturing a coaching culture within the business. Bryan's challenge was how to help new and experienced leaders develop fast key coaching skills like listening, building trust, and asking great questions, to accelerate their growth.

Alex and Bryan met in San Francisco in a week-long AI conference in 2018, and spent hours discussing how AI could be used to enhance human communication and connection, rather than replace humans. They concluded that training key coaching skills is a great place to start and founded Ovida in late 2020.

Ovida is using a unique approach in analysing discussions with the aim to help self-reflection by identifying key moments, using a combination of tools like speech recognition, natural language processing, speed/pace/tonality, and facial movements.

DOI: 10.4324/9781003383741-44

Additionally, Ovida creates transcripts, summaries, and action points using large language models like ChatGPT, and allows through its interface for the coaching or training session to be shared with an expert mentor or supervisor for very fast and efficient feedback.

Ovida also is able to generate objective and observable data from discussions, as well as track progress across sessions, or across a group. And as Ovida is entirely cloud based it is secure and private, and only records data based on full and informed consent from all parties involved. All personal data is never shared nor sold, and is deleted based on the requirements of the users.

During the last year Ovida has been increasingly adopted by leading organisations and universities that train coaches and leaders, as well as corporations that train coaches and managers in coaching skills.

Vision for the future of coaching

Coaching has evolved in the past 30 years from a peripheral practice in a few countries to a multi-billion-dollar industry that spans the globe. This organic growth is testimony to the power of coaching to help individuals and teams within an organisation reach their full potential, achieve their goals, and improve their overall performance and effectiveness. We now know that coaching 'works', not just because of what people say, but because science is increasingly proving it. Numerous peer-reviewed studies show that coaching is remarkably effective in leadership development, team effectiveness, change management, and career development to name a few.

As the need for coaching grows, there are several challenges we must overcome in the future:

(a) First, and arguably the most important one, is fulfilling the need for more and better trained coaches. Users of coaching services are becoming more sophisticated in their understanding and expectations from coaches, and the high diversity of quality across practitioners is becoming increasingly the 'elephant in the room' for users, trainers, corporations, and coaching platforms. It is therefore critical that all coaches are able to continuously improve the standard of their practice through continuous study, practice, and supervision. In a similar way to professional athletes, doctors, or educators, this process of learning and growing should never stop while someone is active as a professional coach.

(b) Second, there is a growing need for managers and leaders to use coaching skills in their daily practice. They don't have to be a qualified coach to learn how to listen more attentively, ask more open-ended questions and facilitate other people's thinking and problem solving, but the impact on their employees of applying these skills is profoundly positive. Organisations are picking up on this trend, as they realise the strong link between productivity, retention, innovation, and overall job satisfaction in employees whose managers are applying these skills. This trend will greatly accelerate, increasing the need for training coaching skills.

(c) Third, the growing power of AI will play an increasingly important role in the coaching industry. AI is extremely unlikely to completely replace humans in coaching. However, we see the application of this powerful technology scale and democratise coaching, coach support and coach training. The benefits of AI in coaching include vastly reduced cost, 24/7 availability and access to coaching services to previously excluded communities, and coaches that are constantly getting better themselves and using AI co-pilots to deliver their full service to their clients will have a competitive advantage.

Vision for the future of Ovida

At Ovida we are pushing the boundaries of using AI to help accelerate people's coaching and communication skills. Our existing algorithms that analyse conversations to improve these skills are based on what is currently known from existing research and increasingly based on the data we are collecting and analysing. Our future vision is to push beyond current knowledge and through robust cutting-edge, high-quality research to understand which methods and approaches are best at detecting and improving coaching and communication skills. We strongly believe in a future of evidence-based, deliberate, and measurable practice.

From sport it is well established that feedback from expert observation dramatically accelerates learning. We are using this concept in coaching to improve the coaching and communication skills of an increasingly diverse group of people beyond coaches. We envision a future where new and experienced coaches, as well as employees at all levels of an organisation use Ovida to improve their communication skills.

New coaches almost always struggle to get feedback on their coaching from experienced supervisors. This is due to the cost and availability of these experts. We see a future where coach training providers use Ovida as a standard part of coach training.

A future where the most experienced and effective mentors and supervisors can help ten or a hundred times more new coaches improve, as AI helps them review sessions, provide better targeted feedback, and measure the progress of their trainees/mentees/supervisees.

Experienced coaches have even fewer opportunities to receive observed feedback on coaching. We see Ovida support the continued growth of coaches by partnering with coaching regulatory and credentialing bodies to provide this service as part of coach membership and continuous professional development.

Employees on all levels of the organisation can massively benefit from better communication skills. This year, more than $1 trillion will be wasted in the US only, because of 'bad bosses'. In most cases this means people that have not learned how to listen, engage, ask great questions, and build trust, all of which are key tools for coaching. We see Ovida playing a pivotal role in training these skills across corporations and organisations.

Eventually we see Ovida help everyone, embrace the proven benefits of a coaching style by helping to create awareness of how people currently communicate and helping them improve.

Conclusion

The key to a more humane future in organisations but also in our personal relationships, is our ability to communicate with each other in a human-centric, thoughtful, and respectful manner. A coaching-skills based communication style has been proven to do just that.

Ovida exists to unlock the communication and coaching potential of people and organisations across the world. We unite human skills with the power of AI to generate data and insights to achieve this, and we commit to doing that in a safe, accessible, and human-centred way.

Index